o.p.

# REGIMENTS OF THE EMPIRE

## A Bibliography of their Published Histories

Compiled by Roger Perkins

1989

PO Box 29   NEWTON ABBOT   Devon   TQ12 1XU

REGIMENTS OF THE EMPIRE
A Bibliography of their Published Histories

Copyright - Roger Perkins 1989
ISBN 0 9506429 1 6

Every reasonable care has been taken by the compiler
to ensure that the information contained herein should
be as complete and accurate as the circumstances of such
a large undertaking might permit.
No responsibility can be accepted, however, for any
inaccuracies or errors which may subsequently
be identified.

By the same author

(for Kenneth Mason, Havant, Hampshire)

GUNFIRE IN BARBARY (1982)(with Capt K J Douglas-Morris RN)

(for Picton Publishing, Chippenham, Wiltshire)

ANGELS IN BLUE JACKETS (1983)(with J W Wilson)
THE KASHMIR GATE (1983)
THE PUNJAB MAIL MURDER (1986)
OPERATION PARAQUAT - THE BATTLE FOR SOUTH GEORGIA, 1982 (1986)
THE AMRITSAR LEGACY (1989)

Published privately
Typeset by the compiler
Produced and printed by Antony Rowe Limited
Bumper's Farm  Chippenham  Wiltshire  (UK)  SN14 6LH

# CONTENTS

Users of this bibliography are urged to familiarise themselves with
the initial explanatory notes (the Introduction), and with the Glossary
and Indexes, before consulting the main body of the entries.

# INTRODUCTION

The rise and fall of the British Empire was arguably the most important political, economic and social historical event of the past two hundred years. In competition with other European nations, and sometimes in conflict with them, the British spread their influence to every quarter of the globe. The continuing vigour of the Commonwealth is today testimony that that influence was fundamentally benign.

The initial motivation for imperial expansion was the quest for trade. Commerce thrives best in a climate of stability. It happened, from time to time, that the activities of British merchant venturers did not meet with the full approval of the diverse peoples with whom they were attempting to deal. It was on such occasions that the presence of an armed and disciplined force had the salutary effect of preserving British interests. Such a force was able also to discourage or repel any intrusion by competitors.

The British Army of the 19th century was too small and too restricted in its capabilities to effectively control all of the lands over which the Union flag was beginning to fly. Extremes of climate and topography, barriers of language and ethnic identity, susceptibility to local endemic diseases, these were some of the factors which made it desirable to recruit and train new regiments from each local populace.

When, in 1893, Joseph Chamberlain spoke of a 'pax Britannica', he was describing a peace based upon the power of the Royal Navy and the many strengths of a polyglot army trained and equipped for a common purpose. It was this military force - composed of soldiers of almost every cultural and ethnic origin - which is the subject of the present volume.

The Dominions, Colonies and Mandated Territories which once formed part of the Empire produced a multitude of military, para-military and police units. Some were mercenary, a few were conscripted, many were composed of volunteers. Over the years, and particularly during the past seventy years, many of these regiments have sponsored the publication of one or more books recounting their past services.

The 'regimental history' is a format which, in broad terms, conforms to a recognised profile. It is a book which tells the story of a regiment during a specified period of time. It contains details of the battles or campaigns in which the unit participated. Ideally, it makes abundant reference to individual officers and men who distinguished themselves in one way or another. The inclusion in the narrative of anecdotes and the minutiae of day-to-day soldiering gives the reader an insight into the spirit of that regiment which is not found in any other type of publication.

Most 'regimental histories' have been intended for presentation or sale to serving and former members of the regiment and to their families and friends. They were rarely intended for a wider readership, so the numbers printed were correspondingly modest. A maximum 'print run' was one thousand, possibly two thousand, rarely more. In some cases it was restricted to just one or two hundreds.

Books, unfortunately, suffer a high rate of attrition. They do not always receive the consideration which, as valuable historical records, they merit. Over the passing years, damp, heat, bookworm, termite, careless handling, all take their toll. The surviving examples of what were always quite rare titles are, in some cases, few and far between. It is a paradox that the military history of the Empire is now attracting the interest of a great many people who never personally served it, or who were born after its demise. For them, locating and gaining access to such books is today often a frustrating task. Demand far exceeds supply.

REGIMENTS OF THE EMPIRE is designed to assist everyone who wishes to know whether a particular regiment or corps has a recorded history and, assuming that they can obtain a copy, whether it is likely to provide the information they require. As a research tool, therefore, this bibliography should be of value to several different categories of user. Apart from its obvious utility to the student of military history in general, it should prove useful to genealogists, sociologists, librarians, publishers, graduates and post-graduates, war-gamers, and collectors of books, campaign medals and militaria.

The book breaks new ground on four major counts. First, nobody had ever attempted to bring all of the available titles within the covers of a single volume. Secondly, it contains far more information regarding each title than is provided in a bibliography of traditional format. Thirdly, it attempts to indicate the quality of authorship to be found in each title and therefore its desirability as a source of reference. Fourthly, and this is possibly the greatest innovation, the project has been a team effort by a number of people sharing a common interest.

When the project was first launched, in 1986, it was evident that no single individual could hope to track down and personally inspect an example of each of the titles qualifying for inclusion. Some are of excessive rarity, there being only a handful of known surviving copies. Many, indeed, are not available in the United Kingdom. The only way to deal with this and similar difficulties was to invite the collaboration of other researchers. The response was excellent and dozens of 'reporters', from fourteen different countries, have generously given their time and expertise to the project. They are listed by name, with the compiler's deep gratitude, in the 'Acknowledgements' section (pages 379-381).

It is inevitable, given the large number of people engaged in this work, that some of their reports will be more or less detailed than others. A second (revised) edition will not be produced before 1995 at the earliest. It would be appreciated, however, if any deficiencies identified in the entries could be brought in the meanwhile to the attention of the compiler so that they may be noted in anticipation of that event.

USER NOTES

The following notes will assist the user of this bibliography to know
how it has been compiled and therefore to obtain from it the maximum
benefit.

1. Each entry commences with the main title of the book in question, and
this is shown in upper-case lettering.

2. The following line, in lower-case, shows the sub-title or title page
preamble.

3. Regimental history books have been written or compiled by a wide range
of people. Some were professional writers, some were amateur editors. Many
worked alone, others formed part of an editorial committee. No attempt
has been made here to differentiate between 'authors', 'editors',
'compilers' or 'committee members'. The entry simply states the name or
names of anyone who has declared himself to be, or who is known to have
been, directly responsible for drafting and assembling the original work.
In the event, it will be seen that many of these books (particularly the
earlier Indian Army histories), flowed from the pen of that most prolific
of authors, 'anonymous'.

4. Stating the name of the publisher is frequently a matter of some
difficulty. A book may have been produced by a publisher, at his own
expense, and as a commercial venture. Then again, he may have been
commissioned by a regiment to produce its 'official history', his
company being responsible for all aspects of the work but the regiment
paying the bill. In many instances, the publisher undertook the design and
supervisory tasks, but then passed the physical production work to a
contract printing firm. From the details given in a book, it is not always
possible to state with certainty what the commercial arrangements might
have been. Many researchers might not regard this as a vital consideration,
but care has been taken nevertheless to state the facts as accurately as
possible.

5. Unless otherwise stated, all listed titles are bound in hardback
(casebound), and covered with some form of natural or synthetic fabric.
The colour of the bindings, embellishments and lettering are as stated,
with additional information if the example seen is thought to have been
rebound at some stage in its life. No reference has been made to dust-
jackets as this point is thought to be of no great interest to the
majority of researchers.

6. There are several ways in which the physical dimensions of a book may
be described. By tradition, librarians and bibliographers have adopted
the nomenclature used by printers and publishers. They have used terms
such a 'folio', 'quarto' and 'octavo'. These words simply indicate the
number of times the original full sheet of paper was folded before being
trimmed and bound into the finished book. It is an imprecise form of
nomenclature because the printer's full sheets may have been of several
different sizes (subject to the paper manufacturer, the country of origin,
and the period in time).

The method adopted for REGIMENTS OF THE EMPIRE is to show the dimensions of the front cover, measured first from top to bottom, and then from the outer hinge to the outer edge, both expressed in inches.

This solution may not please everyone, it being felt by some that one should make a commitment **either** to the traditional nomenclature **or** to the metric system. Both propositions have been resisted, the former on the grounds that it is so imprecise and the latter because it is excessively fussy if applied to books published in the era when the imperial system of measurement was still the norm.

As a general guide, many of the titles listed here will be seen to have one of the following approximate formats: 12.5 x 9.5 inches (quarto), 8.5 x 6.0 inches (octavo), or 5.5 x 4.0 inches (sextodecimo).

7. To the possible disappointment of the true bibliophile, no reference has been made to the finer aspects of the book-designer's art. For example, there is no attempt to state whether end-papers are plain or marbled, whether silk headbands are integral or ornamental, whether coloured plates are protected by tissue leaves, or whether the book has an integral ribbon page-marker. Such matters are no doubt of interest, but to have called for such information would have placed an intolerable burden upon the time and patience of the people who have sought out and recorded many of the titles listed here.

8. The number of pages in each book is indicated in the conventional way. Preliminary pages are shown in lower-case Roman numerals, with the number of narrative and appendix pages in Arabic numerals, e.g. xv/259.

9. The descriptions of appendixes, maps and illustrations are self-explanatory (once the user has consulted the Glossary). It will be noted that this element in each entry is unusually detailed, it being judged that this type of information is particularly important to the researcher. For the same reason, the compiler has been at pains to record the presence or absence of an Index. It is his view that the lack of an Index must, in most cases, severely restrict the value of a 'regimental history' as a work of reference.

Where this type of information is **not** given in an entry, it signifies that the compiler is aware of the existence of the book but has not been able to locate a copy for detailed examination. Such titles are marked 'not seen'.

10. There is a code at the end of each entry which is intended to give an indication of rarity (R) and of research value (V). Both qualities are graded on a scale of one to five. A book of indifferent scholarly merit, easily found, might be rated R/1 V/1. On the other hand, a truly comprehensive account, with detailed appendixes, excellent illustrations and a good Index, will be rated V/5. If it is not easy to acquire a copy, it might be rated R/3 or R/4. These are general and subjective gradings because not all researchers will be working to the same parameters, and a publication easily purchased in Australia might be almost unknown in, say, Canada. Despite such limitations, it is hoped that the gradings will provide a useful guide.

11. The general summary at the end of each entry is intended to tell someone who has never seen a particular book what he or she is likely to find when eventually a copy does come his or her way. To a degree, these summaries reflect the judgement of the individuals who compiled the original reports. It is hoped that they will prove to be objective and informative.

12. In recognition of the contribution made by each 'reporter', his or her initials are shown at the end of each entry (see 'Acknowledgements', pages 380-381).

13. In some cases, there is an additional set of initials at the end of an entry. These indicate the Museum or Library in which the book was found and examined (see page 382). It is hoped that this information may prove helpful to the researcher who is experiencing difficulty in locating one of the rarer titles.

It was intended at one stage to include also the specific catalogue reference numbers for such books, but this plan was abandoned at the request of the Librarians. At least two important military libraries are currently re-cataloguing their holdings and introducing new numbering systems, so any details published in REGIMENTS OF THE EMPIRE would have been outdated and misleading.

14. The general layout of the bibliography has been determined by administrative convenience and the preference of the compiler. No slight is intended to any country which has not received the prominence which its nationals feel it should enjoy. Similarly, when listing the book titles relating to a nation which has achieved independence since 1945, and which has subsequently changed its name, no offence is intended if it is indexed here under its old British Empire name.

15. Over the years, many regiments were amalgamated, disbanded, renamed or reconstituted in one way or another. This was particularly the case in India. The sequence in which Indian Army units are listed here is based mainly upon their titles following the reorganisations of 1922, but also in the chronological (date) order in which their histories were published. Date of publication has determined the order of listing in some other sections also. In the case of Australian, New Zealand and Canadian numbered battalions, it has been found more convenient to list them in numerical order. **The point must be made that this is a book about books. It is not a study of lineages or other aspects of regimental or corps seniority.** Any attempt to arrange the following entries according to an 'order of precedence' would have ended in disaster and is, in any case, irrelevant to the purpose of the work.

16. It will be seen that several national sections of the bibliography commence with one or more 'general interest' titles. These are not 'regimental histories'. They have been included simply as an additional source for the user who may be unfamiliar with the evolution of the Empire's armed forces. There is a huge number of such titles available on the market, and those listed here are no more than a representative sample. Most Librarians and military book dealers will be pleased to supply lists of additional titles.

17. There is no Index of Authors. With so many books having been written anonymously, or by committees of regimental officers, such an Index would have only limited value.

18. As explained earlier, this bibliography is dedicated primarily to 'published regimental histories intended for sale'. There is thus a deliberate exclusion of several other types of source material which might be of interest to a researcher, e.g. Standing Orders, Dress Regulations, recruiting pamphlets, Annual Chronicles, 'commemorative' booklets, unpublished manuscripts, and abridged histories written in the vernacular for the instruction of young soldiers. The compiler has broken his own rule, however, by listing such material in those instances where it is the **only** reference source available, the regiment in question never having succeeded, for one reason or another, in publishing its own history.

19. Reference to the 'Contents' page, and to the 'Index of Indexes' (page 379), will reveal the inclusion of several countries which were never a part of the British Empire, e.g. Iraq, Palestine, Trans-Jordan and China. The reason for listing them here is to permit the inclusion of local forces which were raised by the British for internal security or similar duties.

20. Users of the bibliography may also wonder why Dominion and Colonial police forces have been included in the entries. The explanation is that several of these forces have, at times, fulfilled a para-military role and have shared with their army comrades all the hardships and dangers of one or more campaigns.

21. The only country which has been deliberately excluded is the United Kingdom. Researchers seeking information on the histories of British regiments are recommended to consult A BIBLIOGRAPHY OF THE REGIMENTAL HISTORIES OF THE BRITISH ARMY, originally compiled by Arthur S White (first published in 1965, re-published in expanded form by London Stamp Exchange, 1988).

# GLOSSARY

The following acronyms and abbreviations appear in many of the entries:

| | |
|---|---|
| AIF | Australian Imperial Force |
| Anon | Anonymous |
| Apps | Appendixes |
| BEM | British Empire Medal |
| BOR | British Other Rank |
| Bde | Brigade |
| Bn | Battalion |
| CB | Commander of the Order of the Bath |
| CBE | Commander of the Order of the British Empire |
| CMG | Commander of the Order of St Michael & St George |
| CO | Commanding Officer |
| DCM | Distinguished Conduct Medal |
| DOW | Died of Wounds |
| DSO | Distinguished Service Order |
| Fp | Frontispiece (either coloured or monochrome) |
| H&A | Honours and Awards |
| HEIC | Honourable East India Company |
| idem | the same (the same as before) |
| KIA | Killed in Action |
| LRDG | Long Range Desert Group (WWII, Western Desert) |
| MBE | Member of the Order of the British Empire |
| MC | Military Cross |
| MID | Mentioned in Despatches |
| MM | Military Medal |
| mono phots | monochrome photographs (sepia and/or black and white) |
| MSM | Meritorious Service Medal |
| NCO | Non-commissioned Officer |
| n.d. | no date (date of publication not shown) |
| NZEF | New Zealand Expeditionary Force |
| OBE | Officer of the Order of the British Empire |
| Perfect | Spine of book is glued, not thread-sewn |
| POW | Prisoner of War |
| Regt | Regiment |
| Regtl | Regimental |
| Roll of Honour | names of personnel who lost their lives |
| RSM | Regimental Sergeant Major |
| RPM | Regimental Pipe Major |
| SNCO | Senior Non-commissioned Officer |
| SSM | Squadron Sergeant Major |
| VC | Victoria Cross |
| VCO | Viceroy's Commissioned Officer |
| WIA | Wounded in Action |
| WO | Warrant Officer |

COMPILATION NOTES

Users of REGIMENTS OF THE EMPIRE may be interested to know what facts
and assessments were requested on the forms distributed to 'reporters'
during the survey stage of the project. The questions are not exhaustive,
but the answers do permit the compilation of a clear 'word picture' for
each book examined and recorded. The format may be helpful to users
who are compiling their own records, or who wish to send information to
the compiler of the present work.

Main title (in full, without abbreviations)

Sub-title (or title page preamble)

Author (with full rank, initials, and post-nominals)

Publisher

Printer

Date of publication (as shown, or approximate if not)

Place of publication (city, country)

Number of Volumes (if one of a series)

Type of binding (e.g. casebound, soft card, stiff card)

Colour(s) of casing

Colour of lettering (on exterior of casing)

Detail of embellishment (designs and motifs on casing)

Dimensions of casing (height, then width, in inches)

Number of preliminary pages (e.g. xxiii)

Number of narrative pages (e.g. 259)

Frontispiece (whether included or not)

Number of monochrome photographs (excluding Frontispiece)

Number of coloured plates (excluding Frontispiece)

Number and type of other illustrations

Number and types of map (or plan)

Glossary (list of abbreviations)

Bibliography (or list of author's sources of reference)

Index (with details, if appropriate)

Appendixes (with fullest possible details)

Descriptive observations (with details, especially dates)

Assessment of rarity (e.g. easily found, rare)

Assessment of research value (e.g. fair, good, prime source)

Where and when seen (if in a public archive)

# PART I
Colonies, Protectorates and other Territories

12

For additional information regarding regiments
raised in these Colonies and Territories, see
LAND FORCES OF THE BRITISH COLONIES AND PROTECTORATES
and IMPERIAL SUNSET (pages 350 and 351 respectively)

## WEST INDIES AND BRITISH HONDURAS

THE HISTORY OF THE FIRST WEST INDIA REGIMENT

Major A B Ellis
Chapman & Hall Ltd, London, 1885
Red, gold, regtl crest on front cover, 9.0 x 5.5, xii/336.
Fp, no other illustrations, 14 maps (printed in the text), Index of
personnel (all ranks).

Apps: stations and movements by year (1795-1883), list of former COs.

Served against the Colonials in the American War of Independence
(1779-1781), the expedition to Martinique and Guadaloupe (1794), various
other Caribbean operations (1795-1810), and then the British conquest
and policing of West Africa. A detailed and clearly written narrative,
somewhat dry but hard to fault. R/5 V/4. PCAL. RP.

ONE HUNDRED YEARS' HISTORY OF THE 2nd WEST INDIA REGIMENT FROM DATE OF
RAISING 1795 TO 1898

Colonel J E Caulfield
Publisher not stated, printed by Foster, Groom & Co, London, 1899
Blue and red, gold, 8.5 x 5.5, -/221.
Fp, 2 mono phots, no maps, no Index.

Apps: list of former COs (1795-1892), calendar of movements and locations.

Covers the period from the initial raising of the Bn in 1795 through to
1898. A tedious narrative, but useful for its coverage of little-known
operations in the West Indies and in West Africa.
R/5 V/3. PCAL. RMAS. RP.

WAR DIARY, 1st BATTALION BRITISH WEST INDIES REGIMENT, 1915-1918

Anon (thought to have been Lieut Col C Wood Hill)
Printer's details not known, privately by the Regiment, 1918
Reported in full calfskin, maroon, gold, 'folio', -/245.

Stated to have served in WWI in Egypt, Sinai, Palestine and Syria.
Noted thus in a catalogue. Not seen.

SLAVES IN RED COATS
The British West India Regiments, 1795-1815

Roger Norman Buckley
Yale University Press, The Book Press Inc, Battleboro, Vermont, 1979
Red, gold, 9.5 x 6.25, xi/210.
Fp, no other illustrations, 2 maps (printed in the text), no appendixes,
Bibliography, Index.

In 1795 two regiments of local negroes and creoles were recruited into
British service because freshly arrived regiments from England were
suffering such huge losses from diseases to which they had no acquired
immunity. The force was expanded to a total stength of 13 battalions. The
book traces the evolution of the regiment, its deployments, and its
political, social and economic importance vis-a-vis the Empire and
British attitudes towards the slave trade. Good background reading,
albeit with a discernible 'anti-Colonialism' undertone. Particularly
strong on the period 1795-1806. R/1 V/3. RP.


A SHORT HISTORY OF THE VOLUNTEER FORCES OF BRITISH HONDURAS (NOW BELIZE)

D N·A Fairweather
publisher not stated, apparently produced in Belize sometime in the 1970s
Stiff card, wire-stitched binding, white, black, 9.75 x 6.75, viii/43.
Fp, 7 mono phots, one map printed in text, no Index.

App: list of former COs

A very useful and easily read booklet. Well produced. R/3 V/3. JMAT.

# MIDDLE EAST

THE STORY OF THE ARAB LEGION

Brigadier John Bagot Glubb CMG DSO OBE MC
Hodder & Stoughton, London, 1948
Red, gold, 8.75 x 5.5, -/371.
Fp, 53 mono phots, 7 maps (2 on end-papers, 5 printed in text), Index.

Apps: nil

Glubb Pasha's autobiographical account of the raising of the Arab Legion
and his own services in Trans-Jordan (1921-56). R/1 V/4. RP.

GLUBB'S LEGION

Godfrey Lias
Evans Brothers Ltd, London, 1956
Blue, gold, 8.5 x 5.5, -/230.
Fp, 16 mono phots, 1 map (printed on end-papers), Index.

Apps: nil

Not a conventional history, but good background reading. Covers the
evolution and services of the force up to 1956. R/1 V/3. RP.

THE ARAB LEGION

Brigadier Peter Young DSO MC
Osprey Publishing Ltd, Reading, Berks, 1972
Red and black on white, figure of Arab soldier mounted on camel,
soft card covers with 'Perfect' binding, 9.75 x 7.25, -/40.
31 excellent mono phots, 18 coloured plates drawn by Michael Roffe,
no maps, no Index.

Apps: nil

One of Osprey's 'Men at Arms' series. Very condensed, but easy to read
and consult. All aspects of the regt's history covered through to 1956
when the Legion lost all its British officers and became 'The Jordan
Arab Army'. R/1 V/2. PCAL. RP.

THE IRAQ LEVIES 1915-1932

Brigadier J Gilbert Browne
Royal United Services Institution, London, 1932
Sand brown, gold, regtl crest with two diagonal blue stripes on front
cover, 10.0 x 7.25, vii/88.
Fp, one mono phot, 3 useful folding maps bound in, Index.

Apps: all H&A to British and Indian personnel and to locally-recruited rank and file.

Iraq Levies first formed in 1915 with 40 mounted Arabs as a Field Intelligence unit during the Mesopotamia campaign. Grew to a strength of 6199 officers and men in 1922. A detailed account of an unusual force which helped to keep the peace in Iraq while that country was emerging as an independent nation from the wreckage of the old Ottoman Empire. Served to protect British oil installations and other assets. Majority of officers were British and Indian, dozens of whom are mentioned in the narrative. R/4 V/5. PCAL. RP.


NOTE ON THE HISTORY OF THE CAMEL CORPS
History of the Camel Corps

El Miralai G A V Keays Bey
Sudan Record, Khartoum, 1939
Brown, gold, 9.0 x 6.0, -/103.
No illustrations, no maps, no Index.

Apps: list of former COs, list of former officers, actions and patrols (1884-1930).

A brief history of the Egyptian/Sudan Camel Corps. R/4 V/2. GC.


A JOB WELL DONE
A History of the Palestine Police 1920-1948

Edward Horne BEM
Anchor Press Ltd, Tiptree, Essex, for The Palestine Police Old Comrades Benevolent Association, 1982
Blue, silver, -/616.
39 mono photos, one map printed in text, illustrations of badges and insignia, Index.

Apps: list of former COs, details of rank structure, details of cups, shields and other trophies awarded annually for sport, drill, musketry and turn-out, chart illustrating the great diversity of Jewish political parties in Palestine (1945-48).

A detailed and well-written account covering the whole period. Many individuals named in narrative, many small incidents and engagements interestingly described. An attractive book. R/2 V/4. RP/RLP.


HISTORICAL RECORDS OF THE MALTESE CORPS OF THE BRITISH ARMY

Major A G Chesney
Published in London, 1897
Casebound, cloth, gold lettering, octavo, xii/210.
17 colour plates (mostly of uniforms). Not seen.

# ADEN

ADEN TROOP
A Summary of the War Diary of the Aden Troop 1914-18

Anon
The Pioneer Press, Allahabad, 1921
Maroon, 10.75 x 8.5, -/81.
No illustrations, one map in rear pocket, no Index.

Apps: nil

A very detailed account, in diary form, of the Troop's operations
against the Turks on the Yemen frontier. Good for factual information, but
not 'fleshed out' by reference to personalities. The Aden Troop came
under the administrative control of the Indian Army in Delhi, but enjoyed
a considerable degree of independence during WWI. It consisted of a
Camel Company and an Infantry Company often not exceeding 50/60 men.
The normal complement was 2 British officers commanding a mixed bag of
Indian Army sepoys and sowars who seemingly volunteered for 'special
duties' away from their parent regiments.

This was 'sideshow of a sideshow', the main sideshow being Colonel
T E Lawrence's operations further north. Aden Troop did not see a great
deal of action, and what they did see is described here in a terse
and dry summary form, but it is the only account available for the
period. R/4 V/3. IOL. RGB.

# CEYLON

THE HISTORY OF THE CEYLON GARRISON ARTILLERY
Formerly Ceylon Artillery Volunteers

Sgt V Wijeyesekera and Sgt Ondapji
Times of Ceylon Co Ltd, Colombo, n.d. (c.1952)
Soft card, light blue, black, regtl crest on front cover,
12.0 x 9.0, -/101.
Fp, 39 mono phots, no maps, Index.

Apps: Roll of Honour, H&A, list of former officers, lists of NCOs and
Other Ranks, note on the instructions for war service mobilisation.

A straightforward account of the unit's history from inception in 1888
through to 1952. The narrative relies mainly upon regtl orders and the
regtl diary, therefore somewhat dry. R/4 V/4. IWM/AMOT. PJE/JMAT.


THE HISTORY OF THE CEYLON POLICE, Volume I, 1795-1870

G K Pippet
The Times of Ceylon Co Ltd, Colombo, n.d. (c.1938)
Buff, blue, force cap badge on front cover, 8.5 x 5.5, xii/372.
Fp, large number of portrait sketches of Ceylon Police officers,
no maps, Index.

Apps: H&A, plus a large number of appendixes relating to police ordnances,
instructions, etc.

A very detailed account of the early history, but lacking in 'human
interest'. R/4 V/4. IOL. JA.


THE HISTORY OF THE CEYLON POLICE, Volume II, 1866-1913

A C Dep
The Times of Ceylon Co Ltd, for the Colombo Police Amenities Fund,
n.d. (c.1969)
Light buff, blue, force cap badge on front cover, 8.5 x 5.5, viii/527.
Fp, large number of portrait sketches and photographs of officers,
no maps, Index.

Apps: various reproductions of police ordnances, instructions, etc,
of very limited interest.

Like Volume I, this is a highly detailed account of the development and
services of the force. However, unlike Volume I, it is much more
interesting and contains abundant information regarding the services of
individual officers of the period. R/4 V/5. IOL. JA.

# BURMA AND ASSAM

STANDING ORDERS OF THE SECOND BATTALION THE BURMA RIFLES
With a Short Record of the Battalion

Anon
Gale & Polden Ltd, Aldershot (by Authority), 1948
Dark green, gold, regtl crest on front cover, 9.25 x 7.0, ix/141.
No illustrations, no maps, no Index.

Apps: H&A (for WWII), list of former COs.

The contents precisely as suggested by title. The bulk of the book is
dedicated to the bn's Standing Orders. A very brief history occupies
the last 7 pages, this being a summary in annual diary form.
R/4 V/2. NAM. PJE.


THE HISTORY OF THE ASSAM REGIMENT, Volume I, 1941-47

Capt Peter Steyn MC
Orient Longmans, Calcutta, 1959
Black, white, regtl crest on front cover embellished with the regtl
colours, 8.5 x 5.5, xvii/270.
Fp, 6 mono phots, 14 maps (2 printed on end-papers, 12 printed in text),
Index.

Apps: Roll of Honour (all ranks), H&A (all ranks), list of former COs,
list of Subedar Majors.

Regt was part of the Indian Army, entirely military in nature. Not to
be confused with the Assam Rifles (a Frontier Police regt). Formed in
early 1941 as part of the general wartime expansion of the Indian Army.
It was not then anticipated that it would be required shortly to fight
the Japanese on its home ground. Narrative covers regt's battles at
Jessami, Kohima, Mawbaik, Mandalay and advance to Rangoon. Very readable,
many individuals named, packed with good detail of many major and minor
engagements in which the regt's two battalions took part. R/2 V/5.
IOL/NAM. AN/PJE/RP.


HISTORY OF THE ASSAM RIFLES

Col L W Shakespear CB CIE
MacMillan & Co Ltd, London, 1929. Reprinted by Firma KLM (Pvt) Ltd
for the Tribal Research Institute, Aizawl, Mizoram, 1977. Reprinted by
Spectrum Publications, 1980. Reprinted again in India, 1983.
Original binding, dark green, gold, regtl crest on front cover,
9.0 x 6.0, xxiv/301.
Fp, 84 mono phots, one coloured plate, 6 maps (bound in), Bibliography,
Index.

Apps: list of former COs, notes on affiliation to Gurkha regts, notes
on changes in the Assam Rifles organisation since 1863.

Assam Rifles were Frontier Constabulary first raised in 1824 to control the border between India and Burma. British officers with specially recruited Gurkha rank and file. A very exhaustive history covering the first 100 years. Detailed account of operations in Chin Hills, Naga Hills, Abor, Lushai, etc. Some personnel were transferred to the Assam Regiment when that unit was being formed in 1941. R/4 (for original edition) V/4. IOL/IWM. PJE/RP.


SENTINELS OF THE NORTH EAST
The Assam Rifles

Maj Gen D K Palit VrC FRGS
Palit & Palit, New Delhi, 1984
Cloth and card, stone grey, black, 8.5 x 5.5, xv/329.
Fp, 27 mono phots, 8 maps (one printed on end-papers, 7 bound in), Index.

Apps: H&A (very extensive, all ranks, including service numbers), list of former Inspector Generals and Director Generals, notes on recruitment policy (1835-1982), notes on regtl crest, marching song.

An excellent readable account of the Assam Rifles and its predecessor units. First four chapters are a condensation of Colonel Shakespeare's 1929 history. Narrative then brings the story through to 1982. Good coverage for WWII when Assam Rifles formed part of Force 136 ('V' operations). Only one detected error; portrait photograph of Major Shakespear should be dated c.1920, not c.1890. R/1 V/5. AAM/MCJ.


HISTORY OF THE CHIN HILLS BATTALION, BURMA MILITARY POLICE

Capt A C Moore
Published at Falam, 1934, no other details stated.
Green, brown spine, no lettering or embellishment, 8.0 x 6.0, iii/47.
Fp, one mono phot, 8 coloured sketches, no maps, no Index.

Apps: list of former COs

Readable but very brief condensed history covering 1894-1934. Unit was one of the many which constitued the Burma Military Police until 1937 when Burma was separated from India. Chin Hills Bn then became part of the Burma Frontier Force. Rank and file were recruited in Nepal. Capt Moore was at one time Commandant. R/5 V/3. NAM. PJE.


AMIABLE ASSASSINS
The Story of the Kachin Levies

I Fellowes-Gordon
Robert Hale Ltd, London, 1957
Green, gold, 9.0 x 6.0, -/159.
20 mono phots, no maps, no appendixes, no Index.

Written almost in the form of a novel, but thought to be a good account of the North Kachin Levies during WWII. Reported to be the only unit which remained behind in Burma when the Japanese invaded. R/2 V/3. IWM. PJE.

## FAR EAST

BRITISH AND INDIAN ARMIES IN THE EAST INDIES (1685-1935)

Alan Harfield
Picton Publishing (Chippenham) Ltd, Chippenham, Wilts, 1984
Dark green, gold, 8.5 x 6.0, xv/411.
Fp, 102 mono phots, 8 colour plates, 13 maps (one printed on end-papers,
12 printed in text), Index.

Apps: list of units which served as garrison troops in the Settlements
of Penang, Malacca and Singapore (1805-1915), list of military graves and
burials in the Straits Settlements (1786-1899), medal roll for the
Colonial Auxiliary Forces Long Service medal to the Straits Settlements
Volunteer Force, idem the 1935 Silver Jubilee medal, various muster rolls
(mainly listed in text), Glossary, Bibliography.

A massively researched account of the British conquest, settlement and
administration of the East Indies (comprising Singapore, Malaya, Java,
Sumatra, Sarawak, etc). Not a regtl history, but a goldmine of information
for historians, genealogists and medal collectors. Not a notably 'readable'
book, but containing a vast quantity of information drawn from original
documents and arranged in such a way that it can be easily consulted. An
excellent production. R/1 V/4. RP.


A HISTORY OF THE SINGAPORE VOLUNTEER CORPS 1854-1937
Being also an Historical Account of Volunteering in Malaya

Captain T M Winsley SVC
Government Printing Office, Singapore, 1938
Soft card covers, light green, red, 9.5 x 7.5, xvii/205.
Fp, 51 mono phots, one colour plate, numerous small line drawings, no
maps, Index.

Apps: H&A, list of former COs, list of former officers, list of casualties
for the Singapore mutiny, letters, Warrants, fortifications, Colours,
camp songs.

This is the only published history of the Singapore Volunteers. Contains
many useful notes on the Volunteers of the Federated Malay States and
the Straits Settlements. Published in 1938, and therefore does not
describe the important role played by the Volunteers following the
Japanes invasion (1941-42). R/4 V/4. JLC.


THE MALAY REGIMENT

M C ff Sheppard
Department of Public Relations Malay Peninsula, Kuala Lumpur, 1947
Stiff card covers, stapled and glued, illustrated with photograph of
Port Dickson, deep pink, 9.5 x 7.0, -/52.
28 mono phots, 2 line drawings, 3 maps (one of Malaya tipped in as Fp, one
of Singapore tipped in, one printed in text), no Index.

Apps: Roll of Honour (KIA and WIA for all ranks, British and Malay, with details of where, when and how), H&A (all ranks), list of all British officers serving with the regt in February 1942, list of all Malay officers holding High Commissioner's Commissions (with details of their post-war promotions).

Foreword written by Maj Gen A E Percival who surrendered Singapore to the Japanese in 1942. A story of poor preparation, fierce resistance, and ultimate capture. Not a large work, produced to 'utility' standards, but extremely useful for the appendixes of personnel. Many founder members of the regiment (1933) appear in the group photographs, and are named in the captions. Invaluable for genealogists and medal collectors. R/4 V/4. RMAS. JRS/RP.


HISTORY OF THE MALAY REGIMENT 1933-1942

Dol Ramli
Publisher not stated. Seemingly written by Mr Dol Ramli in Singapore in 1955 as an academic research project, subsequently produced by Life Printers of Kuala Lumpur in 1963.
Green, gold, regtl crest on front cover, 10.5 x 7.0, vi/150.
7 mono phots, 10 maps printed in text, Index.

Apps: list of former COs with biographical notes, list of former officers, H&A, nominal rolls, details of establishments and rates of pay.

A condensed account from the original raising of the regt through to the conclusion of the 1942 campaign. R/4 V/4. AMOT. RP.


HISTORY OF THE MALAY STATES GUIDES 1873-1919

Inder Singh s/o Sgt Ram Singh MSG
Cathay Printers, Penang, c.1965
Soft card covers, photographic illustration of Sergeants with Colours, 8.5 x 5.5, -/122.
Fp, 14 mono phots, one map printed in text, no Index.

Apps: lists of former COs, officers, Subedar Majors, Granthis (priests), notes on the Aden Field Force, notes on food, costumes, sport, Sikh history, etc, Glossary, Bibliography.

The only known record of this Indian-recruited Malay States regt from formation to disbandment. Strong on biographical information. R/4 V/4. JLC.


SPEARHEAD IN MALAYA

J W G Morgan
Peter Davies, London, 1959
Green, 8.0 x 5.0, -/288.
One mono group photograh, no maps, no Index.

Apps: H&A

The story of the Malayan Police Force, concentrating on the Emergency period
(1948-56) and particularly the activities of the Jungle Squads. Largely
autobiographical, but a good insight into police work during that
period.


THE ROYAL BRUNEI MALAY REGIMENT 1961-1976

Major A G Harfield
Star Press, Bandar Seri Begawan, Brunei, 1977
Gold lettering, 10.25 x 7.5, xv/170.
56 mono phots, 3 coloured plates, no maps, Index.

Apps: muster roll at formation, list of officers.

Covers the first 25 years of the regt's history. Strong on ceremonial
and regtl dress. 500 copies printed. R/2 V/4. JLC.


A RECORD OF THE ACTIONS OF THE HONG KONG VOLUNTEER DEFENCE FORCE IN
THE BATTLE FOR HONG KONG, DECEMBER 1941

Known to exist and to have been published in Hong Kong in pamphlet
form (60 pages), but not seen.

# FIJI

PACIFIC COMMANDOS
New Zealanders and Fijians in Action
A History of Southern Independent Commando and First Commando Fiji
Guerillas

C R Larsen
A M & A W Reed, Wellington, NZ, 1946
Yellow, black, dimensions not reported, xiv/161.
12 mono phots, 5 maps printed in text, no Index.

Apps: Roll of Honour, H&A, nominal rolls, list of Commandos engaged
in special raids against the Japanese.

Useful and interesting account of a 'special forces' unit operating
in a little-recognised area of WWII. R/4 V/5. JS.


HISTORY OF THE FIJI MILITARY FORCES 1939-45

Lieut R A Howlett
Published by the Crown Agents for the Colonies on behalf of the Government of Fiji, printed by Whitcombe & Tombs Ltd, Christchurch, NZ, 1948
Stiff card with cloth spine, red and green, black, regtl crest on front
cover, 8.75 x 5.5, -/267.
Fp, 52 mono phots, 2 line drawings, 3 maps (2 printed in text, one large
folding map of Bougainville Island bound in), no Index.

Apps: Roll of Honour (all ranks), H&A (all ranks), list of officers who
served with Fiji forces in WWII, officers of the Fiji Home Guard, plus
numerous other appendixes relating to Fiji Corps of Engineers, Fiji
Corps of Signals, Fiji Artillery Regt, etc.

A very comprehensive account of the Fijian military commitment to the
South Pacific campaign. Three battalions of infantry and ancillary units
saw much action against the Japanese. Training, administration and some
officers were provided by New Zealand  . Corporal Sefanaia Sukanaivalu
was awarded a posthumous VC for rescuing wounded comrades under fire
during the Solomon Islands campaign, June 1944. R/3 V/5. PCL. HEC/RP.


AMONG THOSE PRESENT
The Official Story of the Pacific Islands at War

Anon
Printed by The Whitefriars Press Ltd, for HMSO, London, 1946
Paper cover, illustrated, grey-green, buff, 8.75 x 5.5, -/96.
Fp, 58 mono phots, 4 maps(printed in the text), no appendixes, no Index.

Not a regtl history, and not specifically about Fijian forces, but a
splendid little historical record of behind-the-lines fighting by the WWII
ad hoc native contingents on the Solomon Islands. A fine record of a
little-known campaign. R/2 V/3. HEC/RP.

# CHINA

SHANGHAI DEFENCE FORCES SOUVENIR, Volume I

Anon
North China Daily News, Shanghai, n.d.
Orange, black, illustrated with sketch of soldier, Chinese house and
barbed wire, 15.0 x 10.5, ii/24.
110 mono phots, no maps, no Index
No other volumes reported.

A commemorative booklet relating to the British, US, French, Japanese
and Indian forces which constituted the Shanghai Defence Force
(Shaiforce) 1927. Mainly pictures, with condensed narrative. Major
emphasis on British and Indian units (military, naval and aviation).
Useful background reading. R/4 V/2. GC.


SHANGHAIED - A PICTORIAL RECORD OF THE 1st 16th FOOT, Volume II

Anon
The Willow Pattern Press Ltd, Shanghai, n.d.
Stiff card covers, brown, gold, 9.75 x 7.25, -/33.
80 mono phots, one map printed in text, no Index.

A booklet commemorating the services of the 1st Bedfordshire & Hertfordshire
Regt while part of Shaiforce (1927). The foreword states that Volumes II
and III 'deal with the regiment's experiences in China', while Volume I
(of which 2400 copies are said to have been printed) 'deal, for the greater
part, with the itinerary of the battalion from Malta'. Volumes I and III
not seen, but presumably they have the same format as this Volume II.
R/4 V/2. GC.


THE BUGLE
A Chronicle of the 2nd Bn The Durham Light Infantry
Sialkot to Shanghai

J F M Sumner
Shanghai Mercury, 1927
Paper covers, stapled, light green, black, regtl crest on front cover,
8.5 x 5.5, i/52.
27 mono phots, no maps, no Index.

A useful little book dealing with the services of 1 DLI while part of
Shaiforce. R/4 V/3. GC.


'A' COMPANY S.V.C. (SHANGHAI VOLUNTEER MIH-HO-LOONG RIFLES) 1870-1930

Lieut J Moffat
Publisher/printer shown as 'N.G.D.N.', Shanghai, c.1932
Red, black spine, black, 10.5 x 8.0, i/40.
5 mono phots, no maps, no Index.

Apps: Roll of Honour, list of former COs, list of former officers.

A short history of the Company, first formed as a part-time fire
fighting unit, later trained as military Volunteers following the
Taiping rebellion. Mih-ho-loong (alternatively, Meehouloung) means
'fire eating devil'. A useful source for names and details of former
members. R/5 V/4. NAM. PJE.


EIGHTY YEARS OF THE SHANGHAI VOLUNTEER CORPS, 1853-1938

Anon
The Cosmopolitan Press, Shanghai, n.d. (c.1938)
Seen in alligator (possibly snake) skin binding, black, superb large
gold and silk Corps crest on front cover, 6.0 x 12.0, v/283.
Profusely illustrated throughout with photographs of officers and men
in formal groups, on training exercises, on ceremonial parades, etc.
Numerous captioned individual studio portraits of individual officers.
Two maps, no Index.

Apps: no formal appendixes, but lists of officers appear at various points
in the text.

This was a cosmopolitan unit recruited from the international community
residing in Shanghai between 1853 and 1938. Membership included Americans,
Japanese,Portuguese, Philippinos, White Russians, Chinese, Austrians,
Germans, Italians and British personnel. A highly illustrated book with
many short sections dealing with the sub-units and with the main events of
most years. During their existence, the Volunteers were mobilised on
twenty-five occasions for small wars and to deal with riots in Shanghai
and the North China area. A splendid book, redolent with the spirit of
Empire. R/4 V/5. NAM. PJE.

# PART II
## Africa

For additional information regarding regiments
raised in West, East and Central Africa, see
LAND FORCES OF THE BRITISH COLONIES AND PROTECTORATES
and IMPERIAL SUNSET (pages 350 and 351 respectively)

## WEST AFRICA

THE HISTORY OF THE ROYAL WEST AFRICAN FRONTIER FORCE

Colonel A Haywood CMG CBE DSO and Brigadier F A Clarke DSO
Gale & Polden Ltd, Aldershot, 1964
Blue, gold, regtl crest on front cover, 9.5 x 6.0, xv/540.
Fp, 42 mono phots, 50 maps printed in text, Glossary, Index.

Apps: Roll of Honour (British officers and NCOs), H&A (WWII only),
VC citations, notes on other medals awarded, order of battle for various
years, list of Inspector-Generals, 1903 dress regulations, etc.

A magnificent book, written with great attention to detail and a model
of what a good regtl history should be. Narrative divided into two parts:
first, WAFF evolution and campaigns up to 1919 (concentrating upon the
East Africa operations of 1915-18); second, history from 1920 to
1961 (concentrating upon the Burma campaign of 1943-45). The story
concludes with the Southern Cameroons commitment of 1959-60. One of the
last of Gale & Polden's very high quality publications. R/4 V/5. BCC/RP.

WITH THE NIGERIANS IN GERMAN EAST AFRICA

Capt W D Downes MC
Methuen & Co Ltd, London, 1919
Red, black, 9.0 x 5.5, xiii/352.
Fp, 30 mono phots, 5 maps (4 sketch maps plus one large folding map bound
in at the rear), Index.

Apps: Roll of Honour (British officers and NCOs, KIA, wounded, and
died of disease), H&A (for the Nigerian Brigade for the entire campaign,
all ranks, with dates of awards and a precis of each citation), summary
of British and Indian units in the field at the end of 1916, notes on
effective strengths 1917.

This is the story of Nigerian Brigade - 1st, 2nd, 3rd and 4th Bns The
Nigerian Regt, plus a Nigerian Battery. The Brigade had already served for
18 months in the Cameroons and had returned to Nigeria when, at short
notice, it was remobilised for service in East Africa. Sailed from
Lagos, November 1916. Operations and battles are described in great detail,
with numerous eye-witness accounts by officers who took part. The book
also contains a brief summary of the origins of the regt (evolved from
the Hausa armed police first formed in 1863). R/4 V/5. JRS/RP.

THE GOLD COAST REGIMENT IN THE EAST AFRICAN CAMPAIGN

Sir Hugh Clifford KCMG
John Murray, London, 1920
Brown-grey boards, black leather spine, gold, 8.75 x 5.75, xi/306.
Fp, 7 mono phots, 5 maps (3 printed in text, 2 bound in), Index.

Apps: H&A, regtl strength (tabular form), notes on the history of
the Mounted Infantry of the Gold Coast Regiment.

Covers the services of the regt in East Africa between mid-1916 and
mid-1918. Very readable, a good 'human interest' view of the campaign.
R/3 V/4. BCC.


HISTORY OF THE SIERRA LEONE BATTALION OF THE ROYAL WEST AFRICAN FRONTIER
FORCE

Lieut R P M Davis
Details of the publisher not clear, but thought to have been the
Government Printer, Freetown, 1929
Brown, black, 8.25 x 5.5, ix/147.
no mono phots or other illustrations, one map (printed on rear end-
paper), Bibliography, Index.

Apps: Roll of Honour (all ranks for the Cameroon Expedition 1914-16),
notes on the presentation of Colours (1922), list of officers and
British and African NCOs present on that occasion.

A good detailed history from formation in 1829 as the Sierre Leone Police
through to the 1920s. Covers all the major involvements in punitive
expeditions (Ashanti 1900, Kissi 1905, etc), and the Bn's services
in the Cameroons (1914-16). R/4 V/4. JA.


THE LEOPARD
The Regimental Journal of the West Africa Regiment

Gale & Polden Ltd, Aldershot, 1926-28
Seen in green cloth, casebound, 16.0 x 7.0, -/88 and -/180.
some mono phots, drawings and sketch maps, no appendixes, no Index.

The West Africa Regiment commenced recruiting in 1898 and was disbanded
in August 1928. No formal history was ever published. The Journal
was first issued in October 1926 and ran to eight issues
(until disbandment). This volume is therefore a complete run of the
Journal, arranged in two volumes, each of four issues, the whole bound
in a single casing. It seems likely that Gale & Polden produced a limited
run, in this format, for former officers and their friends circa 1928-29.
Contains all the usual regtl news, with four good articles on
the Cameroons campaign. R/5 V/4. JRS.


ARAKAN ASSIGNMENT
The Story of the 82nd West African Division

Anon
Printed for PR Services (West Africa) by Roxy Press, New Delhi, c.1946
Illustrated paper cover, 8.0 x 5.5, -/44.
Fp, 24 mono phots, one coloured plate, one sketch, one folding map,
no Index.

Apps: order of battle (list of units in the Division), summary of
H&A up to 28 February 1946 (no names).

This is a brief Divisional history useful only as a general background.
R/3 V/3. JRS.


JUNGLE COMMANDO
The Story of the West African Expeditionary Force's First Campaign
in Burma

Anon
Prepared for the Ministry of Information by PR Branch, GHQ West Africa
n.d. (probably c.1944)
Illustrated paper cover, 8.5 x 6.0, vi/34.
Fp, 25 mono phots, Divisional sign inside rear cover, one map (inside
front cover), no appendixes, no Index.

Concerns the 81st (WA) Division in Burma up to July 1944. A 'utility'
war-time publication for general public consumption and therefore
very generalised in content. R/3 V/2. JRS.


A SHORT HISTORY OF THE 1st (WEST AFRICAN) INFANTRY BRIGADE IN
THE ARAKAN 1944-45

Brigadier C R A Swynnerton
Printed by E G Aylmer at Thacker's Press & Directories Ltd, Calcutta,
1945
Stiff card covers, grey with purple cloth spine, 8.75 x 5.75, iii/70.
no mono phots, no other illustrations, 4 maps (bound in at rear),
no appendixes, no Index.

A detailed but rather colourless account of a Nigerian brigade in the
82nd (WA) Division. The period covered is from December 1944 to
May 1945. The only individuals mentioned by name in the narrative are
some of the Other Ranks who gained awards for bravery. This and the
previous two titles (above) are listed here as suggested background
reading because, apart from Haywood and Clarke's book, so little has
been written about West African forces in WWII. R/4 V/3. SB.


HISTORY OF THE 1st Bn THE SIERRA LEONE REGIMENT, ROYAL WEST AFRICAN
FRONTIER FORCE, 1939-45

Anon
No details of publisher stated, c.1947
Seen in casebound cloth, green, white lettering on black label (front
cover), 13.0 x 8.0, -/60 (pages not numbered).
no mono phots or other illustrations, 2 poorly executed maps (bound in),
no Index.

Apps: Roll of Honour (KIA and WIA, all ranks), list of officers, WOs and
BNCOs who embarked at Lagos for India (7 July 1943).

Seen in cyclostyled typescript. Presumably, therefore, some dozens of copies were produced for private circulation, but the work never published formally. Very badly typed and a dull narrative. Useful mainly for the 'personnel' appendix. The battalion served in India and in Burma (Kaladan) from 1943 to 1945. R/5 V/3. RMAS. RP.


THE GOLD COAST POLICE 1844-1938

W H Gillespie
The Government Printer, Accra, Gold Coast, 1955
Stiff card, light blue boards with dark blue spine, black, GCP crest on front cover, 8.5 x 5.75, -/89.
6 mono phots, some line drawings of uniforms, no maps, Index.

Apps: Roll of Honour (1930-1953), H&A (with names and years of award for George Medal, King's Police Gallantry Medal, Colonial Police Medal for Gallantry, Colonial Police Medal for Meritorious Service, etc), list of former officers with biographical details (1894-1953), notes on criminal statistics.

Clear straightforward account of the Force's evolution and operational role. Very good for reference to individuals and to medal entitlements. R/4 V/4. RP.


HISTORICAL RECORDS OF THE ROYAL AFRICA CORPS

J J Crooks
Published in Dublin, 1925
Casebound cloth, octavo, viii/136.

Covers the period 1800 to 1821. Known to exist, but not seen.

# EAST AFRICA

UGANDA VOLUNTEERS AND THE WAR

Capt R S Cholmley
Published by A D Cameron of Kampala, printed by D L Monro of The
Calcutta General Printing Co Ltd, 1917
Brown, gold, 8.75 x 5.5, iv/110.
no photographs, no other illustrations, no maps, no Index.

Apps: nominal roll of the European and Asian members of the UVR,
appointments, promotions, list of Adjutants.

This is the story of the Uganda Volunteer Reserve and its contribution
to the most critical years of the war in East Africa. Excellent source
for details of personnel, but of interest mainly for the notes on the
bewildering range of now forgotten units mentioned in the narrative: The
Baganda Rifles, Uganda Police Service Battalion, Uganda Transport Corps,
Uganda Rifle Corps, Uganda Native Medical Corps, Uganda Medical Service,
Uganda Carrier Corps, Southern Frontier Force, Protectorate Armed Vessels,
East Africa Supply Corps, East Africa Mounted Rifles (Bowker's Horse),
East Africa Transport Corps, Bukakata-Lutobo Ox Transport Corps, Belgian
Advance Ox Transport Corps, etc. R/5 V/4. GC.


K.A.R.
Being an Unofficial Account of the Origins and Activities of the King's
African Rifles

W Lloyd-Jones
Arrowsmith, London, 1926
Maroon, gold, attractive profile sketch of an Askari on the front cover,
9.0 x 5.5, -/296.
Fp, 37 mono phots, one line drawing, one map (printed in text),
Bibliography, Index.

Apps: Roll of Honour (WWI only, British officers and British NCOs only).

The sub-title - 'an unofficial account' - is slightly misleading. This
is a good authoritative description of the regt's root and services
between 1890 and 1925. It covers the anti-slavery and punitive
operations of the period, the campaign against von Lettow-Vorbeck, and
the 1920 campaign against the 'Mad Mullah'. Written in a pleasant readable
style. Many useful commentaries on KAR attitudes and regtl spirit,
with interesting extracts in the narrative from some of the citations
for individual bravery awards. R/2 V/4. DJB/RP.

THE STORY OF THE EAST AFRICAN MOUNTED RIFLES

Capt C J Wilson
The East African Standard Ltd, Nairobi, Kenya, 1938
Dark green, gold, 8.5 x 5.5, viii/130.
25 mono phots, 2 maps (printed on end-papers), 3 topographical sketches, no Index.

Apps: Roll of Honour, nominal roll of all ranks (with some biographical notes and details of honours and awards), list of former COs and other officers, list of important historical dates for the regt.

A very readable account of this locally-raised unit. The lack of an Index is irritating, but the narrative is packed with references to individual members. The nominal roll appendix is particularly useful to medal collectors and genealogists. Reported to be a very accurate and reliable reference source. R/3 V/4. BCC.


THE KING'S AFRICAN RIFLES IN MADAGASCAR

Kenneth Gandar Dower
Published by East Africa Command in conjunction with the Ministry of Information, Nairobi, n.d. (c.1943)
Stiff card, stitched spine, red and sepia, white, 9.0 x 7.0, -/64.
79 interesting but poorly reproduced photographs, 2 excellent coloured maps (bound in), no appendixes, no Index.

Tells the story of the KAR's role in the Madagascar campaign. Covers their services following the initial assault at Diego Suarez on 4 May 1942 through to the signing of the armistice at Ambavalao, 1200 miles further south. A war-time 'utility' standard of production, but the only history available for this little known campaign. R/4 V/2. LM.


WAR JOURNAL OF THE FIFTH (KENYA) BATTALION, THE KING'S AFRICAN RIFLES

W D Draffan and T C C Lewin
Publication details not stated, but seemingly produced c.1946
Blue, gilt, 8.75 x 5.5, -/151.
no photographs, no other illustrations, three folding maps (bound in at the rear), no Index.

Apps: list of former COs (1902-1945).

Deals mainly with WWII (Somaliland, Abyssinia, Madagascar, and the Kabaw Valley operation in Burma). A readable narrative containing plenty of interesting detail, presented in an amateur format.
R/4 V/3. RMAS. RP.

SHORT HISTORY OF THE 6th (T.T.) BATTALION, THE KING'S AFRICAN RIFLES

Lieut Col C J M Watts
The General Printing & Stationery Co Ltd, Port Louis, Mauritius, 1950
Casebound in full Morocco leather, brown, gilt, 7.0 x 5.0, -/23.
no photographs, no other illustrations, no maps, no Index.

Apps: H&A (summary only, but with full citation for Sgt Nigel Leakey's
Victoria Cross).

6th Tanganyika Territory Battalion evolved in 1918-19 with the removal
of that area from German administration. The author gives a sketchy
account of that period and the inter-war years, and then an even sketchier
account of the WWII services of 1/6th, 2/6th and 3/6th Bns. The unique
Kabaw Valley campaign, during the reconquest of Burma, and in which 2/6th
and 3/6th Bns played a gallant part, is covered here in six lines of
narrative. A very inadequate epitaph to a fine regiment. R/5 V/1. RP.


THE KING'S AFRICAN RIFLES
A Short History

Lieut Col H Moyse-Bartlett MBE
Printed by The Regal Press Ltd, Nairobi, for the Regimental Committee,
n.d. (but probably c.1950)
Stiff card, stapled, green, black, 7.25 x 5.0, -/16.
No photographs, no other illustrations, no maps, no appendixes, no Index.

As the Foreword by Maj Gen W A Dimoline explains, the KAR had no
permanent establishment of European personnel. Officers and senior
British NCOs served with KAR on detachment from their parent British
Army units, usually for two or three years, occasionally longer. During
the 1950s, almost all of the Subalterns were National Service officers,
serving in East Africa for only 12 or 18 months. This booklet was
intended to give new arrivals some idea of the KAR's history and regtl
spirit. R/4 V/1. RP.


THE KING'S AFRICAN RIFLES
A Study in the Military History of East and Central Africa 1890-1945

Lieut Col H Moyse-Bartlett MBE
Gale & Polden Ltd, Aldershot, 1956
Black, gold, regtl crest on front cover, 9.75 x 6.0, xix/727.
Fp, 40 mono phots, 58 maps (11 bound in, 47 printed in text), Glossary,
Bibliography, Index.

Apps: battalion locations and movements (1939-45), notes on uniforms,
notes on bands, campaign medallic awards.

Just as Haywood and Clarke's history of the RWAFF is a 'tour de force'
in its field, so does this huge work by Moyse-Bartlett stand head and
shoulders above anything else written about African soldiers. Very deeply
researched, lucidly written, masses of information arranged in digestible
form. Good coverage (from page 475 onwards) of KAR services in the

campaigns in Abysinnia, Somaliland and Eritrea (1941-42), against the Vichy French in Madagascar (1942), and against the Japanese in Burma (1943-45). The lack of an 'Honours & Awards' appendix is a frustration for medal collectors but, with so many battalions raised during WWII, compilation would have been very difficult. However, many officers, and some African Other Ranks, are mentioned in the narrative. A superb book. R/3 V/5. BCC/RP.


THE CHARGING BUFFALO
A History of the Kenya Regiment 1937-1963

Guy Campbell
Leo Cooper in association with Secker & Warburg, printed at The Bath Press, Bath, 1986
Dull orange, gold, 9.5 x 6.25, ix/180.
30 mono phots, one map (printed in text), Bibliography, Index.

Apps: Rolls of Honour (two, one being for 1939-45, the other for 1952-57), list of former officers and list of former Other Ranks (both stated by the author to be incomplete).

The regiment was recruited almost entirely from the European population, and their descendents, who had settled in Kenya in the early 1900s. It fought with distinction against the Italians in Abyssinia and Eritrea, but the bulk of the narrative deals with its specialised role in the suppression of the Mau Mau uprising of the early 1950s. A Territorial Force unit, the regt seems to have kept little in the way of documentation. This book is therefore based largely upon individual anecdotes. The author succeeds, perhaps against the odds, in recounting a dark episode in Kenya's history with flair and humour. R/1 V/4. RP.


THE KENYA POLICE, 1887-1960

M Robert Foran
Robert Hale Ltd, for The Government of the Colony and Protectorate of Kenya, 1962
Blue, silver, 8.75 x 5.5, xvi/237.
68 very good mono phots, 2 maps (printed in the text), Index.

Apps: a brief list of former senior officers.

An excellent readable coverage of the entire period. W R Foran was also author of his autobiographical A CUCKOO IN KENYA, The Reminiscences of a Pioneer Police Officer in British East Africa, published by Hutchinson & Company, London, 1936. Good background reading for the evolution of the Kenya Police and the story of the early settler days. R/3 V/4. RP.

## NORTHERN AND SOUTHERN RHODESIA

THE 2nd RHODESIA REGIMENT IN EAST AFRICA

Lieut Col Algernon Essex Capell DSO
Simson & Co Ltd, London (UK), 1923
Dark blue, gold, 9.25 x 6.0, iv/132.
no photographs, no other illustrations, 7 maps (6 printed in text, one
bound in), no Index.

Apps: Roll of Honour, H&A, list of former COs, summary of casualties,
nominal roll of members.

A well-written detailed account of 2 RR's efforts in East Africa during
WWI. The nominal roll appendix is particularly helpful to medal
collectors and genealogists because it tells the researcher each man's
highest rank held, date of attestation, whether killed or wounded,
and any awards made. RMAS. BCC/RP.


GUNNERS
A Narrative of the Gunners of Southern Rhodesia during the Second
World War

'Tort' (anon)
The Southern Rhodesian Artillery Association, Salisbury, Southern
Rhodesia, 1947
Red, blue, regtl crest on front cover, 8.75 x 5.5, -/383.
Fp, 100 interesting mono phots, 4 maps (printed on end-papers), Glossary,
no Index.

Apps: Roll of Honour (KIA and WIA), H&A, nominal roll of officers and
men who served, roll of members taken POW.

Mainly an account of 4th Rhodesian Anti-Tank Battery and 17th (Rhodesia)
Field Battery in the East Africa, North Africa and Italy campaigns.
A well-written blend of descriptive narrative and personal reminiscences.
Printed on poor quality paper, but nicely bound. R/3 V/4. RP.


THE STORY OF THE NORTHERN RHODESIA REGIMENT

W V Brelsford
The Government Printer, Lusaka, Northern Rhodesia, 1954
Pale olive green, green lettering and regtl crest on front cover,
9.75 x 7.25, viii/134.
61 mono phots, 3 coloured plates (Colours and uniforms), 2 line drawings,
5 maps (bound in), Index.

Apps: H&A (incomplete, for WWII only), list of former COs.

A good general history. Covers the period 1896 to 1953, with good accounts of the regt's services in WWI (East Africa) and WWII (Burma). There is also a helpful explanation of the regt's origins in the early settler days. R/3 V/4. BCC/JBF.


## THE RHODESIAN AFRICAN RIFLES

Christopher Owen
Leo Cooper Ltd, London, produced at The Pitman Press, Bath, 1970
Grey, black, gold, 8.5 x 5.5, vii/75.
8 mono phots, 3 maps (printed in text), Bibliography, no Index.

Apps: Roll of Honour (incomplete).

Useful but superficial little book in the 'Famous Regiments' series. Regt was raised in June 1940 and fought with distinction against the Japanese in Burma, against the Communist insurgents in Malaya, and against the 'liberation' forces during the period of the Ian Smith administration. The author here has dealt only with the Burma campaign. He states that he was obliged to work without full access to official archives. Sadly, it shows in his work. Even sadder, this will probably be the only history ever to be published for a very fine bi-racial regiment. R/1 V/3. AJW/RP.


## SELOUS SCOUTS
Rhodesian War - A Pictorial Account

Peter Stiff
Galago Publishing (Pty) Ltd, Cape Town, 1984
Brown, white, 13.0 x 9.75, vi/170.
Fp, 461 mono phots, 18 coloured phots, various maps, sketches, cartoons and charts, Bibliography, photographic credits, no appendixes, Index.

Good detail and abundant pictures of this specialised 'deep penetration' unit. Very few members named, for obvious reasons. 'Anti-terrorist' operations described in good detail. R/2 V/3. DJB.


## SELOUS SCOUTS  - TOP SECRET WAR

Lieut Col R Reid-Daly, as told by Peter Stiff
A sister volume to the previous entry. Not seen, but reported to be mainly a narrative account (432 pages, 120 colour and mono phots, 10,000 copies printed, easy to acquire in South Africa but less so in UK). R/1. V/3. DJB.

THE ELITE
The Story of the Rhodesian Special Air Service

Barbara Cole
Three Knights Publishing, Pietermaritzburg, South Africa, 1984
Blue, gold, 9.75 x 6.75, x/449.
49 mono phots, 46 coloured plates, 25 maps (printed in text),
Bibliography, Glossary, Index.

Apps: Roll of Honour, chronology of military and political events.

The first 23 pages deal with the origins of the RSAS, the bulk of the
book then concerns 'anti-terrorist' operations during the long years of
the Ian Smith administration. Much detail on specific missions and a
surprising number of individuals mentioned by name. Barbara Cole had
access to privileged 'insider' information when drafting this very
authoritative book. At least two editions have been published, the
first being a 'de luxe' issue of 1500 copies. R/2 V/5. DJB.


CONTACT
A Tribute to Those who Serve Rhodesia

John Lovett
Galaxy Press, Salisbury, Rhodesia, 1977
Grey, black, 11.75 x 9.75, x/228.
Abundantly illustrated (interesting high quality photographs on virtually
every page), coloured Fp, one map, no Index.

Apps: Roll of Honour, H&A.

As the sub-title suggests, this is not a regtl history. However, it
contains such a mass of information on individuals, acts of gallantry,
citations for awards, and anecdotes regarding the military campaign fought
during the UDI period, that it is required reading for any researcher
attempting to understand the country's spirit at that time. Large numbers
were printed, but owners are reluctant to sell. Equally valued is
the successive CONTACT II which covers the years 1978-80. R/3 V/4. AJW.


FRONTIER PATROLS
A History of The British South Africa Police and Other Rhodesian Forces

Colonel Colin Harding
G Bell, London, 1937
Blue, gold, 9.0 x 5.75, xii/372.
Fp, 19 mono phots, 2 maps (bound in), Index.

Apps: sixteen, including Rolls of Honour for 1893, 1896, 1897, and
1914-18.

One of the two classic BSAP histories. R/3 V/4. VS.

BLUE AND OLD GOLD
A Selection of Stories from 'The Outpost', the Regimental Magazine of
The British South Africa Police

by various named former and serving BSAP officers
Howard B Timmins, Citadel Press, Cape Town, n.d. (c.1953)
Beige, blue, regtl crest on front cover, 10.0 x 7.25, -/199.
38 mono phots, one map (printed on end-papers) no appendixes, no Index.

An anthology of articles featured in various earlier editions of
THE OUTPOST. Not a regtl history in the conventional sense, but useful
background reading. The stories cover the period 1890 to 1950.
R/2 V/2. RP.


MEN WHO MADE RHODESIA
A Register of Those Who Served in the British South Africa Company's
Police

Colonel A S Hickman
The British South Africa Company, Salisbury, Rhodesia, 1960
Dark blue and old gold (the regtl colours), BSAC motif on front cover,
10.0 x 6.0, -/462.
Fp, 22 mono phots, 2 maps (bound in), no appendixes, Index.

This is the other classic reference work on the BSACP (vide FRONTIER
PATROLS, previous page). The first 85 pages tell the story of the regt's
origins and their pioneering services from inception in 1890. This was
essentially a para-military force of European mercenaries and adventurers
recruited to fight the Matabele and the Mashona, and to open up Central
Southern Africa for settlement. No stronger in numbers than an army
battalion, and with only limited British Army support, they defeated these
two great warrior tribes and founded a new nation. The bulk of the text
is dedicated to detailed biographical notes on each of the 897 men
enrolled during the early days. An important reference source for
genealogists and for collectors of early Rhodesiana. Available in reprint.
R/2 V/4. RP.


THE WAR HISTORY OF SOUTHERN RHODESIA 1939-45

J F MacDonald
By Authority of the Government of Southern Rhodesia
First published, in two volumes, in 1947 and 1950. Subsequently produced,
in facsimile reprint and with new Introductions, by the excellent
Rhodesiana Reprint Library (as part of their Silver Series, at Bulawayo,
in the 1970s). Not seen, but no doubt very useful background reading.

## BECHUANALAND AND BASUTOLAND

TEN THOUSAND MEN OF AFRICA
The Story of the Bechuanaland Pioneers and Gunners, 1941-46

Major A R Bent
His Majesty's Stationery Office for the Bechuanaland Government,
London, 1952
Red, gold, 8.5 x 5.5, xii/128
Fp, 41 superb mono phots, 3 maps (2 printed on end-papers, one bound in),
Index.

Apps: thirteen, including Roll of Honour (with names and details of
KIA for all ranks), H&A (all ranks), lists of former COs, lists of
former officers, British Warrant Officers and British NCOs.

Per capita of population, Bechuanaland made a major contribution to
the British cause in both world wars. Troops were sent to France in
WWI, but this book tells the story of the WWII generation which served
in Syria, Palestine, Egypt, the Western Desert and Italy. Under British
officers and senior NCOs, soldiers from Bechuanaland fought as Pioneers,
Field Engineers and Heavy Anti-Aircraft gunners. A well-written and
informative account. R/4 V/4. PCL. RP.


BASUTO SOLDIERS IN HITLER'S WAR

Brian Gray
Produced at Morija Printing Works, Morija, for the Basutoland
Government, Maseru, 1953
Red, black, 8.75 x 5.5, x/97.
Fp, 41 mono phots, 6 general regional maps (folding, bound in), detailed
Index.

Apps: H&A (all ranks).

Basuto soldiers volunteered for WWII service in a variety of specialist
and semi-specialist units: Field Artillery, Heavy Anti-Aircraft
Artillery, Field Engineers and Infantry. Their early services were in
Lebanon and Palestine, but their most important campaign services were
in Italy. A well-written and interesting account, produced to a very
good standard. R/4 V/4. PCL. RP.

## SOUTH AFRICA - GENERAL ACCOUNTS

THE HISTORY OF THE SOUTH AFRICAN FORCES IN FRANCE

John Buchan
Thomas Nelson & Sons Ltd, London, 1920
Dark blue, gold, Union motif on front cover, 9.0 x 5.75, -/404.
Fp, 17 mono phots, 22 maps (bound in), Index.

Apps: H&A (for all SA personnel who served in France, with full citations
for all Victoria Crosses to South Africans during WWI), and separate
appendixes with notes on SA Heavy Artillery, Signal Company (RE), Cape
Auxiliary Horse Transport Companies, and medical services.

Deals mainly with the SA Infantry Brigade in France and Flanders
between 1916 (commencing with the Somme) and 1918. Also some coverage
of their earlier campaign in Libya against the Turks and the Senussi.
An attractive book. R/2 V/3. DJB/RP.


DELVILLE WOOD

Ian Uys
Uys Publishers, Rensburg, South Africa, 1983
Khaki, white, 9.5 x 6.75, xi/298.
205 mono phots, 13 line drawings, one sketch, 13 maps (printed in text),
Glossary, Bibliography, Index.

Apps: Roll of Honour, H&A, list of officers.

This is the history of 1st SA Infantry Brigade, comprising 1st, 2nd,
3rd, and 4th SA Infantry Battalions. The author describes their part
in the capture and holding of Delville Wood (14-19 July 1916) when
they lost 766 officers and men killed. A very detailed day-to-day account,
with the fighting analysed at Company level for each Battalion. Many
personal recollections, interspersed with official data. In the space
of five days, the Brigade gained 1 VC, 5 DSOs, 14 MCs, 12 DCMs, and 31 MMs.
R/1 V/4. BCC.

Other books regarding this ferocious battle are: MEMORIES OF DELVILLE WOOD
by J A Lawson (Maskew Miller 1918), DELVILLE WOOD by D Fourie, and
THE SOUTH AFRICANS AT DELVILLE by Richard Cornwall (Militaria 1977).


EAST AFRICAN AND ABYSSINIAN CAMPAIGNS
South African Forces, World War II, Volume I

Neil Orpen
Purnell, Cape Town, 1968
Blue, gold, 10.0 x 6.0, xiv/390
67 mono phots, 14 maps (11 printed in text, 3 bound in), Bibliography,
Index.

Apps: Union Defence Force before 1933, re-organisation 1939, Italian order of battle (East Africa, June 1940), notes on 1st SA Division, 11th African Division, etc.

This is the first of a series of semi-official histories compiled for the SA War Histories Advisory Committee in Johannesburg, and is 'completely authoritative' (based upon SA and Italian records and reminiscences). R/2 V/4. NO.


WAR IN THE DESERT
South African Forces, World War II, Volume III

Neil Orpen
Purnells, Cape Town, 1971
Blue, gold, 10.0 x 6.0, xii/538.
67 mono phots, 20 maps (19 printed in text, one bound in), Bibliography, Index.

Apps: notes on 'Braforce', 2nd SA Division, 1st SA Division, order of battle (17.10.1942), etc.

Complete story of the SA participation in North Africa from December 1940, through Alamein and on to Tunis. Compiled from SA, British, German and Italian records and reminiscences. R/2 V/4. NO.


VICTORY IN ITALY
South African Forces, World War II, Volume V

Neil Orpen
Purnell, Cape Town, 1975
Blue, gold, 10.0 x 6.0, xiv/340.
Fp, 64 mono phots, 14 maps (bound in), no appendixes but some annotations, Bibliography, Index.

Mainly the story of 6th SA Armoured Division (including the British 24th Guards Armoured Brigade) in Italy from the Battle of Cassino through to the end of the war. Much also on the SA Engineer Corps' efforts to restore the wrecked rail and road systems (the Railway Construction Group alone had 10,000 men deployed in Italy). Compiled from SA, British, American and German records and reminiscences. R/2 V/4. NO


THE POLICE BRIGADE
6th SA Infantry Brigade 1939-45

Brigadier F W Cooper DSO
Constantia Publishers, Cape Town, 1972
Soft linen covers, white, black, Divisional sign on covers, 8.5 x 5.5, viii/142.
28 mono phots, 3 maps (printed in text), no Index.

Apps: H&A, list of all officers who served, 14 pages of sketches of all officers and RSMs who served.

A short but complete account of 6th SA Infantry Brigade (comprised of
1st and 2nd SA Police Battalions and the Transvaal Scottish) from
inception in June 1940 to capture at Tobruk in June 1942. R/2 V/2. NO.


INFANTRY IN SOUTH AFRICA, 1652-1976

Capt R J Bouch
Documentation Service, SA Defence Force, Pretoria, 1977
Black, 12.0 x 9.75, v/276.
Numerous mono phots, numerous maps (printed in text), no appendixes,
Bibliography, no Index.

Few details reported, but presumably an account of infantry evolution and
deployments in South Africa during the period stated. Written partly
in English, partly in Afrikaans. R/1 V/3. GB.


SHORT HISTORY OF THE VOLUNTEER REGIMENTS OF NATAL AND EAST GRIQUALAND
PAST AND PRESENT

Colonel Godfrey T Hurst
Knox Publishing Co, Durban, 1945
Green, 8.5 x 5.5, vi/170.
Fp, no illustrations, no maps, Bibliography, no appendixes, no Index.

An anthology of condensed unit histories: Natal Mounted Rifles, Royal
Durban Light Infantry, Royal Natal Carbineers, Umvoti Mounted Rifles,
Natal Naval Corps (RNVR), their predecessors 'and other Corps no longer
extant'. R/3 V/2. VS.

In the context of small local defunct volunteer units, the following
additional titles have been reported but not seen: NATAL COLONIAL SCOUTS
1899-1900 (published in Durban by the 'Natal Mercury'), HISTORY OF THE
NATAL CARBINEERS (no details), and HISTORICAL RECORD OF THE ZULULAND
MOUNTED RIFLES (published by the 'Zululand Times Annual', 1924).

## SOUTH AFRICA – ARTILLERY

PRINCE ALFRED'S OWN CAPE VOLUNTEER ARTILLERY
Handbook of Drills

anon
Murray & St Leger, Cape Town, 1893
109 pages. Not seen.


KHAKI CRUSADERS
With the South African Artillery in Egypt and Palestine

F H Cooper
Central News Agency Ltd, Cape Town, 1919.
Not seen.


A HISTORY OF THE SEVENTY-FIRST SIEGE BATTERY, SOUTH AFRICAN HEAVY ARTILLERY
From July 1915, The Date of its Formation in Cape Town, to the 11th
November 1918, when 'Ceasefire' Sounded at Lesdain, on the Escault Canal,
near Tournai, Belgium.

H Bailey
No publication details available, 55 pages. Not seen.


HISTORY OF THE 72nd SIEGE BATTERY, SOUTH AFRICAN HEAVY ARTILLERY

F J Parsons
Published in Hastings (UK), 1924. Not seen.


THE SOUTH AFRICAN FIELD ARTILLERY IN GERMAN EAST AFRICA AND PALESTINE
1915-1919

Brigadier the Hon F B Adler MC VD ED, Major A E Lorch DSO MC, and
Dr H H Curson FRCVS
J L Van Schaik Ltd, Pretoria, 1958
Pale grey, dark blue, red and blue flash on front cover, 8.5 x 5.5,
xvi/146.
Fp, 14 mono phots (including captioned groups), 2 line drawings of badges,
4 maps (one bound in, 3 in rear pocket), Bibliography, Glossary, Index.

Apps: Roll of Honour (all ranks, with date and place of death), H&A
(all ranks, names but no details), list of former officers, list of
former WOs, NCOs, and artificers).

A clearly-written account which traces the movements and operations of 1st, 2nd, 3rd, 4th, 5th, and 6th Batteries SAFA in East Africa, Egypt and Palestine during WWI. A very professional compilation, presented in a publication of excellent quality. R/1 V/5. RP.


THE HISTORY OF THE TRANSVAAL HORSE ARTILLERY

Major F B Adler MC VD
Transvaal Horse Artillery, Johannesburg, 1927
Dark blue, blue on white, THA crest on front cover, 7.5 x 5.0, ii/101.
Fp, no photographs, no other illustrations, no maps, no Index.


Apps: Roll of Honour, list of former COs, list of former officers, nominal roll of members, list of Instructional and Subordinate Staff, members commissioned into other units, Establishments, annual camps, competitions and trophies, etc.

A brief but authoritative and readable history of the regiment from its formation on 17 March 1904 until the end of 1926. Includes coverage of WWI services and the Rand Revolt of 1922. R/3 V/4. NO.

THE HISTORY OF THE TRANSVAAL HORSE ARTILLERY, 1904-1974

Neil Orpen
Alex White & Co (Pty) Ltd, Johannesburg, for The Transvaal Horse Artillery Regimental Council, 1975
Dark blue, gold, regtl crest on front cover, 10.25 x 5.75, viii/275.
Fp, 101 mono phots, 15 maps, Glossary, Bibliography, Index.

Apps: Rolls of Honour (WWI, Rand Revolt 1922, WWII), H&A (WWI includes awards to former members posted away) for both wars, former COs, former officers, nominal roll of members 1904-1926, notes on helmets and cap badges, eighteen appendixes in total.

One of the best of the several superb regt histories written by the late Neil Orpen, his country's leading military historian. As expected, clear, concise, deeply researched and well laid out. With Adler's book of 1927 (see above) having covered the early years so thoroughly, Orpen concentrates on WWII. Particularly good for the North Africa campaign. An attractive publication. R/2 V/5. DBP-P/BCC.


GUNNERS OF THE CAPE
The Story of the Cape Field Artillery

Neil Orpen
The Standard Press Ltd, Cape Town, for the CFA Regimental Committee, 1965
Prussian blue, gold, regtl crest on front cover, 9.5 x 6.25, xvi/310.
76 mono phots, 8 maps (2 printed on end-papers, 4 printed in text, 2 bound in), 7 line drawings of artillery pieces and unit crest, Bibliography, Index.

Apps: Roll of Honour (Tambookie campaign 1880-81, Langeberg campaign 1897, South African war 1899-1902, WWI, and WWII), H&A (listed under South Africa war 1899-1902, WWI, South West Africa 1914-15, WWII), list of former COs, list of former Honorary Colonels, battle honours, notes on unit designations, list of officers serving at 31.12.1964.

The first of Colonel Orpen's brilliant series of SA regtl histories. The work covers the period 1856 to 1964, but is exceptionally good for the war of 1939-45. R/2 V/5. BCC.

## SOUTH AFRICA - SIGNALS

SUID AFRIKAANS SEINKORPS - SOUTH AFRICAN CORPS OF SIGNALS

Major F J Jacobs, Lieut R J Bouch, Sophia du Preez, Richard Cornwell
Documentation Service, SA Defence Force, No 1 Printing Company,
Pretoria, 1975
Black, 11.5 x 10.0, v/107.
66 mono phots, one map (bound in), apparently no appendixes, Index.

Few details reported, but presumably deals mainly with WWII. Written partly in English, partly in Afrikaans. R/1 V/4. GB.

48

## SOUTH AFRICA - ENGINEERS

THE 8th FIELD SQUADRON
A Brief History of the 8th Field Squadron SAEC, which was a Field
Squadron of the 6th Armoured Division 1939-45

D V Jeffrey
Rostra Printers, Johannesburg, n.d. (c.1946). Not seen.


THE STORY OF THE NINTH
A Record of the 9th Field Company, South African Engineer Corps,
July 1939 to July 1943

J N Cowin
Published by the South African Engineer Corps, Johannesburg, 1948.
Not seen.


NINE FLAMES

Ken Anderson
Purnell & Sons (SA) Pty Ltd, Cape Town, 1964
Dark blue, gold, red blocking on spine, grenade motif (hence the 'nine
flames') on front cover, 9.75 x 6.0, xi/282.
Fp, 16 mono phots, no maps, Index.

Apps: Roll of Honour, H&A (but summary of numbers of awards only, no
names).

A history of SA engineers in WWII, covering their services in East Africa,
North Africa, and Italy. Many individuals and company-sized units are
mentioned in the narrative. R/2 V/4. EDS.


SALUTE THE SAPPERS, Parts I and II
South African Forces, World War II, Volume VIII

Neil Orpen and H J Martin
Published in Johannesburg by the Sappers Association, printed in Cape
Town, Part I being issued as a single volume in 1981, Part II as the
second volume in 1982, the pair then being described as 'Volume VIII'
of South Africa's semi-official war histories
Both volumes in blue, gold, with the SAEC crest on the spines,
10.0 x 6.0, Part I xx/508, Part II xii/424.
Fps, Part I with 69 mono phots, 4 line sketches, 15 maps, and Part II
with 84 mono phots, 5 line sketches, 20 maps, Bibliographies, Indexes.

Apps: Roll of Honour (WWII only), H&A (WWI, WII, and subsequent operations
up to 1982), lists of former COs of all units from the Battle of El
Alamein through to 1945, notes on 8th Army Engineers, order of battle
at 23.4.1945, SAEC organisation at 1982.

A complete and authoritative account covering the period 1859 to
1982, but concentrating primarily upon WWII. R/2 V/5. NO.


## SOUTH AFRICA – CAPE COLOURED TROOPS


WITH THE SECOND CAPE CORPS THRO' CENTRAL AFRICA
A History of the Battalion from its Formation in 1915 Until its Return
from East Africa

A J B Desmore
Citadel Press, Cape Town, 1920
100 pages. Not seen.


THE STORY OF THE 1st CAPE CORPS (1915-1919)

Capt Ivor D Difford
Hortors Ltd, Cape Town, n.d. (c.1921)
Glossy card boards, cloth spine, ivory and brown, gold, Cape Corps
crest on front cover, 10.0 x 7.0, -/448.
Five frontispiece mono phots, 44 other mono phots, 12 maps (printed in
text), Glossary, no Index.

Apps: Roll of Honour (KIA, DOW and WIA), H&A (all ranks), list of former
officers (with details of service), nominal roll (all ranks), record
of service of officers other than while serving with this battalion (very
detailed).

The story of Cape Coloured troops who volunteered for service during WWI.
Virtually unknown outside South Africa, probably largely forgotten now
by many white South Africans. First class as a genealogical and social
reseach source, with a very large amount of biographical detail.
R/4 V/4. RP.

## SOUTH AFRICA - MOUNTED AND MECHANISED

HISTORY OF THE CAPE MOUNTED RIFLEMEN
With a Brief Account of the Colony of the Cape of Good Hope

Anon
John W Packer, for Richard Cannon, London, 1842
Green, blind, 8.75 x 5.75, viii/32.
2 coloured plates (Standard and uniform), no other illustrations,
no maps, no appendixes, no Index.

This is a curiosity, being the only regtl history in the Cannon series
for a Colonial unit. Like most of Richard Cannon's books, it contains
little of substance. The usual redeeming feature of the series are
the pretty and well-executed colour plates. This CMR history is reported
to have had good lithograph prints in the first (1842) edition, but
coarser wood engravings in a later edition. Full details of the latter are
not available, but it is known that the text remained unaltered.
R/5 V/1. VS.


RECORD OF THE CAPE MOUNTED RIFLEMEN

Basil Williams
Sir Joseph Causton & Sons Ltd, London, 1909
Black, gold, regtl crest on front cover, 8.5 x 5.25, iii/138.
no mono phots, 10 coloured plates, one line drawing, one map (bound
in), Index.

Apps: H&A, list of former COs, list of officers still serving.

The first three chapters cover the origins of the regt and describe
the early frontier campaigns. The bulk of the narrative (page 58 onwards)
deals with the regt's role in the Anglo-Boer War (1899-1902).
R/4 V/3. RP.

The history of the CMR is updated in A STORY OF THE CAPE MOUNTED RIFLEMEN,
1st AUGUST 1878 TO 31st MARCH 1913, AND 1st REGIMENT SOUTH AFRICAN
MOUNTED RIFLEMEN, 1st APRIL 1913 TO 1st APRIL 1926, by A E Lorch
(produced by V&R Printers, Pretoria, 1935). Not seen.


MY VERULAM TROOP
Being a Short Account of the Verulam Troop of the Natal Mounted Rifles
and of their Movements and Engagements when they were Seconded to the
Durban Light Infantry in the Zulu Rebellion of 1906

A H Garnett Blamey
South Coast Herald, Port Shepstone
Brown covers, 9.75 x 5.0, -/30.
2 mono phots, one map (bound in), no appendixes, no Index.

The sub-title seems excessively verbose for such a very small book.
Few details reported, but it is thought that it was reprinted in
limited numbers in 1954. Not seen.

HISTORY OF THE NATAL MOUNTED RIFLES

Col Godfrey T Hurst
Knox Printing & Publishing Co, Durban, 1935
Green, 'octavo', 83 pages
'Numerous photographic illustrations'.

Noted in a catalogue thus, but not seen.


ROUGH BUT READY
An Official History of the Natal Mounted Rifles, 1854-1969

E Goetzche
Produced in Durban, for the Regiment, 1972. Not seen.


PREPARE TO MOUNT
The Story of the 6th Mounted Regiment

Albert Plane
Howard Timmins, Cape Town, 1977
'Illustrations', 70 pages, 'table of historical events 1827-1860'.
Reported thus, but not seen.


CARBINEER
The History of the Royal Natal Carbineers

Alan F Hattersley
Gale & Polden Ltd, Aldershot, 1950
Olive green, silver, regtl crest on front cover, 8.5 x 5.5, x/193.
Fp, 12 mono phots, 3 maps (printed in text), Index.

Apps: Roll of Honour (WWII only), H&A (WWII only).

The bulk of the narrative (page 64 onwards) is devoted to WWII services.
The RNC are stated to be the senior regt in South Africa, having been
established in 1855. A workmanlike history. R/2 V/4. MP.


A COMPANY COMMANDER REMEMBERS
From El Yibo to El Alamein

A E Blamey
Publisher's details not stated, produced in Pietermaritzberg, 1963
Green, gold, 8.5 x 5.5, vi/199.
Fps, 12 mono phots, 2 maps (bound in), no Index.

Apps: General Oliver Leese's instruction to 'every driver in XXX Corps'
on D-Day for the Battle of El Alamein.

A readable and accurate story of 1st Natal Mounted Rifles from 8.6.1940
(mobilisation) through East Africa, Abyssinia, and Western Desert. Unit
returned to South Africa after Alamein. R/3 V/3. NO.

THE STORY OF THE IMPERIAL LIGHT HORSE IN THE SOUTH AFRICAN WAR 1899-1902

George Fleming Gibson
G.D. & Company, Johannesburg, 1937
Green, gold, regtl crest on front cover, 9.5 x 6.5, vi/351.
Fp, 18 mono phots, 6 maps (2 printed in text, 4 bound in), no Index.

Apps: H&A.

A detailed readable account of the ILH in the Boer War. R/4 V/4. FRB.


LIGHT HORSE CAVALCADE
The Imperial Light Horse, 1899-1961

Harry Klein
Howard Timmins, Cape Town, 1969
Red imitation leather, gold, 'crossed flags' emblem of the regt on the
front cover ('Imperium et Libertas'), 11.25 x 8.75, xiv/200.

Apps: Roll of Honour, H&A, list of former COs, list of former Honorary
Colonels, list of Colonels-in-Chief, battle honours, notes on dress.

This book amplifies and supersedes the Gibson history listed above,
bringing the story up to date and reporting some of the earlier campaigns
in greater detail. There is, as is usual with books published at about
that time, very good coverage of WWII. The account covers all the
campaigns in which the regt was engaged following inception in 1899:
Boer War (1899-1902), Zulu Rebellion (1906), WWI, the Rand Revolt (1922),
and WWII. The regt fought in the latter in the Western Desert and Italy,
being there amalgamated with the Kimberley Regiment. An armoured regt,
the ILH lost the 'Imperial' from their title when South Africa became a
republic in 1961, and is now The Light Horse Regiment. A good readable
narrative, with exceptionally fine illustrations. R/2 V/5. BCC/GB/FRB.


SPRINGBOKS IN ARMOUR
The South African Armoured Cars in WWII

Harry Klein
Purnell & Sons (SA) Pty Ltd, Cape Town, 1965
Black, silver, SA Tank Corps badge on front cover, 10.0 x 6.0, xvi/338.
Fp, 35 mono phots with 2 large 'pull out' mono group pictures, 6 maps
(4 printed in text, 2 folding bound in), Bibliography, Index.

Apps: Roll of Honour, H&A.

A very readable and authoritative history of the entire SA Tank Corps
from its formation in January, 1940. Covers its activities in the
Abyssinia, Western Desert and Madagascar campaigns, through to the
Corps' disbandment in April, 1943 (when it was absorbed into other
SA and British units). R/3 V/5. NO.

# SOUTH AFRICA - INFANTRY

THE HISTORY OF THE TRANSVAAL SCOTTISH

Captain H C Juta
Hortors Ltd, Johannesburg, 1933
Green, with leather spine and quarters, gold, 10.0 x 7.5, xvii/152.
Fp, 85 mono phots, various line drawings of insignia, 6 maps (2 printed
in text, 4 bound in), Bibliography, Index.

Apps: Roll of Honour, list of former COs, a summary of the history of
4th Bn South African Infantry, summary of the history of the Scottish
Horse (1902-07).

An excellent book. The author covers the early years in good detail. The
WWI account is slightly more generalised, but the overall effect is a
volume full of information probably unobtainable from any other source.
R/4 V/4. BCC.


THE SAGA OF THE TRANSVAAL SCOTTISH REGIMENT, 1932-1950

Carel Birkby
Hodder & Stoughton Ltd, produced by Howard Timmins, Cape Town, 1950
Brown, gold, regtl crest on front cover, 9.75 x 7.5, xxxii/749.
Fp, 202 mono phots, 5 coloured plates, line drawings of uniforms,
27 maps, Bibliography.

Apps: Roll of Honour, H&A, list of former officers, list of former
Warrant Officers, roll of POWs, nominal roll of members.

A massive work, almost more information than the reader can absorb.
Painstakingly researched and reported to be very accurate. Most of the
narrative deals with the WII services of the three fighting battalions
raised by the regt. R/3 V/5. BCC.


THE HISTORY OF PRINCE ALFRED'S GUARD
With Which is Affiliated the Royal Scots Fusiliers, 1856-1938

Major Frank Perridge
E H Walton & Co Ltd, Port Elizabeth, 1939
Red, gold, motif of Zulu war shield on spine and front cover,
9.75 x 6.75, xv/208.
Fp, 10 mono phots, 2 maps (printed on end-papers), no Index.

Apps: list of former officers.

A straightforward accurate history of the regt during the period stated.
R/4 V/3. UWML. BCC.

PRINCE ALFRED'S GUARD, 1856-1966

Neil Orpen
Books of Africa (Pty) Ltd, Cape Town, 1967
Blue, gold, regtl crest on front cover, 9.0 x 6.0, viii/346.
Fp, 80 mono phots, 5 coloured plates, numerous line drawings, 11 maps
(printed in the text), Bibliography, Index.

Apps: Roll of Honour (casualties for Transkei 1877, Basutoland 1880-1881),
Bechuanaland 1897, Anglo-Boer War 1899-1902, WWII), H&A (WWII only),
list of former COs, list of former Honorary Colonels, roll of all officers
who ever served, notes on cap badges.

An authoritative readable account. Particularly interesting descriptions
of the little-known operations in Basutoland (1880) and Bechuanaland
(1897). The PAG was a Volunteer regt recruited from the vicinity of
Port Elizabeth. During WWI is served as infantry in East Africa. In
WWII it re-trained in the armoured role and was equipped with the Sherman
tank. The author gives a good description of the Regt's hard fighting in
Italy (on the Gothic Line) during the winter of 1944-1945.
R/3 V/4. UMWL. BCC.


REGIMENTAL HISTORY OF THE CAPE TOWN HIGHLANDERS
September 1939 - February 1943

W S Douglas
Publisher's details not shown, produced in Cairo, January 1944
Soft card, light brown, black, 1st SA Divisional flash and CTH crest both
on front cover, 8.0 x 5.75, x/54.
31 mono phots, one map (printed on the end-papers).

Apps: Roll of Honour (casualties in the Middle East, June 1941 to
December 1942), H&A, record of battle from 23.10.1942 to 4.11.1942.

A brief readable account of the CTH's doings from September 1939 to
24 February 1943. The Regt was then amagalgamated with First City, becoming
the First City/Cape Town Highlanders. The CTH saw much action in the Desert,
and then, as FC/CTH, more hard action in the Italian campaign. R/3 V/4. NO.


FIRST CITY/CAPE TOWN HIGHLANDERS IN THE ITALIAN CAMPAIGN
A Short History, 1939-1945

L G Murray
Cape Times, for the author, Cape Town, 1946
Light brown, dark brown, 8.5 x 5.75, -/80.
Fp, no other phots, 9 chapter heading sketches, one map (folding,
bound in at the rear, showing FC/CTH route up the Italian peninsula),
no Index.

Apps: Roll of Honour (for Italy), battle honours for both component regts,
notes on their tartans.

A short but sound account of the services in Italy, between late 1942 and mid 1945, of these two newly amalgamated 'kilted' South African regiments. R/4 V/3. NO.


FIRST CITY, A SAGA OF SERVICE

Reginald Griffiths
Howard Timmins, Cape Town, 1970
Dark blue, silver, 9.25 x 6.75, xvi/292.
54 mono phots, 2 maps (bound in), Bibliography, Index.

Apps: Roll of Honour (for Italy), H&A (WWII).

A complete and detailed history from 1875 to 1965, including the 1943 amalgamation with the Cape Town Highlanders for the Italian campaign. Not particularly easy to read because the narrative is much broken up with quotations from letters, nominal rolls, etc, which might have been better arranged as appendixes. The rolls are, however, useful as a reference source for individual services. R/3 V/3. UWML. BCC/NO.


THE CAPE TOWN HIGHLANDERS, 1885-1970

Neil Orpen
Cape & Transvaal Printers Ltd, Cape Town, for the Cape Town Highlanders History Committee, 1970
Green, gold, 9.0 x 6.25, x/396.
Fp, 117 mono phots, 13 maps (printed in text), Bibliography, Index.

Apps: Rolls of Honour (for Anglo-Boer War 1899-1902, WWI, WWII), H&A (ditto, plus 'periodic awards at the Union, 1910'), list of former COs, list of Honorary Colonels, list of Colonels-in-Chief, list of RSMs, battle honours.

A very good regt history, well written, easy to follow. Despite the title, most of the narrative is devoted to WWII. R/2 V/4. BCC.


THE CAPE TOWN HIGHLANDERS, 1885-1985

Neil Orpen
San Printing Press, Simon's Town, for the Cape Town Highlanders Trust, 1988
Green, gold, 8.5 x 6.25, xii/164.
Fp, 99 mono phots, 18 coloured plates, 3 maps (printed in text), Bibliography, Index.

Apps: Roll of Honour (Boer War, WWI, WWII, Angola Border), H&A (all gallantry and bravery awards, all LSGC awards, Efficiency Medals, the John Chard Decoration, Jubilee and Coronation Medals, etc, etc), roll of RSMs, roll of RPMs, notes on regtl band and music, notes on Battalion command and control 1985-86.

This was the last of Colonel Orpen's projects before his final illness. The opening pages summarise the regt's earlier history, but the bulk of the narrative concerns its activities in Southern Angola in the 1970s. The CTH were the first unit of the South African Citizen Force to cross the border. The account is quite bland and straightforward, interesting mainly for its abundant references to individuals and to minor milestones in the regt's daily life. R/1 V/4. RP.

THE STORY OF MEN
A Brief History of Regiment de la Rey and The Witwatersrand Rifles and their Association

S E von Broemsen
The Potchefstroom Herald, 1948
Dark green, black, 8.25 x 5.0, -/130.
3 mono phots, 5 line drawings, no maps, no Index.

Apps: Roll of Honour (WWII), H&A (WWII).

Regiment de la Rey and The Witwatersrand Rifles were amalgamated in the Western Desert on 7 July 1943 as a consequence of the shortage of trained men arriving from South Africa to replace battle casualties. The author covers their previous individual histories (from 1934 for the DLR, and from 1903 for the WR) before giving most of his attention to a brief but readable account of their combined services in Italy. R/4 V/3. NO.

THE HISTORY OF THE KIMBERLEY REGIMENT

H H Curson
Publisher's details not stated,produced in Kimberley, 1963
Black, gold, 9.25 x 6.0, xxiv/284.
Fp, 113 mono phots, 6 maps (printed in text), Bibliography, no Index.

Apps: Roll of Honour (WWII), H&A (WWII), nominal roll of members (WWII), notes on campaigns, local streets named after former officers of the regt.

Covers the period 1876 to 1962, including the amalgamation with the Imperial Light Horse during the Italian campaign (vide ILH entries). The narrative is much disjointed and confusing to read, but it is detailed and accurate, and a good source for the researcher. R/3 V/3. BCC.

RAND LIGHT INFANTRY

Major B G Simkins JCD MM
Howard Timmins, Cape Town, 1965
Royal blue, gold, regtl crest on front cover, 10.0 x 6.5, xiii/357.
Fp, 200 mono phots, 3 coloured plates, 14 maps (12 bound in, 2 printed on end-papers), Index.

Apps: Roll of Honour, H&A, list of former COs, nominal roll for
all ranks: 1914-15, 1922, 1941 and 1943, list of location of burials.

An excellent history. Good coverage for WWI and the 1922 revolt,
but most of the narrative devoted to WWII. R/3 V/4. BCC.


THE DURBAN LIGHT INFANTRY
The History of the Durban Light Infantry, Incorporating that of the
Sixth South African Light Infantry, 1915-1917
Volume I  - 1854 to 1934
Volume II - 1935 to 1960

Lieut Col A C Martin MC VD
Hayne & Gibson Ltd, Durban, 1969
Royal blue, silver, regtl crest on front covers (both Volumes),
9.75 x 7.25 (both Volumes), xx/368 and xvii/487. Coloured fps.
39 mono phots in Volume I, 57 in Volume II (including several captioned
group pictures), 2 coloured plates in each Volume, 6 maps in Volume I,
14 in Volume II (all bound in), Bibliographies, Indexes.

Apps: Rolls of Honour (KIA and WIA for WWI and WWII), H&A (WWI and WWII),
lists of former COs, list of former RSMs and Senior NCOs.

This sumptuous pair of books is a 'tour de force' by the author and a
great credit to the publishers, Hayne & Gibson. Presumably they were
instructed by the Regiment that no expense should be spared, and they
responded in full. All periods of the regt's history are equally well
covered, but some readers particularly admire the section which deals
with the East African campaign (1915-17). A highly desirable possession
for any library or bibliophile. R/4 V/5. UWML. BCC/RP.


THE DUKES
A History of The Duke of Edinburgh's Own Rifles, 1855-1956

Angus G McKenzie
Galvin & Sales (Pty) Ltd, Cape Town, 1957
Red, gold, regtl crest on front cover, 9.0 x 5.5, xii/234.
Fp, 37 mono phots, 2 maps (printed in text), no Index.

Apps: Roll of Honour (WWII only), H&A (WWII only).

Despite the title, 151 pages of the narrative are concerned with WWII,
hence the previous eighty-four years receive scant attention. R/3 V/3. BCC.

A HISTORY OF THE CAPE TOWN RIFLES 'DUKES'

Neil Orpen
Cape Town Rifles Dukes Association, Cape Town, 1984
Blue, gilt, 10.0 x 6.0, vi/325.
Fp, 17 pages of mono phots, 16 maps (printed in the text), Bibliography,
Index.

Apps: Roll of Honour (casualties for 'The Gun War', Basutoland 1880,
Langeberg campaign, Bechuanaland 1897, Anglo-Boer War 1899-1902, WWII,
South West Operational Area 1977-1983), H&A (Anglo-Boer War, WWI, WWII,
'periodical and commemorative awards'), list of former COs, list of former
officers, list of Honorary Colonels, list of Colonels-in-Chief, list of
former Warrant Officers, notes on unit designations, notes on battle
honours.

A very careful, thorough and well-written account which covers an
unusually long period in South African military history (1855 to 1984).
Apart from being a good example of Colonel Orpen's painstaking approach
to the authorship of a regimental record, the book is also an interesting
reflection upon the 'winds of change' which have swept through Southern
Africa during the past 100 years. R/1 V/5. RP.

# SOUTH AFRICA - POLICE

THE MOUNTED POLICE OF NATAL

H P Holt
John Murray, London, 1913
Seen in red and gold, 8.75 x 6.0, xviii/366.
35 mono phots, no maps, Index.

Apps: list of former officers.

A history of the regiment by the officer who raised it and commanded it
for 30 years. His narrative covers the period 1875-1912 and is written
in an informative and entertaining style. R/4 V/4. PCL. LM.


THE REGIMENT
The History and Uniforms of the British South Africa Police

Richard Hamley
Produced by Mardon Printers of Rhodesia for T V Bulpin and Books of
South Africa (Pty) Ltd, 1971
Casebound, colours not reported, 12.0 x 10.0, vi/119.
no photographs, 71 line drawings, no maps, Index.

Apps: notes on badges

The line drawings are reported as well executed and particularly useful
for research on uniforms, badges, insignia, etc. R/2 V/3. DBP-P.
For other titles regarding the BSAP, see NORTHERN AND SOUTHERN RHODESIA.


BOOT AND SADDLE
A Narrative Record of the Cape Regiment, the British Cape Mounted
Riflemen, the Frontier Armed Mounted Police, and Colonial Cape Mounted
Riflemen

P J Young
Maskew Miller Ltd, Cape Town, 1955
Blue, gold, regtl crest on front cover, 8.5 x 5.5, x/193.
7 mono phots, one map (printed in text), Bibliography, Index.

Apps: lists of former COs with biographical notes, lists of former
officers, record of events (1797-1921), list of Commandants of the
Frontier Armed Mounted Police, records of service.

A book which explains the various confusing unit designations found within
the evolution of the Defence Forces of the Cape Colony. The following
were all basically an element of the same Corps: Cape Regiment
(1806-1826), Imperial Cape Mounted Riflemen (1827-1870), Frontier
Armed Mounted Police (1853-1878), Colonial Cape Mounted Riflemen
(1873-1913), and 1st South African Mounted Rifles (1913-1920). The
1st SAMR were unfortunately obliged to surrender to the Germans at
Sandfontein in 1914. They were held POW in South West Africa, were
then freed by General Myburgh, and took part in the suppression of the
Ovambo insurrection of 1916. R/3 V/4. VS/JA.

# PART III
India

Most of the entries recorded in the following pages
(and certainly the Cavalry and Infantry titles)
are listed according to two criteria:
the date order in which they were published, and
in the numerical sequence defined by
the 1922 re-organisations.

Users already familiar with the evolution of the
Indian Army will, it is hoped, quickly detect
these patterns within the arrangement
of the entries.

Reference to the Indexes (pages 358 to 369)
and to the Appendixes (pages 74, 108, 160 and 225)
will serve to clarify the layout of this extensive
and quite complicated section of the book.

Given the complex history of India's armed
forces, however, reference to a specialist work on
regimental lineages is likely to prove helpful.
Major Donovan Jackson's book, INDIA'S ARMY, is the
most convenient source of information on this subject,
and is currently available in reprint format
(see facing page for details).

## INDIA - GENERAL ACCOUNTS

A very large number of books regarding the military history of the Indian
sub-continent has been published over the years. Most of them are helpful,
in one way or another. They are too numerous to list here. The compiler
has selected the following titles on the grounds that they are excellent
'background reading' and are good sources of information on the evolution
and active services of Indian regiments.

INDIA'S ARMY

Major Donovan Jackson
Sampson, Low Marston & Co Ltd, n.d. (c.1940)
Beige, pale blue, 5.5 x 4.5, xxi/584.
Fp, 119 mono phots, 13 coloured plates, numerous good line drawings of
regtl crests (as at 1939), no maps, no appendixes, no Index.

This fat little book is admirable as a 'ready reckoner' for facts, dates
and regtl lineages. It contains a 'potted history' of every regt and Corps
(including the Auxiliary and Princely State forces). The tabular
information - showing each regt's amalgamations, re-organisations and
changes of title in readily understood form - is particularly useful.
R/3 V/5. AMM.
Reprinted by D K Publishing, Delhi, 1986, but without the colour plates.
Stocked by UBS Publishers Distributors Ltd, Harrow, Middlesex.


BRITAIN'S ARMY IN INDIA
From its Origins to the Conquest of Bengal

James P Lawford
George Allen & Unwin, London, 1978
Red, gold, 9.0 x 5.5, -/342.
no photographs, no other illustrations, 17 maps (printed in text),
Bibliography, Index.

Apps: various orders of battle.

Covers the period 1600-1764. A very readable accurate account of the first
150 years of the British in India, particularly the military aspects and
the use of British troops with Indian troops. Good coverage of the
important early battles. R/1 V/4. PJE.


A MATTER OF HONOUR
An Account of the Indian Army, its Officers and Men

Phillip Mason
Purnell Book Services Ltd, London, by arrangement  with Jonathan Cape, 1974
Blue, gold, 9.5 x 6.0, -/580.
27 mono phots, 10 maps (printed in text), Bibliography, Index.

Apps: a brief summary of dates of the main reorganisations.

A magnificent work which, as the sub-title suggests, concentrates upon
the 'changing relations of officers and men and to answer certain
questions about their behaviour'. Covers the entire period of British India
and serves to explain why India's fighting forces gained such a fine
reputation. R/1 V/4. RP.


THE INDIAN ARMY
Boris Mollo
Blandford Press, Poole, Dorset, 1981
Black, gold, 10.0 x 7.5, -/191.
112 mono phots, 66 coloured plates, Glossary, Bibliography, Index.

A meticulous account of the many different uniforms worn by Indian regts
between 1660 and 1947, this information presented within the framework
of changing operational requirements. Beautifully illustrated with rarely
seen photographs and sketches. R/1 V/4. RP.


SWORD OF THE RAJ
The British Army in India 1747-1947

Roger Beaumont
The Bobbs-Merril Company Inc, New York, 1977
Green and beige, gold, 9.25 x 6.25, xiii/237.
39 mono phots, no maps, Bibliography, Index.

Apps: notes on campaign medals, notes on principal battles and other dates.

The sub-title is grossly misleading and can be safely ignored. This is
an American academic's view of the Indian Army, not the British Army.
Based largely upon selected extracts from reports and biographies which
drew the author's eye. A fresh and interesting perspective. R/1 V/3. RP.


THE INDIAN ARMY AND THE KING'S ENEMIES

Major Charles Chenevix-Trench
Thames & Hudson, London, 1988
Red, gold, 9.5 x 6.0, -/312.
Fp, 70 mono phots, 20 maps (printed in text), Bibliography, Index.

Apps: chronology of events.

A useful history of the Indian Army in the 20th century. Based mainly
upon personal accounts of services in WWI, on the North West Frontier
between the wars and in WWII. R/1 V/3. PJE.


THE INDIAN CORPS IN FRANCE

Lieut Col J W B Mereweather CIE and Sir Frederick Smith
John Murray, London, 1919
Maroon, gold, 9.0 x 5.5, xviii/558.
Fp, 19 mono phots, 8 maps (3 printed in text, 5 bound in), Index.

A much under-rated account of the Indian Army's role, between October 1914
and October 1915, in aiding the British and French Armies to halt the
German drives towards Paris and the Channel ports. Packed with vivid
accounts of trench fighting, hundreds of officers and men being mentioned
by name. Detailed coverage of First and Second Ypres, Neuve Chappelle,
Festubert, Givenchy and Loos. The lack of formal appendixes is balanced
by details of casualties and awards in the narrative. The authors complain
bitterly in their Foreword that the War Office applied illogical and
unnecessary censorship to the first edition of their book, a cri de coeur
which strikes a familiar chord with later generations of military historian.
This second (1919) edition is more complete and therefore more desirable.
R/2 V/5. RP.


A ROLL OF HONOUR
The Story of the Indian Army 1939-45

Major General J G Elliott
Cassell & Co Ltd, London, 1965
Beige, red, 8.5 x 5.5, -/392.
32 mono phots, 9 maps (printed in text), Bibliography, Index.

Apps: notes on military terms, order of battle, notes on air supply.

A straightforward factual account of all the campaigns in which Indian
troops served during WWII. Very few individuals mentioned in the text, but
the narrative establishes the framework for further research on the
activities of individual regiments. R/1 V/3. RP.


DEFEAT INTO VICTORY

Field Marshal Sir William Slim
Cassell & Co Ltd, London, 1956
Green, gold, 8.5 x 5.5, xi/576.
Fp, 21 maps (bound in), no appendixes, Index.

Although essentially autobiographical, this is an excellent account of
Allied operations in Burma between the disasters of 1942 and the
destruction of the Japanese in 1945. Very good maps and Index. R/1 V/3. RP.


THE TIGER STRIKES

Anon
The Government of India, Calcutta, 1942
Green cloth, with reversed lettering on white ground, 8.5 x 5.5, xviii/165.
Fp, 65 mono phots, 7 maps (5 bound in, 2 printed on end-papers), no Index.

A detailed and readable account of 4th and 5th Divisions fighting
Italian forces in Somaliland, Eritrea and the Western Desert. Covers
the period from September 1940 to June 1941. Printed on war-time 'utility'
paper, but well bound. There is one appendix, listing all ranks by name
and by regt for Honours & Awards. R/1 V/3. RP.

THE TIGER KILLS
India's Fight in the Middle East and North Africa

Anon
Government of India, Bombay, 1944
Orange, black, 8.75 x 5.5, x/354.
Fp, 66 mono phots, 12 maps (printed in text), no Index.

This work continues the story of 4th and 5th Indian Divisions (mainly 4th)
begun in THE TIGER STRIKES. Lamentably, and despite the fact that the
excellent narrative contains details of many small actions and acts of
individual bravery, there is no Index. There is, however, a good
Honours & Awards appendix. Both of these TIGER Divisional histories are
useful for placing in context the services of individual regiments. Both
books were published while the war was still in progress, but the censors
in Delhi had the good sense to allow history to speak for itself.
R/1 V/4. RP.

Brief histories were published also for the other WWII Indian Divisions,
and they are still quite easily obtainable. However, in terms of presentation and completeness, they cannot be compared with these two TIGER
publications.

# INDIA - BRITISH REGIMENTS ORIGINATING IN INDIA

Nine regiments - one cavalry and eight infantry - at one time
appeared in the British Army's order of battle and yet had their roots
firmly in the armies of the old Honourable East India Company. They
are listed here in the sequence: Bengal - Madras - Bombay.

THE NINETEENTH AND THEIR TIMES
Being an Account of the Four Cavalry Regiments which have borne the
number Nineteen

Colonel John Biddulph
John Murray, London, 1899
Seen in red and gold (probably rebound), 8.75 x 5.5, xxi/330.
no photographs, no other illustrations, no maps, no Index.

Apps: list of former COs, list of former officers.

Part IV, Chapter I, deals quite briefly with the formation, in 1858,
of the Bengal 1st European Light Cavalry, and its transfer, in 1862,
to the British Army. Eventually, in 1922, the regt became 15/19th The
King's Royal Hussars. R/3 V/2. AMM.


THE HISTORY OF THE BENGAL EUROPEAN INFANTRY
Now the Royal Munster Fusiliers and How it Helped to Win India

Lieut Col P R Innes
Simpkin, Marshall & Co, London, 1885
Royal blue, gold, 8.75 x 5.75, xii/572.
Fp, no other illustrations, 4 maps (town plans, bound in), Bibliography,
Index.

Apps: list of former COs, list of former officers, battle honours,
diary of events, notes on war services.

Covers the periods 1644-1756 (pre-formation) and 1756-1861 (regtl history)
in detailed narrative style. Full accounts of the campaigns in which the
regt took part, with some reference to individuals and to casualties.
R/3 V/4. AMM.


THE ROLL OF OFFICERS OF THE 101st AND 102nd FUSILIERS AND ROYAL MUNSTER
FUSILIERS

Lieut Col S T Banning
Published privately in London (no other details shown), 1912
Seen in maroon and gold (rebound), 8.5 x 5.5, ii/47.
no illustrations, no maps, no appendixes, Index.

The book comprises highly condensed data regarding the war services
and promotions (from 1840 onwards) of officers who served in these two
regts (formerly the 1st and 2nd European Bengal Fusiliers respectively).
With historical notes regarding their lineages. R/4 V/3. AMM.

HISTORY OF THE ROYAL MUNSTER FUSILIERS, Volume I, 1652-1860

Captain S McCance
Gale & Polden, Aldershot, 1927
Royal blue, gold, regtl crest on front cover, 10.0 x 7.5, vii/254.
Fp, 32 mono phots, 4 coloured plates, 20 maps, Index.

Apps: H&A, list of former officers, nominal rolls, biographical notes
regarding 10 personalities connected with the regt and 6 VC winners.

Volume I (of two) is divided into two sections: Part I (1652-1860) deals
with the Bengal European Battalion, later the 1st Bengal European Regiment.
Took part in the the battles of Plassey (1757), Deig (1803), Bhurtpore
(1825-26), Ghuznee (1839), and the campaigns for Burma (1852) and the
suppression of the Mutiny (1857-59). Many officers and casualties
mentioned in narrative. Part II (1839-60) deals with the 2nd Bengal
European Regiment. Not as expansive as Part I, but covers the Punjab
campaign (1848-49), Burma (1852) and the Mutiny. Many officers mentioned.
R/4 V/5. AMM.


A SHORT HISTORY OF THE SECOND BATTALION THE ROYAL SUSSEX REGIMENT

Lieut J H Dumbrell
C A Ribeiro, Singapore, n.d. (c.1925)
Card, orange, black, 9.0 x 6.0, -/78.
No illustrations, no maps, no appendixes, no Index.

A brief history covering the period 1853-1861. This was originally, until
1861, the 3rd Bengal European Infantry, but the author gives them only
five pages of narrative. R/4 V/1. PJE


A HISTORY OF THE ROYAL SUSSEX REGIMENT
A History of the Old Belfast Regiment and The Regiment of Sussex 1701-1953

G D Martineau
Moore & Tillyer Ltd, Chichester, Sussex, n.d. (c.1954)
Blue, gold, regtl crest on front cover, 8.75 x 5.5, -/324.
No illustrations, no maps or appendixes relating to India, Bibliography,
no Index.

This author gives even less space to the 3rd Bengal European Regiment
during 1853-61 (just one page, see page 115). R/2 V/1. AMM.


A SKETCH OF THE SERVICES OF THE MADRAS EUROPEAN REGIMENT DURING THE
BURMESE WAR

Anon
Smith Elder & Co, London, 1839
Red, gold, trophy of arms on front cover, 9.0 x 5.75, vii/104.
No illustrations, no maps, no appendixes, no Index.

A good readable account of the regt's part in the Burmese War of
1825-26. Numerous individuals mentioned. R/5 V/3. PJE.

HISTORICAL RECORD OF THE HONOURABLE EAST INDIA COMPANY'S FIRST MADRAS
EUROPEAN REGIMENT
Containing an Account of the Establishment of Independent Companies
in 1645, The Formation into a Regiment in 1748, and its Subsequent
Services to 1842

By a Staff Officer (Brigadier J G S Neill)
Smith Elder & Co, London, 1843
Rust-brown, gold, 9.25 x 6.0, xxiv/575.
Fp, 8 lithograph illustrations, 3 maps (bound in), no appendixes, Index.

The sub-title is self-explanatory. A sound detailed narrative account.
There are probably two separate editions of this work, both dated 1843.
Another version has been noted with the author as 'General J G Smith-Neill,
xxx preliminary pages, 12 plates of portraits and medals'. The differences
would seem to be minimal. R/4 V/4. VS.


SERVICES OF THE 102nd REGIMENT OF FOOT (ROYAL MADRAS FUSILIERS)
FROM 1842 TO THE PRESENT TIME

Colonel Thomas Raikes
Smith Elder & Co, London, 1867
Red, gold, panels, 8.5 x 5.25, i/68.
no illustrations, no maps, no appendixes, no Index.

'Being the sequel to The Services of the Madras European Regiment, by a
Staff Officer', according to the author. This book, in other words, picks
up the story from where Brigadier Neill left it in 1842 (see above).
The period to 1866 is covered in condensed narrative style, with good
accounts of service in Burma and the Mutiny. Casualties and awards are
mentioned in the text (officers only). R/4 V/3. AMM.


REGIMENTAL RECORDS OF THE 1st ROYAL DUBLIN FUSILIERS 1842-1904
Formerly the Madras European Regiment, 1st Madras Fusiliers and 102nd Foot

Anon (known to be Lieut Col S G Bird)
Published privately, produced by Biddle & Shipham, Guildford, 1904
Dark blue, gold, regtl crest on front cover, 8.5 x 5.5, viii/163 & vi.
Fp, 4 mono phots, 5 maps (bound in), no appendixes, Indexes.

This work also picks up where Neill left off, covering 1842 to 1904 in
chronological diary style with details of moves, stations, names of many
officers and men mentioned in the text. Campaigns include Burma (1852)
and the Mutiny (the latter in good detail, with officer casualties).
R/4 V/4. AMM
There is possibly a second edition, with different binding, of this book.
A 1905 version has been noted, the publisher being A C Curtis of Guildford,
being bound in calfskin, and having the sub-title extended with the words:
'By one who has Served over 30 Years in it'. The number of pages is the
same in both instances, suggesting no radical change in content. PJE.

THE REGIMENTAL RECORDS OF THE FIRST BATTALION THE ROYAL DUBLIN FUSILIERS
Formerly the Madras Europeans, The Madras European Regiment, The First
Madras Fusiliers, The 102nd Royal Madras Fusiliers 1644-1842.
By One whose Whole Service was Passed in the Corps and Who had the
Honour of Commanding it.

Anon (reported to be Colonel G J Harcourt)
Hugh Rees Ltd, London, 1910
Dark blue, gold, regtl crest on front cover, 8.5 x 5.5, xiv/152.
Fp, 11 mono phots, 2 maps (bound in), Glossary, Index.

Apps: regtl orders, notes on organisation, memorials, list of former COs,
list of former officers.

This author has gone back to the beginning and covered the same ground
as Neill in his 1843 book. He has re-written that work to 'make it more
clear and less prolix'. Written in detailed chronological diary style. In
presentation and style it conforms neatly with Bird's book of 1904 (see
previous page). Good accounts of all the major battles, with many officers
named. R/4 V/4. AMM/PJE.


NEILL'S BLUE CAPS

Colonel H C Wylly CB
Gale & Polden Ltd, Aldershot, n.d. (but White states 1924)
Blue, gilt, regtl crests on front covers, 9.75 x 7.25.
Three matching volumes published contemporaneously:
Volume I: 1639-1826 (mainly as the HEIC's European Regiment)
Volume II: 1826-1914 (as 1st Madras European Fusilers, etc, then as 102nd
                      Royal Madras Fusiliers, then (1881) transferred
                      to the British Army - see Appendix)
Volume III:- 1914-1922 (now as the Royal Dublin Fusiliers)

Only Volumes I and II relate to India.

Volume I:  -/330, Fp, 16 mono plates, 2 coloured plates, 6 maps (one
folding, bound in), Index, notes on uniforms
Volume II: -/229, Fp, 29 mono plates, 3 coloured plates, 2 maps (bound in),
Index, citations for 4 VC winners.

Colonel Wylly was a professional military historian and author. This
massive book is amongst his finest works, being clear, readable and
informative.  The quality of production is very good, with fine bindings.
R/4 V/5. MP.


THE ROYAL INNISKILLING FUSILIERS
Being the History of the Regiment from December 1688 to July 1914

Anon (the Regimental Historical Records Committee)
Constable & Co Ltd, London, 1928
Violet, gilt, 8.75 x 5.5, xxiii/673.
Fp, 30 mono plates, 16 coloured plates, 21 maps (printed in text), Index.

Apps: eight various, plus list of former COs, Roll of Honour (for
Waterloo and the Anglo-Boer War 1899-1902), H&A (Anglo-Boer War),
list of former officers.

Just one chapter, of 15 pages, deals with the 3rd Madras European Regiment.
The latter was raised in 1853, partly from Europeans already resident in
India and partly by recruitment in Ireland. The regt served in the
suppression of the Mutiny and was then transferred to the British Army
in 1861 as the 108th Regiment of Foot. Re-designated the 2nd Bn Royal
Inniskilling Fusiliers in 1881. R/3 V/3. MP.
Another edition of this book, dated 1934 and having a green binding with
pink lettering, has been reported. The contents are seemingly the same
as the 1928 edition.  AMM.


HISTORICAL RECORDS OF THE ONE HUNDRED AND FIFTH REGIMENT OF LIGHT INFANTRY

Anon
Produced by the Regiment, Meerut, 1871
Rifle green, black, 7.75 x 5.0, -/49.
no illustrations, no maps, no appendixes, no Index.

Compiled in two parts. Part I (1839-61) deals with 2nd Madras European
Regiment and is compiled from General Orders, Dress Regulations, extracts
from Regimental Records, etc. Part II (1861-71) deals with 105th Madras
Light Infantry, again from official and regtl records, but in greater
detail. Useful rather than stimulating. R/5 V/4. AMM.


THE HISTORY OF THE KING'S OWN YORKSHIRE LIGHT INFANTRY, Volume II

Colonel H C Wylly
Percy Lund, Humphries & Co Ltd, London, n.d.
Royal blue, gold, regtl crest on front cover, 9.0 x 6.0, vii/710.
Fp, some illustrations but not relating to India, Index.

This is essentially a KOYLI history. The author has given just 17 pages
to the 2nd Madras European Regiment from raising in 1839 to British Army
transfer in 1861. R/3 V/2. PJE.


THE KING'S OWN YORKSHIRE LIGHT INFANTRY
Register of Officers, 1755-1945

C P Deedes
Lund, Humphries & Co, London, 1946
Royal blue, gold, 9.0 x 6.0, -/247.
no illustrations, no maps, no appendixes, no Index.

A remarkable work of compilation. A list of officers, with biographical
notes, for the entire period. This includes officers who served with the
old 2nd Madras European Regiment. R/3 V/3. PJE.

RECORDS OF HM'S 1st REGIMENT OF BOMBAY EUROPEAN INFANTRY 'FUSILIERS'
Containing a Brief Account of its Formation in 1662 and Services to 1861

Anon (Lieut H Woodward)
Published privately, printed at the Observer Press, Poona, 1861
Originally in paper covers, seen rebound in blue and black, 8.5 x 6.0, -/40.
no illustrations, no maps, no Index, one appendix consisting of two
speeches given to the regt by Gen Sir Charles Napier.

Arranged in three short parts. Part I (1662-1794) a record by Lieut
Woodward and first published by the East Indian United Services Journal
in 1838. Part II (1662-1843) first published in Bombay General Orders in
1843. Part III (1843-1861) compiled from regtl records. This latter part
consists of only 4 pages, but it gives an account of the Punjab and Mutiny
campaigns with several officers being named. R/4 V/3. AMM.
The same little book was published contemporaneously in England, in 1861,
at the press of T Kentfield, Newport, Isle of Wight. This latter differs
in slightly smaller page sizes (8.25 x 5.25) and a slightly different
wording to the title. Contents are identical. AMM.


HISTORICAL RECORDS OF THE 103rd ROYAL BOMBAY FUSILIERS

Anon
Published privately, produced by A H Swiss, Devonport, n.d. (c.1876)
Royal blue, gold, Royal Coat of Arms, 8.75 x 5.5, -/81 & ix.

Apps: list of former COs, list of former officers (1824-76), strength
returns, succession of Adjutants (1798-1876).

Covers the period 1661-1876, being a detailed history of (successively)
1st Bombay Europeans (1661-1862), and 103rd Foot (Royal Bombay Fusilers)
(1862-1876). Written in diary style, giving stations, moves, etc, with
some officers named. Covers the major campaigns: Seringapatam (1799),
Mahratta War (1817-1818), Aden (1839), and Punjab (1848-1849). The
Mutiny is covered only sketchily. R/4 V/4. AMM.


CROWN AND COMPANY
The Historical Records of the 2nd Batt Royal Dublin Fusiliers, formerly
1st Bombay European Regiment, 1661-1911

Major Arthur Mainwaring
Arthur L Humphreys, London, 1911
Green, gold, regtl crest on front cover, 10.25 x 7.5, xxii/437.
Fp, 21 mono plates, 7 coloured plates, one map (folding, bound in at rear),
no Index.

Apps: 12, including list of former COs, list of former officers.

Well written and well produced. The regt became the 2nd Bn Royal Dublin
Fusiliers in 1881. R/3 V/3. MP.

THE DURHAM LIGHT INFANTRY

W L Vane
Gale & Polden, London, 1914
Dark green, gold, regtl crest on front cover, 10.0 x 7.0, xii/334.
Some illustrations (details not known), Index.

Apps: list of former COs, list of former officers.

This book deals mainly with the pre-war DLI. Just 12 pages are devoted
to the 2nd Bombay Light Infantry, this information being based upon regtl
records. There is some account of the Kolhapur (1844), Persia (1856)
and Mutiny (1857-59) campaigns. One of the few published sources available.
R/3 V/3. PJE.


FAITHFUL
The Story of the Durham Light Infantry

S G P Ward
Published by Regimental Headquarters, Durham Light Infantry, London 1962
Rifle green, silver, regtl crest on front cover, 10.0 x 6.0, xx/574.
Various illustrations, maps, appendixes, etc, but none relevant to the HEIC
except one map (showing India in 1862, printed in text).

A reasonably detailed account of the services of 2nd Bombay European Light
Infantry between 1839 and 1862. Covers the same material as Vane (above),
but with some officers' names added to the narrative and the Persia
campaign perhaps better described. R/1 V/3. AMM/PJE.


THE HISTORY OF THE PRINCE OF WALES'S LEINSTER REGIMENT (ROYAL CANADIANS)
Volume I (of two)

Lieut Col Frederick Ernest Whitton CMG
Gale & Polden Ltd, Aldershot, n.d. (c.1924)
Blue with broad band of green, gold, regtl crest on front cover,
8.75 x 5.5, xii/483.
Various illustrations, etc, but none relevant to the HEIC except one map.

Chapters XIV to XX cover the period 1600-1864 and especially the services
of the 3rd Bombay European Regiment (1853-1862). Good readable narrative,
particularly good for the Mutiny (when the regt served under Sir Hugh Rose
and distinguished themselves at the capture of Jhansi).Volume II of this
attractive pair covers the POW's Leinster Regiment in WWI. R/4 V/4. AMM/MP.

*****************************

Researchers experiencing difficulty with these former HEIC regiments
are recommended to consult A REGISTER OF THE REGIMENTS AND CORPS OF THE
BRITISH ARMY (The Ancestry of the Regiments and Corps of the Regular
Establishment of the Army), by Arthur Swinson, The Archive Press,
London, 1972.

For immediate reference purposes, the following simplified version of the
lineages may be of some assistance.

## APPENDIX I

Simplified lineages of British Army regiments formerly of the
armies of the Honourable East India Company

101st Royal Bengal Fusiliers (formerly 1st Bengal Europeans)
linked to
104th Bengal Fusiliers (formerly 2nd Bengal Europeans)
to form
THE ROYAL MUNSTER FUSILIERS (disbanded 1922)

107th Bengal Infantry (formerly 3rd Bengal European Light Infantry)
linked to
35th Royal Sussex Regiment of Foot
to form
THE ROYAL SUSSEX REGIMENT (now 3rd Bn THE QUEEN'S REGIMENT)

102nd Royal Madras Fusiliers (formerly 1st Madras European Fusiliers)
linked to
103rd Royal Bombay Fusiliers (formerly 1st Bombay European Fusiliers)
to form
THE ROYAL DUBLIN FUSILIERS (disbanded 1922)

105th Madras Light Infantry (formerly 2nd Madras Light Infantry)
linked to
51st (Yorkshire West Riding) Regiment
to form
THE KING'S OWN YORKSHIRE LIGHT INFANTRY (now THE LIGHT INFANTRY)

108th Madras Infantry (formerly 3rd Madras Infantry)
linked to
27th (Inniskilling) Regiment of Foot
to form
THE ROYAL INNISKILLING FUSILIERS (now THE ROYAL IRISH RANGERS)

106th Bombay Light Infantry (formerly 2nd Bombay Light Infantry)
linked to
68th (Durham Light Infantry) Regiment
to form
THE DURHAM LIGHT INFANTRY (now THE LIGHT INFANTRY)

109th Bombay Infantry (formerly 3rd Bombay Europeans)
linked to
100th (Prince of Wales's Royal Canadian)Regiment.
to form
THE PRINCE OF WALES'S LEINSTER REGIMENT (ROYAL CANADIANS) (disbanded 1922)

# INDIA - THE PRESIDENTIAL ARMIES

THE PRESIDENTIAL ARMIES OF INDIA

Lieut Col S Rivett-Carnac
W H Allen & Co, London, 1890
Red, gold, Imperial Crown with 'Vivat Imperatrix' on front cover,
9.0 x 5.5, xxiii/442.
no illustrations, no maps, Index.

Apps: notes on Lord Napier of Magdala, operations in Upper Burma
(1885-86), the native armies of India.

The early chapters cover Anglo-Indian history in general terms from the
earliest days through to 1748, and then India's military history from
1748 to 1886. There are chapters on HEIC artillery, cavalry and infantry,
but the style is neither very readable nor very informative. R/3 V/1. AMM.


THE BENGAL NATIVE INFANTRY
An Historical Account from its first Formation in 1757 to 1796 when the
Present Regulations took place, with Supplementary Notes to the Year 1814,
together with a Detail of the Services on which several Battalions have
been employed during that period

Capt John Williams
John Murray, London, 1817
Leather spine with marbled boards, gold, 8.75 x 5.25, -/387.
Fp, 4 coloured plates, no maps, no Index.

Apps: list of officers (for 1760 only).

A useful secondary source for the early conquest of Northern India and
the raising and organisation of the BNI. The narrative is as ponderous
as the sub-title (which must be one of the longest on record). R/3 V/3. RP.
A facsimile reprint of this book was produced in 1970 by Frederick
Muller Ltd of London, in a limited edition of 550 copies.


HISTORY OF THE RISE AND PROGRESS OF THE BENGAL ARMY, Volume I

Capt Arthur Broome
W Thacker & Co Ltd, Calcutta, 1850
Red, gold, ornamental motif of flags with drum, gun and soldier on front
cover, 9.0 x 5.5, vi/629/lxxvi (the last being the appendixes).
no illustrations, 6 plans and a map (in rear pocket), no Index (but
good detailed chapter headings).

This was seemingly the only Volume published. Covers the period 1589-1767.
The narrative is patchy, some sections being good reading and stimulating,
other sections being tedious and over-written. R/3 V/3. AMM/LM.

A SKETCH OF THE SERVICES OF THE BENGAL NATIVE ARMY
To the Year 1895

Lieut F G Cardew
Superintendent of Government Printing, Calcutta, 1903
Dark green, gold, 8.5 x 5.5, v/576/ii.
2 coloured plates, no other illustrations, no maps, Bibliography, Index.

Apps: chronological list of Corps, idem Corps at 1895, idem list of services.

Although it deals with the entire Bengal Native Army, the book  is
particularly good as a source for the Bengal Artillery (including Punjab
Frontier Force). Compiled originally by Cardew in 1890-91, but then
revised and corrected by G W de Rhe-Philipe prior to publication.
R/4 V/4. AMM.


THE BENGAL NATIVE INFANTRY, 1796-1852
Its Organisation and Discipline

Amiya Barat
F K L Mukhoppadhyay, Calcutta, 1962
Light red, black, 9.0 x 5.5, xii/341.
4 mono phots, 2 maps (printed on end papers), Bibliography, Index.

Apps: list of former Commanders-in-Chief (Bengal), list of officer
strengths for BNI in various years.

A good secondary reference source. Early history and mutinies are dealt
with in a fresh perspective. R/1 V/3. PJE.


HISTORY OF THE MADRAS ARMY FROM 1746 TO 1826
With an Account of the European Artillery, Engineers and Infantry up
to their Amalgamation with the Royal Army in 1861, and of the Native
Cavalry and Infantry up to 1887

Lieut Col W J Wilson
Government Press, Madras, between 1882 and 1889
published in five Volumes, all 8.75 x 5.5, red, gold, full Morocco

Vol I:   1746-1780 vi/396
Vol II:  1780-1799 iv/383
Vol III: 1799-1816 vii/408
Vol IV:  1817-1826 ix/552, with Index for all four volumes
Vol V:   14 maps and plans, all relating to Vols I - IV

Apps: various tables of Returns, summaries of casualties, etc

A comprehensive factual account. Few individuals mentioned by name.
The period 1817-1826 is described in great detail, and a final chapter
in Vol IV summarises the events from 1827 to 1887. R/4 V/4. AMM.

THE MADRAS SOLDIER

Lieut Col E G Phythian-Adams OBE
Government Press, Madras, 1948
Light blue, dark blue and red vertical bands, green spine, dark blue
lettering, 10.0 x 6.25, xii/215.
Fp, no other illustrations, 2 maps (folding, bound in), Bibliography,
a limited Index.

Apps:list of Madras units 1939-46, H&A (nominal roll for 1939-46), notes
on recruiting, dress and uniforms.

A condensed but complete history covering a long and complex period
of time. Particularly useful for the WWII appendixes. R/3 V/3. TA.


HISTORY OF THE BOMBAY ARMY

Sir Patrick Cadell CSI CIE VD
Longmans, Green & Co, London, 1938
Red, gold, 8.75 x 5.5, xv/362.
Fp, one other coloured plate, no mono phots, 11 maps (printed in text),
Bibliography, Indexes.

Apps: campaigns of the Bombay Army (with details of units engaged),
chronological list of regiments (all arms), list of regiments raised
during WWI, amalgamations, class composition of Bombay regiments in
1895 and 1935.

Covers the period 1662-1937 in a general but thorough way. Very readable.
Few individuals named in text, but many regiments featured.  An
excellent over-view, with good appendixes. R/2 V/4. AMM/LM.

## INDIA - THE BODYGUARDS

HISTORICAL RECORDS OF THE GOVERNOR-GENERAL'S BODY GUARD
Historical Records of the Viceroy's Body-Guard

Lieut V C P Hodson
W Thacker & Co, London, 1910
Red, gold, regtl crest and battle honours on front cover, 10.0 x 7.5,
xiv/414.
Fp, 7 coloured plates, 12 mono phots (including reproductions of
lithographic portraits), no maps (but 2 of the coloured plates are
town plans), Bibliography, Glossary, Index.

Apps: 16 various, including war services of the Corps, notes on the origins
of the Corps, alphabetical list of officers who have served, nominal roll
of officers for each year, biographical notes of British combatant officers,
idem medical officers, idem veterinary officers, idem European Riding
Masters and NCOs, notes on Native Officers, etc.

Described as 'an unofficial history' of the Body Guard from its formation
in 1773 to the end of 1908. Extremely detailed, and certainly ranks as a
formal history. Minutes from Secret Consultations describe the formation
and organisation of the unit, and the differences of opinion between Warren
Hastings and General Clavering. Much interesting detail on actions in
which the Body Guard took part, including such little known affairs as
the Battle of St George, 23 April 1774. The Glossary and Bibliography are
unusually detailed, including many sources and terms not easily found
elsewhere. The Corps fought in several major campaigns: Mysore (1811),
Mahratta Wars (1815-18), First Burmese War (1824-26), Gwalior (1843), the
Sikh Wars (1845-46 and 1848-49), and the Burmese War of 1886.

Occasionally there is confusion over the title of this excellent book.
The outer casing refers to THE VICEROY'S BODY-GUARD (the sole instance
of the hyphenated spelling in the entire volume). The title page and the
body of the narrative refer to THE GOVERNOR-GENERAL'S BODY GUARD. At the
Durbar held at Allahabad on 1 November 1858, it was proclaimed that HM the
Queen would assume henceforth the Government of India, and that the
Governor-General would be styled 'Viceroy and Governor-General'. The
Body Guard, however, did not change its title until the mid-1860s. As the
dedication at the front of the book is to The Earl of Minto, 'Viceroy and
Governor-General of India', it would seem that, even as late as 1910,
the author felt it prudent to hedge his bets by using both titles.
R/4 V/4. NAM. IOL. PJE/BR.
The India Office  Library holds a short article from THE CAVALRY
JOURNAL, dated 1939, and entitled INDIA'S HOUSEHOLD CAVALRY, THE BODY-
GUARDS, which may be useful for additional research.


SERVICES OF THE MADRAS BODY GUARD AND ITS OFFICERS

H Morgan
Published at Fort St George, Madras, 1866
Brown leather, gold, scrolled edgings, 9.5 x 6.0, -/23.
no illustrations, no maps, no appendixes, no Index.

Composed mainly of extracts from General Orders between 1783 and 1859.
The text gives a concise but clear account of the unit's services during
that period (although, with only 23 pages, it is very superficial).
R/4 V/2. BM. PJE.


SERVICES OF THE BODY GUARD OF HIS EXCELLENCY THE GOVERNOR OF MADRAS

Anon
Lawrence Asylum Press, Madras, 1886
Dark green, gold, armorial bearings of the Baron Ampthill on inside front
cover, 8.25 x 5.25, -/34.
No illustrations, no maps, no Index.

Apps: list of former Adjutants, list of former Commandants.

A short history of the Corps, based upon General Orders, from its
inception in February 1783 to 1886. The strength of the Corps
averaged 200 officers and men, half being cavalry and half light
infantry, arranged in two sub-units under command of a Captain or Major,
with a Lieutenant as Adjutant. R/4 V/3. IOL. RGB.


RECORDS OF THE BODY GUARD OF HIS EXCELLENCY THE GOVERNOR OF MADRAS

Capt L W C Kerrich
Addison & Co, Madras, 1894
Maroon, gold, 9.0 x 5.5, -/47.
no illustrations, no maps, no Index.

Apps: list of former COs, list of former Adjutants.

Based mainly upon official reports. Lacks human interest. The period
covered is 1783-1894. R/4 V/3. NAM. PJE.


RECORDS OF THE BODY GUARD OF H.E. THE GOVERNOR OF MADRAS

Capt R B Worgan
Hoe & Co, The Premier Press, Madras, 1910
Red, gold, regtl crest on front cover, 8.5 x 5.0, -/75.
no illustrations, no maps, no Index.

Apps: list of former COs (from 1783), list of former Adjutants (from
1826).

The compiler has collected an interesting assemblage of official
documents, arranged chronologically, regarding uniforms, pay, etc.
In its early days, the unit was by no means purely ceremonial in its
function. It accompanied Lord Cornwallis in the war against Tippoo Sahib
in 1791-92, and later distinguished itself in the campaign of 1801 against
the Poligars in Southern Madras. R/4 V/3. JRS.

HISTORICAL RECORD OF THE BODY GUARD OF H.E. THE GOVERNOR OF MADRAS

Capt A E G Maconochie
Vest & Co, Madras, 1922
Red, gold, 8.5 x 5.5, -/95.
no illustrations, no maps, no Index.

Apps: list of former COs, list of former Adjutants.

This is simply an update on the previous works by Kerrich and Worgan.
The author sticks rigidly to the established format, and thereby misses
the opportunity to breath life and human interest into the story. A curiously
old-fashioned effort for a book published in 1922. R/4 V/3. NAM. PJE/RP.

## INDIA - CAVALRY - GENERAL BACKGROUND

THE INDIAN CAVALRY
History of the Indian Armoured Corps until 1940

Maj Gen Gurcharn Singh Sandhu PVSM
Vision Books, New Delhi, 1981
Black, gold, 10.0 x 7.5, -/473.
Fp, 8 mono phots, one coloured plate, 15 maps (printed in text),
Bibliography, Index.

Apps: a series of seven extremely useful tables detailing the date of
raising and title changes and disbandment dates of early Cavalry regts,
notes on early Volunteer Cavalry units, battle honours, etc.

Covers a very broad field but includes details of individual regiments,
war services, and many of the finer points. Description of the sillidar
system, and the transition from horsed cavalry to mechanised cavalry prior
to WII. A most useful book packed with interesting information. Sadly,
the publishers have taken little care with their type-setting and the
quality of paper and binding is not good. Even so, a first class source
of reference. R/1 V/4. CJP.


THE INDIAN ARMOUR
History of the Indian Armoured Corps, 1941-1971

Maj Gen Gurcharn Singh Sandhu PVSM
Vision Books (incorporating Orient Paperbacks), Delhi, 1987
Black, yellow, 9.5 x 7.0, -/570.
48 mono phots, 19 maps (printed in text), Bibliography, Index.

Apps: list of former COs, regtl titles (1922-1971), list of armoured
fighting vehicles (cars and tanks), class composition of units,
training establishments (1937-1971).

Full of interesting information concerning the Indian Armoured Corps
during WWII, including the occupation of Japan. Also an account of events
at Partition and subsequently. Like the author's first book (above),
this is a very well researched and well written work. R/2 V/4. CJP.

## INDIA - CAVALRY REGIMENTS

A SHORT HISTORY OF THE 1st DUKE OF YORK'S OWN LANCERS (SKINNER'S HORSE)
1803-1908

Major H Roberts
Indian Daily Telegraph Press, Lucknow, 1908
Paper, green, black, 8.5 x 5.5, -/26.
no illustrations, no maps, no appendixes, no Index.

A general record, mainly a quick reference source. Presumably produced
for the instruction of newly joined young officers. R/4 V/1. NAM. PJE.


SKINNER'S HORSE
The History of the 1st Duke of York's Own Lancers and the 3rd Skinner's
Horse, now amalgamated under the designation, The 1st Duke of York's
Own Skinner's Horse

Major A M Daniels OBE
Hugh Rees Ltd, London, 1925
Blue, gold, 8.5 x 6.0, xvi/181.
no illustrations, no maps, no Index.

Apps: H&A, list of officers serving at 1923, notes on the evolution
of the regt.

A useful summary of services. Includes extracts from the Bengal Army Lists
for 1839, 1844, 1857, 1879, 1897, 1914 and 1923, in respect of both
original regts. R/4 V/3. UWML. BCC.


THE LAST DAYS OF HORSED CAVALRY
An Account of Skinner's Horse between the wars

Lieut Col E G Haynes
Never formally published, facsimile typescript, dated 1974
Seen in black soft card binding, 12.0 x 8.0, -/26.
no illustrations, one map (showing stations), no Index.

Apps: list of former officers.

The author was Adjutant of the regt from 1932 to 1936. This is a very slim
work, but it describes the typical activities of a cavalry regt in India
during that period. R/5 V/2. IOL. CRDG.


SKINNER'S HORSE

Christopher Rothero
Almark Publishing Co Ltd, New Malden, Surrey, printed by Staples Printers,
Kettering, 1979
Stiff illustrated card, red, yellow, blue, green, sketch of four standing
figures (officers and sowars), 7.25 x 8.25, -/48.
17 pages of good black-and-white sketches, 6 pages of colour drawings
of uniforms, Glossary, Bibliography, no Index.

This is not a regimental history in the conventional sense. Only 3 pages
of narrative are devoted to former services and lineage. The value of
the book lies in its excellent account of all the types of uniform,
equipment and accoutrements (including saddlery) used by the regt.
The coloured plates are particularly attractive and helpful. R/2 V/4. CRDG.


SWORN TO DIE

Lieut Col M A R Skinner
Lancer International, for the regiment, New Delhi, 1984
Patinated boards, red lettering, full colour illustration of a mounted
sowar, 10.75 x 7.25, -/252.
20 mono phots, one coloured plate, 34 line drawings and sketches,
3 maps (printed in text), Index.

Apps: Roll of Honour (WWII and 1971), H&A (WWII and 1971), list of British
and Indian officers serving at the time of amalgamation (May 1921), roll
of recipients of the 1935 Jubilee medal, idem 1937 Coronation medal,
list of former COs, list of former officers (1921-1939), etc.

The first 61 pages cover the period from amalgamation in 1921 through to
1939. The main part of the narrative deals with WWII (Eritrea, Egypt,
Libya, Persia and Italy). There is also a short final section on the
Indo-Pakistan war of 1971.

The author was great-great-grandson of the regt's founder, Colonel James
Skinner CB. This was the first serious attempt to produce a comprehensive
history of Skinner's Horse in readable narrative form. His predecessor (see
previous page, Major Daniels) lost his suitcase containing all his notes
and research material, hence Lieut Col Skinner had a more than usually
difficult task. His book is in fact informative and readable, the WWII
section being based upon the personal recollections of most of the officers
who served during that time. R/3 V/4. RP


A BRIEF HISTORY OF THE 2nd LANCERS (GARDNER'S HORSE)
From 12th May 1809 to 12th May 1909

Anon
Pioneer Press, Allahabad, 1909
Royal blue, gold, 7.5 x 5.0, -/53.
no illustrations, no maps, no Index.

Apps: list of former officers, notes on the life of Lieut Col W L Gardner,
nominal roll of British officers and VCOs serving in May 1909.

The text is based mainly upon regtl records, and lacks human interest.
Essentially a summary of stations and engagements in diary form. NAM.
R/4 V/2. PJE.

DIGEST OF SERVICES OF IV CAVALRY

Anon
Punjab Frontier Press, Peshawar, 1920
Red, black, 7.0 x 5.5, -/138.
no illustrations, no maps, no Index.

Apps: list of former COs, list of former officers, 'Who's Who' of
IV Cavalry.

A basic historical record, written in both English and Hindi. The regt
traces its origins back to 1838 and the Irregular Cavalry of the Oude
Auxiliary Force. Absorbed into the Bengal Army in 1840 as the 6th Bengal
Irregular Cavalry. R/5 V/3. USII. NKR/OSS.


A HISTORY OF THE 2nd LANCERS (GARDNER'S HORSE) FROM 1809 TO 1922

Capt D E Whitworth MC
Sifton Praed & Co Ltd, London, 1924
Khaki, regtl colour stripes (blue and light blue), regtl crest on
front and back covers, 8.5 x 5.5, xi/228.
no illustrations, 8 maps (5 printed in text, 3 bound in), no Index.

Apps: H&A (WWI), war services of officers, summary of operations with
Mhow Cavalry Brigade (November-December 1917), notes on horses, notes
on sillidar cavalry.

The first 45 pages are a synopsis of the period 1809-1914. The bulk of
the narrative then deals with WWI services in good informative detail.
R/4 V/4. NAM. CSM/RGH.


A HISTORY OF THE 2nd ROYAL LANCERS (GARDNER'S HORSE)

Brigadier E W D Vaughan CB DSO MC
Printed by The Harrow Observer, Harrow, for Sifton Praed & Co Ltd,
London, 1951
Blue, gold, regtl crest on front cover, 8.5 x 5.5, xi/196.
no illustrations, 4 maps (bound in at rear), no Index.

Apps: Roll of Honour (WWII), H&A (WWII), list of former COs, lists of
former British officers and VCOs, nominal rolls officers and men taken POW
with details of those who escaped.

The narrative mainly deals with WWII fighting in the Western Desert
where the regt was twice destroyed (El Mechile and Bir Hachiem). Later
re-formed and saw service in Palestine, Iraq and Iran. A sound readable
book and the Western Desert maps are very helpful, but the lack of an
Index and the poor quality of paper tend to diminish its overall worth.
R/3 V/3. NAM. RP.

ARMY LISTS - 5th CAVALRY

Anon
Printed by Dhoomi Mal Dharam Das, Military Printers, New Delhi,
presumably for the regiment, n.d. (c.1922)
Seen in blue and gold (rebound), 9.75 x 5.5, i/63.
no illustrations, no maps, no appendixes, no Index.

This is nothing more than a reprint of Bengal and Indian Army lists for
the 5th Cavalry between April 1841 and January 1922. British officers are
listed, Indian native officers are not, and this fact severely limits
the worth of the book as a reference source. R/4 V/1. CJP.


NOBODY'S OWN
The History of the 3rd Cavalry and its Predecessors, 1841-1945

Brigadier H W Picken
published privately in Eastbourne,  no details shown, 1962
Sky blue, gold, regtl crest on front cover, 10.25 x 8.0, vi/209.
7 mono phots, one black-and-white sketch, one diagram showing the
parade arrangements for the execution of Mutineers, 8 maps (printed in
text), no appendixes, no Index.

A comprehensive and humorous account for the stated period, but marred by
the lack of any appendixes and the absence of an Index. The 5th Cavalry
and 8th Cavalry were amalgamated in 1922 to form the 3rd Cavalry. The regt
was the only Indian cavalry unit to be captured by the Japanese at the
surrender of Singapore. Four hundred and fifty officers and men survived
imprisonment and the regt was re-constituted in 1945. R/3 V/3. NAM. PJE.


10th DUKE OF CAMBRIDGE'S OWN LANCERS (HODSON'S HORSE)
Nominal Roll 1857-1912

Anon
Thacker Spink & Co, Calcutta, 1913
Royal blue with red quarters, gold, 10.0 x 6.5, i/94.
no illustrations, no maps, no appendixes, no Index.

This is a compendium of extracts from official Indian Army lists, showing
the roll of officers serving in each year, and the stations at which the
regt was serving. Very bare and basic. R/4 V/2. NAM. PJE.


WITH HODSON'S HORSE IN PALESTNE

Anon (shown as 'C.H.R.')
Thacker & Co Ltd, Bombay, n.d. (c.1919)
Paper covers, red cloth spine, black, 7.0 x 5.0, -/57.
no illustrations, 5 maps (folding, bound in), no Index.

Apps: H&A (WWI).

The regt served in Palestine from March 1918, and it is evident that the
author was one of the officers who was there throughout that time.
Quite useful in a limited way. R/5 V/3. NAM. RJW.

NARRATIVE OF WAR SERVICE, 9th HODSON'S HORSE, 1914-21

Anon
Never formally published, facsimile typescript, n.d. (c.1922?)
Seen casebound, black, gold, 13.0 x 9.0, -/54 (appendix pages not
numbered),no illustrations, one map,  no Index.

Apps: H&A, list of former officers, a selection of letters and orders,
an account of the Battle of Cambrai.

A good account of the WWI period, brief but clear. The H&A appendix is
helpful. R/4 V/3. NAM. PJE.


HODSON'S HORSE

Major F G Cardew OBE
William Blackwood & Sons Ltd, Edinburgh and London, 1928
Blue, gold, Lancer motif on front cover, 9.5 x 6.5, viii/402.
Fp, 8 mono phots, 14 maps (6 printed in text, 8 bound in), Glossary, Index.

Apps: H&A (for all campaigns, from Mutiny to WWI), list of former COs (with
biographical notes), list of former officers (with some biographical notes),
list of former Risaldar-Majors, notes on casualties, etc.

A magnificent history of a famous regiment. Well written and attractively
produced. Good accounts of the Mutiny, the Second Afghan War, and WWI
(France and Mesopotamia). R/3 V/5. NAM. RGH/RP.


HODSON'S HORSE [LATE HODSON'S HORSE AND 10th D.C.O. LANCERS (HODSON'S
HORSE)]
Nominal Roll of Officers who have served with the Regiment, 1857-1928

Anon
Printed by The Civil & Military Gazette Press, Lahore, presumably for the
regiment (no other details shown), 1929
Blue boards with red spine, gold, 10.0 x 6.75, -/330.
no illustrations, no maps, Glossary, no Index.

A compendium of extracts from Bengal Lists and Indian Army Lists,
detailing all British officers who served with the original and
amalgamated regts during the stated period. Risaldar-Majors are listed
from 1864 onwards, and all Indian officers from 1877 onwards. Very comprehensive, and most useful when tracing services and promotions.
R/5 V/4. CJP.


A SHORT HISTORY OF HODSON'S HORSE, 1857-1940

Lieut Cdr the Hon Charles Willoughby RN
Gale & Polden, Aldershot, 1946
Stiff card, blue, black, regt crest on front cover, 8.0 x 5.5, iii/57.
Fp, no illustrations, no maps, no Index.

Apps: list of former COs, list of Honorary Colonels.

A very condensed and easily readable version of the regt's history and lineage, intended presumably for the instruction of newly joined war-time officers. Two other editions of this booklet have been reported, bearing the dates 1941 and 1945. R/3 V/2. PJE/RP.


HISTORICAL RECORD OF THE SERVICES OF THE 11th BENGAL LANCERS (LATE 1st SIKH IRREGULAR CAVALRY) 1857-1872
With Supplement, Historical Record of the Services of the 11th Prince of Wales's Own Bengal Lancers from March 1870 to March 1876

Anon
Government Central Press, Calcutta, n.d. (c.1876)
Paper covers, pink, black, 9.5 x 7.5, -/16/ii.
no illustrations, no maps, no appendixes, no Index.

Composed of two sections. Part I briefly covers the services of 11th Bengal Lancers (1857-1870) in chronological diary form and including all stations and moves (service in the Mutiny, Second China and Umbeyla campaigns).Part II deals mainly with the change of title and the Prince of Wales as Honorary Colonel. R/5 V/3. AMM.


REGIMENTAL LISTS, XI KING EDWARD'S OWN LANCERS (PROBYN'S HORSE), 1857-1907
1st Regiment of Sikh Irregular Cavalry, XI Prince of Wales's Own Bengal Lancers

General Sir W R Birdwood GCMG KCB KCSI CIE DSO
Government of India Central Printing Office, Delhi, 1907
Red, gold, 9.5 x 6.5, i/234.
no illustrations, no maps, no appendixes, no Index.

A compendium of extracts from Indian Army Lists which made reference to the regt between 1857 and 1907. Dry and dusty reading, but totally reliable. The author (later Field Marshal) commanded the regt from 1875 to 1884. His hand-written note in a surviving 'presentation' copy states that he prepared the extracts 'on the occasion of the celebration of the jubilee of my regiment at Rawalpindi in March 1907'. R/4 V/3. NAM. PJE/CJP.


NOTES ON THE WAR SERVICES OF THE XII CAVALRY

Anon
The Civil & Military Gazette Press, Lahore, 1908
Black, gold, regtl crest on front cover, 7.0 x 5.0, -/21.
no illustrations, no maps, no appendixes, no Index.

A very, very brief description of war services in the Mutiny, Abyssinia and Second Afghanistan campaign. R/4 V/1. NAM. PJE.

A HISTORY OF THE XI KING EDWARD'S OWN LANCERS (PROBYN'S HORSE)

Capt E L Maxwell
A C Curtis Ltd, Guildford, Surrey, 1914
Light maroon and dark red, gold, regtl crest on front cover, 10.0 x 8.0,
xi/163.
one mono phot, 18 line drawings, 4 maps (bound in), no Index.

Apps: list of former COs (1857-1909), letters selected from the original
letter book.

Originated as a textbook for the regtl school, then expanded for publication.
Suffers from 'the incomplete nature of the records'. Good detail on
the raising of the regt in 1857, the death of Capt Whale, the appointment
of Maj D M Probyn as Commandant, service in China under Hope Grant, and the
Umbeyla expedition of 1863. The regt also served in the Second Afghan war,
the Chitral relief force, and the Malakand Field Force. Long on fine detail,
short on historical perspective. R/4 V/4. NAM. BRW/RGH.


THE HISTORY OF PROBYN'S HORSE (5th KING EDWARD'S OWN LANCERS)

Major C A Boyle DSO
Gale & Polden Ltd, Aldershot, 1929
Maroon, with a very fine crest on the front cover in silver, gold, blue
and scarlet, 10.0 x 7.5, xv/98.
Fp, no other illustrations, 9 maps (bound in), no Index.

Apps: Roll of Honour, H&A, list of former officers, notes on the services
of General Sir D M Probyn VC, idem Sir Hugh Gough VC.

The narrative covers the entire period from the Mutiny through to
amalgamation in 1922 in just 81 pages, hence there is little detail.
R/4 V/3. IOL. RGH.


PROBYNABAD STUD FARM
The Property of Probyn's Horse (5th King Edward VII's Own Lancers)

Lieut Col E S MacL Prinsep
The Civil & Military Gazette Ltd, Lahore, April 1938
Full calfskin, brown, gold, with ribbon having the regtl colours pasted
diagonally across the front cover, 9.0 x 5.5, -/88.
2 mono phots, no other illustrations, no maps, no appendixes, no Index.

Covers an aspect of horsed cavalry soldiering often overlooked. This is
the stud book for the regt's own breeding programme for the entire period
from 1864 to 1938. Probynabad was located at Bannu, on the North West
Frontier. The book gives details of all the sixty-six different brood mare
lines maintained at the farm, and of all the stallions which stood there.
An interesting volume for horsemen or specialist cavalry researchers.
R/5 V/4. RMAS. RP.

AN ACCOUNT OF THE OPERATIONS IN BURMA CARRIED OUT BY PROBYN'S HORSE
DURING FEBRUARY, MARCH AND APRIL, 1945

Major B H Mylne MBE
Publisher's details not shown, printed in Rangoon, 1945
Seen in black boards, with red spine, probably rebound, 10.0 x 6.0, -/76.
5 mono phots (of poor quality), 19 maps (bound in, being crudely printed
but showing excellent detail and being very useful for reference),
no Index.

Apps: Roll of Honour (all ranks), H&A (all ranks), list of officers who
served in the campaign.

The regt was equipped with Sherman tanks and the narrative describes their
advance to Meiktila and then Rangoon. A well written account, with
good detail and many references to individuals. R/4 V/5. RMAS. RP.


HISTORY OF THE 13th DUKE OF CONNAUGHT'S LANCERS (WATSON'S HORSE), FORMERLY
THE 4th SIKH CAVALRY FROM THE DATE THEY WERE RAISED IN MARCH 1858 TO
SEPTEMBER 1908

Publisher and printer unknown due to damage to the only copy seen, but
probably written anonymously and produced for the instruction of young
officers, n.d. (c.1909?),  6.5 x 5.0, -/38.
no illustrations, no maps, no Index.

Apps: list of former COs, notes on the war services of the regt.

No more than a brief sketchy pamphlet, but one of the very few sources
available. The regt has an interesting and complex  history but, sadly, it
never appointed an author and publisher to produce a formal detailed
account.   It may be noted that, according to a former officer of the regt,
it was known as 'Watson's Horse' only between 1859 and 1862, and then again
after 1909. The addition of 'Duke of Connaught' to its title was the
result of a dashing charge by the regt at Tel-el-Kebir in 1882 which was
witnessed by the Duke and caused him to ask if he could become the regt's
Colonel. R/5 V/2. NAM. PJE/RS.


THE 6th DUKE OF CONNAUGHT'S OWN LANCERS IN ITALY
September 1943 - May 1945

Major F Brock
Published privately, printed by William Brown & Davis, Durban, 1948
Soft card covers, fawn, black, 8.5 x 5.5, i/48.
no illustrations, 5 maps (folding, bound in), no Index.

Apps: H&A, summary of casualties.

A readable accurate account, with many junior officers and other ranks
named in the narrative. Based on the regtl war diary. R/4 V/4. AGB.

THE 28th LIGHT CAVALRY IN PERSIA AND RUSSIAN TURKISTAN, 1915-1920

Major J A C Kreyer and Captain G Uloth
Slatter & Rose Ltd, for the Regiment, Oxford, 1926
Dark blue, gold, regtl crest on front cover, 9.0 x 6.5, xx/203.
Fp, 47 mono phots, 2 maps, no Index.

Apps: H&A, list of British officers who served, idem Indian officers,
notes on casualties, unit strengths, notes on uniforms, summary of events.

A good easily readable account for the period stated. This is the only
published history for what became, in 1922, the 7th Light Cavalry.
R/4 V/4. NAM. PJE.


DIARY OF THE SERVICES OF THE 1st MADRAS LANCERS, AND A TROOP EACH OF
THE 3rd AND 4th MADRAS LIGHT CAVALRY ATTACHED DURING OPERATIONS IN
UPPER BURMA, 1886-87 AND 1887-88

Anon (but stated to be Lieut H L B Acton)
Lawrence Asylum Press, Madras, 1889
Black boards with brown spine and quarters, gold, regtl crest on front
cover, 9.5 x 6.5, -/234.
no illustrations, no maps, no Index.

Apps: list of men invalided back to India, idem men who died of disease
in Burma, idem horses which died in Burma.

A straightforward factual account of the regt's part in the operations
in Burma, based upon regtl records and the war diary. R/4 V/3. NAM. PJE.


HISTORY OF THE 30th LANCERS (GORDON'S HORSE)
Formerly 4th Nizam's Cavalry, 4th Hyderabad Contingent, and 4th Lancers
Hyderabad Contingent

Major E A W Stotherd
Gale & Polden Ltd, Aldershot, 1911
Dark green, gold, regtl crest on front cover, 7.5 x 5.0, vi/207.
Fp, 15 mono phots, one map, no Index.

Apps: list of officers who served in the regt (arranged in chronological
order), list of officers serving in 1911.

The 4th Nizam's Cavalry was first raised in 1826 by Sir John Gordon, an
officer of the Coldstream Guards. Thereafter it took part in many
campaigns and underwent numerous changes of title. As always with these
old Indian regiments, the researcher is recommended to consult Donovan
Jackson's INDIA'S ARMY in order to follow the convoluted lineages.
R/4 V/4. NAM. IOL. RGB/RP.

A SUMMARY OF THE WAR DIARY OF THE 26th (K.G.O.) LIGHT CAVALRY, AUGUST
1915 TO OCTOBER 1918

Anon
The Pioneer Press, Allahabad, 1918
Royal blue boards, brown spine and quarters, gold, 8.5 x 5.5, -/92.
no illustrations, one map (folding, bound in at rear), no Index.

Apps: H&A, list of officers attached to the regt.

An unadorned account, based upon the war diary, of the regt's WWI services
in Mesopotamia. R/4 V/3. NAM. PJE.


HISTORY OF 8th KING GEORGE V's OWN LIGHT CAVALRY
[Until 1922, 26th Light Cavalry and 30th Lancers (Gordon's Horse)]

H G Rawlinson CIE
Gale & Polden Ltd, Aldershot, 1948
Light green, gold, regtl crest on front cover, 8.75 x 5.5, ix/142.
Fp, 4 mono phots, 8 maps (printed in text), Index.

Apps: Roll of Honour (WWII only), H&A (WWII only), list of former
officers, copy of Order of the Day, 2.4.1946.

The author was a military historian and professional writer. This
is one of his usual excellent works, and the best available on the regt.
He includes an informative account of the regt's services in Burma
against the Japanese.R/3 V/4. NAM. IOL. RGB.


HISTORY OF THE 1st LANCERS, HYDERABAD CONTINGENT, FROM 1816 TO 1903

Anon
The Times of India Press, Bombay, 1903
Limp covers, green, 8.25 x 5.5, -/29.
no illustrations, no maps, one appendix (roll of officers at July 1903),
no Index.

As with so many of these little books produced by many Indian regts at
the turn of the century, it is hard to know what they were hoping to
achieve. To attempt to span nearly 90 years of active service in the
space of 29 pages is a project doomed to failure from inception. For
the record, 1st Lancers became 20th Deccan Horse in 1903, the title then
changing to 9th Royal Deccan Horse in 1922. R/4 V/1. NAM. VS/RP.


A HISTORY OF THE HYDERABAD CONTINGENT

Major Reginald George Burton
Office of the Superintendent of Government Printing, Calcutta, 1905
Green, gold, regtl crest on front cover, 8.75 x 5.5, -/320/xc.
Fp, one sketch (Mahratta camel gun in action), 9 maps and plans (bound in).

Apps: statements of unit strength, notes on active service, list of British Residents in Hyderabad, list of former COs, notes on Treaties, etc.

A well organised and most useful book. Covers all arms of the Hyderabad Contingent from the earliest days through to 1903. Clear explanation of its evolution and the reorganisation of 1853 when it was absorbed into the HEIC army. Detailed account of its role in the suppression of the Mutiny (pages 143 to 245) with liberal mention of casualties and awards. Troops from the Contingent served in Burma (1886-87) and in Central Africa to suppress the slave trade (1891-92). The last three chapters are summaries of each regiment of the Contingent, with details of uniform and equipment. R/3 V/5. CJP.


THE ROYAL DECCAN HORSE IN THE GREAT WAR

Lieut Col E Tennant
Gale & Polden Ltd, Aldershot, 1939
Green boards, with Morocco spine and quarters, regtl crest on front cover, 10.75 x 7.5, xvii/181.
Fp, no mono phots, 2 coloured plates, 5 maps (folding, bound in), no Index.

Apps: Roll of Honour, H&A, list of former COs, list of former officers.

The narrative deals with the WWI services of the Royal Deccan Horse and 29th Lancers (Deccan Horse) in France and Palestine. Well written, and a sumptuous quality of production, but sadly diminished by the absence of an Index. R/4 V/4. RP.


ROYAL DECCAN HORSE
Account of Operations in Burma, January to May 1945

Anon
Thacker's Press and Directories Ltd, Calcutta, n.d. (c.1946)
Soft card cover, green and yellow, black, regtl crest on front cover, 8.5 x 5.5, ii/43.
5 mono phots, 2 maps (bound in, one folding), no appendixes, no Index.

Although very brief, this is a superb read. Written in the form of a highly detailed war diary, and obviously compiled while memories were still fresh. R/5 V/4. RJW.

HISTORICAL RECORD OF THE SERVICES OF THE (QUEEN'S OWN) CORPS OF GUIDES
1846-77

Anon
J Gray, Military Department Press, Lahore, February 1877
Yellow, black, 12.5 x 8.0, -/42.
no illustrations, no maps, no formal appendixes, no Index.

This is the earliest published account of the famous Corps first raised
in 1846. Typically of the period, the text is based upon formal regtl
records. Untypically, these are interesting, informative,liberally sprinkled
with references to individual officers and men, and lists of casualties
and awards. Some good descriptions of fighting actions on the North West
Frontier. R/4 V/4. NAM. PJE.


HISTORICAL RECORDS OF THE SERVICES OF THE (QUEEN'S OWN) CORPS OF GUIDES
1846-85

Anon
Civil & Military Gazette Press, Lahore, 1885
Yellow, black, 12.5 x 8.0, -/62.
two mono phots, no maps, no formal appendixes, no Index.

Like the 1877 edition (above), this account is based upon regtl records
and quotations from official despatches. Again, it is well interspersed
with details of casualties, awards, and officers' comings and goings. The
story is updated to include details of the Second Afghan War. R/4 V/4.
NAM. PJE/DBP-P.


RECORDS OF THE SERVICES OF THE QUEEN'S OWN CORPS OF GUIDES

Anon
Publisher and printer details not shown, 1888
Red, gold, 12.5 x 8.0, -/63.
no illustrations, no maps, no appendixes, no Index.

This book is substantially the same as the 1885 edition (above). However,
it is one page longer (updating the story to 1887), the binding is quite
different, and the title is slightly different. R/4 V/4. NAM. PJE.


THE STORY OF THE GUIDES

Colonel G J Younghusband
Printed by R Clay & Sons Ltd, for MacMillan & Co Ltd, London, 1908
Maroon, gold, regtl crest on front cover, 9.0 x 5.75, xvi/207.
Fp, 15 mono phots (of indifferent quality), no maps, no appendixes, Index.

This is arguably the most widely distributed regtl history ever produced.
At least five editions were published (see end of entry) and each was
printed in large numbers. Its success owes more to the dash and brilliance
of the actions which it describes than the writing style of the author. He
makes only limited reference to individual officers and men, and the lack

of appendixes is a disadvantage. However, despite Younghusband's ponderous prose, the book is a complete and informative account of an extraordinary fighting force. The inspiration of Sir Henry Lawrence, raised and led by Lieut H B Lumsden (later Sir Harry) in 1846, it fought in both Sikh Wars, heroically in the suppression of the Mutiny, and in almost every campaign on the Afghan frontier. Until WWI it consisted partly of cavalry and partly of infantry. The latter were then transferred to 12th Frontier Force Regiment (see Index). R/1 V/3. HLL/RGB/WEL/RLP/RP.

A 1909 edition appears frequently at auction and in dealers' catalogues. It is slightly longer than the first edition (having xvi/217 pages). Two years later (1911) an expanded 'One Shilling' popular edition was published, to be followed (in 1918) by an even larger version (xvi/245). Finally, in 1921, a 'schools' edition was published, the text having been abridged by J E Parkinson.


THE HISTORY OF THE GUIDES, 1846-1922, Volume I

Anon (compiled by various serving officers)
Gale & Polden Ltd, Aldershot, 1938
Buff, gold, regtl crest on front cover, 9.75 x 7.25, xv/347.
Fp, 18 mono phots, 18 maps (11 bound in, 7 in rear pocket), no Index.

Apps: fourteen various, including list of former COs, list of former officers (1858-1922), lists of attached officers (1858-1914 and 1914-1922), lists of Risaldar-Majors and Subadar-Majors, list of former medical officers, H&A (1914-1921, with details of recipients of the VC and the Indian Order of Merit), notes on regtl organisation.

A full and detailed history of the Corps for the period stated. Originally a Corps of Pathan volunteers recruited from the area of Mardan on the North West Frontier, it served subsequently in almost all the 19th century campaigns in India, and then in Mesopotamia, Persia, Palestine and Syria during WWI. R/3 V/5. IOL. RGB/HLL.


THE HISTORY OF THE GUIDES, 1922-1947, Volume II
10th Cavalry (QVO Guides), 5/12 Frontier Force Regiment (QVO Guides Infantry)

Lieut Gen Sir George MacMunn KCB KCSI DSO
Gale & Polden Ltd, Aldershot, 1950
Buff, gold, regtl crest on front cover, 9.75 x 7.25, xv/208.
Fp, 25 mono phots, 2 coloured plates, 8 maps (bound in), Index.

Apps: list of former COs and Risaldar-Majors (Cavalry) and Subadar-Majors (Infantry), list of former Honorary Colonels, various lists of former officers (both Cavalry and Infantry), H&A (with details of Captain Robert Shebbeare's VC action at Delhi which was not mentioned in Volume I).

This work continues the history of the Corps from 1922 to 1947. Principal operations were Waziristan (1937) and WWII in Persia, Iraq, Syria and North Africa. A detailed and comprehensive narrative, with very useful maps. R/3 V/5. IOL. RGB/WEL.

HISTORY OF THE 1st PUNJAB CAVALRY

Anon
The Civil & Military Gazette Press, Lahore, 1887
Red, gold, 9.0 x 5.5, -/83/viii.
no illustrations, no maps, no Index.

Apps: Roll of Honour, H&A (Indian officers and Other Ranks who received
the Order of British India and the Order of Merit),list of former officers.

This is a short history for the period 1849 to 1883. Covers the composition
of the regt, services during the Mutiny, Frontier actions and the Second
Afghan War. The text is based mainly upon official reports, and mentions
many British and Indian officers. R/5 V/3. IOL. BDM.


HISTORY OF THE THIRD REGIMENT, PUNJAB CAVALRY

Anon
Punjab Printing Co, for W Ball & Co, Lahore, 1887
Black, black on white label, 10.0 x 6.5, -/10.
no illustrations, no maps, no appendixes, no Index.

A short factual history covering the period 1849-1885. Based upon official
reports and regtl orders, but lacking in detail. R/5 V/1. NAM. PJE.


HISTORY OF THE 23rd CAVALRY (FRONTIER FORCE), LATE 3rd REGIMENT
PUNJAB CAVALRY

Anon (compiled by officers of the Regiment)
Publisher's details not shown, n.d. (c.1910)
Dark blue, black on white label, 9.5 x 6.5, -/17.
no illustrations, no maps, no Index.

Apps: list of personnel, list of Inspections (1849-1908), list of Stations.

A short and sketchy history, year by year, from date of raising (1849)
to 1909. Containsvery little information. R/5 V/1. IOL. NAM. RGB/PJE.


SHORT HISTORY OF THE P.A.V.O. CAVALRY (11th FRONTIER FORCE)

Anon
Publisher's details not shown, n.d. (c.1936)
Brown boards with black spine, gold, 7.5 x 5.5, -/21.
no illustrations, no maps, no appendixes, no Index.

This title is even less useful than the c.1910 booklet listed above. It
attempts to cover the entire period 1849-1935 in just 21 pages. It does
not succeed. R/5 V/1. RP.

REGIMENTAL RECORDS, 5th REGIMENT, PUNJAB CAVALRY

Anon
W Ball & Co, Lahore, 1886
Black, no lettering, 9.5 x 6.5, -/69.
no illustrations, no maps, no appendixes, no Index.

Based upon official records. A very short factual history lacking in
detail. R/5 V/1. NAM. IOL. USII. PJE

HISTORY OF THE SECOND PANJÁB CAVALRY
From 1849 to 1886

Anon
Kegan, Paul, Trench & Co, London, 1888
Red boards, leather spine, gold, 12.0 x 10.0, -/71.
16 mono phots, no maps, no Index.

Apps: H&A, list of former officers, stations, list of British officers
wounded in action.

Very little detail, but a good readable account and a good selection of
photographs of British and Indian officers. R/5 V/3. IOL. NAM. PJE.

REGIMENTAL RECORDS FROM 1886 TO 1912, 25th CAVALRY (FRONTIER FORCE)

Anon
Rai Sahib M Gulab Singh, Calcutta, 1912
Black, white, 9.75 x 6.25, -/47.
no illustrations, no maps, no appendixes, no Index.

A compendium of selected extracts from the regt records for the period stated.
Useful only when used in conjunction with other sources. R/5 V/1. VS.

2nd PUNJAB CAVALRY, REGIMENTAL HISTORY

Anon(written by various officers of the Regiment)
An unpublished typescript, compiled c.1920, 13.0 x 8.0, pages not
numbered, listed here because it is one of the very few accounts on record.

The narrative is a 'digest of services' in two sections. Part I covers
1849 to 1900 and is sparse but readable. Part II covers 1900 to 1919,
and is a compendium of official records. A moderately useful source of
reference. R/4 V/3. NAM. PJE.

SAM BROWNE'S CAVALRY (FRONTIER FORCE)

Anon
An unpublished typescript and, as with the above title, included here solely
because the regiment (like Prince Albert Victor's Own) never produced a
formal regtl history. The typescript is in two folders: Part I covers 1849
to 1880, Part II covers 1886 to 1933. Good detail. R/5 V/3. NAM. PJE.

22nd SAM BROWNE'S CAVALRY (FRONTIER FORCE)
Extracts from Official Lists giving the Names of Officers who have Served
in the Regiment from 1849 onwards (through to 1940)

Anon
Publisher's details not stated, n.d.
Brown leather, gold, regtl crest on front cover, 13.0 x 8.5, -/142.
no illustrations, no maps, no appendixes, no Index.

Again, this is a 'one off' book held by the National Army Museum which is
listed here solely because there is so little material available to
the researcher concerning this regiment. The volume consists of entries in
the Indian Army Lists which have been extracted and then pasted into a
scrapbook. R/5 V/2. NAM. PJE.


JOURNAL OF THE LATE GENERAL SIR SAM BROWNE VC GCB KCSI 1840-1898

Autobiography (published posthumously on the initiative of his daughter
following his death in 1901)
William Blackwood & Sons Ltd, Edinburgh and London, 1937
Blue, gold, 9.0 x 6.0, -/80.
Fp, no other illustrations, no maps, no appendixes, no Index.

A terse but very interesting account by Sam Browne of his life and
service in India. Packed with references to the great and famous of
mid-19th century India. He won his VC, and lost his left arm, during the
Mutiny. The sword belt which he designed to overcome the absence of the
limb is now in display in The India Room, at the RMA Sandhurst. His
narrative describes the Second Sikh War, the Annexation of the Punjab,
the Mutiny, and various Frontier skirmishes. The regt which bore his name
ceased to be part of the Order of Battle in 1933 and became a Training
Establishment. R/3 V/3. WMTM.


A BRIEF HISTORICAL SKETCH OF HIS MAJESTY'S 31st DUKE OF CONNAUGHT'S
OWN LANCERS, INDIAN ARMY

Colonel G F Newport-Tinley CB
Bombay Gazette Electrical Printing Works, Bombay, 1910
Grey boards with green quarters, gold, 9.75 x 6.75, iii/57.
no illustrations, no maps, no Index.

Apps: H&A (for the Order of British India and the Order of Merit),
list of formers COs, list of former officers, list of campaigns, notes on
uniforms, notes on class compositions, stations and movements.

The fatal words 'brief' and 'sketch' in the title of a regtl history are
usually a sure sign of inadequacy in the contents. This little book is an
exception to that rule. Although very slim, it is full of useful facts.
The story covers the period from 1817,when the regt was first raised as
the 1st Regiment Bombay Light Cavalry, through to 1910. R/5 V/4. NAM. VS/RGH.

RECORD BOOK OF THE SCINDE IRREGULAR HORSE, Volumes I and II

General John Jacob
Smith Elder & Co, London 1856
Reversed calfskin, brown, gold, regtl crest on front cover, 13.0 x 8.0,
Volume I - 340 pages, Volume II - 284 pages
Reported as having no illustrations or maps.

Volume I covers the period 8.8.1839 to 1.10.1851. Volume II covers the
period 8.10.1851 to 13.6.1855. Not seen.


RECORD BOOK OF THE SCINDE IRREGULAR HORSE, Volumes I and II

Reprinted (Volume I) by S M Soleiman & Sons, at Sukkur, 1902, and
(Volume II) by Victoria Printing Press, Sukkur, 1903, both stated to be
with dark brown boards, light brown leather spine and quarters, iv/355 and
-/283 respectively.
no illustrations in either Volume, but Volume I now having 2 maps and an
Index.

Although these 1902-03 editions have more pages than the equivalent 1856
edition, the contents would appear to be the same. Both are based upon
Gazette extracts and regtl documents. The text is dry and basic, but
contains ample detail of battles and the regt's evolution. R/5 V/3.
NAM. PJE.


A SHORT HISTORY OF THE 35th SCINDE HORSE

Captain E D Giles
Publisher's details not stated, Peshawar, 1909
Stiff card covers, olive green, dark green, regtl crest on front cover,
8.25 x 5.5, -/21/ii.
Fp, no other illustrations, no maps, no appendixes (apart from some brief
notes on medals and trophies),no Index.

This is a short history compiled by the Adjutant of the 35th Scinde
Horse, and was written for the instruction of newly-joined personnel
(those, presumably, who spoke English). Written in terse and bombastic
language. There is a brief and basically unhelpful mention of each of
the campaigns and battles in which the regt took part. First raised in
1839 as the 1st Sind Horse. R/5 V/1. IOL. RGB.
An identical version has been reported, showing all the same details, but
with the publisher being declared as Thacker & Co Ltd of Bombay.


PRINCE OF WALES'S OWN
The Scinde Horse 1839-1922

Colonel E B Maunsell
Butler & Tanner Ltd, London, for the Regiment, 1926
Green, gold, regtl crest on front cover, 10.0 x 7.5, xx/348.
Fp, 49 mono phots, 22 maps, Index.

Apps: H&A, list of former COs, list of former officers (for WWI, with
details of casualties), notes on the sillidar system.

A very readable narrative, and probably the best of the available titles
for this regt for that period. R/4 V/4. NAM. IOL. PJE.


THE SCINDE HORSE
14th Prince of Wales's Own Cavalry, 1922-1947

Lieut Col K R Brooke
Deighton's Embassy Press, Haslemere, for the Scinde Horse Association, 1957
Green, gold, 9.75 x 7.5, xiv/90.
13 mono phots, no maps, no Index.

Apps: list of former officers (WWI only), list of former COs, list
of Risaldar-Majors (1921-47), battle honours.

The author states that this is a 'regimental biography' rather than a
'regimental history'. His meaning is obscure, but the book is in the event
pleasantly readable and helpful. The period covered runs from amalgamation
in 1921 (35th Scinde Horse and 36th Jacob's Horse) through to Partition.
There is brief mention of the regt's time at Quetta in the 1930s, and the
pre-war displays of horsemanship on Meeanee Day. The regt became an
armoured unit in 1938 and then served in Persia, Egypt and Syria in WWII.
R/3 V/4. NAM. PJE/TM.


THE SCINDE HORSEMAN
Special War Number, Autumn 1940 to January 1946

Major F G Foster
Printed in Bombay, privately for the Regiment, 1946
Paper covers, off-white, green, regtl crest on front cover with diagonal
strips of green-red-green, 9.25 x 7.0, vii/110/v.
36 mono phots, one map (bound in), no appendixes, no Index.

This is a combined publication of the regt's usual annual chronicles,
produced to commemorate its return to India in 1946. It includes some
rolls of officers, good 'action' photographs of soldiering against the
Waziri tribesmen in 1940 and later service in Syria. The text was
transposed verbatim by Brooke for his formal history (see entry above).
R/4 V/3. CJP.


REGIMENTAL STANDING ORDERS, 17th CAVALRY

Capt D D Wilson
Hugh Rees Ltd, London, 1909
Dark blue boards, cream spine, gold, regtl crest on front cover,
8.25 x 5.25, -/98.
no illustrations, no maps, no Index.

This is exactly what its title states. It is a compendium of Standing
Orders dealing with the duties of British and Indian officers, Native
NCOs and Sowars, administration duties and organisation of the line of
march, the care of horses and mules, etc. The book has no historical
content, but is of interest in revealing the daily routine work of a
cavalry regiment during that period. R/5 V/2. AMM.


THE STAR AND CRESCENT
Being the Story of the 17th Cavalry from 1858 to 1922

Major F C C Yeats-Brown
Printed by the Pioneer Press, Allahabad, privately for the author, c.1927
Dark blue boards, with blind white pigskin spine, gold, regtl crest on
front cover, 9.75 x 6.5, xii/359.
Fp, 57 mono phots, one map (folding, bound in), no Index.

Apps: Roll of Honour, H&A, list of former officers.

The author was 'the' Yeats-Brown, best known for his LIVES OF A BENGAL
LANCER, but also Editor of THE SPECTATOR and a skilled writer on a range
of subjects. This history is slightly chaotic because many different sources
regarding the various predecessor units have been quoted in parallel.
However, the result is a superb history book. Almost half of the book
is devoted to the appendixes, the most fascinating of which is that
which lists all the British and Indian officers, gives full details of
their service careers, and most of which are accompanied by a portrait
photograph. The book was the author's own personal project, and the
number of copies printed probably did not exceed 100 (each being impressed
with an individual serial). The three copies noted for this bibliography
carry the numbers 6, 42 and 88. A very desirable history. R/5 V/5. NAM.
RJW/RGH


HISTORICAL RECORDS OF THE 2nd MADRAS LANCERS, NOW 27th LIGHT CAVALRY

Colonel J B Edwards
Christian Mission Press, Jubbulpore, 1907
Black, gold, 8.5 x 5.5, -/132.
no illustrations, no maps, no Index.

Apps: list of former officers, regtl establishment (1819), notes on
horses, Dress Regulations (1820 and 1846).

Based on regtl records and Standing Orders. Fairly informative for the
specialist researcher, but lacking in human interest.
R/5 V/2. USII. NAM. PJE.


HISTORY OF THE 16th LIGHT CAVALRY (ARMOURED CORPS)

Lieut Col C L Proudfoot
Publisher's details not shown, thought to have been produced in Calcutta,
c.1976
Blue, white, regtl crest in silver on front cover, 8.5 x 6.0, viii/202.
Fp, 16 mono phots, no maps, no Index.

Apps: Roll of Honour (KIA and WIA, WWII only), H&A (WWII only),
list of officers serving at the end of WWII, plus some of the earlier
appendixes from Colonel Edward's history (see previous entry).

A well-written history, dealing mainly with WWII. R/4 V/4. UWML. IOL. BCC.


HISTORICAL RECORDS OF THE SERVICES OF THE 3rd (QUEEN VICTORIA'S OWN)
REGIMENT OF BOMBAY LIGHT CAVALRY

Major A P Currie and Captain M H Anderson
Publisher's details not stated, produced at Poona, 1911
Green with black spine, gold, 9.5 x 6.5, -/208.
no illustrations, no maps, no Index.

Apps: list of Subadar-Majors and Risaldar-Majors, postings of British and
Indian officers in and out of the regt.

A history book with a chequered history of its own. It is a much expanded
and updated version of a 26-page booklet produced by Major Currie in 1877
(which was printed at The Education Society's Press, Bombay). Presumably
the regt was not happy with this 1911 work, because Captain (soon to be
Major) M H Anderson immediately made another complete revision with the
aid of his brother, Lieut Col E S J Anderson. Their new version was
published two years later, in 1913, with vii/274 pages. Both editions are
based mainly upon regtl orders and records, but give a useful account
of the regt's part in the First and Second Afghan Wars, Sind, the
Mutiny, Persia and Abyssinia campaigns.R/5 V/4. USII. RGB/NKR/OSS.


HISTORICAL RECORDS OF THE POONA HORSE, 1882

Major G C Hogg and Major C M Erskine
Printed at The Education Society's Press, Bombay, n.d. (c.1882)
Black, gold, 13.0 x 8.5, vii/36.
3 mono phots, no maps, no Index.

Apps: list of former COs, list of former officers.

Based upon official records and reports. Very brief indeed, and, like
several other short Indian regtl histories published during that period,
no more than a token effort. R/5 V/1. NAM. RP.


THE HISTORICAL RECORDS OF THE 34th (PRINCE ALBERT VICTOR'S OWN) POONA HORSE

Major G M Molloy
Hugh Rees Ltd, London, 1913
Dark blue boards, light blue spine, gold, 9.0 x 6.0, ix/139.
Fp, 5 mono phots, no Index.

Apps: list of former COs, list of former officers, list of Honorary Colonels.

A readable and fairly informative narrative, although only a general record. R/4 V/3. IOL. NAM. PJE.


## HISTORICAL RECORD OF THE 33rd (QUEEN VICTORIA'S OWN) LIGHT CAVALRY

Anon (compiled by officers of the Regiment)
Printed by The Orphanage Press, Poona/Aurangabad, for the Regiment, 1913
Olive green, gold, 10.25 x 6.25, vii/274.
5 mono phots, 12 maps (bound in), Index.

Apps: list of former COs, list of former officers, notes on campaigns.

Covers the period 1820-1913. A detailed account of the various campaigns in which the regiment served. The maps are better than average in preparation and reference value. R/4 V/4. IOL. RGB.


## WITH THE 33rd Q.V.O. LIGHT CAVALRY IN MESOPOTAMIA

Major M H Anderson
Publisher's details not stated, printed in Quetta, 1915
Cloth and leather, dark green, black, 9.75 x 6.25, -/49.
Fp,sketch, no other illustrations, no maps, no appendixes, no Index.

An unusual little book. It is Major Anderson's diary, edited and published for private circulation by his brother, written during his services against the Turks between November 1914 and April 1915. R/5 V/2. IOL. RGB.


## THE POONA HORSE (17th QUEEN VICTORIA'S OWN CAVALRY) 1817-1931
Volume I  : 1817-1913
Volume II : 1914-1931

First volume by Major M H Anderson, Lieut Col E S J Anderson and Colonel G M Molloy OBE
Second volume by Colonel H C Wylly CB
Both volumes published (contemporaneously) by the Royal United Service Institute, London, 1933
Green boards with red spines, gold, 10.0 x 7.5, xxiv/276 and xviii/235.
Fps, 11 mono phots in Vol I, 12 mono phots in Vol II, 11 maps in Vol I (10 printed in text, one bound in), 15 maps in Vol II (all printed in text), Indexes (both volumes).

Apps: lists of former officers (with full individual details of campaigns in which they took part and their regtl services).

These two beautiful books are in a totally different category to the usual run of Indian Cavalry histories noted elsewhere in this bibliography. Well written, well printed, and well bound, they cover a long period of time in detailed informative prose.      R/4 V/5. NAM. IOL. RP.

HISTORY OF THE 6th KING EDWARD'S OWN CAVALRY

Colonel W R Birdwood
Publication details not known due to damage to the only example seen (c.1909)
Rebound in black, gold, 9.25 x 6.25, -/47/Lxviii.
no illustrations, no maps, no Index.

This book is divided into two parts. The first 47 pages are a well-
written regtl diary containing much useful information. The author has
arranged his narrative under the headings of stations at which the regt
served between 1842 and 1909. Some of the information is purely technical
(unit strengths, class compositions, arms, equipment, uniforms, etc), but
the passages describing actions in which the regt fought, and how it
survived the Mutiny, are very lucid. He lists the Indian personnel who
remained loyal in 1857 and gives details of their services and awards. The
second half is an extract from the Bengal and Indian Army Lists for each
year (1.4.1842 to 1.1.1909) showing all British Officers serving.
The senior Risaldars are listed from January 1858 onwards, and all Indian
officers from January 1877. R/5 V/4. CJP.


REGIMENTAL HISTORY OF THE 18th KING EDWARD VII's OWN CAVALRY

Lieut Col L Lawrence-Smith
The Station Press, Meerut, 1938
White, silver, regtl crest on front cover, 10.0 x 6.5, ii/46.
Fp, 2 mono phots, no maps, no Index.

Apps: list of former COs, movements of the regt.

A short history from 1921 to 1938. Mainly compiled from official records.
R/4 V/2. PJE.


A SHORT HISTORY OF THE 18th (P.W.O.) TIWANA LANCERS, 1858-1908

Anon
Superintendent of Government Printing, Calcutta, for the Regiment. 1908
Red with white diagonal stripe, gold, regtl crest on front cover,
9.5 x 6.5, vi/146.
2 mono phots (mounted and bound in), no maps, no appendixes, no Index.

Only six pages are devoted to the regt's history in conventional terms.
The other 140 pages are simply extracts from Bengal and Indian Army Lists
of items relating to the regt. R/4 V/1. NAM. PJE.


ARMY LISTS - 19th LANCERS (FANE'S HORSE)

Anon
Publication details not shown, n.d. (c.1922)
Blue, gold, 10.0 x 6.5, -/222.
no illustrations, no maps, no appendixes, no Index.

This is simply a compendium of extracts from quarterly Bengal and Indian
Army Lists from January 1860 to January 1922 (less July and October 1920,
which are ommitted). Indian officers are included from October 1876
onwards. R/4 V/1. CJP.


HISTORY OF THE 19th KING GEORGE'S OWN LANCERS
Formerly 18th King George's Own Lancers and 19th Lancers (Fane's Horse),
Amalgamated in 1921

General Sir H Hudson GCB
Gale & Polden Ltd, Aldershot, 1937
Dark blue, three regtl crests on front cover, red and grey embellishment,
gold, 10.0 x 7.0, xiv/370.
Fp, 31 mono phots, 2 coloured plates, 6 maps (folding, bound in),
Bibliography, no Index.

Apps: numerous, including Roll of Honour (KIA, WIA and missing), H&A
(with citations, where applicable, for the entire period 1858-1921), list
of former COs, list of former officers, list of Honorary Colonels.

A superb publication, beautifully prepared and presented. The only
expense spared was the cost of paying someone to compile an Index, an
astonishing failure in a book of this quality. For the rest, it has
everything which one could hope to find in a regtl history. The narrative
covers the period 1858-1921, including the Mutiny, Second Afghan War,
North West Frontier (Tirah campaign), and WWI (France and Palestine).
R/3 V/5. IOL. RP.


19th KING GEORGE'S OWN LANCERS - WAR NEWS
September 1939 - December 1945

Anon
Publication details not shown, n.d. (c.1948)
Black, yellow, regtl crest on front cover, 10.0 x 7.25, ii/88.
78 mono phots, one map (bound in), no Index (but a good 'Contents' page).

Apps: Roll of Honour, H&A, list of officers who served in WWII, notes on
recruiting, notes on VCOs, officers' marriages.

Covers the period 1940-1945 in great detail, with many individuals named
throughout. The Regt served in India, Arakan, India again, and finally
Malaya. The photographs are interesting, but are small and poorly printed.
After Partition, the Regt was re-designated 19th Lancers, Pakistan Army.
R/5 V/4. AMM.


THE SPIRIT OF A REGIMENT
Being the History of the 19th King George V's Own Lancers, 1921-1947

Brigadier J G Pocock
Gale & Polden, Aldershot, 1962
Blue, gold, regtl crest on front cover, 9.5 x 7.5, xvi/114.
Fp, 29 mono phots, 6 maps, Index.

Apps: Roll of Honour, list of former COs, list of former officers, battle honours.

A very good workmanlike history for the period stated. R/4 V/5. NAM. PJE.


15th LANCERS (CURETON'S MULTANIS), 1858-1908

Anon
The Superintendent of Government Printing, Calcutta, 1910
Full Morocco, green, gold, with regtl crest and a list of the main title changes all on the front cover, 10.75 x 7.5, xxviii/172.
no illustrations, no maps, Index.

Apps: H&A, list of former COs, list of former Risaldar-Majors, list of former officers (with their war services), notes on regtl organisation.

The book is essentially a compendium of extracts from official Lists and reports. However, its greatest value lies in the descriptions of the original formation of the regt, and the passages regarding the Multani Pathans of the Derajat and the Baluch tribes of the Sind Sagar Thal. R/5 V/4. NAM. CJP.


KING GEORGE V'S OWN CENTRAL INDIA HORSE
The Story of a Local Corps

Major General W A Watson CB CMG CIE
William Blackwood & Sons Ltd, Edinburgh, 1930
Fawn boards, with red spine and quarters, gold, regtl crest on front cover, 9.0 x 6.0, x/474.
Fp, 4 mono phots, 4 maps (bound in), Index.

Apps: H&A (WWI only, all ranks), list of former officers (WWI only).

An excellent quality of production and very readable narrative. Many individuals mentioned in the text. Covers the Mutiny, Second Afghan War, Tirah campaign, and WWI service in France and Palestine. R/4 V/5. NAM. IOL. RP.


KING GEORGE V'S OWN CENTRAL INDIA HORSE
The Story (Continued) of a Local Corps, Being Volume II of a Regimental History

Brigadier A A Filose
William Blackwood & Sons Ltd, Edinburgh, 1950
Red, gold, 10.0 x 7.5, x/435.
Fp, 9 mono phots, 2 coloured plates, 13 maps (one bound in, 12 printed in text), Index.

Apps: H&A (WWII only, all ranks).

Although the format and dimensions of this book are slightly different to
General Watson's work (see previous entry), it is effectively the second
Volume of a two-part series (as the sub-title claims). The first half of
the book deals with the regt's activities during the inter-war years, the
second half then covering its services in WWII (Eritrea, Western Desert
and Italy). A well-written narrative, full of interesting detail,
with many individuals of all ranks freely mentioned. To quote a former
officer of the Regiment: 'It is a model for the story of an Indian
cavalry regiment, having been written by a man whose prose was excellent
and who had the advantage of the publication being paid for by a
benevolent Maharaja of Bahawalpur, an Honorary Officer of the Central
India Horse'. R/4 V/5. NAM. RP.
As a footnote, it should be mentioned that the Nawabs of Bahawalpur were
friends and allies of the British from the 1840s onwards, supplied troops
and treasure to most of Great Britain's campaigns and wars through to 1947,
and still maintain friendly contacts with this country. Bahawalpur State
was absorbed into Pakistan when that country attained Independence.


THE CENTRAL INDIA HORSE - NEWSLETTERS 1 TO 24, JULY 1940 TO FEBRUARY 1946

Lieut Col R W Peters
Published by the Regiment, for private circulation, printed by C Murphy
at Thacker's Press, Bombay, n.d. (c.1947)
Seen in blue cloth, gold, with regtl crest on front cover, and seen
also in full green Morocco, 9.25 x 8.25, -/231.
no illustrations, 7 maps (bound in), no Index.

Apps: numerous, all to be found at the end of each Newsletter instead of
at the rear of the binding, the most useful being H&A and lists of officers.

As the title suggests, this is a compendium of the regt's customary
quarterly Newsletters, reproduced and bound together as a commemorative
volume at the end of the war. A detailed diary of moves, battles, honours
and awards, casualties, daily events, etc. It is clear that Brigadier Filose
drew heavily upon this source for his formal history (see previous entry),
but much of the detail which lack of space obliged him to ignore is to
be found here. For example, most of the citations for gallantry awards
(British and Indian) are quoted in full in the Newsletters. A very
useful publication. R/4 V/5. CJP.


A SHORT HISTORY OF THE 75th REGIMENT, INDIAN CAVALRY

Lieut Col H L Mostyn-Owen
HQ, Luckdist Press, Lucknow, n.d. (c.1946)
one map, viii/87, with appendixes.

This was a short-lived war-time regt. Not seen.

HISTORICAL RECORD OF THE FOURTH 'PRINCE OF WALES'S OWN' REGIMENT, MADRAS
LIGHT CAVALRY

Lieut Col W J Wilson
Printed by C Foster & Co, Madras, for the Regiment, 1877
Soft card covers, rather crudely sewn, blue, black, 9.5 x 6.0, -/96.
no illustrations, no maps, no Index.

Apps: analysis of casualties by type of casualty, rank and regiment, for
the battle of Bangalore (6.3.1791), idem Assaye (23.9.1803), idem
Mahidore (21.12.1817), notes on the composition of 4th Regt of Cavalry at
March 1811 and October 1825, tables detailing entitlements to gratuity,
batta, pensions, etc.

A competent history compiled from records in the offices of the Government
and the Adjutant General, supplemented with regtl records. Much useful
information on the internal organistion of the regt from the earliest
years. Some superficial coverage of the early campaigns (Third and
Fourth Mysore War, Second and Third Mahratta Wars), but comprehensive
coverage of the Mutiny period. The regt was one of several senior
Indian Army cavalry regiments disbanded in 1877. This is the only known
record of their services. R/5 V/5. IOL. NAM. RGB/CJP.

## APPENDIX II

### Designation of Indian Cavalry regiments
### following the Re-organisations of 1922

Skinner's Horse (1st Duke of York's Own Cavalry)

2nd Royal Lancers (Gardner's Horse)

3rd Cavalry

Hodson's Horse (4th Duke of Cambridge's Own Lancers)

Probyn's Horse (King Edward VII's Own Lancers)

6th Duke of Connaught's Own Lancers (Watson's Horse)

7th Light Cavalry

8th King George's Own Light Cavalry

The Royal Deccan Horse (9th Horse)

The Guides Cavalry (10th Queen Victoria's Own Frontier Force)

Prince Albert Victor's Own (11th Frontier Force)

Sam Browne's Cavalry (12th Frontier Force)

13th Duke of Connaught's Own Lancers

The Scinde Horse (14th Prince of Wales's Own Cavalry)

15th Lancers

16th Light Cavalry

The Poona Horse (17th Queen Victoria's Own Cavalry)

18th King Edward VII's Own Cavalry

19th King George V's Own Lancers

20th Lancers

The Central India Horse (21st King George V's Own Cavalry)

# INDIA - INFANTRY

HISTORY OF THE 2nd MADRAS INFANTRY
Volume I: 1759-1902    Volume II: 1902-1908

Lieut Col R M Rainey-Robinson (both Volumes)
Thacker Spink & Co, Calcutta, Vol I: 1904  Vol II: 1909
Dark green and gold (Vol I), olive paper and black (Vol II)
no illustrations, no maps, no Index.

These two very slim volumes, consisting of 63 and 14 pages respectively,
are based upon extracts from official reports and regtl records. The
information provided is very spare and of a general nature. R/4 V/1. PJE.


A BRIEF HISTORY OF THE 3rd BATTALION, 1st PUNJAB REGIMENT
Formerly 76th Punjabis, 16th Madras Native Infantry, 2nd Bn 5th Madras
Native Infantry, 16th Madras Bn, 16th Carnatic Bn or Lane's Battalion.

Anon
Gale & Polden Ltd, Aldershot, 1927
Green, gold, blind spine, regtl crest on front cover, 7.5 x 5.0, v/56.
no illustrations, no maps, no Index.

Apps: Roll of Honour (officers only, KIA and WIA), H&A, list of former COs.

Published to commemorate their 150th anniversary. There is a short summary
of their services in the 19th century, and then the WWI operations in which
the regt gained seven battle honours (mainly Mesopotamia). Served also
in the Third Afghan War and the Waziristan troubles. R/4 V/4. NAM. RJW.


HISTORY OF THE 1st BATTALION, 1st PUNJAB REGIMENT

C W Sanders
The Civil & Military Gazette Press, Lahore, 1937
Dark green, gold, 6.5 x 5.0, ii/45.
Fp, no other illustrations, no maps, no appendixes, no Index.

A very brief history based upon official records. A version having 61 pages
has been noted, but not seen. R/4 V/1. NAM. PJE.


AN OUTLINE HISTORY OF THE FIRST PUNJAB REGIMENT

Anon
Gouldsbury Press, Jhelum, n.d. (c.1945)
Khaki, black, 9.5 x 6.0, i/80.
Fp (picture of regtl badges), no other illustrations, no maps, no Index.

Apps: H&A (WWII only), changes of unit titles.

As the title states, this is an 'outline' history. The narrative is
readable, but of a general nature. The book's main value is probably to
be found in the appendixes. R/4 V/2. NAM. PJE.

THE FIRST PUNJABIS
History of the First Punjab Regiment, 1759-1956

Major Mohammed Ibrahim Qureshi
Gale & Polden Ltd, Aldershot, 1958
Green, gold, regtl crest on front cover with red embellishment,
9.5 x 6.25, xix/484.
Fp, 48 mono phots, 50 maps (43 printed in the text, 5 bound in, 2 printed
on the end-papers), Index.

Apps: H&A (WWII only, all ranks), list of former COs, list of former
Honorary Colonels, notes on past and present unit titles.

Marking the 200th anniversary of the founding of the regt, publication of
this handsome book was the first serious attempt to tell its story.
Major Qureshi is an excellent historian and this book is a tour de force.
His narrative is interesting and informative, and a great deal of care has
been taken with regard to presentation, indexing and the maps. Gale &
Polden's staff responded with an excellent quality of printing and
binding. R/3 V/5. NAM. IOL. RP.


EXTRACT FROM THE REGIMENTAL RECORDS OF THE 74th PUNJABIS
Regimental History, 4/2nd Punjab Regiment (on outer cover only)

Anon
Thacker & Co, Bombay, n.d. (c.1922)
Dark green, gold, regtl crest on front cover, 7.25 x 5.0, -/45.
no illustrations, no maps, no appendixes, no Index.

A very brief account based upon regtl records. It covers the period 1776
to 1922, and is useful only as a source for important dates. R/4 V/2. PJE.


HISTORY OF THE 1st BATTALION, 2nd PUNJAB REGIMENT
Late 67th Punjabis, and originally 7th Madras Infantry, 1761-1922

Colonel H Ogle and Lieut Col H W Johnston
W Straker Ltd, London, n.d. (c.1923)
Green boards with dark green spine, blind, 10.5 x 8.5, ii/86.
no illustrations, 3 maps, no Index.

Apps: H&A, list of former COs, list of former officers, battle honours,
notes on badges and insignia.

This is a hybrid between the 'old fashioned' type of Indian Army regtl
history and the newer and more informative style which replaced it. The
text is based upon official reports and regtl records, but the authors
have expanded certain sections with their own narrative. Although brief,
the result is informative and readable. R/4 V/3. NAM. PJE.

EXTRACTS FROM THE REGIMENTAL HISTORY OF 5th BN, 2nd PUNJAB REGIMENT

Anon
G Narayam & Co, Secunderabad, n.d. (c.1923)
Grey paper covers, black, 8.5 x 5.5, -/9.
no illustrations, no maps, no Index.

Apps: notes on casualties (WWI), H&A (WWI), notes on recruiting areas.

Very basic and brief. R/5 V/1. NAM. PJE.


REGIMENTAL HISTORY OF THE 3rd BATTALION, 2nd PUNJAB REGIMENT

Colonel H C Wylly CB
Gale & Polden Ltd, Aldershot, 1927
Green, gold, 9.0 x 7.25, v/69.
Fp, 4 mono phots, no maps, no appendixes, Index.

This is the only published history for 3rd Bn. Although based mainly
upon official report and records, it does include numerous references to
officers and other ranks, with detils of their awards. The period
covered is 1746 to 1923 (operations against Hyder and the French, the
surrender of Cuddalore, the Second Mahratta War, First and Third Burma
Wars, Frontier operations, and WWI service in Egypt and Palestine). The
author was a much-respected military historian, and it is surprising that
he did not include any maps or appendixes in this work. R/4 V/4.
NAM. IOL. DM/RP.


THE GOLDEN GALLEY
The Story of the 2nd Punjab Regiment, 1761-1947

Lieut Col Sir Geoffrey Betham KBE CIE MC and Major H V R Geary MC
Printed by Charles Batey, at the Oxford University Press, for the
2nd Punjab Regt Officers' Association, 1956
Green, gold, regtl crest on front cover, 8.25 x 5.25, ix/330.
Fp, 22 mono phots, 9 maps (bound in), no appendixes, Index.

This is a well-illustrated account of all of the battalions of 2nd Punjab
Regt, covering the period 1761 to 1947, with much informative detail. More
than half of the narrative is devoted to WWII operations. The pre-war
coverage is fairly cursory and relates mainly to stations, movements and
Frontier skirmishes. There is good detail regarding the Regimental Centre,
recruiting policy, class/race compositions, etc. The lack of appendixes is
to be regretted in an otherwise impressive work. R/2 V/4. SB/DBP-P.
There is a second edition of this book, printed in Delhi in 1975.
This lacks the regtl crest on the front cover, has 19 monochrome
photographs (versus 22 in the first edition), and the general production
quality is mediocre. However, the second edition contains three coloured
plates not found in the first edition. SB.

## HISTORICAL RECORDS OF THE XIII MADRAS INFANTRY

Lieut R P Jackson
W Thacker & Co, London and Calcutta, 1898
Red, gold, motif of flags on front cover, 10.5 x 6.5, xv/319.
9 coloured plates (uniforms and badges), no maps, Bibliography, no Index.

Apps: list of former COs, list of former officers, stations, recruitment
policy, notes on dress and uniform.

A reasonably full history, readable and informative. R/4 V/3. NAM. PJE.
Another edition, of uncertain date, has been noted with Frontispiece, eight
additional coloured plates, nine maps, and having cream-coloured covers.
Not seen.

## HISTORY OF THE 83rd WALLAJABAD LIGHT INFANTRY

Lieut Col J C W Erck
Printed at The Central Jail, Cannanore, 1910
Black, gold, 8.0 x 5.5, i/75.
no illustrations, no maps, no Index.

Apps: incomplete list of former officers, list of stations.

Compiled from regtl records, and covers the period 1794-1910. A brief
history providing few details. Deals with the campaigns against Tippoo
Sultan 1799, Mahratta Wars of 1817-18 and 1844-45. In 1922, this unit
became 4th Bn 3rd Madras Regt, but was then disbanded. R/3 V/2. NAM. PJE.

## MADRAS INFANTRY 1748-1943

Lieut Col E G Phythian-Adams OBE
The Superintendent at the Government Press, Madras, 1943
Stiff card, rifle green, white, embellished diagonally with regtl colours
on front cover (red and white), 9.5 x 6.0, x/136.
Fp, one mono phot (Assaye Day Parade, 23.9.1942), no maps, no appendixes,
no Index.

A very detailed and very readable narrative. Although the book has no
appendixes, there is liberal mention of personnel (British and Indian) in
the text, with notes on battle honours. The descriptions of small-scale
actions are particularly good. R/3 V/4. SDC.

## NOW OR NEVER
The Story of the 4th Bn The Madras Regiment in the Burma Campaign

Major G D Garforth-Bles and Capt S D Clarke
Printed by E G Aylmer at Thacker's Press and Directories Ltd, Calcutta,
October 1945
Rifle green. gold, regtl crest on front cover, 10.0 x 7.5, vii/45.
Fp, 11 mono phots, 3 coloured plates, 2 maps (printed in text), no Index.

Apps: Roll of Honour, list of all British and Indian officers who served.

A very readable narrative account of the unit's services between October 1943 (when it joined 20th Indian Division in the Kabaw Valley) and June 1945 (when it finally entered Rangoon). During those two years of hard fighting, the battalion took part in operations at Imphal, the capture of Ava Bridge, Mount Poppa, and the final destruction of Japanese land forces in Burma. R/5 V/4. SDC.


SHORT HISTORY OF THE MADRAS REGIMENT

Anon
Printed by 'M.P.H.', Madras, n.d. (c.1951)
Dark green, gold, regtl crest on front cover, 9.0 x 6.0, -/30.
no illustrations, no maps, no Index.

Apps: H&A (WWII only), list of COs (WWII).

A very, very short history dealing with the entire period 1758 to disbandment in the 1920s. The author then provides condensed histories for each battalion after the regt was re-raised for WWII. R/5. V/1. PJE.


THE MADRAS REGIMENT, 1758-1958

Lieut Col E G Phythian-Adams OBE
Printed by C D Dhody & Sons of Wellington, for the Defence Services Staff College Press, 1958
Green, gold, 9.0 x 6.0, viii/338.
Fp, 8 mono plates, 5 coloured plates, 7 maps (bound in, one folding), Bibliography, Index.

Apps: H&A, precis of unit services.

A very readable and detailed history. The best available source for this regt, especially when read in conjunction with the same author's THE MADRAS SOLDIER 1746-1946, (xii/215), published in Madras in 1948 (see page 77). R/3 V/5. NAM. PJE/RP.


HISTORICAL RECORD OF THE SECOND OR PRINCE OF WALES'S OWN GRENADIER REGIMENT, BOMBAY NATIVE INFANTRY

Colonel Stanley Edwardes
The Education Society's Press, Bombay, 1878
Royal blue in full Morocco, gold, regtl crest and the words 'Military Records Bombay Native Infantry' embellished on front cover, 13.5 x 11.0, ii/122.
Fp, (print photograph of the Koreygaum Monument), 28 mono phots (print photographs of British and Indian officers, and four group pictures, all captioned with names and ranks), no maps, no Index.

Apps: list of former officers, list of officers of British regts and the Staff Corps who have served with the regt.

The text is based upon official reports and regtl records, and therefore lacks human interest. The value of this book is to be found in the appendixes and the captioned photographs. The use of original prints would suggest that it was produced in very limited numbers, i.e. sufficient only for 'presentation' copies to be given to serving officers and friends of the regiment. The copy seen was given to Field Marshal Lord Napier (then at the School of Oriental and African Studies, University of London). R/5 V/4. NAM. PJE.


HISTORICAL RECORD OF THE SERVICES OF THE FIRST REGIMENT, BOMBAY INFANTRY GRENADIERS.

Colonel H S Anderson
First Grenadiers Regimental Press, Poona, 1885
Red, gold, 9.5 x 8.0, i/69.
no illustrations, no maps, no Index.

Apps: list of former COs, list of former officers (post-1863), list of Medical Officers, separate list of officers (pre-1863).

Text based upon official reports and regtl records. It provides only the barest details.  R/5 V/2. NAM. IOL. PJE.


OUTLINE HISTORICAL RECORD OF THE PRINCE OF WALES'S OWN GRENADIER REGIMENT OF BOMBAY INFANTRY

Anon
The Education Society's Press, Bombay, 1887
Pink paper, black, 8.5 x 5.5, -/9.
no illustrations, no maps, no Index.

Apps: general state and composition of the regt, list of campaigns, battles and seiges.

Only 9 pages in length, this is obviously very incomplete and superficial. Probably written for newly joined British subalterns and English-speaking Indian Other Ranks. R/5 V/1. NAM. PJE.


HISTORICAL RECORDS OF THE 8th REGIMENT, BOMBAY INFANTRY

Capt Sandwith
The Education Society's Steam Press, Bombay, 1894
Dark maroon, gold, -/85/iii/31.
2 large plates consisting of sketches of soldiers (folding, bound in), no maps, no Index.

Apps: three pages (iii) of stations and movements, 31 pages then contain extracts from Regtl Standing Orders for 1896 and music for the regtl march.

Text covers the period 1768-1894. Not very detailed, and lacks human
interest. However, there is a large folding page showing the genealogy
of the regt, compiled by Capt J C Swann in 1891 and bound in at the rear,
which is extremely useful. The unit later became the 108th Infantry and
then the 4/4th Bombay Grenadiers. R/4 V/2. NAM. RJW.


REGIMENTAL HISTORY OF THE 1st BN 4th BOMBAY GRENADIERS

Major A Thompson
Shri Ramtatya Prakash Printing, Belgaum, n.d.
Green, black, -/21.
no illustrations, no maps,  no appendixes, no Index.

A very condensed account of no more than general interest. Probably
compiled for newly-joined junior officer. R/5 V/1. NAM. PJE.
Another version, printed in Roman Urdu, has been noted. This consists of
22 pages and is bound in blue cloth, presumably for the instruction of
Indian recruits.


HISTORICAL RECORD OF THE SERVICES OF THE 2nd PRINCE OF WALES'S OWN
BOMBAY NATIVE INFANTRY

Anon
The British India Press, Bombay, 1909
Dark green, gold, 10.5 x 8.5, -/124.
no illustrations, no maps, no Index.

Apps: list of former officers, list of former Medical Officers.

This is another 'hybrid' history, composed partly of extracts from
official records and partly personal anecdotes and private letters.
A better-than-average effort for that period. R/4 V/3. NAM. PJE.


5th BATTALION 4th BOMBAY GRENADIERS (CXII INFANTRY)
Historical Record 1798-1923

Anon
Publisher's details not stated, n.d. (c.1924), probably never published.
Seen in a black folder, 13.0 x 9.0, -/163 pages (not numbered)
Fp, 13 mono phots, 8 maps, no appendixes, no Index.

This is a typescript narrative, of which no more than two or three copies
were probably ever produced. Presumably the author failed to find a
publisher. A useful detailed account of the part played by the battalion
in Mesopotamia and elsewhere between 1915 and 1918. R/5 V/4. USII. OSS.

THE 101st GRENADIERS
Historical Record of the Regiment, 1778-1923

Colonel H A Anderson, revised in 1927 by Captain A Frankland
Gale & Polden Ltd, Aldershot, 1928
Dark blue, gold, 10.0 x 7.5, vi/138.
Fp, 7 mono phots, 2 coloured plates (uniforms), 9 maps, Index.

Apps: list of former COs, list of former officers, idem Medical Officers,
idem other units at times attached to the Regt, notes on the Siege of
Mangalore, notes on the return from Maiwand.

This is essentially an updated version of the history written by Anderson
and first published in 1885 (see page 114). Again, it is based mainly
upon extracts from official reports, but does include some personal
accounts. It is stated to be very accurate, but superficial. R/4 V/3. PJE.


2nd BATTALION, 4th BOMBAY GRENADIERS (KING EDWARD'S OWN)
Formerly the 102nd King Edward's Own Grenadiers: Historical Record of
the Regiment, 1796-1933

Major J T Gorman
Lawrence Brothers Ltd, Weston Super Mare, Somerset, 1933
Dark blue, gold, 2nd Bn badge on front cover, 10.0 x 7.5, vi/173.
Fp, 11 mono phots, 10 maps (bound in), Bibliography, no Index.

Apps: list of former officers, notes on the regtl Colours, idem regtl
music, idem other units at times attached to the Bn.

This book was first published in 1877 (1st edition not seen). The 1933
version is stated to be basically the same as that 1st edition, but having
additional information to cover WWI. Based largely upon official reports,
but with officers' letters and comments woven into the text (a technique
which certainly adds to the interest). A good quality production,
detailed and informative. R/4 V/4. NAM. IOL. PJE.


5th BATTALION, 4th BOMBAY GRENADIERS (CXII INFANTRY) HISTORICAL RECORDS
1798-1923

Anon
Probably never published, seen only in typescript, n.d. (c.1940)
Seen in pink and white patterned cloth, pages not numbered
Fp, 12 print photographs, one line drawing, 8 maps, no Index.

Apps: H&A, list of former COs, list of former officers, extracts from
Bombay Army Lists (1799 and 1800), stations and movements, list of
Adjutants, Quartermasters and Subedar-Majors.

Based upon regtl records, but quite complete and informative. Good
descriptions of battles. This item has a strong resemblance to the last
entry on the previous page. It seems to be an updated version (c.1940)
with additional appendixes. R/5 V/4. NAM. PJE.

THE GRENADIERS
A Regimental History

Brigadier Rajendra Singh
Army Educational Stores, New Delhi, 1962
Green, black, grenade motif on front cover, 10.0 x 7.5, xvi/328.
Fp, 16 mono phots, one coloured plate, 15 maps, Index.

Apps: Roll of Honour, H&A, list of former COs, notes on the Colours,
notes on dress, uniforms and regtl music.

This is the first history of the regt since Independence. There are
reported to be some inaccuracies in the narrative, but it was the best
attempt so far at describing the story of all of the Grenadier battalions
in detailed readable form. R/3 V/4. NAM. PJE/RP.


THE GRENADIERS: A TRADITION OF VALOUR
A Historical Record of the Grenadiers

Colonel R D Palsokar MC
Printed in Poona, for The Grenadiers Regimental Association, Jabalpur,
n.d. (c.1980)
Black, gold, grenade motif on front cover, xxiv/538.
Fp, 120 mono phots, 5 coloured plates, 49 maps (printed in text),
Bibliography, Index.

Apps: H&A, list of former COs, idem Subedar-Majors.

The author is one of India's best known military historians, and he has
compiled here a comprehensive history covering all the Grenadier bns
between 1779 and 1880. The photographs have not reproduced well, but
there are plenty of them and the maps are helpful. The Bombay Grenadiers
were renamed The Indian Grenadiers in 1945 and then, in 1947, The Grenadiers.
Their post-Independence services are described in detail. R/1 V/4. NAM. MCJ.


HISTORICAL RECORD OF THE 3rd BOMBAY LIGHT INFANTRY

Anon
Printed by the Caxton Steam Press, Bombay, for the Adjutant General's
Office, Poona, 1892
Blue, gold, regtl crest on front cover, iv/109.
no illustrations, no maps, no appendixes, no Index.

Covers the period 1768-1891. Based upon regtl orders and records. Very
dry, sparse and superficial. There is brief mention of the operations and
battles in which the unit was engaged, but most of the text is devoted
to stations, movements, and the postings of officers. R/5 V/2. NAM. PJE.

HISTORICAL RECORD OF THE 16th REGIMENT BOMBAY INFANTRY

Anon
Publication details not shown, n.d. (c.1911?)
Red, gold, embellishments on front cover, 10.0 x 6.5, -/24.
Fp, no other illustrations, one map (folding, bound in), no appendixes,
no Index.

Covers the period 1800-1910. The usual melange of extracts from 'official
sources'. Brief, sparse and not very helpful. Only the references to
the Second Afghan War might be useful to a researcher. R/5 V/1. NAM. PJE.


CHRONOLOGY OF THE 114th MAHRATTAS, Parts I and II

Anon
Printed by The Times of India Press, Bombay, published privately, 1922
Royal blue, gold, 7.0 x 5.25, -/55.
no illustrations, no maps, no Index.

Apps: H&A (all ranks), list of officers, lists of former COs(1800-1922).

Part I covers the period 1800-1914 in diary form (14th Bombay Native
Infantry from 1800 to 1903, and then 114th Maharattas post-1903).Makes brief
reference to the Pindari Wars, Scinde (1843), the Mutiny, and Abyssinia
(1867-68). Part II covers the period 1914-1922, including WWI on the
Frontier (Tochi 1914-15), Mesopotamia (1915-18), and Iraq (1920). Stations
and movements are described in great detail. R/4 V/3. AMM.


HISTORICAL RECORD OF THE 4-5th MAHARATTA LIGHT INFANTRY

Capt A R Solly
The Civil & Military Gazette Press, Lahore, 1924
Light green boards with dark green spine, black, 9.0 x 6.0, -/67.
no illustrations, no maps, no Index.

Apps: H&A, list of former COs, list of officers (1914-21), Mutiny orders
and correspondence, list of former Adjutants, stations and movements.

Covers sparsely and inadequately the period 1801-1924. Based, as usual, upon
official orders and records. The sections dealing with the Second Afghan
War and the 1901 operations in East Africa are possibly useful.
R/4 V/2. NAM. IOL. USII. PJE.


A FAMOUS INDIAN REGIMENT, THE KALI PANCHWIN
2/5th (Formerly the 105th) Mahratta Light Infantry, 1768-1923

Colonel Sir Reginald Hennell CVO DSO OBE
John Murray, London, 1927
Green, gold, regtl crest on front cover, 8.75 x 5.5, xi/292.
Fp, 11 mono phots, 2 maps (printed in text), Index.

Apps: H&A (1799-1919), list of former COs, list of former officers, notes on uniforms, idem regtl ceremonies, idem the Colours, etc.

This excellent history was written by Hennell, and then edited and prepared for publication by his sister-in-law, Mrs Mary Hennell. The narrative is interesting and clear, with plenty of good descriptions of campaigning in China (1860-61), Burma (1886-88), Aden (1901), and in Mesopotamia and Palestine (1916-18). The appendixes are very good. 'Kali Panchwin' means 'The Black Fifth'. R/3 V/4. NAM. IOL. RP.
A facsimile reprint was produced in India, by B.R. Publications, in 1985.


HISTORICAL RECORD, 110th MAH(A)RATTA LIGHT INFANTRY (NOW 3rd BATTALION 5th MAHRATTA LIGHT INFANTRY) DURING THE GREAT WAR, 1914 TO 1918

Anon ('Three officers who wish to remain anonymous')
Government of India Press, Calcutta, 1927
Green, gold, regtl crest on front cover, 10.0 x 7.25, ix/109.
one mono photo (captioned group of officers, 1914), 12 maps (bound in), no Index.

Apps: Roll of Honour (British officers and VCOs only), H&A, tables relating to the siege of Kut.

The regt was destroyed at Kut, but was later reformed and saw action with the Egyptian Expeditionary Force in Palestine. The 3/5th MLI now forms part of the Indian Army's Order of Battle under its new title, 2nd Parachute Regt, but still retains many of the traditions of the old unit. R/4 V/4. NAM. CSM.


HISTORY OF THE 1st BATTALION 5th MAHRATTA LIGHT INFANTRY (JANGI PALTAN)

Anon
Government of India Press, Calcutta, 1930
Dark green, gold, 10.0 x 8.0, viii/88.
no illustrations, 14 maps (2 printed in text, 12 folding and bound in), no Index.

Apps: list of former officers, list of stations.

Covers the period 1768 to 1929. A short readable history which concentrates upon those engagements for which the regt was awarded battle honours: Mysore (1789), Scinde (1799), Arabia (1821), Mooltan, Gujerat and Punjab (1848-49), Abyssinia (1867-68), Mesopotamia (1915-16). It is stated that the number of copies printed was one hundred. R/5 V/3. NAM. IOL. PJE.


EXTRACTS FROM THE DIGEST OF SERVICES OF THE 10th BOMBAY LIGHT INFANTRY
Compiled at Poona, October 1892

Lieut Col L F Heath and Lieut H C B Dann
Printed by G Claridge & Co Ltd, Bombay, with imprint '1938'
Dark green, gold, regtl crest on front cover, 9.75 x 6.5, -/51.
no illustrations, no maps, no appendixes, no Index.

The contents are a simple diary of events between 1797 and 1887. Despite the date mentioned in the sub-title, this booklet seems not have been published until 1938. Whatever the explanation for the long delay, the final result is virtually worthless as a source of reference.
R/5 V/1. RMAS. RP.


A BRIEF HISTORY OF THE MAHRATTA LIGHT INFANTRY

Major J S Barr
Printed by G Claridge & Co, Bombay, 1945
Green, gold, regtl crest on front cover, 9.75 x 7.25, vi/65.
Fp, no other illustrations, no maps, no appendixes, no Index.

As the title states, this is indeed a brief history. The first century and a half of the regt's life are dealt with in the opening eleven pages. The remainder of the narrative then deals sketchily with the WWII services of each of the MLI battalions in North Africa, Italy, Assam and Burma. Chapter VIII gives a numerical summary of honours and awards gained by MLI officers and men, but very few are mentioned by name in the text.
R/4 V/2. LDR.


VALOUR ENSHRINED
A History of the Maratha Light Infantry, 1768-1947

Lieut Col M G Abhyankar
Orient Longman, New Delhi, 1971
Green, white, 9.5 x 6.5, xx/546.
Fp, 35 mono phots, 13 coloured plates, 70 maps (printed in text), no Index.

Apps: H&A, list of former COs, idem Subedar-Majors, notes on the origins of the regt, notes on archival sources.

This is yet another instance of a fine old Indian Army regiment receiving scant attention from British historians. Colonel Abhyankar has done the job for them, and done it well. This is a book which provides uniformly good coverage for all periods and battalions between 1768 and 1947. The maps are helpful and the photographs are well reproduced. Unfortunately, the general quality of production and binding is disappointing, and the lack of an Index difficult to understand in such a well-researched work.
R/3 V/4. NAM. MCJ/RP.


HISTORICAL RECORDS OF THE 23rd REGIMENT (2nd Bn RIFLE REGIMENT) BOMBAY INFANTRY, FORMERLY 1st Bn/12th NATIVE INFANTRY

Capt W A M Wilson
Printed at The Education Society's Steam Press, Bombay, 1894
Green, gold, regtl crest on front cover, 9.0 x 6.0, -/84.
no illustrations, no maps, no Index.

Apps: list of former COs, list of former officers, idem Adjutants, idem Medical Officers, list of stations and movements, etc (ten appendixes in total).

Although brief, this is a useful and well arranged book. R/5 V/4. RGH.

HISTORY OF THE 13th RAJPUTS (THE SHEKHAWATI REGIMENT),
FROM THE TIME OF ITS ORGANISATION AS PART OF THE SHEKHAWATI BRIGADE
IN A.D. 1835 TO A.D. 1907

Lieut Col W Prior
Traill & Co, Calcutta, 1908
Full calfskin, brown, gold, 10.0 x 6.5, ii/84.
7 mono phots, one sketch, one map (printed in text), no Index.

Apps: list of former officers, details of class composition and recruiting
districts, list of Native Officers for various years post-1848, notes on
the life of Colonel Harry Foster CB.

A brief but readable history for the period stated. With a description
of the problems in Rajputana which prompted the original raising of the
regt. A good account of the Battle of Aliwal (1846). R/4. V/4. NAM.PJE.


HISTORICAL RECORDS, 122nd RAJPUTANA INFANTRY

Anon
The British India Press, Bombay, 1908
Green, gold, regtl crest on front cover, 9.0 x 5.5, -/110.
Fp, 6 mono phots, 9 sketches, no maps, no Index.

Apps: list of former COs, list of former officers, stations and movements,
list of Native Officers, notes on dress and uniforms, extracts from Army
Lists for 1805-08, 1857, 1862 and 1900.

A brief history containing only superficial accounts of campaigns and
battles. Based largely upon regtl orders and records. Useful only for
its appendixes. R/4 V/2. RMAS. NAM. RP/PJE.


BRIEF HISTORY OF THE 125th NAPIER'S RIFLES

Lieut H J Huxford
Publication details not shown, 1912
Stiff card, olive green boards with red cloth spine, black, 6.5 x 5.25, i/28.
no illustrations, no maps, no Index.

Apps: stations and movements, notable events in the regt's history.

'Brief' is certainly an appropriate prefix. An extract of official records
covering nearly two hundred years (1817-1921) in 28 pages. Fundamentally
useless as a source of reference. R/5 V/1. NAM. PJE/RP.


NAPIER'S RIFLES
The History of the 5th Battalion 6th Rajputana Rifles

H G Rawlinson
Printed at The Weslyan Mission Press, Mysore, for the Oxford University
Press, 1929
Fp, 7 mono phots, 3 sketches, 13 maps (8 printed in text, 5 folded and
bound in), Index.

Apps: H&A (WWI only), list of former COs, list of former officers,
notable events in the bn's history, stations and movements, battle honours.

This is one of the better Indian Army histories. Good descriptions of the
3rd Mahratta War,  the Sind campaign, the Mutiny, and services in WWI.
R/4 V/3. NAM. IOL. PJE.


OUTRAM'S RIFLES
A History of the 4th Bn 6th Rajputana Rifles

H G Rawlinson CIE
Oxford University Press, 1933
Green, gold, regtl crest on front cover, 8.5 x 5.5, viii/218.
Fp, 11 mono phots, 7 maps (5 printed in text, 2 bound in), Bibliography,
Index.

Apps: Roll of Honour (British and Indian officers for WWI), H&A (WWI, all
ranks, with some details for earlier campaigns), list of former COs,
list of officers at August 1914, list of former Adjutants.

Like all of Rawlinson's works, this is a sound, reliable and readable
history. He covers the period 1818 to 1922, with good coverage for the
Persian War, the Mutiny, Second Afghan War, Third Burmese War, Aden,
the Persian Gulf, and WWI (Egypt and Palestine). Many individuals
mentioned in the narrative. R/3 V/5. NAM. RP.


THE HISTORY OF THE 2/6th RAJPUTANA RIFLES (PRINCE OF WALES'S OWN)

H G Rawlinson CIE
Oxford University Press, London, 1936
Green, gold, 8.5 x 5.5, x/195.
Fp, 8 mono plates, 10 maps (9 printed in text, one bound in), Index.

Apps: Roll of Honour (officers only), H&A (WWI only), list of former COs,
list of former officers (WWI only), list of Honorary Colonels, list of
former Adjutants, idem Subedar-Majors, idem Jemadars, battle honours,
stations and movements.

Covers the period 1817-1922. Good account of the Mutiny period, but deals
mainly with WWI (Mesopotamia, the Battle of Ctesiphon and the disaster
at Kut-al-Amara). Many officers mentioned in the narrative. There is also
a very useful summary of casualties in the text, with citations for H&A.
R/2 V/4. NAM. IOL. MP.


HISTORY OF THE 1st BATTALION 6th RAJPUTANA RIFLES (WELLESLEY'S)

Lieut Col F H James OBE MC
Gale & Polden Ltd, Aldershot, 1938
Dark green, silver, regtl crest on front cover, 10.0 x 7.5, xx/277.

Fp, 20 mono phots, 4 coloured plates, 20 maps (4 printed in text, 16 bound
in), Index.

Apps: H&A (WWI only), list of former COs, list of former officers, list of Honorary Colonels, idem Adjutants, idem Subedar-Majors.

One of the best Indian Army infantry histories. Very detailed and a mine of information. Covers the period 1771-1937, with the first half of the book dealing objectively with their early history, and the second half devoted to Mesopotamia (particularly the debacle at Kut-al-Amara). R/3 V/5. NAM. IOL. RP.


THE RAJPUTANA RIFLES
A History of the Regiment, 1775-1947

Major M G Abhyankar
Printed by S C Ghose at the Calcutta Press, for Orient Longmans, 1961
Green, white, regtl crest on front cover, 9.75 x 6.5, xxiv/468.
Fp, 20 monochrome plates, 5 coloured plates, 53 maps (printed in the text), Index.

Apps: H&A, list of former COs, notes on battle honours, notes on dress and regtl customs.

A large-scale comprehensive work which gives full details of the Regt's evolution (the story of the early Bombay Regiments which evolved into the Rajputana Rifles), with their services under Wellesley. Good accounts of the Sikh Wars, the Sind campaign, First and Second Afghan Wars, Persia, the Mutiny, Abyssinia, Third Burmese War, East Africa, and the two world wars. R/4 V/5. USII. BCM/OSS.


TRADITIONS OF A REGIMENT
The Story of the Rajputana Rifles

Lieut Gen A M Sethna PVSM AVSM and Lieut Col Valmiki Katju
Lancer Publishers, New Delhi, 1983
Black, gold, 10.0 x 6.5, xiv/243.
44 mono phots, 25 maps (printed in the text), Bibliography, Index.

Apps: H&A (full details for post-1947, with some pre-1947 awards noted in the narrative), lists of COs and Subedar-Majors (post-1947), notes on battle honours.

This is a generalised account of the Regt's history, but is nevertheless most useful. The accounts of campaigning lean mainly towards post-1947 engagements, but there are good explanations of the raising of various battalions which are particularly helpful with regard to war-time bns raised specifically for WWII. The author covers all of the 'battle honour' actions: Bourbon (1809), Kirkee (1817), Meeanee (1843), Aliwal (1846), Bushire (1856), Keren (1941), and Djebel Garci (1943), each being accompanied by an explanatory map. R/1 V/3. NAM. MCJ.

## SERVICES OF 2nd NATIVE LIGHT INFANTRY, LATE 31st NATIVE LIGHT INFANTRY

Anon
P P Blaney, at the Kaiser Baugh Press, location not stated, n.d. (c.1863)
Stiff card, grey, black, 8.0 x 5.5, -/39.
no illustrations, no maps, no appendixes, no Index.

Extracts of reports by the CO to the Adjutant General during the Mutiny in
Central India. R/5 V/2. NAM. PJE.


## HISTORY OF THE 2nd REGIMENT, BENGAL NATIVE INFANTRY
From its Formation in 1798

Lieut Col W B Shawe

Publisher's detail not shown, Julpigoree, 1872
Seen rebound in blue cloth, blind, 11.0 x 8.0, -/100 (approx),
no illustrations, no maps, no Index.

Apps: list of former officers, idem Medical Officers.

The historical content is extremely brief, but the appendix of former
officers and their services (running to 87 pages) is very useful. Covers
the period 1798-1870. R/5 V/3. IOL. NAM. PJE.


## HISTORICAL RECORD OF SERVICES OF 2nd REGIMENT NATIVE LIGHT INFANTRY

Anon (Officers of the Regiment)
Central Government Press, Calcutta, 1877
Bound in with other fragments, brown, gold, 9.75 x 7.0, -/11.
no illustrations, no maps, no appendixes, no Index.

A short pamphlet which deals mainly with services during the Mutiny. One
of the very few sources recorded. Also known as The 2nd Queen's Own
Bengal Light Infantry, formerly the 31st Native Infantry. R/5 V/1. IOL. RGB.


## HISTORICAL RECORDS OF THE XI RAJPUTS

Capt E D Roberts
The Pioneer Press, Allahabad, 1913
Red, black, 9.0 x 5.5, -/194.
no illustrations, no maps, no formal appendixes, no Index.

This is a very brief history covering the period 1825-1912. The bulk of
the book is a compendium of extracts from annual Army Lists, showing the
names of officers serving with the regt. R/5 V/2. NAM. PJE.

HISTORICAL RECORDS OF THE 5th BATTALION, 7th RAJPUT REGIMENT
(LATE 11th RAJPUTS)

Capt E D Roberts, revised by Capt P C Scudamore MC
The Pioneer Press, Allahabad, 1925
Reversed calfskin, brown, gold, regtl crest on front cover,
7.5 x 5.0, -/223.
no illustrations, no maps, no formal appendixes, no Index.

The initial 45 pages describe the period from the Sikh Wars through to the
Third Afghan War. Very superficial, therefore. The remainder of the book
is a direct reprint from various issues of the Army Lists. R/4 V/2. NAM. PJE.


ARMY LISTS, 8th RAJPUTS

Anon
Publication details not shown, n.d. (c.1928?)
Black, gold, 11.0 x 8.0, -/220.
no illustrations, no maps, no Index.

This is a 'one off' melange held by the NAM which consists of nothing more
than extracts from various Army Lists dated between 1847 and 1927, showing
the names of serving officers. The only merit in the work is that it
demonstrates the continuity of service under the many changes of title:
59th Regt N.I.(1847-62), 8th Regt N.I.(1863-82), 8th Regt (Bengal Inf)
(1885-97), 8th Rajput Regt of Bengal Inf (1898-1901), 8th Rajput Inf
(1902-03), 8th Rajputs (1907-12), then 7th Rajput Regt (1925-27).
R/4 V/2. NAM. PJE.


THE SEVENTH RAJPUT REGIMENT IN THE INDIAN MUTINY OF 1857

J W B T Tindall
S.P.G.Mission Printing Pres. Ahmednagar, 1936
Yellow, black, 8.5 x 5.5, -/56.
no illustrations, no maps, no Index.

Apps: H&A, summary of casualties by rank, notes regarding the regtl
monument at Lucknow.

As the title suggests, this is a summary of the activities of each bn of
7th Rajput Regt during the Mutiny (1857-59). R/4 V/2. NAM. PJE.


THE HISTORY OF THE 3rd BATTALION, 7th RAJPUT REGIMENT (DUKE OF
CONNAUGHT'S OWN)

H G Rawlinson CIE
Oxford University Press, London, 1941
Green, gold, with regtl crest in black/yellow/red on front cover,
10.0 x 7.5, x/223.
Fp, 30 mono phots, 15 maps (14 printed in text, one bound in), Index.

Apps: Roll of Honour (WWI), H&A (NWF 1936-37 only), list of former COs, list of former Subedar-Majors.

Amidst so much literary mediocrity, the work of authors such as Rawlinson stands out as a shining example. The historian can only regret that more Indian Army regiments did not employ the services of professional writers/ researchers of his calibre. This book is another of his lucid and informative accounts, with helpful maps and a good Index. He covers the period 1778 to 1939, with many individuals and small actions mentioned in the narrative. The main campaigns for the regt were: Second China War (1860), Egypt (1882), Aden and Mesopotamia (WWI), and numerous engagements on the North West Frontier. R/3 V/5. RP.

HISTORY OF THE 1st Bn 7th RAJPUT REGIMENT

Colonel A H McCleverty
Unpublished typescript, n.d. (c.1964)
Contained in looseleaf folder, 14.0 x 8.0, pages not numbered
no illustrations, no maps, no appendixes, no Index.

It is a pity that Colonel McCleverty failed to find a publisher. This is a full and useful history of the Bn, covering the period 1798-1918, with additional notes for the period 1911-1964. The papers are basically a narrative account, although some lists of serving officers are included, with Honours and Awards for Lushai (1889-1902) and China (1900). R/5 V/3. NAM. PJE.


5th BURMA BATTALION

Anon
The Civil & Military Gazette Press, Lahore, 1928
Blue, gold, Bn crest on front cover, 10.5 x 7.0, -/19.
no illustrations, no maps, no appendixes, no Index.

This very slim booklet refers to 5th Bn 8th Punjab Regiment (Burma), to give it its full 1922 designation. Formerly it was 33rd Burma Infantry until 1903, and then 93rd Burma Infantry. The text consists of extracts from Standing Orders interspersed with brief narrative descriptions of engagements (including the attempted relief of Kut). R/5 V/1. NAM. PJE.


REGIMENTAL HISTORY, 3rd Bn 8th PUNJAB REGIMENT, LATE 91st PUNJABIS

Anon
No publication details shown, n.d. (c.1934)
Mauve boards with brown spine and quarters, black on white label, 6.0 x 5.25, -/14.
no illustrations, no maps, no appendixes, no Index.

A sketchy outline history for the period 1759-1934. NAM. PJE.

REGIMENTAL HISTORY, 1914-1920, 93rd BURMA INFANTRY

Anon
Printed by William Lewis, Cardiff, n.d. (c.1921)
Cream, gold, regtl crest on front cover, 9.0 x 6.0, ii/138.
no illustrations, 13 maps (folding, bound in at rear), no Index.

Apps: Roll of Honour.

A full and readable account of the regt's five and a half years overseas
during WWI: Egypt, France and Mesopotamia. R/4 V/5. NAM. PJE.


HISTORY OF THE 1st BATTALION, 8th PUNJAB REGIMENT

Col N M Geoghegan DSO and Capt M H A Campbell OBE
Gale & Polden Ltd, Aldershot, 1928
Dark blue, gold, blind spine, regtl crest on front cover,
10.0 x 7.25, xii/82.
Fp, 9 mono phots, 10 maps (9 printed in text, one on end-papers), no Index.

Apps: Roll of Honour (British and Indian officers only), H&A.

This bn was originally the 29th Regt Madras Native Infantry, then 29th
Madras Infantry, then 89th Punjabis. The narrative here is confined mainly
to their WWI services which were exceptionally varied. Between 1914
and 1920, they campaigned in South West Arabia, Egypt, Gallipoli, France,
Mesopotamia, back to India for the North West Frontier, back again to
Mesopotamia, then Salonika, the Caucasus and, finally, Constantinople.
R/4 V/5. IOL. NAM. CSM.


HISTORICAL RECORD OF THE SIXTH REGIMENT OF BENGAL NATIVE INFANTRY
Compiled for use in the Regimental School

Major C H Westmorland
The Pioneer Press, Allahabad, 1896
Green, gold, regtl crest on front cover, 5.25 x 4.5, i/40.
no illustrations, no maps, no appendixes, no Index.

As the title states, this is a very basic account prepared for the
teaching staff in the Regimental School. It covers the period 1803 to
1905. R/5 V/1. NAM. PJE.
A second edition, having off-white paper covers and expanded to 52 pages,
was published in 1909.


119th REGIMENT, HISTORICAL RECORDS

Anon
Higginbotham & Co, Madras and Bangalore, n.d. (c.1909)
Red, gold, 9.75 x 6.5, -/147 (see below).
no illustrations, no maps, no Index.

A strange 'one off' volume held by the NAM and apparently the only source available for this regt. Pages 1-32 are a printed history for 1817-1907, pages 33-53 are a typescript  account for 1908-13 pasted in, pages 54-132 are totally blank, and pages 133-147 are appendixes listing former officers and their awards. R/5 V/2. NAM. PJE.


WAR SERVICES OF THE 9th JAT REGIMENT

Lieut Col W L Hailes MC
Gale & Polden Ltd, Aldershot, 1938
Blue, gold, regtl crest on front cover, 10.0 x 7.25, xii/185.
Fp, 3 other coloured plates, no mono phots, 6 maps (folding, bound in), no Index.

Apps: H&A (WWI only, with London Gazette dates and theatres of war for which awarded), notes on the Colours.

A straightforward well-produced history, with good maps, but spoiled by the lack of an Index. Covers the period from 1803 (the Mahratta Wars) through 1937 (Waziristan). The central third of the book  is devoted to WWI services, with many individuals named in the narrative.
R/4 V/4. PCAL. RP/DBP-P.


HISTORY OF THE 4/9th JATS

Anon
No publication details shown, n.d. (c.1945)
Yellow, gold, 13.0 x 8.5, -/24.

A sad and incomplete typescript narrative. The bn was raised in 1940, trained in India, sent to Malaya, and there captured by the Japanese a few weeks later. R/5 V/2. NAM. PJE.


STANDING ORDERS FOR WAR, M.G. Bn 9th JAT REGIMENT

Anon
Printed at the Luckdist Press, Lucknow, for HQ Lucknow District, 1943
Stiff card, grey boards with blue cloth spine, black, 7.5 x 5.0, iv/64.
no illustrations, no maps, no appendixes, no Index.

An oddity, as very few Battalion Standing Orders for that period seem to have survived the years. Of interest because it is one of only two known publications relating to the bn, and contains much information regarding tactics and procedures for an Indian Army unit in WWII. Former aviators will savour the Order which states: '**All** low-flying aircraft will be engaged by machine-gun fire'. R/5 V/2. RP.

A BRIEF HISTORY OF THE MACHINE GUN BATTALION, THE JAT REGIMENT
1941-46

Lieut Col E Johnson
Printed by Higginbothams, Bangalore, for the Regiment, 1947
Red, gold, Bn badge on front cover, 8.75 x 5.5, iv/86.
5 mono phots, 2 maps (printed in text), no Index (but a good Contents
page).

Apps: H&A (all ranks), list of officers who served (with their addresses
at 1947).

A very good account of their services from formation in 1941 to disbandment
in 1946. Narrative based partly upon the War Diary and partly upon the
personal recollections of officers who served with the Bn in Burma
between 1942 and 1945. Being a MG regt, its operations were widely
spread as Companies were detached for service with a variety of other
Indian, British and Gurkha units. The narrative follows the adventures of
each Company throughout each stage of the Burma campaign: First Arakan,
Imphal, forcing of the Irrawaddy, the advance to Rangoon, and the final
annihilation of Japanese troops attempting to escape from the Pegu Yomas.
After VJ Day, the Bn was flown to Saigon where, for six months, it
supported French anti-insurgency operations. A remarkable story of a
remarkable unit. R/4 V/5. AMM.


HISTORY OF THE 9th JAT REGIMENT, 1937-46

Major J Ross
Unpublished typescript, n.d. (c.1948)

This is the draft of a large-scale WWII history and appears to have formed
the basis for the book compiled by Colonel Hailes and published in
1965 (see following entry). R/5 V/4. NAM. PJE.


WAR SERVICES OF THE 9th JAT REGIMENT
Volume II:  1937-48

Lieut Col W L Hailes and Major J Ross
Sapphire Press Ltd, London, 1965
Dark blue, gold, regtl crest on front cover, 10.0 x 7.5, v/227.
Fp, 4 mono phots, 6 maps (printed in text), no Index.

Apps: H&A (WWII), list of officers who served, summary of casualties,
notes on recruiting, notes on the experiences of personnel taken prisoner.

A full and informative history detailing the services of all 9th Jat
battalions between 1937 and 1948: Near East, Malaya, Burma, and India
at Partition. The narrative is a continuation of the story told in Colonel
Hailes' history published in 1938 (see page 128). R/4 V/4. IOL. NAM. MP.

THE JAT REGIMENT
A History of the Regiment 1803-1947

Lieut Col W L Hailes MC and Major J Ross
Published by The Commandant, Jat Regimental Centre, Bareilly, 1967
Blue, gold, regtl crest on front cover, 10.0 x 7.5, xxi/401.
Fp, 19 mono phots, 6 coloured plates, 13 maps (printed in text), no Index.

Apps: H&A, notes on the Colours.

A splendid combined edition of the two previous Volumes (published in 1938
and 1965) in a single binding. This is probably the best of the available
titles concerning the Jat Regiment, but sadly it still lacks an Index.
R/4 V/4. IOL. NAM. PJE.


RECORDS OF THE 27th OR 1st BELOOCH REGIMENT LIGHT INFANTRY

Lieut Col H Beville
United Services Institute of India Journal, Volume II, No 11

A ten-page article held by the NAM, and listed here only because so little
has been written about the regt's early years (1844-72). Based upon
regtl records, but providing possibly useful information regarding the
postings in and out of officers. R/5 V/1. NAM. PJE.


THE HISTORICAL RECORDS OF THE 127th BALUCH LIGHT INFANTRY
Compiled from the Official Records, 1844 to 1905

Anon ('The Officers of the Regiment')
William Clowes & Sons Ltd, London, 1905
Dark green, colour of lettering not recorded, 8.5 x 5.5, ix/180.
Fp, 21 mono phots, 6 coloured plates, no maps, no Index.

Apps: H&A, list of former COs, lists of former officers.

Essentially a narrative history based upon annual reports and official
documents. The text is concerned mainly with administrative detail and
the comings and goings of officers. Very little coverage of battles or
campaigns. The most interesting aspect of the book is the assemblage of
photographs. They seem to have been drawn from many different sources, and
relate to several regts other than 127th BLI. Of probable interest to
students of dress, insignia and regalia. R/5 V/3. IOL. NAM. RGB.


THE FOURTH BATTALION (DUKE OF CONNAUGHT'S OWN) TENTH BALUCH
REGIMENT IN THE GREAT WAR
129th D.C.O. Baluchis

W S Thatcher
Cambridge University Press, Cambridge, 1932
Black (seen also in dark blue), gold, regtl crest on front cover,
8.5 x 5.5, xix/290.
Fp, 3 mono phots, 9 maps (3 printed in text, 6 bound in), Index.

Apps: H&A (for all ranks, with citations), list of former British and
Indian officers,roll of personnel recommended for awards, etc.

The Bn served with distinction in France and East Africa, and this is
an excellent account of their adventures. Well-written, and containing
much detail regarding individuals. R/4 V/5. NAM. IOL. CSM/DBP-P.


THE 10th BALUCH REGIMENT
The First Battalion, Duchess of Connaught's Own (late 124th D.C.O.
Baluchistan Infantry) and the Tenth Battalion (late 2/124th Baluchistan
Infantry)

O A Chaldecott
Printed at The Times of India Press, Bombay, n.d. (c.1935)
Maroon, gold, regtl crest on front cover, 8.75 x 5.5, xiii/250.
Fp, 2 mono phots, 11 maps (loose in rear pocket), Index.

Apps: ten, including Roll of Honour (WWI), H&A (WWI), notes on lineage,
notes on class composition, stations (1820-1934), list of former COs
(1820-1934), etc.

This is a well-produced history of the 1st and 10th Battalions of
the 10th Baluch Regiment which were reconstituted as such in 1922. The
narrative gives a perfunctory review of the earlier campaigns (mainly
the Mutiny and Second Afghan War) before concentrating upon WWI:
Mesopotamia (1916-18), Palestine (1918-20), South Persia (1918-19, for the
siege of Shiraz). R/3 V/5. NAM. IOL. RGB.


A SHORT HISTORY OF THE 3rd BATTALION, 10th BALUCH REGIMENT (QUEEN MARY'S
OWN), JULY 1941 - SEPTEMBER 1943

Anon (presumably by serving officers of the Regiment)
Printed by Societê Orientale de Publicité, Cairo, 1945
Stiff card, cream, black, regtl crest on front cover, 8.0 x 6.0, -/54.
3 mono phots, one sketch, 2 maps (printed in text), no appendixes,
no Index.

Although brief, this is an informative and detailed account of their
services in Iran, Iraq, the Western Desert, and Sicily. R/5 V/3. NAM. PJE.


CAPITAL CAMPAIGNERS
The History of the 3rd Battalion (Queen Mary's Own), The Baluch Regiment

Lieut Col W E Maxwell
Gale & Polden Ltd, Aldershot, 1948
Dark green, gold, regtl crest on front cover, 8.5 x 6.0, iv/167.
Fp, 6 mono phots, 4 maps (2 printed in text, 2 printed on end-papers),
Bibliography, Index.

Apps: list of former COs.

A readable and fairly informative history of the Bn and its predecessors from 1844 to 1947. R/3 V/3. NAM. IOL. PJE.


THE TENTH BALUCH REGIMENT IN THE SECOND WORLD WAR

W S Thatcher (completed by his daughter, published posthumously)
The Baluch Regimental Centre, Abbottabad (Pakistan), 1980
Brown, gold, 10.0 x 7.5, ix/565.
no illustrations, 6 maps (printed in text), no Index.

Apps: H&A, list of COs.

The regt raised 12 active service bns for WWII, and they served in four theatres of war: 1st Bn (NWF, Iraq, Iran), 2nd Bn (Malaya), 3rd Bn (Iran, Western Desert, Sicily), 4th Bn (Eritrea, Western Desert, Italy), 5th Bn (Burma), 6th Bn (NWF), 7th Bn (Burma), 8th Bn (Burma), 9th Bn (NWF), 14th Bn (Burma), 16th Bn (Burma), 17th Bn (Iraq). Two VCs were gained by the regt, Sepoy Bhandari Ram and Naik Fazal Din. Although there are stated to be some minor inaccuries in the narrative, and despite the lack of an Index, this is a fine reference source for a distinguished regt. R/3 V/4. JPR.
A history of the 5th Bn, possibly written pre-1939, has been reported, but not seen. It may exist only in limited facsimile typescript, and in very limited numbers.


35th SIKHS REGIMENTAL RECORD, 1887-1900

Anon
Printed by H & J Pillans, Edinburgh, 1902
Olive green, gold, 10.0 x 7.5, -/70.
no illustrations, no maps, no formal appendixes, no Index.

A very brief narrative history in the first 15 pages, the remainder of the book then consisting of extracts from Indian Army Lists and showing the postings in and out of officers. R/5 V/1. NAM. PJE.


A SHORT HISTORY OF THE 14th  PRINCE OF WALES'S OWN SIKHS

Anon
The Khalsa Press, Kohat, 1908
Yellow, black, 8.0 x 6.0, -/43.
no illustrations, no maps, no appendixes, no Index.

A very brief history covering the period 1846 to 1907 and based upon regtl orders. R/5 V/1. NAM. PJE.

35th SIKHS REGIMENTAL RECORD, 1887-1922

Colonel J C Freeland
Sham Lall & Sons, Peshawar, 1923
Green, gold, regtl crest on front cover, 10.0 x 7.5, i/103.
no illustrations, no maps, no Index.

Apps: list of former COs, former officers (British and Indian), and
Subedar-Majors.

The regt saw only limited service in the 1897 Frontier campaign and did
not leave India during WWI. It had the task of raising drafts for the
47th Sikhs in France, Mesopotamia and Palestine. The first half of the book
is a narrative account of these events, the second half being extracts
from annual Indian Army Lists. R/3 V/3. NAM. MP.


REGIMENTAL HISTORY OF THE 45th RATTRAY'S SIKHS DURING THE GREAT WAR
AND AFTER. 1914-1921.

Lieut Col R H Anderson
Sifton Praed & Co, London, for the Regiment, 1925
Dark blue, gold, regtl crest on front cover, 9.0 x 6.0, -/266.
no illustrations, 16 maps (folding, bound in), no Index.

Apps: H&A, list of the British and Indian officers who served, returns
of casualties.

A very careful and informative narrative of the regt's services during WWI,
mainly in Mesopotamia. After 1922, they were re-designated 3rd Bn, 11th Sikh
Regiment (Rattray's Sikhs). A useful source, which would have been much
improved by the inclusion of illustrations and an Index.
R/3 V/4. NAM. PJE.
This book has been reported also with grey covers, but seemingly
identical in all other respects.


47th SIKHS, WAR RECORDS, THE GREAT WAR 1914-18

Anon
Never formally published, but seen in facsimile reprint in various
forms of binding, n.d. (c.1925), 10.0 x 8.0, -/303.
no illustrations, 2 maps (bound in), no Index.

Apps: Roll of Honour, H&A, list of officers who served.

The regt was raised in 1901, but saw little active service before 1914.
They then had two bns, serving in France, Mesopotamia and Palestine.
A good narrative account, apparently written by an officer who served
throughout. After 1922, they became 10th Bn, 11th Sikh Regiment.
R/5 V/4. RMAS. IOL. VS/DBP-P.

HISTORY OF THE 45th RATTRAY'S SIKHS
Volume I: 1856-1914

Colonel H StG M McRae
Robert Maclehose Co Ltd, Glagow, Scotland, 1933
Dark blue, gold, regtl crest on front cover, 9.0 x 6.0, xxiv/480.
Fp, no other illustrations, 10 maps (folding, bound in), Bibliography,
no appendixes, no Index.

This is a very full and readable history. The regt's main campaigns were
the Mutiny, the Second Afghan War, and various Frontier operations.
Inexplicably in such a thorough work, the author has provided neither
appendixes nor an Index. R/3 V/3. NAM. IOL. PJE.
There is no record of a Volume II ever having been published.


THE 14th KING GEORGE'S OWN SIKHS 1846-1933
The 1st Bn (K.G.O.)(Ferozepore Sikhs), The 11th Sikh Regiment

Colonel F E G Talbot
Printed by Butler & Tanner Ltd, Frome and London, for the Royal United
Services Institute, 1937
Maroon, gold, regtl crest on front cover, 9.75 x 7.5, viii/164.
Fp, no other illustrations, 8 maps (printed in text), no Index.

Apps: list of former COs, list of former British officers, idem Subedar-
Majors, notes on casualties.

Although the book covers the period through to 1933, the main title of
this well-written history refers to the Bn's pre-1922 designation. The
sub-title is the post-1922 designation. Approximately one third of the
narrative is devoted to their pre-1914 history and evolution, most of
the remainder then dealing with WWI. A good general record.
R/3 V/4. USII. IOL. NAM. RGH.
An edition of this book with the imprint 1935 has been noted. Not seen.


OPERATIONAL HISTORY OF THE M.G. BN, THE SIKH REGIMENT

Anon
Unpublished typescript, foolscap, 11 pages, no illustrations, no maps, no
Index, appendixes for H&A and officers who served.

A brief but usefully detailed account of the Bn's raising in 1942 and
its services in Burma in 1944-45. Included here because it is the only
known source. R/5 V/2. IWM. PJE.


A BRIEF HISTORY OF THE 11th SIKH REGIMENT

Anon
The Military Steam Press, Nowshera, n.d. (c.1945)
Green, gold, regtl crest on front cover, 9.5 x 6.5, -/60.
no illustrations, no maps, no appendixes, no Index.

This is a sketchy history which attempts to cover the period 1843-1943,
drawing only upon regtl records, in the space of 60 pages. A token
war-time effort to cover their centenary. R/4 V/1. IWM. PJE.


1st KING GEORGE V'S OWN BATTALION, THE SIKH REGIMENT
The 14th King George's Own Ferozepore Sikhs, 1846-1946

Lieut Col P G Bamford DSO
Gale & Polden Ltd, Aldershot, 1948
Dark green, gold, regtl crest on front cover, 9.75 x 7.75, -/172.
Fp, 24 mono phots, 11 coloured plates, 17 excellent maps (printed in text),
no Index.

Apps: Roll of Honour (all officers killed and wounded in all campaigns
during the period stated), H&A (for all ranks and all campaigns
during the period, with some details of place and year), list of former COs,
idem Subedar-Majors, notes on regtl titles, summary of casualties for
all ranks for all campaigns.

A very handsome book, well presented, with exceptionally good maps.
The narrative is clear and informative, and deals with the regt's
services from the Mutiny through to Malaya (WWII). R/3 V/4. DBP-P.


THE SIKH REGIMENT IN THE SECOND WORLD WAR

Colonel F T Birdwood OBE
Jarrold & Sons, Norwich, n.d.
Red, gold, 9.0 x 6.0, xviii/462.
no illustrations, 18 maps (bound in), no Index.

Apps: H&A.

A very full history of the part played by the regt's nine battalions
during WWII. R/3 V/3. NAM. PJE.


A DIARY OF 5th Bn (D.C.O.) THE SIKH REGIMENT IN THE MALAYAN CAMPAIGN
8 December 1941 to 15 February 1942

Anon
Publication details not shown, n.d.
Light blue, gold, 13.0 x 8.5, -/27.
no illustrations, no maps, no Index.

Apps: H&A.

A brief but useful day-by-day account of events leading up to the
surrender. R/5 V/2. NAM. PJE.

SARAGARHI BATTALION - ASHES TO GLORY
History of the 4th Battalion The Sikh Regiment (XXXVI)

Colonel Kanwaljit Singh and Major H S Ahluwalia
Lancer International, New Delhi, 1987
Black, gold, 8.75 x 5.5, -/300.
28 mono phots, 11 maps (3 bound in, 8 printed in text), Bibliography,
Index.

Apps: Roll of Honour, H&A (WWI only), list of former COs.

A good readable history of the first 100 years, 1887-1987. The narrative
is based upon regtl orders, war diaries, and personal accounts. A
sound source of reference. R/1 V/5. PJE.


HISTORY OF THE 1st SIKH REGIMENT 1846-1886

Anon
Thacker, Spink & Co, Calcutta, 1887
Dark brown, gold, 10.0 x 6.5, -/184
no illustrations, no maps, no Index.

Apps: Roll of Honour, H&A, lists of former officers, list of former Subeda-
Majors, list of cantonments.

The text is based upon extracts from regtl records and includes
descriptions of the regt's services during the Mutiny and on the NWF.
R/4 V/2. NAM. PJE.


HISTORY OF THE 1st SIKH INFANTRY 1846-1886, AND 51st SIKHS (FRONTIER FORCE)
1903-1920 (1st Bn 12th FRONTIER FORCE REGIMENT, PRINCE OF WALES'S OWN,
[SIKHS])

Anon
The Diocesan Press, Vepery, various dates (see below)
Dark green, gold, 10.0 x 6.75
Published in 3 volumes, all with maps, with appendixes, no illustrations,
no Indexes, thus
Volume I:   1887, 225 pages, amended and reprinted in 1903 with 171 pages
Volume II:  1903, 101 pages, reprinted in 1929
Volume III:1929, 225 pages.
All three volumes were produced in 1929 within a single binding consisting
of 497 pages. The following notes refer to the 1929 combined edition.

Apps: Roll of Honour (with full details), H&A (detailed, for all ranks,
British and Indian), lists of former officers (with details of services).

This is a very full narrative history, the WWI period being presented as a
War Diary. The appendixes are exceptionally useful, and the 8 folding maps
bound into the 1929 edition are good.    R/3 V/5. NAM. PJE/RJW.

THE HISTORICAL RECORD OF THE 4th SIKH INFANTRY, PUNJAB FRONTIER FORCE

Anon ('By Authority')
The Punjab Government Press, Lahore, 1887
Red, gold, regtl crest on front cover, 10.5 x 7.0, v/90.
no illustrations, no maps, no formal appendixes, no Index.

Covers the period 1847-1885. A very brief history, based upon regtl
records and orders. The account deals mainly with the Mutiny and various
Frontier operations. Useful mainly with regard to the many officers
mentioned by name in the text. R/4 V/3. USII. NAM. PJE.


THE HISTORICAL RECORD OF THE 2nd (OR HILL) SIKH INFANTRY, PUNJAB FRONTIER
FORCE

Anon ('By Authority')
The Punjab Government Press, Lahore, 1887
Red, gold, 10.5 x 7.0, -/46.
no illustrations, no maps, no appendixes, no Index.

A short and very superficial history based upon regtl records.
R/4 V/2. IOL. USII. NAM. PJE.


HISTORICAL RECORDS OF THE 3rd SIKH INFANTRY, PUNJAB FRONTIER FORCE

Anon ('By Authority')
The Punjab Government Press, Lahore, 1887
Red, gold, 10.5 x 7.0, v/75.
no illustrations, no maps, no appendixes, no Index.

Another in the 'PFF Regiments' series (see above two entries), but one
of the better volumes. Covers the period 1847-87 in useful detail,
the text based upon regtl records. Written in chronological diary form.
Gives stations and moves, with numerous British and Indian personnel
being named in the text (together with some details of their awards).
Detailed accounts of operations during the Mutiny, Umbeyla (1863), Jowaki
(1877-78), and Afghanistan (1879-80), with details of casualties.
R/4 V/4. IOL. NAM. AMM/PJE.
A corrected and much expanded edition (-/165 pages) was published
by the same source in 1903. This has black boards, leather spine, and
gold lettering with the regtl crest on the front cover. Clearly the more
useful and desirable of the two versions.


HISTORICAL RECORD OF THE 52nd SIKH FRONTIER FORCE
Late the 2nd (or Hill) Sikh Infantry, Punjab Frontier Force

Anon
M Gulab Singh & Sons, Lahore, 1905
Red boards with leather spine and quarters, gold, regtl crest on front
cover, 9.5 x 6.0, -/63.
no illustrations, no maps, no appendixes, no Index.

This is an expanded version of the 1887 edition (see previous page) which
covers the period 1846-1904. A brief history based upon regtl records,
but with many individuals mentioned in the text. R/3 V/3. IOL. NAM. PJE.


HISTORY OF THE 54th SIKHS, FRONTIER FORCE REGIMENT
Previously designated 4th Sikhs, Punjab Frontier Force, 1846-1914

Captain S R Shirley
Gale & Polden Ltd, Aldershot, 1915
Dark green, gold, 7.0 x 5.0, xiv/219.
no illustrations, 9 maps (loose in rear pocket), no Index.

Apps: H&A, list of former COs, list of former officers, list of campaigns.

A narrative history which covers the period up to 1914 in fair detail.
Good descriptions of services in the First Burma War, the Mutiny, and
various Frontier campaigns. R/4 V/4. NAM. PJE.


HISTORICAL RECORDS OF THE 3rd SIKHS, 1847-1930

Lieut Col C I Shepherd
Pardy & Son, Bournemouth (UK), 1931
Black, gold, regtl crest on front cover, 9.5 x 6.5, -/313.
no illustrations, no maps, no Index.

Apps: Roll of Honour (WWI only, British and Indian officers), H&A (with
full citations for IOMs, DSOs, MCs, etc), list of former officers
(1847-1930), list of battles in which engaged (WWI).

This is a record of dates rather than a full-blown history. The book is
divided into three sections: Part I - 3rd Sikhs PFF (origins and battle
honours) 1847-1903, Part II - 53rd Sikhs FF 1914-18, Part III - 3rd Bn,
12th Frontier Force Regt 1922-1930. The overall effect is extremely
tedious. The main value to a researcher is the references to officers
being posted in and out, and the personnel appendixes. R/4 V/3.
IOL. NAM. RMAS. HLL/RP.


HISTORY OF THE 2nd SIKHS, 12th FRONTIER FORCE REGIMENT, 1846-1933

Captain C W May
E C Davis at The Mission Press, Jubbulpore, for the Regiment, 1933
Full Morocco in black, gold, regtl crest on front cover, 10.0 x 7.25,-/153.
17 mono phots, 5 maps (loose in rear pocket), no Index.

Apps: Roll of Honour (WWI), H&A (WWI), lists of former British and Indian
officers, former COs, former Adjutants, Quartermasters and Subedar-
Majors, notes on dress and uniform, notes on battle honours, notes on
organisation, etc.

A well-written narrative in an attractive binding. Good coverage of
Frontier campaigns, the Mutiny, Second Afghan War, Somaliland (1903), and
WWI (when they served on the Frontier and also found drafts for the 56th
and 59th Rifles). R/4 V/4. NAM. BDM/RP.

THE FRONTIER FORCE REGIMENT

Brigadier W E H Condon OBE
Gale & Polden Ltd, Aldershot, 1962
Khaki, gold, regtl crest on front cover, 9.75 x 7.25, xxii/592.
Fp, 19 mono phots, 36 maps (26 printed in text, 10 bound in),
Bibliography, no Index.

Apps: Roll of Honour (WWII only, officers only), H&A (WWII only, with
citations for VCs), notes on changes of title (1846-1956).

An excellent book, the best on the regt, marred only by the lack of an
Index. More than half of the well-written narrative is devoted, in
great detail, to WWII services. Deals with 2nd Bn (Q.V.O. Corps of Guides),
3rd Bn (1st P.O.W. Own), 4th Bn (2nd Dogra Paltan), 5th Bn (3rd Royal Bn),
6th Bn (4th Burmah Paltan), 8th Bn, 9th Bn, and the Pakistan National
Guard (post-1956 designation). There are good accounts of soldiering in
Malaya (1942), Italy and Burma. Many British officers are mentioned in the
text by name. R/2 V/5. IOL. NAM. DJB/RP.


THROUGH THE MUTINY WITH THE 4th PUNJAB INFANTRY, PUNJAB IRREGULAR FORCE

Surgeon-General J Fairweather
Apparently an unpublished facsimile typescript, presumably drafted from
an original manuscript, n.d.
Seen casebound in green, gold, 10.0 x 8.0, -/61.
no illustrations, no maps, no appendixes, no Index.

An autobiographical account of his experiences with the regt during the
Mutiny. Covers the period 1855 to 1858. A useful secondary source.
R/5 V/2. NAM. PJE.


HISTORY OF THE VI PUNJAB INFANTRY, PUNJAB FRONTIER FORCE, FROM 1843 TO 1885

Lieut Col T Fraser Bruce
The Civil and Military Gazette Press, Lahore, 1886
Stiff card, sand, with red spine and corners, black, 6.75 x 4.5, iv/30.
no illustrations, no maps, no appendixes, no Index.

Gives in outline diary form the history of the Scinde Camel Corps (1843-53),
then the Scinde Rifle Corps (1853-56), then the VI Punjab Infantry. Details
of stations, moves, postings, and campaigns (Sutlej, Mutiny, Umbeyla,
and Jowaki). All in very condensed form, but with some British officers
mentioned in the text. R/4 V/2. AMM.


HISTORICAL RECORD OF THE 5th PUNJAB INFANTRY, PUNJAB FRONTIER FORCE

Anon ('By Authority')
The Punjab Government Press, Lahore, 1887
Red, gold, 10.5 x 7.0, v/79.
no illustrations, no maps, no appendixes, no Index.

This is a fairly typical example of the books being produced by the authorities in Lahore in 1887. It is based upon regtl and other official records, and is concerned mainly with stations, movements, and the comings and goings of officers. Covers quite superficially the period 1849 to 1866, in chronological diary form. R/4 V/3. USII. OSS.


DIGEST OF SERVICES OF THE 1st (COKE'S) REGIMENT, PUNJAB FRONTIER FORCE

Colonel Theo Higginson
The Simla Chronicle Press, Simla, 1888
Brown, gold, 9.5 x 6.5, -/122.
no illustrations, 5 maps (folding, bound in), no Index.

Apps: notes on casualties, stations and movements.

Based upon extracts from regtl orders with copies of some despatches interspersed. Covers the period 1849-1887. R/4 V/3. USII. NAM. PJE.


HISTORY OF THE 4th REGIMENT, PUNJAB INFANTRY

Anon
Thacker Spink & Co, Calcutta, 1894
Mauve, gold, 10.0 x 6.5, ii/66.
no illustrations, no maps, no formal appendixes, no Index.

Again, this book is based upon regtl records and orders. Deals with the Mutiny and North West Frontier operations in fairly cursory style. Some rolls of officers are included in the text. R/4 V/2. IOL. NAM. PJE.


HISTORY OF THE 2nd PUNJAB INFANTRY

Anon
Publisher's details not shown, n.d. (c.1903)
Dark green, gold, 9.5 x 6.5, -/126.
no illustrations, no maps, no Index.

Apps: H&A, list of former officers (British and Indian), stations and movements, notes on casualties.

Based upon regtl records and orders, and covers the period 1849-1902. Deals with Frontier actions and the Second Afghan War. R/4 V/3. IOL. PJE. An earlier edition, dated 1889 and covering events up to 1887, has been noted, but not seen.


HISTORY OF THE 55th COKE'S RIFLES, FRONTIER FORCE
Formerly known as the 1st Panjab Infantry, Panjab Frontier Force

Captain J P Villiers-Stuart
Harvey & Co, Waterford, 1908
Green boards, red spine, 2 regtl crests on front cover, 10.5 x 6.5, ii/119.
no illustrations, 6 maps (bound in), no appendixes, no Index.

A brief history covering the period 1849 to 1908 and based upon regtl
records. Devoted mainly to the Mutiny and Frontier operations. Lists of
Native Officers are included in the text. R/4 V/2. NAM. PJE.


REGIMENTAL HISTORY OF THE 6th ROYAL BATTALION, 13th FRONTIER FORCE RIFLES
(SCINDE), 1843-1923

Captain D M Lindsay
Gale & Polden Ltd, Aldershot, 1926
Dark green, gold, (seen also in full Morocco), 9.75 x 7.25, -/145.
Fp, 30 mono phots, 8 maps (folding, bound in, very detailed), no Index.

Apps: no Roll of Honour, but lists of casualties are included in the text,
H&A, list of former COs, list of former officers and dates of service with
other details, notes regarding the designation 'Royal'.

A sound narrative history covering the period 1843 (when still the Scinde
Camel Corps) through various reorganisations to WWI (France 1914-15,
Mesopotamia 1916-17, and Palestine 1918) as 59th Scinde Rifles (F.F.).
Many individual officers are mentioned in the text. R/4 V/4. PCAL. RP.


HISTORY OF THE 5th BATTALION, 13th FRONTIER FORCE RIFLES, 1849-1926

Colonel H C Wylly CB
Gale & Polden Ltd, Aldershot, 1929
Green, gold, regtl crest on front cover, 10.0 x 7.25, vii/135.
Fp, 12 mono phots, 6 maps (loose in rear pocket), no Index.

Apps: Roll of Honour (WWI only, British and Indian officers only),
H&A (WWI), list of former officers.

A good narrative account of the entire period, with much interesting
detail. The unit was formerly the 5th Punjab Infantry and then 58th
Vaughan's Rifles. R/3 V/4. CSM.


REGIMENTAL HISTORY OF THE 4th BATTALION, 13th FRONTIER FORCE RIFLES
(WILDE'S)

Anon
Butler & Tanner, Frome and London, apparently for the Regiment, n.d.(c.1930)
Fawn boards with blue spine, gold, regtl crest on front cover,
8.5 x 5.5, vii/235.
Fp, 3 mono phots, one map (bound in at rear), no Index.

Apps: list of former COs, list of former officers (for the period 1849-
1930, some having biographical details noted).

A good narrative history with plenty of substance. Many individuals and
minor actions mentioned in the text, together with details of casualties
and awards. Deals with the Mutiny, Frontier operations, WWI services
(approximately half of the book), and the Third Afghan War (a complete
chapter). R/4 V/4. RMAS. NAM. RP.

THE HISTORY OF COKE'S RIFLES

Colonel H C Wylly
Gale & Polden Ltd, Aldershot, 1930
Dark green, gold, regtl crest on front cover, 10.0 x 7.5, iii/164.
Seen also in a 'de luxe' binding, full Morocco with marbled end-papers
and gold-blocked all around
Fp, 10 mono phots, 2 sketches, no maps, Index.

Apps: list of former COs, list of former Subedar-Majors (with details of
their distinctions and awards).

A good readable history for the period 1849-1928. Covers the campaigns on
the Frontier, Second Afghan War, and WWI (East Africa and South Persia).
Many individuals mentioned in the text, with direct quotations from their
personal experiences. A nicely presented book.
R/3 V/5. RMAS. NAM. RP/PJE.


HISTORY OF THE 2nd BATTALION, 13th FRONTIER FORCE RIFLES, 1849-1931

Anon
Groom & Son Ltd, Bury St Edmunds (UK), 1933
Dark green, gold, 8.25 x 6.75, -/74.
Seen also in dark blue, and with and without leather spine.
no illustrations, no maps, no appendixes, no Index.

A very nicely printed and well bound book, but the contents are simply a
calendar of stations and movement, with very little detail. The Bn
served in Egypt and Aden in 1914-15, and in Syria and Palestine in 1918-19.
Possibly useful as a secondary source. R/4 V/3. RMAS. NAM. RP/PJE.


A RECORD OF THE 58th RIFLES, FRONTIER FORCE, IN THE GREAT WAR, 1914-19

Colonel A G Lind DSO
The Commercial Steam Press, Dera Ismail Khan, 1933
Dark green, gold, 10.0 x 7.5, i/155.
no illustrations, 7 maps (loose in rear pocket), no Index.

Apps: H&A, notes on casualties, notes on reinforcements, orders and letters.

A good straightforward account of the Bn in WWI. R/4 V/4. IOL. NAM. PJE.


REGIMENTAL HISTORY OF THE 6th ROYAL BATTALION (SCINDE), 13th FRONTIER
FORCE RIFLES, 1843-1934

Anon (but possibly Captain D M Lindsay)
Gale & Polden Ltd, Aldershot, 1935
Dark green, black, 9.75 x 7.25, xi/117.
no illustrations, no maps, no Index.

Apps: H&A (WWI only), list of former COs.

The narrative is an updated version of that published in Lindsay's
history of 1926 (see page 141). It continues the history through to
1934, but, unlike the 1926 edition, it has no illustrations, no maps,
and no succession rolls of officers. It was at the time intended to
produce a 'de luxe' edition, incorporating these features, in time for the
centenary in 1943. This plan was shelved during the war and then overtaken
by Partition. Instead, a new history, covering 1934 onwards, was published
in 1951 (see following entry). The Lindsay works are both good in their
own ways, but researchers working on the period 1920-40 may need to
consult both (rather than one or the other). R/3 V/3. NAM. CSM/RJW/RP.


REGIMENTAL HISTORY OF THE 6th ROYAL BATTALION (SCINDE), 13th FRONTIER
FORCE RIFLES, 1934-1947

Brigadier N L St P Bunbury DSO
Gale & Polden Ltd, Aldershot, 1951
Dark green, gold, regtl crest on front cover, blind spine, 8.5 x 5.5,
vii/116.
Fp, no other illustrations, 5 maps (bound in), no Index.

Apps: Roll of Honour (British officers only), H&A, list of COs, list of
officers who served.

A useful and readable account, devoted mainly to WWII services in
the Middle East and Italy. There is also good coverage of operations
on the North West Frontier. R/3 V/4. NAM. CSM.


REGIMENTAL HISTORY, 13th FRONTIER FORCE RIFLES

W H H Young
Publisher's details not shown, Abbottobad, 1945
Green, black, 9.0 x 5.5, v/121.
no illustrations, no maps, no appendixes, no Index.

This is a brief summary of the history of each bn in the 13th FFR, intended
mainly for the instruction of young officers. R/4 V/2. NAM. PJE.


2nd Bn 13th FRONTIER FORCE RIFLES
War History (Unofficial)

C J Weld
No publication details shown, seen in facsimile typescript,  foolscap,
bound in yellow cloth, black, -/90.

This is a full and readable account of the Bn's services in Burma and
Sumatra between 1942 and 1946. Presumably it was cyclostyled in limited
numbers for circulation to officers who served,as a memento.
R/5 V/4. NAM. PJE.

THE FRONTIER FORCE RIFLES

Brigadier W E H Condon OBE
Gale & Polden Ltd, Aldershot, 1953
Green, silver, regtl crest on front cover, 10.0 x 7.0, xix/461.
Fp, 21 mono phots, 26 maps (7 bound in, 19 printed in the text), no Index.

Apps: Roll of Honour (WWII only, officers only), H&A (WWII, for all ranks, including Commendations, with full citations for their 6 VCs), statistical summary of casualties for Other Ranks.

A highly detailed, extremely well-written and well-produced history. It covers the period 1857-1946, but concentrates mainly upon WWII. Includes accounts of the services of all the FFR battalions: Coke's Rifles, Wilde's Rifles, Vaughan's Rifles, Scinde Rifles, and the war-time battalions. Between them, they saw service in Malaya, Syria, Eritrea, North Africa, Italy and Burma. This book is comparable with his other major work, THE FRONTIER FORCE REGIMENT (see page 139), but in neither case did Condon produce an Index, and this is most regrettable in books of such scale and complexity. R/2 V/4. IOL. RP.


A SUMMARISED HISTORY OF THE 13th FRONTIER FORCE RIFLES DURING THE SECOND WORLD WAR, 1939-1946

Lieut Col A D Fitzgerald MBE
Printer's details not shown, produced privately for the author, 1985
Facsimile typescript, bound in a plastic folder, 8.75 x 11.75, 'badges and battle honours' motif on front cover, iv/13.
no illustrations, no maps, no appendixes, no Index.

Stated to be a brief but useful record of 13 FFR in WWII, covering the services of all 15 active service bns, the Regtl Centre, and the Garrison Companies. Still available from the author. R/1 V/2. FWST.


HISTORY OF THE 20th (DUKE OF CAMBRIDGE'S OWN) INFANTRY, BROWNLOW'S PUNJABIS
From its Formation, in 1857, to 1907

Anon (presumably a Regtl Committee to commemorate their 50th anniversary)
Swiss & Co (Army & Navy Printers), Devonport (UK), n.d. (c.1910)
Buff cloth boards, green leather spine and quarters, gold, regtl crest embossed in gold on leather quarter, 9.6 x 6.0, -/147.
Fp, 13 mono phots, one plan (bound in), no Index.

Apps: expeditions in which the Regt (or units of) has taken part (with lists of participating British and Indian officers), list of former COs, list of former Subadar-Majors, notes on stations and movements, extracts from Indian Army Quarterly Lists (October 1909 and January 1910), lists of former officers (British and Indian) at various dates between 1858 and 1901, notes on changes in unit designation.

This is a history of the regiment from its formation in 1857 through to
1907, with detailed accounts of the 16 campaigns in which it served in
India and overseas during that time. These accounts include descriptions
of specific actions, extracts from despatches, casualty lists, medals and
clasps awarded, subsequent battle honours awarded. There are interesting
short biographies for their founder, ultimately Field Marshal Sir Charles
Brownlow GCB, and Subadar-Major Mauladad Khan CIE, Sirdar Bahadur. The good
photographs include several studio portraits of individual senior officers
and captioned group pictures of officers, NCOs and Other Ranks. This is a
book which covers a great deal of ground in 147 pages. It might have been
even better if the narrative had been longer, but it is nevertheless
an excellent source of reference. R/4 V/4. BWR/RGH.


RECORDS OF THE I/XXI PUNJABIS

Major P Murray
Gale & Polden Ltd, Aldershot, 1919
Green, gold, regtl crest on front cover, 7.5 x 5.0, -/107.
no illustrations, 3 maps (folding, bound in), no Index.

Apps: list of former COs, list of former officers, war services of each bn.

A very brief history based upon regtl documents for the period 1857-1919.
Deals with Frontier actions, the Mutiny, and WWI. R/4 V/3. NAM. PJE.


THE 40th PATHANS IN THE GREAT WAR

Anon
The Civil & Military Gazette Press, Lahore, 1921
Paper covers, green, black, 9.0 x 6.0, -/73.
Fp, 2 mono phots, 3 maps (folding, bound in), no Index.

Apps: H&A (WWI), notes on casualties.

Again, a fairly sketchy history, this time based upon the Bn War Diary.
Often known as 'the Forty Thieves', the Bn served in Hong Kong and
East Africa during WWI. R/4 V/3. NAM. PJE.


HISTORICAL RECORDS OF THE 20th (DUKE OF CAMBRIDGE'S OWN) INFANTRY,
BROWNLOW'S PUBJABIS, Volume II: 1909-1922

Anon
Butler & Tanner, Frome and London, for the Regiment, 1923
Khaki, green spine, gold, regtl crest on front cover, 9.0 x 6.0, viii/86.
Fp, 3 mono phots, 6 maps (folding, bound in), no Index.

Apps: Roll of Honour (all ranks for WWI), H&A (all ranks, WWI), list of
former COs (1908-1922), list of officers who served in WWI, list of former
Subedar-Majors (1908-1922), Indian personnel awarded the OBI and the IOM
(1863-1922), stations and movements.

This is a detailed readable narrative history dealing mainly with WWI.
The Bn served in Mesopotamia, Egypt and Palestine.
R/4 V/4. RMAS. NAM. RP/PJE.


WAR RECORDS OF THE 24th PUNJABIS, 4th BATTALION, 14th PUNJAB REGIMENT

Brigadier A B Haig
Gale & Polden Ltd, Aldershot, 1934
Dark green, gold, regtl crest on front cover, 10.0 x 7.25, xi/84.
Fp, one mono phot (group portrait of all British and Indian officers at
October 1914), 9 maps (bound in), no Index.

Apps: Roll of Honour (British and Indian officers), H&A, list of former
officers.

This is a WWI history. The Bn was destroyed by the Turks at Kut (there
is a chapter devoted to the experiences of the imprisoned survivors).
Later it was reformed. A brief but useful account. R/4 V/4. CSM.


REGIMENTAL HISTORY OF THE 3rd BATTALION, 14th PUNJAB REGIMENT, 1857-1922

Lieut Col W F R Webb
Unpublished typescript, foolscap, seen bound in green, gold, -/222.
Appendixes for H&A, former COs, officers who served, dress regulations,
8 maps.

The NAM holds a copy of this full and detailed history which, as far as
can be determined, was never formally published. R/5 V/3. NAM. PJE.


HISTORY OF THE 5th BATTALION (PATHANS), 14th PUNJAB REGIMENT
Formerly 40th Pathans, 'The Forty Thieves'

Major R S Waters OBE
James Bain Ltd, London, 1936
Green, gold, regtl crest on front cover, 10.0 x 9.0, xxii/398.
Two fps, 22 mono phots, 7 maps (folding, bound in), Index.

Apps: 60 pages of detailed appendixes, including Roll of Honour (WWI, British
and Indian officers only), H&A (WWI, all ranks), list of former COs,
biographical notes on certain senior officers who formerly served with the
Bn, notes on dress and uniform, war memorials, etc.

A very thorough narrative, with excellent appendixes. Covers the period
1780-1936 in great detail, but particularly good for their WWI services
(France and East Africa). An exemplary work. R/4 V/5. RMAS. IOL. VS/RP.


CONTINUATON OF THE HISTORY OF THE 5th BATTALION (PATHANS), 14th PUNJAB
REGIMENT, 1937-1942

Major R S Waters
Lund Humphries, London, n.d.
Paper covers, olive green, black, 7.0 x 4.5, -/81.
no illustrations, one map (folding, bound in at rear), no Index.

The narrative deals mainly with the Bn's services in Malaya in 1941-42, culminating in the surrender. There is much detail, including information on casualties and the route followed by the Bn during the campaign. R/5 V/4. NAM. PJE.


FOURTEENTH PUNJAB REGIMENT
A Short History, 1939-1945

Anon
Lund Humphries, London, n.d.
Dark green, gold, regtl crest on front cover, 9.0 x 6.0, ii/111.
no illustrations, 3 maps (printed on end-papers), no Index.

Apps: H&A (numerical summary only), list of officers who served.

This is a brief description of the activities of the various bns, in and out of India, during WWII. Very little detail. R/4 V/2. NAM. PJE.


HISTORY OF THE 1st BATTALION, 14th PUNJAB REGIMENT, SHERDIL-KI-PALTAN
(LATE XIX PUNJABIS)

G Pigot
The Roxy Printing Press, New Delhi, 1946
Green, black, regtl crest on front cover, 11.0 x 8.0, iv/243.
no illustrations, 11 maps and 24 sketch plans (bound in), no Index.

Apps: list of former COs, extracts from Bn Standing Orders,
stations and movements.

Covers the period 1857-1946. A good readable narrative, with plenty of informative detail. R/4 V/4. NAM. PJE.


7th Bn 14th PUNJAB REGIMENT
Regimental History of Active Service during WWII

Anon
The Northern Army Press, Nowshera, n.d. (c.1947)
Stiff card, light green, black, 10.0 x 6.0, -/63.
no illustrations, no maps, no Index.

Apps: Roll of Honour, H&A, notes on casualties.

A good readable narrative account covering the period 1942-47 (mainly actions in Burma). R/5 V/4. NAM. PJE.

NINTH BATTALION, FOURTEENTH PUNJAB REGIMENT
Raised 1st April 1941, Disbanded 8th July 1947

Lieut Col J R Booth and Lieut Col J B Hobbs
Western Mail & Echo Ltd, Cardiff, 1948
Green, gold, regtl crest on front cover, 9.0 x 6.0, -/132.
Fp, 9 mono phots, 2 maps (one printed on end-papers, one folding and
bound in), no Index.

Apps: Roll of Honour, H&A, list of VCOs who served.

An interesting and informative narrative account of the Bn's campaign
in Burma, incorporating numerous eyewitness accounts. R/5 V/4. NAM. PJE.


SOUVENIR,CENTENARY, 8th Bn THE PUNJAB REGIMENT
1857-1957 (28th BENGAL INFANTRY 1861)

Anon
No publication details shown, n.d. (c.1957)
Red, black, 6.5 x 8.5, -/36.
Fp, 17 mono phots, one sketch, no maps, no Index.

Apps: H&A, battle honours, stations, list of officers serving at 1957.

This is only a brief souvenir booklet which was not intended as a regtl
history. However, the appendixes contain many names, and this makes the
publication a useful secondary source. R/4 V/2. NAM. PJE.


A SHORT HISTORY OF THE 27th PUNJABIS

Anon
No  publication details shown, n.d. (c.1902)
Pale buff cloth on soft boards, red, 8.5 x 6.0, -/25.
no illustrations, no maps, no formal appendixes, no Index.

The regt was raised in June 1857 for service in the suppression of the
Mutiny, but saw little action. Then went overseas for the Second China
War but, again, had little opportunity to distinguish itself. This is a
very brief and basically unhelpful account  of some Frontier actions
and a record of dates, stations and movements through to 1902. A few
individual officers are mentioned by name. R/5 V/1. RP.


A HISTORY OF THE 26th PUNJABIS, 1857-1907

Lieut P S Stoney
The Pioneer Press, Allahabad, 1908
Brown boards with red spine and quarters, red, 7.5 x 5.0, iv/51.
no illustrations, no maps, no Index.

Apps: list of former officers, list of Subedar-Majors, records of
Inspections, notes on musketry and signalling.

Compiled from a Digest of Services and regtl office records. Very brief, but useful for checking important dates. R/4 V/2. NAM. PJE.


A HISTORY OF THE 26th PUNJABIS, 1857-1923
Compiled from the Digest of Services and Other Official Records

Lieut Col P S Stoney
Gale & Polden Ltd, Aldershot, 1924
Red, gold, regtl crest on front cover, 7.5 x 4.75, xii/144.
Fp, 15 mono phots, 4 maps (bound in), no Index.

Apps: Roll of Honour (WWI, British and Indian officers), H&A (WWI and Waziristan 1921-23), list of former officers (with details of those wounded), Inspection Reports, notes on musketry and signalling, list of former Subedar-Majors, extracts from Army Lists for 1858, 1907, and 1922, notes on final postings in 1923.

Stoney was the author of the 1908 edition (see previous entry), but this is a much more detailed book. A good useful history, with many individuals mentioned. The Bn served in Mesopotamia in WWI. The maps are of above-average quality. R/4 V/4. RMAS. MGHW/RP.


A SHORT HISTORY OF THE 4th BATTALION, 15th PUNJAB REGIMENT

Anon
Thacker & Co, Bombay, n.d. (c.1923)
Black, blind, regtl crest on front cover, 4.0 x 6.5, -/15.
no illustrations, no maps, no Index.

Apps: H&A (WWI only), list of former COs.

An extremely skimpy account, being mainly notes regarding stations, movements and postings. Possibly useful for dates and awards.
R/4 V/2. NAM. PJE.


HISTORY OF THE 1st BATTALION, 15th PUNJAB REGIMENT, 1857-1937
Compiled from the Battalion's Digest of Services and Other Official Documents

Lieut Col J E Shearer MC
Gale & Polden Ltd, Aldershot, 1937
Dark blue, gold, regtl crest on front cover, 8.5 x 5.25, xi/100.
Fp, 17 mono phots, no maps, no Index.

Apps: H&A, list of former COs, list of former officers, changes of unit designation, battle honours.

Despite being a fairly short narrative, this is a very useful history with all periods covered equally well. The photographs are good, and include several formal group pictures of officers (named in the captions). Originally the Lahore Punjab Bn, then the 17th Punjab Regt, then the 25th Regt of Bengal Native Infantry, then the 25th Punjabis. R/4 V/4. NAM. IOL. CSM/AMM.

NO GONGS FOR HEROES

Helene and John Scott
Unpublished facsimile typescript, 1979
Seen bound in yellow cover, 11.5 x 8.5, viii/149.
18 mono phots, 8 maps (bound in), Bibliography, no Index.

Apps: H&A, list of officers (British and Indian).

This is an excellent description of SARFOR (Sarawak Force), of which
2/15th Punjab Regt was the main part. The narrative deals with their
services in the early part of WWII, and the experiences of the survivors
as prisoners of the Japanese. R/5 V/4. NAM. PJE.


THE STORY OF THE 33rd PUNJABIS, 1857-1925

Anon
Scottish Mission Industries, Poona, 1925
Black, gold, regtl crest on front cover, 6.25 x 5.0, i/31.
no illustrations, no maps, no appendixes, no Index.

This is a brief summary of their history, based upon formal regtl
records. The WWI coverage is the most useful element for reference
purposes. R/4 V/2. NAM. PJE.


REGIMENTAL HISTORY: VAN COURTLAND'S LEVY
Afterwards called Bloomfield's Sikhs, 23rd Punjab Regiment, 35th Punjab
Infantry, 31st Punjabis, 2nd Bn 16th Punjab Regiment

Brig Gen A G Kemball
Thacker & Co Ltd, Bombay, 1926
Green, gold, 8.25 x 6.0, -/48 (last 10 pages not numbered)
Fp, 7 mono phots, no maps, no Index.

Apps: H&A (WWI only, all ranks), lists of former British and Indian
officers (for 31st Punjabis only).

At Ferozepore, in May 1857, Deputy Commissioner van Courtland received
orders to raise three companies of Sikhs for service against mutinied
regiments of the Bengal Army. He gave the task to Capt G C Bloomfield,
hence the unit's initial titles. This book is mainly a condensed diary
of events for the period 1857-1918. Although very brief, it is a
useful source of reference, and the photographs (tipped in) are
particularly good. R/5 V/3. RMAS. RP.


HISTORICAL RECORDS OF THE 4th BATTALION 16th PUNJAB REGIMENT

Anon (but probably a Regtl Committee of Maj C C Jackson, Lieut Col G D
Martin MC, and Col H H Smith DSO)
Gale & Polden Ltd, for the Regiment, Aldershot, 1931
Red, gold, 9.0 x 5.5, x/173.
line drawings of badges on title page, no other illustrations, 8 maps
(bound in), Index.

Apps: Roll of Honour (WWI), H&A (WWI), list of former COs, list of former officers, list of Honorary Colonels, notes on units which supplied drafts during WWI.


This was a local corps until 1903 and did not take part in any major campaigns apart from a minor role in the Second Afghan War. The greater part of the narrative is devoted to WWI services in France and Mesopotamia, and these are described in good detail. R/3 V/4. NAM. MCJ.


I AM READY
The Story of the 2nd and 3rd Battalions, 16th Punjab Regiment

Anon
Unpublished typescript, n.d.
Seen in card covers, khaki, black, 13.0 x 8.5, -/42.
no illustrations, 7 maps (bound in), no Index.

Apps: Roll of Honour, H&A.

This is a very good description of the part played by the 2nd Bn in Malaya and its subsequent experiences in Japanese captivity. R/5 V/4. NAM. PJE.


SOLAH PUNJAB
The History of the 16th Punjab Regiment

Lieut Col J P Lawford MC and Major W E Catto
Gale & Polden Ltd, Aldershot, 1967
Green, gold, regtl crest on front cover, 8.75 x 5.5, xiii/302.
30 mono phots, 28 maps (26 printed in text, 2 printed on end-papers), no Index.

Apps: H&A (WWI only).

A good clear narrative account which covers the period 1818 to 1945. Devoted (page 29 onwards) to WWI services (France, Mesopotamia, East Africa and Palestine), and to WWII services (Abyssinia, North Africa, Italy, Malaya and Burma). The book itself is an 'economy' production in terms of paper and binding quality, but the story is well researched and gives a comprehensive account of each of the regt's various battalions. R/1 V/4. NAM. IOL. RP.


30th PUNJABIS

James Lawford MC MA
Osprey Publishing Ltd, Reading, Berks (UK), 1972
Soft card covers, 'Perfect' binding, 9.75 x 7.25, -/40.
28 mono phots, 22 coloured illustrations, no maps, no appendixes, no Index.

This booklet is mainly of interest to students of dress, uniform,
insignia and equipment. Some excellent coloured drawings (including
a fine depiction of a Sepoy on the front cover) by Michael Youens.
The black-and-white photographs are also helpful. The author provides
a condensed but very interesting account of the Bn's services through to
operations in Java in 1946. The 30th Punjabis were re-designated the
1st Bn 16th Punjab Regt. R/2  V/3. PCAL. RP.


HISTORY OF THE 46th PUNJABIS
A Memoir

Brigadier A F F Thomas CIE
Unpublished facsimile typescript, n.d. (but probably c.1970)
Seen casebound in green, black, 13.0 x 8.0, iii/17/11.
no illustrations in the copy seen, no maps, no Index.

Apps: lists of officers serving in 1900, 1914 and 1921.

This memoir contains 17 pages of narrative (mainly regarding the period
1914-1922), with 11 pages of appendixes. Although very brief, it is a
good source for references to individual officers. R/5 V/3. RMAS. MGHW.


THE STORY OF THE 1st AND 2nd BATTALIONS, 41st DOGRAS
Volume I: October 1900 to December 1923, and October 1917 to March 1922

Anon ('Officers of the Regiment')
Thacker & Co, Bombay, for the Regiment, n.d. (c.1923)
Full Morocco, black, gold, regtl crest and battle honours on front cover,
9.25 x 7.0, -/146.
Fp, 14 mono phots, 5 maps (bound in), Index.

Apps: Roll of Honour (British and Indian officers only), H&A (all ranks),
list of former COs, list of former officers (British and Indian).

The regt was formed at Jullundur in 1900 and the two Bns saw service
in France, Egypt and Mesopotamia. This is an excellently prepared and
presented book, with an attractive binding. The narrative is well-
written, and the appendixes are particularly useful for biographical
research (the H&A section includes details of all IDSM and IOM awards,
foreign awards, full citations where appropriate, and details of
Recommendations). R/3 V/5. NAM. RP.


THE DOGRA QUARTERLY
The War Years
Colonel R C B Bristow and Lieut Col R W D Gloyne
The Civil & Military Gazette Press, Lahore, 1946
Paper covers, ivory, blue, regtl crest on front cover, 8.5 x 5.5, iii/184.
7 mono phots, no maps, no Index.

Apps: Roll of Honour, H&A.

This is an excellent account of the activities and achievements of the
17th Dogra Regt in WWII. The narrative covers the services of the
regular battalions (1st, 2nd and 3rd), the war-raised battalions
(4th, 5th, 6th, 7th MG, 25th and 26th), and the Regtl Training Centre.
Contains all the usual information of interest to members of the regiment
at that time: promotions, awards, casualties, personalities, etc.
R/5 V/4. HRC.


A HISTORY OF THE 1st (P.W.O.) BATTALION, THE DOGRA REGIMENT, 1887-1947
37th Dogras 1887-1922, 1st (P.W.O.) Bn, 17th Dogra Regt 1922-1945

C T Atkinson
Printed by the Camelot Press Ltd, Southampton, for the Regiment, 1950
Blue, gold, 8.0 x 5.5, xiii/210.
Fp, 39 mono phots, 28 maps (printed in text), Index.

Apps: H&A, list of former COs, idem officers who served, idem Subedar-
Majors.

A narrative account which provides a moderately good coverage for the
period 1887-1914, a more detailed account of WWI services in France, and
then excellent coverage of WWII services. The photographs are particularly
good. An essential reference source for this bn. R/4 V/4. IOL. MCJ.


HISTORY, 2nd Bn THE DOGRA REGIMENT (1891-1942)

Lieut Col W B Cunningham and Lieut Col J N Phelps
Krishan Sudama Press, Ferozepore, n.d. (c.1958)
Blue, gold, 3 regtl badges on front cover, 10.0 x 6.5, iii/334.
no illustrations, no maps, no Index.

Apps: H&A, list of former COs, list of former officers, stations and
movements, notes on casualties (1891-1931).

A readable and detailed history of the Bn for the period stated, but
dealing mainly with WWI and operations on the North West Frontier.
R/3 V/3. NAM. PJE.


THE DOGRA REGIMENT, A SAGA OF GALLANTRY AND VALOUR
A Historical Record 1858-1981

Colonel R D Palsokar MC
The Dogra Regimental Centre, Faizabad, 1982
Black, gold, regtl crest on spine, 10.0 x 7.0, iv/590.
Fp, 179 mono phots, 2 coloured plates, one line drawing of early uniform,
55 maps (printed in text), Bibliography, Index.

Apps: H&A, list of former COs, list of former Subedar-Majors, notes on the
regtl march.

This is a readable and informative unified history of all the various
Dogra battalions. The maps are well presented; the many photographs have
not reproduced well (due to the usual difficulties with equipment and
paper in Indian publishing houses). Colonel Palsokar is a well-known
military historian and it is stated that his narrative contains only a few
minor inaccuracies. He covers the Frontier campaigns and Chitral, then
WWI operations in France, Mesopotamia, Aden and Palestine. Dogras were
engaged in the Third Afghan War, Waziristan 1921-23, Khajuri Plain,
the Burma Rebellion, and Waziristan 1936-39. The WWII section covers the
activities of all 17 battalions which served. The final section describes
Dogra Regt involvements in the various post-1947 campaigns. Although the
book is said to have been printed in limited numbers, copies are to be
found in all the main military libraries. R/3 V/4. NAM. IOL. RMAS. HRC.


HISTORICAL RECORD OF THE 39th ROYAL GARHWAL RIFLES
Volume I: 1887-1922

Brig Gen J Evatt DSO
Gale & Polden Ltd, Aldershot, for the Regiment, 1922
Rifle green, gold, regtl crest on front cover, page marker riband in
regtl colours, 10.0 x 7.25, xiv/215.
Fp, 89 mono phots, 16 maps (11 bound in, 5 loose in rear pocket),
Bibliography, no Index.

Apps: Roll of Honour (British officers with details of war service,
Indian officers named if KIA but without such details), H&A (for 1887-
1922, with citations), list of former officers (British and Indian),
notes on the 1/50th Kumaon Rifles and the Tehri Imperial Service Sappers.

This is a very handsome book, well-written and admirably produced. Despite
dates given in the sub-title, much of the narrative is devoted to WWI
services (France and Mesopotamia). A package of 'addenda and corrigenda'
slips was sent out to all subscribers about one year after publication,
but these slips are now rarely seen. A copy of the book with the slips
in place is clearly preferable to one without. Some of the books were
sold with an additional page bound in, showing the name of an individual
officer and headed 'In honoured memory of ...'. These may have been
presentation copies (from the Regiment) to the next-of-kin of officers
who died. R/4 V/5. NAM. IOL. RP.
The original 1922 edition was reprinted at Lansdowne, Garhwal, sometime
around 1975. It is a facsimile reprint, having 215 pages and all the
same contents including the bound-in maps, but lacking the loose maps
in a rear pocket. This edition is bound in black cloth with gold lettering.
The overall quality is very good.


STANDING ORDERS OF THE 18th ROYAL GARHWAL RIFLES

Anon
The Pioneer Press, Allahabad, 1928
Dark green boards, red spine, gold, 10.0 x 6.5, vi/104.
no illustrations, no maps, no Index.

Apps: customs and traditions in rifle regiments, notes on sports trophies, Hindu holidays, notes on dress and uniform (all ranks), notes on common Garhwali Rajput names, clans and castes, showing their phonetic spelling with equivalent Roman and Devanagri characters.

This is a typical volume of Standing Orders which has been included here because so little has been written about Garhwali soldiers, and some of the appendixes could certainly be of interest to the researcher. R/5 V/3. LBR.


WITH THE ROYAL GARHWAL RIFLES IN THE GREAT WAR
From August 1914 to November 1917

Brig Gen D H Drake-Brockman CMG
Publication details not shown, n.d. (c.1934)
Dark green, gold, 10.0 x 7.25, -/164.
33 mono phots, 14 maps (13 printed in text, one bound in at rear), no Index.

Apps: H&A, list of officers who served, copies of orders for various operations.

The interesting and informative narrative was written, according to the Preface, 'by someone who was there', and it certainly has a sound feeling of authenticity. The regt had two active service Bns in WWI, and the services of both are well described. R/3 V/4. NAM. IOL. CSM.


HISTORICAL RECORD OF THE ROYAL GARHWAL RIFLES
Volume II: 1923-1947

Lieut Gen Sir R B Deedes
The Army Press, Dehra Dun, 1962
Black boards, green spine, gold, regtl crest on front cover, 9.5 x 7.5, xxxv/276.
Fp, 27 mono phots, 26 maps (folding, bound in), no Index.

Apps: Roll of Honour, H&A, list of former officers, notes on battle honours for WWII.

This volume continues the history commenced by Evatt in his 1922 volume (see page 154). It has a good readable narrative with plenty of interesting detail. R/3 V/4. NAM. PJE.


HISTORY OF THE HYDERABAD CONTINGENT

Major R G Burton
The Superintendent of Government Printing, Calcutta, 1905
Dark green, gold, regtl crest on front cover, 9.0 x 6.0, vi/410.
5 sketches, no other illustrations, 6 maps (folding, bound in), Index.

Apps: list of former COs, list of former Residents, notes on the cost, strengths and services of the Contingent.

A readable and informative history for the period pre-1806 through to 1903 when the Contingent was disbanded. The researcher should consult Donovan Jackson and/or Philip Mason for details of the unit's roots and evolution. R/5 V/3. IOL. USII. NAM. PJE.


STANDING ORDERS FOR THE 3/19th HYDERABAD REGIMENT, 19th INDIAN INFANTRY GROUP

Anon
The Commercial Press, Quetta, 1924
Red, black, 9.5 x 7.0, -/92.
no illustrations, no maps, no appendixes, no Index.

This is simply a compilation of Standing Orders issued by the Commanding Officer, with amendments issued thereafter. It has been included here because it is the only known publication referring specifically to this battalion. R/5 V/2. USII. OSS.


REGIMENTAL HISTORY OF THE 2/19th HYDERABAD REGIMENT (BERAR)

Lieut Col J de L Conry
Gale & Polden Ltd, Aldershot, 1927
Dark green, gold, regtl crest on front cover, 7.25 x 5.0, -/32.
no illustrations, no maps, no appendixes, no Index.

A very superficial history covering the period 1780 to 1922.
Based upon regtl records. There is mention of the Bn's services in the Mutiny campaign, in Burma, and in Mesopotamia in WWI. R/4 V/2. NAM. PJE.


HISTORY OF THE 1st BATTALION, 19th HYDERABAD REGIMENT (RUSSELL'S)

Anon
Gale & Polden Ltd, Aldershot, 1928
Dark green, gold, regtl crest on front cover, 7.25 x 5.0, ii/31.
no illustrations, no maps, no appendixes, no Index.

Like the previous entry, this one refers also to a brief summary for a very long period (1813-1928). Based upon regtl orders. There is reference to services in the Deccan under, first, the Nizam, and, later, under the British. The Bn served in Mesopotamia in WWI. R/4 V/2. NAM .PJE.


THE STORY OF THE 97th DECCAN INFANTRY

Major W C Kirkwood
The Government Central Press, Hyderabad, 1929
Dark green, gold, regtl crest on front cover, 10.0 x 7.0, iii/165.
Fp, 20 mono phots, one map (bound in), no Index.

Apps: Roll of Honour (WWI), H&A (WWI), list of former officers.

This is a readable and reasonably detailed history. It covers the early
wars in Southern India and then the Bn's services in Mesopotamia in WWI.
R/4 V/3. NAM. PJE.


A HISTORY OF THE 4th BATTALION, 19th HYDERABAD REGIMENT

G G C Bull
Gales & Polden Ltd, Aldershot, 1933
Dark green, gold, regtl crest on front cover, 7.5 x 5.0, iv/57.
no illustrations, no maps, no Index.

Apps: list of former COs, list of former Adjutants, stations and movements.

A generalised account of the period 1788-1933. There is some description
of the Bn's services during the Mutiny, on the Frontier, and in East
Africa during WWI. R/4 V/2. RMAS. NAM. MGHW.
The Preface states: 'This History replaces a previous edition printed in
1929'. Another edition, dated 1939, has also been reported (with identical
features to the 1933 version described above). Neither of these variants
have been seen.


VALOUR TRIUMPHS
A History of the Kumaon Regiment

K C Praval
The Thompson Press (India), Faridabad, 1976
Green, gold, 10.0 x 6.5, xv/443.
Fp, 49 mono phots, 26 maps (bound in), Bibliography, Index.

Apps: H&A, list of former COs, list of former Subedar-Majors.

A readable and detailed history covering the period 1813-1972. The first
160 pages deal with pre-1947 services. The Kumaon Regiment is descended
from the old Hyderabad Contingent, later the 19th Hyderabad Regiment,
being renamed Kumaon Regiment in 1945 and the prefix '19' being then
discarded. Praval is an excellent military historian, and he has included
in this fine book some very interesting early photographs of Viceroy's
Commissioned Officers, a picture of Lord Robert's orderly (Boer War),
and pictures of regtl badges. R/2 V/5. IOL. NAM. MCJ.


STANDING ORDERS OF THE SECOND BATTALION, THE BURMA RIFLES
With a Short Record of the Battalion

Anon
Gale & Polden Ltd, Aldershot, 1948
Green, gold, dimensions not known, x/142.
Noted thus in a catalogue, but not seen. The Bn was first raised in 1917
as 2/70th Burma Rifles.

HISTORY OF THE MAHAR REGIMENT

Major B N Mittra
Printed by The Statesman Press, New Delhi, for the Regiment, 1972
Brown, white, 9.5 x 6.5, vi/216.
97 mono phots, 5 coloured plates, 6 sketches, 2 maps (printed on end-
papers), no Index.

Apps: Roll of Honour, H&A, list of former COs, notes on the music of the
regt, list of old units in which Mahars served prior to 1941, notes on
cap badges and shoulder titles.

Major Mittra was serving with the regt at the time when he compiled this
book. It is a good narrative account of the Regt's origins and evolution,
particularly with regard to the early days. His account formed the basis
for the professionally written FOREFRONT FOR EVER (see following entry).
R/2. V/4. JWW.


FOREFRONT FOR EVER
History of the Mahar Regiment

V Longer
Printed by Allied Publisher Pte Ltd, New Delhi, for the Regiment, 1981
Maroon, gold, 9.5 x 6.5, v/300.
130 mono phots, 19 coloured plates, 5 sketches, 9 maps (one printed on
end-papers, 8 bound in), no Index.

Apps: Roll of Honour (for all ranks and all post-1947 campaigns),
H&A (WWII and all post-1947 campaigns), list of former COs, notes on
regtl music, notes on old units in which Mahars served prior to 1941,
notes on badges and shoulder titles.

A readable, accurate and well-documented narrative which describes not only
the history of the regt but also its development in the context of the
history of India and the history of the Indian Army. The regt was first
raised at Belgaum on 1 October 1941 by Brigadier H J R Jackson. The 1st
Bn served mainly on internal security duties in India during WWII, 2nd Bn
served in Burma and then, in late 1945, in Iran and Iraq. The 3rd Bn
was on the NWF throughout the war. Recruiting was restricted initially
to the Mahars, the indigenous low-caste Hindu people of the old Bombay
Presidency.  Mahars had been recruited for their martial qualities by
various regts in the 19th century, but the practice was discontinued in
1892. Recruitment recommenced briefly in 1917 with the formation of the
111th Mahars, but they were disbanded in 1922. Today the Mahar Regt is an
important component of the Indian Army. R/2 V/5. JWW.


HISTORICAL RECORD OF THE 88th CARNATIC INFANTRY

Anon
Printed at The Edward Press, Cannanore, 1913
Soft card covers, grey, black, 8.0 x 5.0, -/139.
no illustrations, no maps, no Index.

This is a dry and somewhat terse summary of engagements between 1798 and 1909. The main campaigns were: Travancore (1809), the Mahratta Wars (1815-1818), First Burma War (1825-1826), the Mutiny (1857-1859), Third China War (1900, occupation duties at Tientsin and Tongshon). There are no formal appendixes in this book, but the final seven chapters fulfil the same purpose. They contain notes on uniforms and weaponry, alterations to the unit's establishment, notes on badges and insignia, names of officers who distinguished themselves, names of officers killed and wounded, stations and movements. The Regt was disbanded after WWI, and this is its only known published history. R/4 V/4. BM. IOL. PJE/RGB.

## MERCENARY INFANTRY

### HIS MAJESTY'S REGIMENT DE MEURON

Julian James Cotton, Madras Civil Service
Printed by The City Press, Calcutta, for the author, 1903
Red, gold, 9.0 x 5.5, -/43.
no illustrations, no maps, no appendixes, no Index.

A readable and informative history, probably the only one ever written, of this Swiss professional mercenary regiment founded by Charles Daniel de Meuron, at Neuchatel, in 1781. The regiment was raised for service under the Dutch East India Company in Ceylon. When that island was captured by the British in 1795, de Meuron negotiated successfully with their agents for the transfer of his entire regiment into temporary Crown service. Four years later it took part in the assault at Seringapatam under the command of Colonel Arthur Wellesley. Subsequently it served in North America, but was then disbanded in 1817. The narrative contains the names of many individual officers, and gives details of numerical strengths and national compositions at different dates. R/5 V/4. SSL. TA.

## AIRBORNE FORCES

### INDIA'S PARATROOPERS
A History of the Parachute Regiment of India

K C Praval
Thomson Press (India) Ltd, Faridabad, 1974
Blue, yellow, 8.75 x 5.75, xiv/366.
Fp, 50 mono phots, one sketch, 30 maps, Bibliography, Index.

Apps: H&A (1947-1948), list of former COs, notes on aircraft used.

A good narrative account of the raising of 50th Indian Parachute Brigade in 1941, and its subsequent services in Burma. A medical sub-unit served with the Commonwealth forces in Korea, and the Regt has taken part in India's other post-1947 campaigns. R/1 V/3. MCJ.
Published also by Leo Cooper, London, 1975.

**APPENDIX III**

Designation of Indian Infantry regiments
following the Re-organisations of 1922

1st Punjab Regiment

2nd Punjab Regiment

3rd Madras Regiment

4th Bombay Grenadiers

5th Mahratta Light Infantry

6th Rajputana Rifles

7th Rajput Regiment

8th Punjab Regiment

9th Jat Regiment

10th Baluch Regiment

11th Sikh Regiment

12th Frontier Force Regiment

13th Frontier Force Rifles

14th Punjab Regiment

15th Punjab Regiment

16th Punjab Regiment

17th Dogra Regiment

18th Royal Garhwal Rifles

19th Hyderabad Regiment

20th Burma Rifles

# INDIA - PUNJAB FRONTIER FORCE

A BRIEF ACCOUNT OF THE PUNJAB FRONTIER FORCE FROM ORIGINATION IN 1849 TO REDISTRIBUTION ON 31.3.1903

Rai Sahib Boydo Nath Dey
W Newman & Co, at the Caxton Press, Abbottobad, 1903
Dark red, gold, 7.5 x 5.0, -/85.
no illustrations, no maps, no Index.

Apps: notes on regts and batteries (when, where and by whom raised), list of former COs, with lists of former Assistant Adjutants-General, Principal Medical Officers, and other senior officers.

The author was the former Head Clerk to the Force. The PFF was first raised by the Marquis of Dalhousie to guard the 600 miles of Punjab Frontier. Known colloquially as 'the Piffers', the force was under the direct control of the Lieutenant Governor of the Punjab until 1886 when it was assigned to the Indian Army. Although brief, this is an excellent history, with many individuals (British and Indian) named in the text. It is useful also for tracing the evolution of the Force. R/3 V/3. USII. NAM. IOL. RGB/BDM/LD.

Several examples of this book have been seen. The 1903 edition (as described here) seems to have been published in both cloth and leather. A 1905 version (apparently identical) has been reported in blue cloth.

THE PUNJAB FRONTIER FORCE
A Brief Record of their Services, 1846-1924

R E F G North
The Commercial Steam Press, Dera Ismail Khan, 1934
Dark green, gold, 10.5 x 7.5, xi/95.
no illustrations, one map (loose in rear pocket), Bibliography, no Index.

Apps: H&A, list of former permanent Commandants, note on the Frontier Force War Memorial(1914-1918).

This is a very brief and very condensed history, arranged under a series of headings for each component unit, with only one or two lines devoted to the annual activities of each unit. Useful as a source for checking important dates in the life of a particular unit, but otherwise quite limited in its scope. R/3 V/2. NAM. PJE.

ONE HUNDRED GLORIOUS YEARS
The History of the Punjab Frontier Force, 1849-1949

Major General M Hayand Din
The Civil & Military Gazette Press, Lahore, 1950
Red, black, front cover embellished with regtl colours, 9.0 x 7.0, iv/36.
no illustrations, no maps, Bibliography, no Index.

Apps: H&A, list of former Commandants (to 1903 only), notes on the
raising of particular component units, battle honours, notes on regtl music.

The author attempts to cover 100 years and numerous units in the space
of 36 pages. Many individuals are named in the text, but there is very
little in the way of detail. R/2 V/2. NAM. PJE.


THE WARDENS OF THE MARCHES
A History of the Piffers, 1947-71

Major General M Attiqur Rahman MC
Wajidalis, Lahore, 1980
Dark green, gold, 9.0 x 6.0, xv/255.
Fp, 19 mono phots, 12 maps (bound in), Index.

Apps: Roll of Honour, H&A, list of former COs, battle honours, notes on
changes of title.

Only a small proportion is dedicated to pre-1947 services. The rest is a
full account of the Indo-Pakistan and Bangladesh wars. R/1 V/3. PJE.

INDIA - PIONEERS

32nd SIKH PIONEERS
Volume I: Delhi 1857, Waziristan 1902

Lieut Col H R Brandon
Thacker, Spink & Co, Calcutta, 1906
Red, black, 7.5 x 5.0, x/204.
Fp, no other illustrations, no maps, no Index.

Apps: notes on the Mahzbi (Muzbee) Sikhs, notes on the Delhi Pioneers and
the Punjab Pioneers, extracts from Army Lists.

Originally a scratch force of civilian canal-diggers, raised hurriedly in
1857 to assist in the siege operations at Delhi, the Muzbee Sikhs
evolved into one of the Indian Army's most famous fighting regts. This
account covers the period 1857 to 1902, and is informative and interesting.
R/4 V/3. USII. OSS.


32nd SIKH PIONEERS
Volume II: Sikkim and Tibet 1903-04

Lieut Col H R Brandon
Edward Stanford, London, 1905
Red, black, 7.25 x 5.0, -/105.
one topographical sketch, 4 maps (folding, bound in), no Index.

Apps: Roll of Honour (British officers only, 1857-1904), list of former
COs, stations and movements (1857-1904), recipients of the Indian Order
of Merit (1858-1904) with details.

An excellent account of the regt's role in the Tibet campaign. Many
individuals mentioned in the narrative, with details of their actions and
awards. R/4 V/5. RMAS. USII. NAM. RP.


THE HISTORY OF THE SIKH PIONEERS
(23rd, 32nd, 34th)

Lieut Gen Sir George MacMunn KCB KCSI DSO
Printed by Purnell & Son Ltd, for Sampson Low, Marston & Co Ltd, n.d.(c.1936)
Red, gold, four regtl crests on front cover, figure of a standing
Pioneer soldier on the spine, 9.5 x 6.25, xvi/560.
Fp, 45 mono phots, 4 maps (2 bound in, 2 printed on end-papers), Index.

Apps: list of former COs, biographies of 9 famous members of the regt.

A magnificent work, giving uniform and detailed coverage from 1857 through
to 1932. Incorporates much of the material to be found in Brandon's two
volumes (see previous entries), but updated to include WWI. A very desirable
book. R/4 V/5. NAM. IOL. RP.

A SHORT HISTORY OF THE 23rd SIKH PIONEERS

Captain H M Pirouet
G F Amary, Finchley, London, 1927
Brown, dark brown, 5.0 x 4.5, -/68.
11 mono phots, no maps, no Index.

Apps: Roll of Honour, list of former COs, list of former officers.

A fairly condensed account of the period 1857 to 1923. Informative.
R/5 V/3. USII. OSS.


RECORDS OF THE IV MADRAS PIONEERS (NOW 64th PIONEERS) 1759-1903

Major H F Murland
Higginbothams Ltd, Bangalore, 1922
Dark blue, gold, 11.25 X 8.5, -/314.
no illustrations, no maps, Bibliography, no Index.

Apps: list of former COs, list of former officers, idem Warrant Officers.

A history in expanded diary form. The author gives particular attention
to the origins and evolution of the regt, and to its earlier campaigns:
Haidar Ali (1760s), Pondicherry (1778), and Tippoo Sahib (1792-99).
There is also good coverage of various Frontier campaigns and the Third
China War. A very helpful reference source. R/4 V/4. IOL. RGB.


REGIMENTAL RECORDS OF 2nd BATTALION, 1st MADRAS PIONEERS, 1903-25

Anon ('Committee of the Regiment')
2nd Bn 1st Madras Pioneers Press, Madras, 1926
Dark blue, gold, 10.5 x 8.25, -/235.
no illustrations, no maps, no formal appendixes, no Index.

A very detailed history in diary form, dedicated mainly to the WWI period.
The Bn served in Mesopotamia and Palestine (1916-1919), Persia (1919-
1921), and then in the suppression of the Moplah Rebellion (1921-1922).
There are no appendixes, but Chapters IV and V contain comprehensive lists
of British officers who served (1903-1925) with biographical notes for
each. Lists of Indian officers are also included in the narrative.
R/4 V/4. IOL. USII. RGB.


BAILLIE-KI-PALTAN
Being a History of the 2nd Battalion, Madras Pioneers (Formerly the
IV Madras Pioneers), 1759-1930

Lieut Col H F Murland
Higginbothams, Madras, 1932
Blue, gold, regtl crest on front cover, 10.0 x 8.5, viii/602.
Fp, no other illustrations, 24 maps (4 folding and bound in, 20 printed in
the text), Bibliography, partial Index (British officers only).

Apps: list of former COs, list of former officers (British and Indian), a selected list of senior other ranks.

A comprehensive and detailed history, well laid out, in five parts for ease of reading and reference. The maps are particularly well executed. The regt was disbanded in 1933. R/4 V/4. NAM. IOL. TA.


HISTORICAL RECORD OF THE 21st REGIMENT, BOMBAY NATIVE INFANTRY OR MARINE BATTALION

Anon ('A Committee of the Regiment')
The Education Society's Press, Bombay, 1875
Light blue, gold, 9.5 x 6.0, -/57.
no illustrations, no maps, no appendixes, no Index.

A simple compendium of reports, stations, etc. Originally raised in 1777 for maritime duties in the Arabian Sea and Persian Gulf, hence the secondary title (Marine). Was at that time attached to the Bombay Marine (HEIC Navy). Converted in 1818 into a regular regiment of Pioneers (121st Pioneers in 1903, 10th Bn 2nd Bombay Pioneers in 1922). Served against pirate forces in the Gulf and fought in the Mahratta War of 1817-18. R/4 V/2. IOL. RGB.


PIONEERS ON FOUR FRONTS
Being a Record of the Doings of the 107th Pioneers, now 1/2 Regiment of Pioneers, in the Great War

Edwin Haward
The Civil & Military Gazette Press, Lahore, 1923
Dark green, gold, 8.75 x 5.5, -/63.
no illustrations, 4 maps (bound in at rear), Index.

Apps: Roll of Honour, H&A (1914-20), lists of COs, officers, Adjutants, and Subedar-Majors from inception in 1796 to 1923, etc.

A dry but quite detailed summary of WWI services in France, Mesopotamia, Waziristan and East Persia. Useful mainly for the detailed appendixes of personnel. R/4 V/3. NAM. IOL. RGB.


HISTORY OF THE BOMBAY PIONEERS, 1777-1933

Lieut Col W B P Tugwell
The Sydney Press Ltd, Bedford, 1938
Half leather, half cloth, blue, gold, regtl crest on front cover, 8.75 x 5.5, xix/439.
Fp, 43 mono phots, 8 coloured plates, 17 maps (14 printed in text, 3 bound in), Bibliography, Index.

Apps: too numerous to list here, all excellent.

One of the most comprehensive and handsomely produced of all Indian
unit histories. The narrative covers the period from 1790 through to the
Waziristan campaign of 1920-22, with good coverage of the First Afghan
War, the Mutiny, Abyssinia, Second Afghan War, Frontier operations, and
Somaliland 1902-04. The second half of the book is devoted entirely to WWI
services in France, Mesopotamia, Palestine and Persia. The regt was
disbanded in 1932. R/3 V/5. NAM. RP.


HISTORY OF THE 121st PIONEERS

W B P Tugwell
The Regimental Printing Press, Meerut, 1918
Stiff card covers, olive green, gold, 7.25 x 5.5, i/33.
no illustrations, no maps, no appendixes, no Index.

A readable but extremely superficial account of the period 1777 to 1917.
All the major campaigns during that time are mentioned, but with very
little detail. R/4 V/1. NAM. PJE.


A BRIEF HISTORY OF THE 106th HAZARA PIONEERS

Brig Gen N L S P Bunbury
Unpublished typescript, 1949
Seen in card covers, multi-coloured, ink lettering, 9.0 x 7.0, -/25.

After 1922, this regt became the 1st Bn 4th Hazara Pioneers, and this
brief unpublished typescript is their only known recorded history.
Copies are held by several military libraries, and it is a useful
reference source. The narrative is well-written and includes a list of COs
and a list of officers serving in July 1913. The period covered is 1903-
1933, and includes reference to WWI services and to operations in Siberia.
R/5 V/2. IOL. NAM. PJE.

## INDIA - ENGINEERS AND SAPPERS & MINERS
## GENERAL ACCOUNTS

THE MILITARY ENGINEER IN INDIA
Volume I

Lieut Col E W C Sandes
Mackays Ltd, Chatham, for the Institution of Royal Engineers, 1933
Red, gold, Corps crest on front cover, 9.5 x 6.5, xxiii/594.
Fp, 17 mono phots, 18 maps (12 printed in text, 6 loose in rear pocket),
Index.

Apps: notes on each of the component Corps (Bengal, Madras and Bombay),
notes on the abolition of the Pioneers.

An excellent and very full historical account, in great detail, for the
period 1640 to 1932. Covers every campaign in which HEIC and Indian Army
forces took part. R/4 V/5. USII. NAM. PJE.


THE MILITARY ENGINEER IN INDIA
Volume II

Lieut Col E W C Sandes
Mackays Ltd, Chatham, for the Institution of Royal Engineers, 1935
Red, gold, Corps crest on front cover, 9.5 x 6.5, xxi/392.
Fp, 40 mono phots, 9 maps (5 printed in text, 4 loose in rear pocket),
no appendixes, Index.

An excellent and very full historical account of all aspects of the civil
and marine engineering work carried out in India by Engineers and by
Sappers & Miners. Covers the period 1800 to 1930. R/4 V/5. NAM. PJE.


THE INDIAN SAPPERS & MINERS

Lieut Col E W C Sandes
W & J Mackay & Co Ltd, Chatham, for the Institution of Royal Engineers,
1948
Red, gold, Corps crest on front cover, 9.5 x 6.0, xxx/726.
Fp, 30 mono phots, 55 maps (52 bound in, 3 loose in rear pocket), Index.

Apps: condensed histories of: Queen Victoria's Own Madras Sappers & Miners,
King George V's Own Bengal S&M, Royal Bombay S&M, Burma S&M, Indian State
S&M, Railway S&M, Indian Submarine Mining & Defence Light Units S&M,
Indian Signals Unit S&M.

Possibly the most complete Corps history ever written. The Index section
alone runs to 18 pages. The highly readable narrative is packed with
references to individuals, minor actions and small units. The story covers
the period 1759 to 1939 in uniform detail, and the maps are exceptionally helpful. An incomparable source of reference. R/3 V/5. NAM. RP.

HISTORY OF 10th INDIAN DIVISIONAL ENGINEERS IN ITALY

Lieut Col G F Hutchinson
Publication details not shown,1946
Black, gold, 9.5 x 6.0, ii/63.
no illustrations, 14 maps (RE Survey maps bound in), no Index.

Apps: lists of officers, notes on casualties.

A good readable narrative which covers the period from May 1944 to
May 1945. Based upon War Diaries, and full of informative detail.
R/5 V/4. NAM. PJE.


THE INDIAN ENGINEERS 1939-47

Lieut Col E W C Sandes
The Institution of Military Engineers, Kirkee, 1956
Red, gold, 4 Corps crests on front cover, 9.5 x 6.5, xxx/534.
Fp, 20 mono phots, 25 maps, Index.

Apps: notes on the condition of the Madras, Bengal and Bombay Engineer
Groups at the outbreak of war, 1939.

A very good readable history for the WWII period and a good description of
the impact of Partition. R/3 V/3. USII. NAM. BDM.


THE CORPS OF INDIAN ENGINEERS 1939-47

Major S Verna and Major V K Anand
The Controller of Publications, for the Historical Section, Ministry
of Defence, Delhi, 1974
Green, gold, 10.0 x 6.5, xii/486.
20 mono phots, 8 maps (bound in), Bibliography, no Index.

Apps: no less than 38 appendixes, and too many to list here. Most are
concerned with organisation and technical matters, although one is headed
'Officers who held senior engineering appointments in India during WWII'.

This book covers the same ground as Sandes' work (see previous entry), but
appears to enter more into technical engineering details than he did.
Deals with the campaigns in North Africa, East Africa, Italy, Malaya, Burma
and South East Asia. Extremely detailed, but perhaps mainly of interest
to the researcher of engineering subjects. R/2 V/4. IOL. RGB.


THEIR FORMATIVE YEARS
History of the Corps of Electrical and Mechanical Engineers (Volume I)

Lieut Col Rufus Simon
Vikas Publishing House PVT Ltd, New Delhi, 1977
Red, gold, Corps crest on front cover, 8.75 x 5.75, xxx/486.
Fp, 13 mono phots, 1 coloured plate, 3 maps (printed in text),
Bibliography, Index.

Although well-written and neatly presented, the narrative is fairly
hard work for the non-specialist. There is an astonishing total of 47
appendixes, all dealing with organisational and technical matters.
This Volume was the first of a planned four-Volume series, all to be
published by the Director of Electrical & Mechanical Engineers, Army HQ,
Delhi. It covers the evolution of the Corps, commencing with the
appointment in 1895 of Capt W E Donohue as the first Inspector of Ordnance
Machinery in the Indian Ordnance Department, and ending in mid-1945. The
second Volume in the series, to be entitled MANY SPLENDOURED ACTIVITY, was
intended to decribe the services of the IAOC Workshop Branch and IEME
units during WWII, but plans for this publication seem to have been
later abandoned (see following entry). R/2 V/5. IOL. RGB.


HISTORY OF THE CORPS OF ELECTRICAL AND MECHANICAL ENGINEERS, 1943-1971

Colonel Shushil Jagota VSM
Produced at the College of Electrical & Mechanical Engineering,
Secunderabad, for the Corps, 1981
Black, gold, 9.0 x 5.57, xxii/444.
Fp, 13 pages of mono phots, 5 coloured plates, 7 charts, 19 maps
(bound in), Bibliography, Index.

Apps: three in number, organisational and technical.

As the title indicates, this book covers the history of the Corps from
its inception in May, 1943, through to 1971. It is divided into four
sections, the first being a condensed version of THEIR FORMATIVE YEARS by
Simon (see previous entry), the second being an account of its WWII and
post-war occupation forces activities through to 1947, and the two
other sections then covering the post-Independence period. The result is a
very comprehensive Corps history containing all the information which
any researcher in this field is likely to require.
R/1 V/5. ESS.

# INDIA - SAPPERS & MINERS
## UNIT HISTORIES

HISTORY AND DIGEST OF SERVICE OF THE 1st KING GEORGE'S OWN SAPPERS & MINERS

Anon
1st King George's Own Press, Roorkee, n.d. (c.1911)
Marbled blue board, brown spine and quarters, black, 13.0 x 8.5, -/75.
no illustrations, no maps, no appendixes, no Index.

A brief summary of stations, movements and campaigns, covering the period
up to 1908. R/5 V/2. NAM. PJE.


A SHORT HISTORY OF THE CORPS OF KING GEORGE'S OWN BENGAL SAPPERS
& MINERS DURING THE WAR, 1914-18

Colonel A H Cunningham
Publication details not shown, 1930
Light blue boards, black spine and quarters, black, 13.0 x 8.5, -/85.
no illustrations, no maps, no Index.

Apps: H&A, list of officers who served (with details of record of
service), notes on unit strengths.

A brief account of WWI services based upon orders and records, with very
little detail. R/4 V/2. NAM. PJE.


REGIMENTAL HISTORY OF THE KING GEORGE'S OWN BENGAL SAPPERS & MINERS

Anon
HQ Printing Press, KGO Bengal Sappers & Miners Press, Roorkee, 1937
Stiff card covers, black boards, brown spine, black, 13.0 x 8.0, iii/38.
no illustrations, no maps, no appendixes, no Index.

Printed in English and Urdu (38 pages of print for each). It was used
until 1939 for the instruction of Indian Other Ranks, and covers all
the campaigns in which the Corps was engaged between 1803 and 1930. It
also deals with organisational matters up to 1933. Although brief, it
contains considerable detail (including instances of personal gallantry
during WWI). R/5 V/3. DCSD.


CALENDAR OF BATTLES, HONOURS AND AWARDS
King George V's Own Bengal Sappers and Miners from 1803 to 1939

Captain K S Rahmat Ullan Khan
Publication details not shown, n.d. (c.1945)
Blue, gold, gold embellishment, 13.0 x 8.5, -/63.
no illustrations, no maps, no appendixes, no Index.

As the title suggests, this is a compendium of information regarding all honours and awards gained by the regt and by regtl personnel in all the campaigns in which it took part during the period stated. Many, many names are listed. R/4 V/2. NAM. PJE.

BRIEF HISTORY OF THE KING GEORGE V's OWN BENGAL SAPPERS & MINERS GROUP R.I.E. (AUGUST 1939 - JULY 1946)

Lieut Col G Pearson
Publisher's details not shown, Roorkee, 1947
Dark blue, gold, Corps crest on front cover, 9.5 x 6.5, vi/153.
11 mono phots, 7 maps (bound in at rear), no Index.

Apps: H&A.

A detailed history of the Corps' involvements in the West Desert, Malaya, Burma and Italy. R/4 V/4. NAM. PJE.

HISTORICAL RECORD OF THE 'QUEEN'S OWN' SAPPERS AND MINERS
Containing an Account of the Establishment of Companies of Pioneers in 1870, the Formation of these Companies in Corps of Sappers and Miners in 1831, and the History of their Service from 1780 to 1876

Lieut Col W J Wilson
The Government Press, Madras, 1877
Card, grey, black, 9.25 x 6.5, -/104.

Apps: list of former COs, extracts from Madras Army Regulations (relating to Sappers & Miners), rules for tasks in trade testing.

A narrative account, arranged chronologically, covering the period 1780 to 1876. Many officers named in the text, with details of stations, movements and campaign services. R/5 V/3. IOL. AMM.

THE MILITARY HISTORY OF THE MADRAS ENGINEERS AND PIONEERS
From 1743 up to the Present Time, Volumes I and II

Major H M Vibert
W H Allen & Co, London, 1881 and 1883
Red, gold, 9.0 x 5.5 (both Volumes), xxiii/602 and xiv/627.
Fps, no illustrations, 23 maps in Volume I, 26 maps in Volume II, Bibliography in Volume I (but no Index), no Bibliography but an Index in Volume II (relating to both Volumes).

Apps: Roll of Honour (officers only), H&A (British and Indian officers), list of former Commandants and Chief Engineers, list of former officers.

Volume I covers the period 1743-1829, Volume II covers 1829-1879. This is a handsome and very well produced pair of books, with many individual officers mentioned in the narrative and with admirably full descriptions of battles and campaigns. R/4 V/5. IOL. AMM.

172

HISTORICAL RECORD OF THE 2nd 'QUEEN'S OWN' SAPPERS & MINERS
Volume I: 1780 to 1909

Lieut Col C H Roe
2nd 'Q.O.' Sappers & Miners Press, Bangalore, 1909
Dark red, gold, 9.5 x 6.5, -/486.
no illustrations, no maps, no Index.

Apps: Roll of Honour, H&A, list of former COs, list of former officers,
stations and movements.

The text is based upon regtl orders and records but, unusually, is full of
details of all kinds. It covers almost all Indian campaigns for the period
stated in the sub-title. R/4 V/5. IOL. AMM.


HISTORICAL RECORD OF THE 2nd 'QUEEN VICTORIA'S OWN' SAPPERS & MINERS
Volume II: 1910 to 1919

Lieut Col C H Roe
Sisters of the Good Shepherd Press, location not shown, 1950
Dark red, gold, Corps crest on front cover, ii/305.
no illustrations, no maps, no Index.

Apps: Roll of Honour, H&A, list of former COs, details of former officers,
stations and movements.

This (second) Volume has been given a separate entry here because, as can
be seen, the dimensions and printer details are slightly different to
those of Volume I. Both books are written, however, to the same high
standard. The narrative is somewhat dry and dusty, but it is extremely
comprehensive and is said to be a very reliable source of reference.
R/4 V/5. NAM. PJE.
It would seem that Volume I may have been reprinted in limited numbers in
1919 and sold to some purchasers of Volume II as a single combined volume,
i.e. the two productions stitched into the same binding.


HISTORICAL RECORD OF THE 2nd 'QUEEN VICTORIA'S OWN' SAPPERS & MINERS
FROM 1914 TO 1919

Lieut Col R L McClintock
2nd 'Q.V.O.' Sappers & Miners Press, Bangalore, 1921
Stiff card, yellow, black, 10.0 x 6.5, -/39.
no illustrations, no maps, no Index.

Apps: Roll of Honour, H&A, list of officers who served.

A brief narrative based upon official records. Quite detailed with regard
to their services in the Middle East, very few personnel mentioned in
the text. R/4 V/2. NAM. PJE.
The above entries have also been seen in a single binding, but marked
Vol I: 1780-1909, Vol II, Part 1: 1910-1914, Part II: 1914-1919,
Vol II (2): 1919-1923, Vol IV: 1923-1928, Vol V: 1929-1939.

QUEEN VICTORIA'S OWN SAPPERS & MINERS IN FRANCE AND IRAQ. 1914-1920

R Hamilton
Publisher's details not shown, Bangalore, n.d. (c.1922)
Brown, black, 10.0 x 6.5, iv/78.
6 mono phots, 9 maps (2 printed in the text, 7 folding, bound in at the
rear), no appendixes, no Index.

Although again brief, this is a better record than the previous entry.
Based upon the unit's War Diary, it is a reasonably informative account of
their services in France, Mesopotamia and Iraq. R/4 V/3. NAM. PJE.


A SHORT HISTORY OF QUEEN VICTORIA'S OWN MADRAS SAPPERS AND MINERS DURING
WORLD WAR II, 1939-1945
Compiled from War Diaries and Unit Histories completed up to December 1947

R A Lindsell
Publisher's details not shown, Bangalore, 1947
Seen partly rebound, but thought to have been produced originally in
paper covers, stapled and glued very poorly, blue, 8.5 x 5.5, -/148.
Fp, 26 mono phots, 7 maps (stapled in at rear), no Index.

Apps: Roll of Honour (all ranks), H&A (all ranks), list of former COs.

A good narrative account, with plenty of interesting detail, of services
in Abyssinia, Egypt, Western Desert, the Aegean, Italy, Greece, Malaya,
Burma and Indo-China. There are some good biographical notes on many
officers of the Corps. The number of copies printed is stated to have been
1000. The number now surviving is likely to be low due to inadequacy
of the assembly and binding. R/4 V/4. RMAS. RP.


SHORT HISTORY OF THE SERVICES OF THE 3rd SAPPERS & MINERS

Anon
No publication details shown, n.d. (c.1910)
Black, gold, 8.0 x 5.5, -/18.
no illustrations, no maps, no appendixes, no Index.

A very brief history based upon regtl orders. Covers the period 1820-
1910, with some passing description of their services in Persia, the
Mutiny, Second Afghan War, Third China War, and on the Frontier.
R/4 V/1. NAM. PJE.


A BRIEF HISTORY OF THE ROYAL BOMBAY SAPPERS & MINERS

Anon
Royal Bombay Sappers & Miners Press, Kirkee, 1924
Red, black, 8.0 x 5.5, i/38.
no illustrations, no maps, no formal appendixes, no Index.

A very brief account produced for use in the Corps schools. Based upon
official records, and including a section on honours and awards.
R/5 V/1. IWM. PJE.

HISTORY OF THE 20th (FIELD) COMPANY, ROYAL BOMBAY SAPPERS & MINERS,
Great War: 1914-1918

Major H W R Hamilton DSO MC
Reprinted from a feature article first published in the Royal Engineers
Journal, n.d.
Stiff card, white boards with blue spine, black, 9.75 x 6.0, -/51.
no illustrations, 6 maps (large folding flimsies, bound in), no
appendixes, no Index.

To quote the Introduction: 'Compiled mainly from the War Diary of the
Company, supplemented by the memory of the writer'. An interesting
narrative account, with many British officers mentioned in the text,
of services in France (1914-15), Mesopotamia (1916-17, Relief of Kut),
and Palestine (1918). R/5 V/3. NAM. RP.


 SHORT HISTORY OF THE 17th AND 22nd FIELD COMPANIES, THIRD SAPPERS &
MINERS, IN MESOPOTAMIA, 1914-1918

Brig Gen U W Evans CB CMG, Col F A Wilson CB, Lieut Col E J Loring MC,
Maj K B S Crawford, Maj K D Yearsley, and others
Publisher's details not shown, Kirkee, 1932
Calfskin, dark blue spine with medium blue boards, gold, 8.5 x 5.5, vii/131.
Fp, no other illustrations, 10 maps (bound in), Index.

Apps: H&A (British and Indian, all ranks), statistics on casualties
(KIA, WIA, POW), notes on the organisation of Field Companies.

A very detailed account of two typical Indian Army Field Companies in WWI.
Many British and Indian personnel (all ranks) mentioned in the text, with
excellent coverage of several little-known actions. NAM. ED.


SHORT HISTORY OF THE JAIL LABOUR CORPS

Anon
W B Lane
The Government Press, Baghdad, 1920
Paper covers, beige, black, 13.0 x 8.25.

This is a series of pamphlets which deal with a most unusual Corps. In order
to augment the logistical manpower on the lines of supply in Mesopotamia,
and to free the Sappers & Miners for more skilled work,seven Jail Labour &
Porter Corps units were recruited from the inmates of the prisons of
India. They were: 11th (Bombay) Jail Corps, 6th (Punjab) Jail Labour
Corps, 8th (United Provinces) Jail Porter Corps, 10th (Punjab) Jail
Porter Corps, 10th (Madras) Jail Porter Corps, 5th (United Provinces)
Jail Porter Corps, 12th (Burma) Jail Porter Corps. The pamphlets, all
identical in format and presentation, describe the services of each unit,
with appendixes regarding deaths, invalids, offences, desertions, bonuses
paid and work done. R/5 V/4. IWM. PJE.

# APPENDIX IV

Designation of Indian Sappers & Miners
following the Re-organisations of 1922


King George's Own Bengal Sappers & Miners
formerly
1st King George's Own Sappers & Miners (Great War period)
formerly
1st Sappers & Miners (1903)
formerly
Bengal Sappers & Miners


Queen Victoria's Own Sappers & Miners
formerly
2nd Queen Victoria's Own Sappers & Miners (Great War period)
formerly
2nd Queen's Own Sappers & Miners (1903)
formerly
Queen's Own Madras Sappers & Miners


Royal Bombay Sappers & Miners
formerly
3rd Sappers & Miners (Great War period)
formerly (and still)
3rd Sappers & Miners (1903)
formerly
Bombay Sappers & Miners


N.B. The Burma Sappers & Miners were formed c.1922, but no published
history has been traced (see page 167).

INDIA - ARTILLERY
GENERAL ACCOUNTS


THE HISTORY OF THE ROYAL AND INDIAN ARTILLERY IN THE MUTINY OF 1857

Colonel Julian R J Jocelyn
John Murray, London, 1915
Blue, gold, embellished on front cover with facsimile of an Indian Mutiny
medal, 9.25 x 6.0, xxvi/520.
Fp, one mono phot, 14 engravings, 11 maps (some coloured), Bibliography,
Index.

Apps: list of officers who served, summary of casualties, notes on
organisation, notes on battles and sieges, etc.

An excellent book, full of detail, which deals almost exclusively with
the period 1857-58, but with a short chapter taking the story through
to the amalgamation (in 1862) of the Royal and HEIC artilleries.
R/4 V/5. RAI. AMM.


THE HISTORY OF THE INDIAN MOUNTAIN ARTILLERY

Brig Gen C A L Graham DSO OBE
Gale & Polden Ltd, Aldershot, 1957
Dark blue, gold, 9.0 x 5.75, xvi/470
Fp, 15 mono phots, 8 maps (bound in), Glossary, Index.

Apps: extensive notes on Indian States Mountain Artillery, garrison batteries,
survey units, etc.

An excellent overall history. Covers the entire period from inception in
1840 through to post-WWII operations in Indo-China (1946). The author
succeeds in striking a good balance between the evolution of the Corps,
its campaigns, and some important technical factors. Many officers, and
some Other Ranks, are mentioned in the text. R/2 V/5. BCC.


BATTERY RECORDS OF THE ROYAL ARTILLERY, 1859-1877
Including HEIC (Foot) Artillery Companies, 1748-1862

Lieut Col M E S Laws OBE MC
Royal Artillery Institution, Woolwich, 1970
Dark blue, gold, RA arms on front cover, 8.75 x 11.0, vi/312.
no illustrations, no maps, Index.

Apps: notes on the Bengal Artillery, Madras Artillery, and Bombay Artillery.

This book (Volume II in a long-term series) deals principally with
batteries of the RA. In 1862, fifty-two Companies of Artillery which
formerly had been in HEIC service were transferred to the RA, hence their
records are included in this volume. The appendixes give details
of formation dates, changes in title, battle honours, and other matters
of interest. R/1 V/5. RAI. AMM.

HISTORY OF THE REGIMENT OF ARTILLERY, INDIAN ARMY

Brig Gen Y B Gulati and Maj Gen D K Palit VrC
Palit & Dutt, Dehra Dun, 1971
Black, gold, 8.75 x 5.75, xiii/342.
Fp, 12 mono phots, 3 coloured plates, 11 maps (printed in text), Index.

Apps: H&A (WWII only, possibly incomplete), notes on nomenclature, units
sent overseas in WWII, notes on anti-aircraft and coastal defence,
allocation of units at Partition, etc.

From 1862 to 1924, the only regular artillery units in the Indian Army
were the mountain batteries, but in the latter year even they became part
of the Royal Artillery. Then, in 1935, the Indian Regiment of Artillery
was formed. The mountain batteries were transferred from the RA to the
new Regt in 1939. There was rapid expansion after 1939 and the regt served
overseas in many roles. In August 1945, King George V granted it the title
of Royal Indian Artillery (the prefix being discarded upon the proclam-
ation of the Indian Republic in January 1950). This very comprehensive book
has one chapter on the history of Indian gunnery prior to 1935, then a very
detailed account of the raising of new units and new branches in WWII, with
an even more detailed account of the post-1947 campaigns. The narrative
concentrates mainly upon the origins and services of each unit and is
thereby an excellent reference source. R/1 V/5. NAM. IOL. MCJ/BCC/RGB/AMM.
Reprinted by Leo Cooper, London, 1972, red, gold, 9.0 x 6.0, xiii/342.


TALES OF THE MOUNTAIN GUNNERS
An Anthology, Compiled by Those who Served with Them

C H T MacFetridge and J P Warren
William Blackwood, Edinburgh, 1973
Fawn, gold, 10.0 x 7.0, xix/327.
Fp, 20 mono phots, 9 maps (printed in the text), no appendixes, no Index.

A very good secondary source, especially when read in conjunction with
General Graham's book (see page 176). R/1 V/3. RP.


HONOUR TITLES OF THE ROYAL ARTILLERY

Maj Gen B P Hughes
Royal Artillery Institution, Woolwich, 1976
Blue, gold, 8.5 x 6.0, xii/222.
2 mono phots, 20 sketches, 21 maps (printed in the text), Bibliography,
Index of Units, Index of Persons.

An excellent and readable book which describes the circumstances which led
to the award of an honour title to certain batteries of the RA. Twenty-five
of them were (at the time of the event leading to the award) part of the
HEIC artillery (pre-1862). The book has a section for each battery,
arranged chronologically, stating its evolution and services. Roughly one
quarter of the maps and illustrations relate to HEIC services. R/1 V/5. AMM.

THE ANTI-AIRCRAFT BRANCH OF THE INDIAN ARTILLERY, 1940 TO 1947

Major H Y Sawyer
No publication details shown, facsimile typescript, dated 1983
Seen in cardboard covers, blue, blind, 11.5 x 8.5, -/42.
no illustrations, no maps, Bibliography, no Index.

Apps: list of Heavy AA Regts, list of Light AA Regts.

A useful and detailed history of the various Regts and Batteries
of the Anti-Aircraft, Indian Army. The only known source dealing
specifically with this subject. R/5 V/3. NAM. PJE.


THE KAYE'S 2nd ANTI-TANK REGIMENT
Later 7 Fd 'The Gola of Gabot' - Some Facts and Experiences

M A Gani SJ
Publisher's details not shown, Islamabad, 1977
Plasticated soft card, dark red, gold, regtl crest on front cover,
9.5 x 7.25, iii/88.
Fp, 14 mono phots, one map (printed in text), no appendixes, no Index.

An expansive account written by an Indian officer who served with the
regt and eventually commanded it. The unofficial title of 'The Kaye's'
derives from the fact that, when the regt was raised in 1940, the first
CO was Lieut Col J W Kaye RA. It consisted of 5, 6, 7 and 8 Indian Anti-
tank Batteries. On 15 August 1947, it was transferred to the Pakistan Army.
A very readable and interesting account of campaigning in Burma (1942-
1944), Java (1945), and Kashmir (1947-1948). R/1 V/4. RAI. AMM.

## INDIA - BENGAL ARTILLERY, BENGAL HORSE ARTILLERY, BENGAL FOOT ARTILLERY

MEMOIR OF THE SERVICES OF THE BENGAL ARTILLERY
From the Organisation of the Corps to the Present Time, with Some Account
of its Internal Organisation

Capt E Buckle and J W Kaye
William H Allen & Co, London, 1852
Leather spine, wine red boards, gold, 9.0 x 5.5, xvi/592.
18 engravings (10 of medals, 18 of gun carriages), no maps, no Index.

Apps: H&A, lists of former officers.

A detailed and invaluable account of the period 1748-1849. Some details
of individual officer's services are stated to be inaccurate, but this
book is basically a very reliable source of reference. R/4 V/4. RAI. AMM.


HISTORY OF THE ORGANISATION, EQUIPMENT AND WAR SERVICES OF THE REGIMENT
OF BENGAL ARTILLERY, in 3 volumes

Lieut Col Francis W Stubbs
Henry S King & Co, London, 1877/1895
Red, gold, 8.5 x 5.5
no illustrations, many maps and plans, Bibliography, no Index.

Apps: many miscellaneous, including lists of former officers, statistics
of ammunition expenditure for various sieges, etc.

These three volumes all have the same dimensions and conform to the same
production format. An invaluable reference source for the Bengal Artillery,
but including some facts concerning the Madras and Bombay Artilleries not
easily found elsewhere.
Volume I (1748-1813):    published 1877, 35 maps and plans, xx/354
Volume II (1814-1826):   published 1877, 16 maps and plans, viii/274
Volume III (1838-1860): published 1895, 37 maps and plans, xii/615
R/5 V/5. RAI. AMM.


LIST OF OFFICERS WHO HAVE SERVED IN THE REGIMENT OF THE BENGAL ARTILLERY
(1748-1860)

Maj Gen F W Stubbs
C Seers, Bath (UK), 1892
Rust red, gold, 11.25 x 8.75, iii/72.
no illustrations, no maps, Bibliography, Index.

Apps: notes on establishments, list of officers commissioned from the ranks.

The work lists all officers of the Bengal Artillery, with details of their
decorations, promotions, and dates of death (but no details of war
services). R/4 V/3. RAI. AMM.

STATEMENT OF THE SERVICES OF 'C' BATTERY, 'C' BRIGADE R.H.A. (FORMERLY
SHAH SOOJAH'S HORSE ARTILLERY)

Anon (thought to be Capt W J Finch)
Publisher's details not shown, London, n.d. (c.1878)
Paper covers, light blue, black, 8.5.x 5.5, -/8.

A pamphlet which covers the period 1838-1877, but which deals
primarily with 1838-1862. The unit originally consisted of two Troops of
Shah Soojah's Artillery which were amalgamated in 1843 to form 5th Troop
(Native) 1st Brigade, Bengal Horse Artillery. The text is a diary of
stations, movements and battles. R/5 V/2. RAI. AMM.


RECORDS OF 3rd TROOP, 2nd BENGAL HORSE ARTILLERY (NOW No1 DEPOT R.F.A.)

Anon (Maj Gen F W Stubbs)
Publication details not shown, Woolwich, 1904
Card covers, grey, black, 7.0 x 5.0, -/28.
no illustrations, no maps, no Index.

Apps: H&A (officers only), list of former officers, stations, notes on
equipment and unit designations.

Covers the period 1825-1862. Although brief, it is written in Stubbs'
usual concise narrative style and is a useful source of reference.
R/5 V/3. RAI. AMM.


A SKETCH OF THE HISTORY OF 'F' BATTERY, ROYAL HORSE ARTILLERY
Formerly 1st Troop, 1st Brigade, Bengal Horse Artillery

Major A S Tyndale-Biscoe
Spottiswoode & Co Ltd, London, 1905
Red, black, 7.5 x 4.75, ii/64.
Fp, 2 mono phots, 3 sketches, no maps, no Index.

Apps: list of former COs, list of former officers.

Half of the text is devoted to the period 1800-1862 when, as 1/1 BHA,
the unit was in HEIC service. The narrative is based upon notes originally
prepared by Maj Gen F W Stubbs, and gives details of stations, movements,
changes in command, active services in the field, etc.
R/4 V/3. RAI. AMM.

The same information can be found in THE STORY OF 'F' TROOP, by Lieut Col
C B Findlay (published by William May & Co Ltd, Aldershot, 1932, iv/84).

A SHORT HISTORY OF 'S' BATTERY, 1826-1926

Anon ('O.T.F.')
The Cabot Press, Bristol, 1926
Seen only in photostat form, 11.5 x 8.25, -/36.

The battery was first raised as 3rd Troop, 3rd Brigade, Bengal Horse
Artillery, and this brief history makes some reference to those early
years. R/4 V/1. NAM. PJE.


143rd (TOMBS'S TROOP), ROYAL ARTILLERY, A SHORT HISTORY
Formerly 2nd Troop, 1st Brigade, Bengal Horse Artillery

Major A M Macfarlane
Published privately, Woolwich, 1968
Stiff card, Royal blue, gold, battery crest (Tiger's Head) on front cover,
8.0 x 5.5, -/64.
4 mono phots, no maps, Bibliography, no Index.

Apps: H&A, list of former COs, list of former officers, nominal roll
for the siege of Delhi (1857), etc.

The first nine pages cover the period 1825-1862 when the unit was in
HEIC service. Although brief, the very readable narrative is packed with
informative detail and interesting anecdotes. Only 500 copies printed.
A model of its kind. R/2 V/5. RP.


THE BENGAL HORSE ARTILLERY, 1800-1861
The Red Men, A 19th Century Corps d'Elite

Maj Gen B P Hughes
Arms & Armour Press, London, 1971
Ochre, gold, 10.0 x 7.5, xiv/184.
20 mono phots, 4 coloured plates, 14 maps (printed in the text),
Bibliography, Index of persons, Index of units.

Apps: extensive notes on uniforms, arms and armament, tactics, campaigns,
medals, organisation and administration, etc.

The regt took part in all the major campaigns in India and was then
absorbed into the Royal Artillery in 1862. This is a very good narrative
history, with most of the text being devoted to campaign services. It is
regarded as the best overall history of the BHA. R/1 V/5. MJC/BCC/JSA.


HISTORY OF THE 22nd (RESIDENCY) FIELD BATTERY, ROYAL ARTILLERY
Formerly 2nd Company, 3rd Battalion, Bengal (Foot) Artillery

Capt P A Brooke MC
The Pioneer Press, Allahabad, 1931
Royal blue, gold, 7.5 x 5.0, v/47.
Fp, no other illustrations, 3 maps (bound in), no Index.

Apps: list of former COs, battles and sieges, stations and movements.

This book is arranged in two sections: pages 1-32 cover the period 1786-1862, while pages 34-42 apply to the period 1862-1930. It is the first section which deals with HEIC service, and it is devoted mainly (and interestingly) to the campaign to suppress the Mutiny (Lucknow). Few individuals are mentioned by name, but the narrative is otherwise clear and informative. R/4 V/4. RAI. AMM.


FROM RECRUIT TO STAFF SERGEANT
The Bengal Horse Artillery of Olden Time

N W Bancroft. late Sergeant, Bengal Horse Artillery
Ian Henry Publications, London, 1979
Illustrated stiff card, red, black and white, 8.75 x 5.5, 24/ii/97/xiv.
one mono phot, one map (printed on end-papers), Bibliography, no Index.

Apps: list of former COs, list of former officers, correspondence (1900) from the HM the Queen's Secretary, record of service of the author.

Three editions of this book are known to have been produced (1885, 1900 and 1979). The third edition, as recorded above, is the best and most complete. It includes an Introduction of 24 pages by Maj Gen B P Hughes which describes the Bengal Artillery of the day, and an Epilogue by Hughes which comments upon Bancroft himself. These are excellent commentaries upon the times. Although a personal record (and the only one written by a soldier of the regt), the book is largely a history of 2nd Troop, 1st Brigade, Bengal Horse Artillery from 1841 to 1859. R/1 V/5. AMM.

## INDIA - MADRAS ARTILLERY AND MADRAS HORSE ARTILLERY

HISTORY OF THE SERVICES OF THE MADRAS ARTILLERY
With a Sketch of the Rise of the Power of the East India Company
in Southern India, Volume I

Major P J Begbie
Franck & Co, at the Christian Knowledge Society's Press, Madras, 1852
Seen re-bound in green, blind, 8.75 x 5.25, xviii/275.
no illustrations, no maps, no Index (but detailed chapter heads),
no appendixes, Bibliography.

This is one of two matching Volumes, the second being published a year
later (1853),and having identical dimensions and format (-/257/lxvi).
Volume I covers the period 1600-1810, one chapter being dedicated to the
founding and growth of the HEIC, the other chapters dealing exclusively
with the Madras Artillery. Although in many respects a prime source,
the narrative is sometimes confusing because individual units are not
identified by name or number. Volume II partly compensates for this
deficiency with a massive appendix (41 pages) which lists all officers who
served between 1748 and 1852 and gives details of their services and
awards. R/5 V/4. RAI. AMM.


LIST OF THE OFFICERS WHO HAVE SERVED IN THE MADRAS ARTILLERY FROM ITS
FORMATION IN 1748 DOWN TO 1861

Maj John Henry Leslie
Publication details not shown, possibly printed in Derbyshire, 1900
Card, buff, black, 11.5 x 8.75, iv/65.
Fp, no other illustrations, no maps, Index.

Apps: list of former COs, list of former officers.

A useful source, listing all officers who served with the Madras Artillery.
Gives their decorations,dates of promotion, and death, but no details
of war services. R/5 V/3. RAI. AMM.


CAMEL HOWITZER BATTERY
Planned, Raised and Commanded by Captain J H Frith, Madras Artillery,
Raised January 1819, Disbanded 15 May 1821

Capt J H Frith
'Lithographed' at the Artillery Depot, Madras, 1837
'Six plates'.
Noted in a catalogue, but no other details available. Not seen.

THE HISTORY OF 'F' BATTERY, 'B' BRIGADE, ROYAL HORSE ARTILLERY
Formerly 'A' Troop, Madras Horse Artillery

Capt G E Wyndham Malet
F J Cattermole, Woolwich, 1878
Royal blue, gold, regtl crest on front cover, 7.25 x 4.75, iv/41.
Fp, no other illustrations, no maps, no Index.

Apps: list of former COs, list of former officers, notes on changes in
unit designation, notes on the unit's war service (1808-59).

Half of the narrative deals with the period 1767-1861 when the Troop
was in HEIC service. The text is an annual diary of stations, movements,
changes in command, active service, etc, and relies heavily upon
Begbie's book (see page 183). R/5 V/4. RAI. AMM.
The above description refers to the second (1878) edition. A year
earlier, the first edition had sold out so quickly that a re-print became
necessary. The 1878 edition is to be preferred because some of the minor
errors found in the first edition were meantime corrected.


THE HISTORY OF 'J' BATTERY, ROYAL HORSE ARTILLERY
Formerly 'A' Troop, Madras Horse Artillery

Major G E W Malet
Charles Good & Co, London, 1903
Fp, no other illustrations, one map, no Index.

Apps: list of former COs, list of former officers.

A good reference work, based upon regtl orders but with a lot of detailed
information included. R/5 V/4. NAM. PJE.
This is the third and updated version of two earlier editions (1877 and
1898).


SOME NOTES UPON THE ORIGIN, FORMATION AND SUBSEQUENT DEVELOPMENT
(1805 TO 1861) OF THE MADRAS HORSE ARTILLERY

Maj John H Leslie
Printed by W H Lead, Leicester, for The Royal Artillery Institution, 1907
Card, grey-green, black, 9.5 x 6.0, ii/8.
Fp, 9 mono phots (all of uniforms), no maps, appendixes, no Index.

The title page refers to 'J', 'M', 'P' and 'R' Batteries, Royal Horse
Artillery, as represented in the year 1907. Of these, 'J' and 'P' still
exist today (1989). This very slim volume is, in fact, a reprint of
an article published in the Royal Artillery Journal and is of interest
mainly for its notes on uniforms (1805-1819). R/5 V/1. RAI. AMM.


No published histories have been traced in respect of the Madras Foot
Artillery.

## INDIA - BOMBAY ARTILLERY AND BOMBAY HORSE ARTILLERY

THE BOMBAY ARTILLERY
List of Officers (1748-1862)

Colonel F W M Spring
William Clowes & Sons Ltd, London, 1902
Royal blue boards with cream-white spine, gold, bearings on front cover,
8.5 x 5.5, xii/135.
Fp, 5 sketches, no maps, Index.

Apps: H&A, list of former COs, list of former officers, numerous lists
and tables within the body of the book.

This was the last of the three Lists of Officers of the HEIC artilleries
to be published (see pages 179 and 183), and is by far the best. After an
outline chronology of the Corps, the author provides long lists of
officers in various appointments, Troops and Companies. Each of the latter
is also listed, with details of its services and title changes. There is
a large section of 50 pages giving the records of service of every officer
who served with the Bombay Artillery (including his campaign medals and
honours). R/4 V/5. RAI. AMM.


RECORDS OF 'E' BATTERY, 'C' BRIGADE, ROYAL HORSE ARTILLERY
4th Troop, Bombay Artillery, 1824-1876

Anon (reported to be Major T M Holberton)
Unpublished facsimile typescript, copied from a manuscript first
drafted in 1876, 11.5 x 8.5, -/63.

This is a good history, well-written, with useful additional notes on
former officers, stations and movements, and changes of designation.
Covers the following campaigns: Mahratta Wars, First Afghan, Persia and
Mutiny. Based partly upon regtl records and partly upon personal
experiences. R/5 V/3. NAM. PJE.


HISTORY OF THE 'E' BATTERY, 'D' BRIGADE, ROYAL HORSE ARTILLERY, FROM
1820 TO 1876
Formerly 2 Troop, Bombay Horse Artillery

Major Hubert Le Cocq
Curtis & Beamish, Coventry, n.d. (c.1876)
Paper covers, grey, black, 8.0 x 5.25, -/19.
no illustrations, no maps, no Index.

Apps: list of former COs, list of former officers.

Covers the period 1820-1862. Written in narrative style, with details of
stations,movements, services, and changes in title. Good coverage for the
Mutiny period (although only 4 pages). R/5 V/3. MODL. AMM.

RECORDS OF 'D' BATTERY, 'C' BRIGADE, ROYAL HORSE ARTILLERY
Late 3rd Troop, Bombay Horse Artillery

Lieut Col T M Holberton
F J Cattermole, Woolwich, 1878
Seen in yellow, black, 9.5 x 6.0, -/64.
no illustrations, no maps, no Index.

Apps: list of former COs, list of former officers, list of actions
fought, personal reminiscences of actions.

A full and readable account for the period 1824 to 1872, which gives
some detail of their involvement in the First Afghan War and the Mutiny.
A good usable reference source. R/5 V/4. NAM. PJE.


A SHORT HISTORY OF THE EAGLE TROOP, R.H.A.
Formerly 1st Troop, Bombay Horse Artillery

Anon
Publisher's details not shown, Hohne, West Germany, 1955
Paper covers, buff, blue, Battery crest (an eagle) on the front cover,
8.0 x 7.0, ii/40.
no illustrations, no maps, no Index.

Apps: list of former COs, notes on actions fought, stations and movements,
changes in designation.

Two chapters(12 pages) cover the period 1811-1862 when the Troop was in
HEIC service (Deccan, First Afghan, Scinde and Mutiny). The narrative
was presumably written while the author was serving in Germany and
therefore had limited access to original sources (hence the many gaps).
Not entirely satisfactory, but the only published source specifically for
this unit. R/3 V/3. RAI. AMM.


No published histories have been traced in respect of the Bombay Foot
Artillery.

# INDIA - MOUNTAIN ARTILLERY

No3 (PESHAWAR) MOUNTAIN BATTERY, PUNJAB FRONTIER FORCE, BATTERY HISTORY
Formerly the Peshawar Mountain Train

Anon
The New Albion Press, Lahore, 1886
Red, gold, picture of 7 pdr RML gun on front cover, 8.25 x 5.75, i/78.
no illustrations, no maps, no Index.

Apps: list of former COs, list of former officers, list of Indian
officers, H&A (only one man named), notes on origins of unit, war services
of the unit. N.B. these appendixes are arranged as sections throughout
the body of the book.

Covers the period 1853-86. The total number of pages is 159, but half were
left blank so that future members of the Battery could add their own
annotations. An excellent reference source. R/4 V/4. MODL.AMM.


THE HISTORICAL RECORDS OF No1 (KOHAT) MOUNTAIN BATTERY, PUNJAB FRONTIER
FORCE
Formerly No2 Light Field Battery, P.F.F.

Anon
The Punjab Government Press, Lahore, 1886
Royal blue, gold, 'gun and crown' motif on front cover, 10.5 x 6.75, v/45.
no illustrations, no maps, no appendixes, no Index.

This is another of the useful 'Historical Records of the Regiments of the
Punjab Frontier Force', all of which seem to have been commissioned and
published at around the same time. This one covers the period 1851-1886
in detailed diary form, naming all officers who served (with dates), and
with notes of stations and movements, and campaign services.
R/4 V/4. MODL.AMM.


THE HISTORICAL RECORD OF No5 (OR GARRISON) BATTERY, PUNJAB FRONTIER FORCE
Formerly No4 (or Garrison) Company, P.F.F.

Anon
The Punjab Government Press, Lahore, 1886
Royal blue, gold, 'gun and crown' motif on front cover, 10.5 x 6.75, i/8.
no illustrations, no maps, no appendixes, no Index.

Covers the period 1851-1885. It includes the usual details of stations,
movements, officers' postings, etc, but no details of active service (for
the simple reason that it did not see any, hence the total history of
eight pages). R/5 V/3. MODL.AMM.

THE HISTORICAL RECORD OF No4 (HAZARA) MOUNTAIN BATTERY, PUNJAB FRONTIER
FORCE
Formerly the Hazara Mountain Train

Anon
The Punjab Government Press, Lahore, 1888
Royal blue, gold, battery crest on front cover, 10.0 x 6.0, x/97.
no illustrations, no maps, no Index (but a detailed Contents page)

Apps: stations and movements (1848-1887), establishments and rates of pay.

Again, an excellent example of the PFF series of publications of that
period. Covers the period 1849-1887 in detailed diary form, giving full
details of battery services, names of officers in the text, and an account
of the unit's involvement in the Second Afghan War and various Frontier
operations. R/3 V/4. RAI. AMM.


HISTORICAL RECORD OF No2 DERAJAT MOUNTAIN BATTERY, PUNJAB FRONTIER FORCE
Formerly No3 Light Field Battery P.F.F.

Anon
W Ball & Co (successors to The Punjab Printing Co), Lahore, 1887
Dark brown, black on white label, 9.75 x 6.25, i/20.
no illustrations, no maps, no appendixes, no Index.

Though very similar in content to the 'standard' PFF series, it is quite
different in outward appearance (due to having a different printer).
It covers the period 1849-1886 in detailed diary form, with all the
expected information regarding stations and movements, officers posted in
and out, campaign services, etc. An excellent reference source.
R/4 V/4. RAI. AMM.
This work was updated to 1905 and re-published in that year (The Albion
Press, Lahore, i/41). It was then updated again, still with the same
title and format, in 1921 (The Pioneer Press, Allahabad, ii/94, with
appendixes for campaign services and campaign medal entitlements). Of the
three versions, the 1921 edition would appear to be the most useful for
research purposes.


BATTERY HISTORY, 106th JACOB'S PACK BATTERY
Formerly No2 (Bombay) Mountain Battery

Anon
The Pioneer Press, Allahabad, 1923
Buff boards with black spine, black, 6.0 x 4.75, -/15.
no illustrations, no maps, no appendixes, no Index.

This is a narrative account of the battery's services 1843-1923 and is
disappointing for its lack of detail. There is the usual information on
stations and movements, but in fairly imprecise terms. The best aspect
of the story is the account of services at Maizar (1897) and in WWI
(Gallipoli 1915, and Mesopotamia 1916-19). R/5 V/3. RAI. AMM.

MOUNTAIN BATTERY, BURMA 1942

Pat Carmichael
Devin Books, Bournemouth (UK), 1983
Buff, gold, 8.75 x 5.75, v/246.
13 mono phots, one map (printed in the text), no appendixes, Bibliography,
no Index.

A very graphic autobiographical account by a war-time RA officer,
describing his service with 23 Indian Mountain Battery RIA in Burma from
autumn, 1941, to his evacuation, late 1942. R/1 V/2. RAI. AMM.


ACTION IN BURMA, 1942-1945

Colonel J C Chaplin DSO OBE
Publisher's details not shown, London, 1984
Blue, gold, 8.5 x 6.0, xiii/212/xxii.
Fp, 48 mono phots, 22 maps (bound in), no formal appendixes, Glossary,
Index.

This is the war history of 21 Mountain Regiment RIA (consisting of 1, 6
and 37 Mountain Batteries) in Burma. Compiled by the officer who commanded
it from August 1944 to late 1945. A clear graphic narrative, with many
individuals mentioned, and including numerous citations for gallantry
awards (especially the MC). A very good reference source.
R/1 V/4. RAI. AMM.


REGIMENTAL HISTORY, 29th INDIAN MOUNTAIN REGIMENT, ROYAL INDIAN ARTILLERY

Anon
The Edwardes Press, Razmak, 1946
Card, blind, 8.0 x 6.0, i/39.
no illustrations, no maps, no Index.

Apps: Roll of Honour, H&A, list of COs, diary of events 1942-1945.

This was a pre-war formed regt consisting of 9 (Murree), 14 (Rajputana),
and 38 Mountain Batteries. The booklet comprises 23 pages of narrative
followed by a diary of events and other appendixes. Probably printed in
very limited numbers as a memento for officers who served.
R/5 V/4. RAI. AMM.

190

INDIA - VOLUNTEER FORCES - BENGAL


SERVICE AND ADVENTURE WITH THE KHAKEE RESSALAH OR MEERUT VOLUNTEER
HORSE DURING THE MUTINIES OF 1857-58

R H W Dunlop BCS
Richard Bentley, London, 1858
Light red, gold, 'Winged Victory and Vanquished Foe' motif on front cover,
7.75 x 4.75, xi/168/xi (plus 32 pages of advertisements)
Fp (attractive coloured print showing 'A Volunteer of the Meerut Khakee
Ressalah', mounted, in field dress), 6 mono plates, 2 coloured plates,
one line drawing ('The Wallace Guard', an arm protector for sabre
fighting, no maps, no Index (but a very good 'Contents' page).

Apps: 'A List of Corps which have Mutinied or been Disarmed' (5 pages).

This was one of several bodies of mounted militia or vigilantes which
spontaneously sprang into existence in the immediate aftermath of the
outbreak at Meerut and the fall of Delhi. Despite the misleading title,
the Meerut Volunteer Horse was disbanded in October, 1857. Mr Dunlop wrote
his account over the winter and the book was published in London in
1858, an excellent example of good commercial marketing. The term
'ressalah' loosely describes any formed body of horsemen, and forces such
as this consisted of anyone willing and able to wield a sabre against
the mutineers: European civilians, officers whose regiments had mutinied,
loyal Indian troopers. The story reflects a tragic and very violent period
in Anglo-Indian history. R/5 V/5. CJP.


MEMORANDUM OF THE BENGAL YEOMAN CAVALRY, 1857-58

Anon (known to be John Tulloch Nash)
J F Bellamy at The Englishman Press, Calcutta, n.d. (c.1859)
Seen rebound, details of original binding not known, 9.75 x 7.0, i/28.
no illustrations, no maps, no formal appendixes, no Index.

This is a narrative account of a Volunteer unit raised officially in
Calcutta for service against the mutineers. It was recruited from the
local European civil population and was sent up to Amorah, on the
Oudh/Behar frontier in October 1857. It formed part of Brig Gen Rowcroft's
Sarun Field Force and had several encounters with disaffected sepoys.
The text includes details of establishment, rates of pay, a nominal roll
of all members, and lists of killed and wounded. R/5 V/5. NAM. TA.
Another volume, entitled VOLUNTEERING IN INDIA, OR A NARRATIVE OF THE
MILITARY SERVICES OF THE BENGAL YEOMAN CAVALRY DURING THE INDIAN MUTINY
AND SEPOY WAR, has been noted but not seen. It was published in London
in 1893 (viii/136), and is presumably a much expanded version of the
c.1858 edition recorded here.

THE HISTORY OF LUMSDEN'S HORSE
A Complete Record of the Corps from Formation to Disbandment

Henry H S Pearse
Longmans Green & Co. New York and Bombay, 1903
Red, gold, regtl crest on front cover, 10.0 x 7.5, xii/508.
Fp, 78 mono phots, one map (bound in), Index.

Apps: nine in total, including notes on mobilisation, Adjutant's notebook,
accounts and funds.

Lieut Col D M Lumsden was on leave in Australia when, in December
1899, he received news of the war in South Africa. He wrote to the
authorities in India, offering £50,000 of his own money and his 'own
personal services' to raise a regt of cavalry for service against the
Boers. The offer was accepted. He returned to Calcutta and recruited
two squadrons from the local British civil population. Recruitment was
based upon an applicant's experience with one of the Mounted Volunteer
units and his perceived social standing (there were many complaints of
snobbery). The regt departed Calcutta in February 1900, returned
January 1901, and was then disbanded. An extremely detailed,
comprehensive and useful source of reference. R/4 V/5. IOL. VS/RGB.


LUMSDEN'S HORSE, SOUTH AFRICA 1900 AND JUBILEE MEMORIAL REGISTER
1900-1950

Major H O Pugh
The Welsh Gazette, Cardiganshire, 1952
Paper covers, grey, blue, 8.5 x 5.5, -/39.
Fp, 2 mono phots, no maps, no formal appendixes, no Index

A readable account of the regt's short history, with two lists of former
members: those now dead and those still living  (at 1951). R/5 V/2. NAM. PJE.


HISTORY OF THE BEHAR LIGHT HORSE
From Formation in 1862 to 1908
The Oldest Volunteer Regiment in Bengal

Major G W Disney
Edinburgh Press, Calcutta, 1908
Purple, silver, 'musical notation' motif on front cover, 7.5 x 5.0, -/80.
no illustrations, no maps, no Index.

Apps: notes on Fort Pill Box (1857), nominal roll of the Soubah Behar
Mounted Rifles 1862 (this being the original name when first formed),
nominal rolls for various other years through to 1906 (when the unit was
transferred from the Government of Bengal to C-in-C India).

Covers the period 1862-1907. This was a small Corps of gentleman
Volunteers (merchants, doctors, etc) which saw no action during the
stated period other than 'The Basantapur Cattle Rescue Riots' of 1893.
R/4 V/3. IOL. RGB.

HISTORY OF THE BEHAR LIGHT HORSE
From Formation in 1862 to 1918

Major G W Disney and Major T R Filgate
Thacker Spink & Co, Calcutta, 1921
Ochre, gold, regtl crest on front cover, 7.5 x 5.0, vi/180.
Fp, one mono phot, no maps, no Index.

Apps: list of former officers, extracts from Indian Army Lists, results
of competitions.

This is basically an updating of Major Disney's work of 1908 (see page
191), with details up to 1918. R/4 V/3. NAM. PJE.


HISTORY OF THE BEHAR LIGHT HORSE
The Most Senior and Oldest Volunteer Cavalry Unit in India

Lieut Col W N R Kemp ED
Thacker's Press & Directories Ltd, Calcutta, 1948
Stiff card, light grey, gold, 7.5 x 5.0, xx/240.
Fp, no other illustrations, no maps, no formal appendixes (but see below),
no Index.

The book is divided into three sections: 1857-1903, 1903-1919, and 1920-
1947. Each section has many appendixes, compiled in immense detail.
The narrative is tedious, but the book is a first-class reference source
for individual names. R/3 V/4. NAM. IOL. RJW.


A CONCISE HISTORY OF THE BIHAR LIGHT HORSE
Taken from Disney's, Filgate's, and Kemp's Histories

F A C Munns
Cheriton Press, Folkestone (UK), n.d. (c.1958)
Paper covers, dark blue, white, regtl crest on front cover, 8.5 x 5.5,-/31.
no illustrations, no maps, no Index.

Apps: list of former COs, list of officers (at 1951), list of Adjutants,
idem Chaplains.

A very brief 'summary' history of limited value. The lists of officers
may possibly be of interest to the researcher. R/4 V/2. BM. PJE.


COSSIPORE ARTILLERY VOLUNTEERS
A Brief History

Lieut Col D A Tyrie VD
Thacker Spink & Co, Calcutta, 1912
Brown, gold, 7.25 x 5.0, -/34.
no illustrations, no maps, no Index.

Apps: list of all officers who served, 1883-1910.

This is not a book in itself, but a 34-page short history bound within a
volume entitled PAMPHLETS MILITARY AND NAVAL and held by the IOL.
It is the only known published account for this unit. The Cossipore
Artillery Volunteers were a half-battery of gentlemen-volunteers who saw
no  active service but who manned the guns on ceremonial occasions on
the old Calcutta Forts. R/5 V/3. IOL. RGB.


CALCUTTA LIGHT HORSE A.F.(I)., 1759-1881-1947

Anon ('A Committee of the Regiment')
Gale & Polden Ltd, Aldershot, 1957
Dark blue, gold, regtl crest on front cover, 8.75 x 5.5, xv/175.
Fp, 40 mono phots, 4 line drawings, one coloured plate, no maps,
no Index.

Apps: Roll of Honour (WWI and WWII), H&A (WWII), lists of former officers,
notes on sporting trophies, nominal roll (all ranks, 1914, 1939, 1947).

The regt was essentially a military and sporting club for the British
male community in Calcutta. However, it took its military commitments
seriously and many members were detached for full-time active service with
other regts during WWI and WWII. The unit is famous for its clandestine
attack on Axis shipping in the harbour of neutral Goa in 1943. This episode
does not appear in this book ('suppressed for reasons of security', to
quote the text). An interesting and useful work, particularly for research
into individual careers. R/2 V/4. IOL. NAM. RGB/CSM.


BOARDING PARTY
Calcutta Light Horse

James Leasor
Heineman, London, 1978
Blue, silver, 8.75 x 5.5, xv/204.
Fp (map), 22 mono phots, one other map (printed in text), no appendixes,
Index.

The CLH was formed in 1759 as the Calcutta Volunteer Cavalry and underwent
several changes of title over the years. Apart from occasional actions 'in
aid to the civil power', it saw no active service until March 1943 (and
even then the action was 'unofficial'). A party consisting of 15 members
of the CLH, and 4 of the Calcutta Scottish, sailed a hopper barge into
Goa harbour and caused the sinking of three German merchantmen (Ehrenfels,
Drachenfels and Braunfels), and an Italian ship (Anfora). James Leasor's
book is a dramatised version of that event, based upon interviews with
several participants. His narrative contains a number of 'howlers' and
exaggerations, but is basically factual. His story was later made into
a film entitled THE SEA WOLVES. Although not a regtl history as such,
this volume is a graphic record of a unique military operation.
R/1 V/3. CLL/RGB/RP.

194

THE CALCUTTA AND PRESIDENCY BATTALION, A.F.(I), 1857-1938

Anon
Wilsone & Son, Calcutta, n.d. (c.1938)
Green, gold, 9.0 x 5.5, i/30.
Fp, 3 mono phots, no maps, no formal appendixes, no Index.

A short readable account of one of the auxiliary battalions which were
raised after the Mutiny for 'internal security' duties during time
of emergency. R/5 V/2. NAM. PJE.
There is mention in this volume of 'the original history of the Battalion
written in 1934 by Lieut Col A H Bishop'. Not seen.


INDIA - VOLUNTEER FORCES - GENERAL

THE VOLUNTEER FORCE OF INDIA: ITS PRESENT AND FUTURE

Major E H H Collen
The United Services Institution of India, 1883
Red, gold, 10.0 x 6.5, -/39.
no illustrations, no maps, no Index.

Apps: notes on the strength and organisation of the Volunteer Force.

This prize-winning essay was written by Major Collen in 1883. In it he
presents a concise history of the evolution of the Volunteer movement in
India and argues the case for its continuation. It would seem to be the
only general account ever published. R/5 V/3. USII. OSS.

## INDIA - VOLUNTEER FORCES - MADRAS

A SHORT HISTORY OF THE MADRAS VOLUNTEER GUARDS FROM 1857, THE DATE OF
FORMATION, TO 1907, THE JUBILEE YEAR OF THE CORPS

James Robert Coombes
The Lawrence Asylum Press, Madras, 1907
Stiff card, light grey/green, black, 8.5 x 5.5, xiv/223.
4 mono phots, no maps, no Index.

Apps: list of former officers, notes on comparative strengths 1857/1907.

A very readable and detailed history covering the period from 1857 to
1907. R/4 V/3. USII. IOL. NAM. OSS/PJE.

This edition has been seen also in a blue leather binding with gold
lettering. There is known to be an earlier edition, published in 1883,
which has fewer pages (xii/140). The 1883 edition was produced by
The Mail Press, Madras, and has a full red Morocco binding with, again,
gold lettering. Not seen.


THE KOLAR GOLD FIELDS BATTALION, MYSORE

Anon
Publication details not shown, n.d.
Yellow, black, 7.5 x 6.0, -/4.
no illustrations, no maps, no appendixes, no Index.

With only four pages, this item barely qualifies as a regtl history.
However, it is the only known published history for the unit. The period
covered is 1847 to 1947. There is some mention of the occasions when the
unit was mobilised for Aid to the Civil Power duties and during the
Moplah Rebellion of 1921-1922. R/5 V/1. NAM. PJE.

## INDIA - VOLUNTEER FORCES - BOMBAY

'J' (THE SCOTS) COMPANY, BOMBAY VOLUNTEER RIFLES
First Annual Report, 1915-1916

Captain N F Paton
Printed by The Times Press, Bombay, for the Regiment, 1916
Yellow, black, 7.5 x 5.0, -/71.
4 mono phots, no maps, no formal appendixes, no Index.

Five pages refer to the raising of the Company, the remaining pages then
consist of a report on their first year's activities. Many individuals are
named in the text, but the volume is of limited interest.
R/5 V/2. NAM.PJE.


THE BOMBAY VOLUNTEER RIFLES
A History

Samuel T Shepherd
The Times Press, Bombay,1919
Brown, gold, regtl crest on front cover, 9.75 x 6.75, iii/199.
Fp, 18 mono phots, no maps, Index.

Apps: list of former COs, idem Adjutants, idem Sergeant-Majors, idem
staff and officers in late 1916, biographical notes on officers, roll
of members who saw active service with other regts during WWI.

A comprehensive and interesting account of the unit's history between
1799 (then the Bombay Fencibles) through to the end of the Napoleonic wars
(when they were allowed to fade away). The story then resumes in
1860 when they were re-activated as the Bombay Volunteer Rifle Corps, one
of many such units resulting from the sense of anxiety caused by the
Mutiny. Apart from occasional riot-control duties, they saw no active
service until 1914 when a detachment of volunteers from the regt sailed
for East Africa to take part in the campaign against von Lettow-Vorbeck.
R/4 V/5. IOL. NAM. RGB.


THE BOMBAY LIGHT HORSE AND ITS SUCCESSOR, THE BOMBAY MOTOR PATROL A.F.(I)

Anon (known to be Major J S R Spelman)
Cranford Press (Croydon) Ltd, Croydon (UK), 1966
Dark blue, silver, regtl crest on front cover, 9.75 x 6.25, -/47.
Fp, 6 mono phots, no maps, no Index.

Apps: Roll of Honour (WWI and WWII), list of former COs, list of officers
serving during the period 1914-1918.

Although very slim, this little volume contains much scarce information
regarding the organisation, administration, equipment and uniforms of a
typical Mounted Volunteer regt. The author was the last CO, and he gives
a brief resume of their services and eventual disbandment in 1947.
Only 150 copies printed. R/5 V/4. IOL. NAM. RJW/RGB.

## INDIA – VOLUNTEER FORCES – ASSAM

THROUGH FIFTY YEARS
A History of the Surma Valley Light Horse

The Rev W H S Wood MC
The Assam Review Publishing Co, Calcutta, 1930
Black, gold, 10.0 x 6.5, xi/89.
31 mono phots, no maps, no Index (but good Contents page).

Apps: H&A, list of former COs, list of former officers, roll of permanent
instructional staff (all ranks).

Covers the period 1857-1930. Written in an easy readable style, many names
being mentioned in text, with some excellent captioned group and portrait
photographs. The unit served on the North East Frontier in 1891 (Manipur)
and in South Africa (when it formed 'B' Company of Lumsden's Horse).During
WWI, many members were detached for service with other regts.
R/5 V/5. MODL. AMM.


ASSAM-BENGAL RAILWAY BATTALION, AUXILIARY FORCE INDIA
Annual Report 1940-41

Major J H Bavin
Publication details not shown, 1941
Card covers, olive green, black, 9.0 x 5.5, -/16.
no illustrations, no maps, no Index.

Apps: list of former Adjutants and RSMs (for the period 1903-1941),
notes on Bn strength for 1901 and 1940, various competition results.

As an Annual Report, this document understandably contains little
'history', but it is the only published item which has been traced for
the regt. Presumably it was also the last such document, given the
events of the following year. R/5 V/3. NAM. PJE.

## INDIA – POLICE, ARMED POLICE AND TRIBAL MILITIAS

THE INDIAN POLICE

J C Curry
Faber & Faber, London, 1932
Dark blue, gold, 8.5 x 5.5, -/353.
no illustrations, one map, Index.

Apps: tables of statistics and establishments.

A useful general history, but particularly strong on matters relating to
the structure and organisation of Indian police departments. Of interest
to the specialist, but not very stimulating for the general reader.
R/3 V/3. IOL. JA.


TO GUARD MY PEOPLE
The History of the Indian Police

Sir Percival Griffiths KBE CIE
Ernest Benn Ltd, London,1971
Brown, gold, 8.75 x 5.5, xii/431.
38 mono phots, 2 line drawings, one map (bound in), Index.

Apps: Roll of Honour (gazetted officers only), H&A, Index.

A superb work, deeply researched and well-written. The narrative
covers more than 200 years of police work in India and Burma, and is
full of incident with many individuals named in the text. The evolution of
the Indian Police reflected not only changing patterns of criminality
but also the emergence of nationalism. The work is therefore of interest
to researchers of Indian politics. The H&A section is most useful for
medal collectors. R/1 V/5. RP.
It is reported that the book was re-printed in 1972.


POLICE AND CRIME IN INDIA

Sir Edmund C Cox
Stanley Paul & Co, London, n.d. (c.1910)
Dark blue, gold, Force crest on front page, 9.0 x 6.0, -/328.
Fp, 21 mono phots, no maps, no appendixes, no Index.

A long, detailed, and very readable book devoted mainly to the Bombay
Presidency Police, but with much information regarding the law, criminal
activities, and police responsibilities in general. R/4 V/4. NAM. PJE.

A BRIEF HISTORY OF THE OLD POLICE BATTALIONS IN THE PUNJAB

H L O Garrett
The Government Printing Press, Lahore, 1927
Yellow, black, 10.0 x 7.5, iii/23.
no illustrations, no maps, no appendixes, no Index.

This is a short history of the ten Police Battalions raised in the
Punjab from 1849 onwards. With details of their services during the
Mutiny through to their disbandment in July 1861 (when they were replaced
by the Frontier Militias). Lacking in detail, but a useful secondary
source. R/5 V/3. NAM. PJE.


THE WHITE BELTS
History of the Corps of Military Police

Lieut Col R Ganapathi
Lancer Publishers, New Delhi, 1982
Black, gold, 8.5 x 5.75, xii/560.
56 mono phots, 8 pages of line drawings of badges and insignia,
11 maps (printed in text), Bibliography, Index.

Apps: Roll of Honour, H&A, list of former Commandants, notes on the
evolution of the Corps badges.

A comprehensive and interesting narrative account of the work and
evolution of 'the Provost' in India. Covers the entire period from the
days of the HEIC through to the formation of the CMP(I) in 1939, then
its services in WWII. The story continues with post-1947 developments
through to 1981. The photographs have not reproduced well, but there
are many individuals mentioned in the text. The only reported reference
source for the Military Police in India. R/1 V/4. AN.


THE FOUNDING OF THE NORTH WEST FRONTIER MILITIAS

Thomas D Farrell
Journal of the Royal Society for Asian Affairs (offprint), n.d. (c.1973)
Seen in stapled paper covers, 9.5 x 6.0, -/14.
no illustrations, no maps, no appendixes, Bibliography, no Index.
A brief but useful account of the reason for raising the NWF Scouts and
Militias. Included here as it may be a useful secondary source when read
in conjunction with Garrett's booklet (see this page). R/3 V/2. NAM. PJE.


FRONTIER SCOUTS

Colonel H R C Pettigrew
Published privately, Selsey, Sussex, n.d. (c.1966)
Stiff card, brown, illustrated, 8.5 x 6.5, ii/122.
Fp, 33 mono phots, 8 line drawings, one map (folding, bound in), no
appendixes, no Index.

An interesting account of this Irregular Corps, consisting of: Pishin Scouts, Zhob Militia, South Waziristan Scouts, Tochi Scouts, Kurram Militia, Samana Rifles,Khyber Rifles, Chitral Scouts, and Gilgit Scouts. The Corps was administered under the Frontier Corps Ordinance by the Administration of the North West Frontier Province, all officers being seconded from regular units of the Indian Army. The period covered in this largely anecdotal narrative is from 1900 (date of first raising of the Scouts) through to 1950. R/4 V/4. JHG/JRS.


THE FRONTIER SCOUTS

Charles Chenevix Trench
Jonathan Cape, London, 1985
Blue, gold, 9.25 x 6.25, xxii/298.
38 mono phots, 11 maps (printed in text), Glossary, Bibliography, no appendixes, Index.

This is a formalised history of the Scouts, containing much more detail than appears in Pettigrew's work (see above), but including much of Pettigrew's material (for which the author makes due acknowledgement). The individual units covered are those named in the Pettigrew entry. R/1 V/5. JHG/JRS.


DOSTAN (FRIENDS)
A Personal View of the North West Frontier

Major Dick Corfield
Published privately, no details shown, 1986
Soft card, 'spiral' spine, green, black, 11.5 x 8.25, ii/197.
21 mono phots, 3 line drawings, Bibliography, Glossary, no Index.

Apps: notes on the major tribes and sub-tribes.

An interesting autobiographical account by a British officer who joined the Tochi Scouts from the Frontier Force Rifles in 1945, and who served later with the South Waziristan Rifles and Khyber Rifles. Useful background material when read in conjunction with Pettigrew and Chenevix Trench. R/1 V/3. FWST.


THE MEYWAR BHIL CORPS

Lieut H L Showers
Printed by Cotton & Morris, Simla, for the United Service Institution of India, 1891
Journal of the United Service Institution of India, Vol 20, pages 87-97.

Although not a published history in the conventional sense, this article is noted here as being the only known record of this militia-cum-police unit. It was raised in 1841 for peace-keeping duties in Rajputana, remained loyal during the Mutiny, and took part in numerous actions against bands of mutineers and scavengers. A good description of the Bhil people and their country. R/2 V/3. PJE.

A SHORT HISTORY OF THE MALWA BHIL CORPS

Lieut Col A Poingdestre
Publisher's details not shown, Lucknow, 1905
Paper covers, cream, black, 8.0 x 5.0, -/5.
no illustrations, no maps, no appendixes, no Index.

A very short but accurate history of the Corps from 1840 to 1905.
Took part in the suppression of the Mutiny and was responsible for
maintaining law and order in Bhopawar Agency, Central India.
R/5 V/3. PJE.


A MEMOIR OF THE KHANDESH BHIL CORPS

A H A Simcox
Thacker & Co, Bombay, 1912
Blue with green edgings, gold, 'Queen Victoria head' motif embellishment
on front cover, 10.0 x 7.0, iv/281.
Fp, 4 mono phots, one map (in rear pocket), no Index.

Apps: list of former officers.

An excellent full history, with interesting descriptions in general terms
of Khandesh and the Bhil people. The Corps was raised in 1825, saw
service during the Mutiny, and was then converted into an armed police
unit in 1862. This book is apparently the only in-depth description
of a Bhil Corps unit, of which there were several. R/4 V/4. IOL. PJE.


THE FRONTIER

Maj Gen J G Elliot
Cassell, London, 1968
Yellow, black, 8.5 x 6.0, xii/306.
20 mono phots, 8 maps (bound in), Bibliography, no appendixes, Index.

This is not a regtl or Corps history, but a very readable and fairly full
account of police and military actions on the North West Frontier over a
period of 108 years. It provides useful additional background reading
for any study of the Frontier Scouts and Militia.R/1 V/3. PJE.

## INDIA - IMPERIAL SERVICE TROOPS AND INDIAN STATES FORCES
## OF THE PRINCELY STATES

A HISTORY OF THE IMPERIAL SERVICE TROOPS OF THE NATIVE STATES
With a Short Sketch of Events in each State, which have led to their
Employment in Subordinate Co-operation with the Supreme Government

Brigadier General Stuart Beatson CB
Office of the Superintendent of Government Printing, Calcutta, 1903
Blue, gold, 9.0 x 6.0, xvi/180.
no illustrations, one map (loose in rear pocket), no Index.

Apps: notes on 'the Ruling Chiefs', statistics on numerical strength
of Imperial Service Troops (at 1903), designation of British officers,
names of officers, notes on H&A, Bibliography.

Despite the patronisingly pompous title and sub-title, this is a good
summary of the structure and organisation of the IST system as it stood
in 1903. There is a short chapter describing the IST of each of the
twenty-three Princely States involved in the scheme. The full value of
the IST (re-designated Indian State Forces c.1922) was demonstrated in
1914 and confirmed in 1939. R/5 V/4. BDM/AM/RP.


A SHORT HISTORY OF THE SERVICES RENDERED BY THE IMPERIAL SERVICE
TROOPS DURING THE GREAT WAR, 1914-18

Major General Sir Harry Watson KBE CB CMG CIE MVO
Government of India Central Publications Branch, Calcutta, 1930
Seen rebound, details of original binding not known, 8.5 x 5.5, vii/68.
no illustrations, no maps, no Index.

Apps: H&A (stated to contain some inaccuracies).

This is a very useful narrative account, packed with detail. It includes
the names of many British officers seconded for duty with IST, with
details of stations, movements, and services, plus statistics regarding
casualties. R/5 V/4. AM.


THE INDIAN STATES FORCES
Their Lineage and Insignia

His Highness the Maharajah of Jaipur
Produced by Orient Longmans Ltd, printed in India, distributed in the
UK by Leo Cooper Ltd, 1967
Green, gold, 8.5 x 5.5, xxi/122.
Fp, 4 mono phots, 172 line drawings of badges, no maps, no appendixes, an
Index for each State.

To date, this is the only work to have been published which attempts to
deal with the Indian States Forces as a whole. The narrative is reported
to contain some inaccuracies, and the drawings of badges are unreliable.
A brave attempt to cover a large and complicated subject. R/1 V/3. AM.

HISTORY OF THE 15th (IMPERIAL SERVICE) CAVALRY BRIGADE DURING THE GREAT
WAR, 1914-1918

Anon
Printed by Harrison & Son, for His Majesty's Stationery Office,London,1919
Seen only in facsimile form, original binding and dimensions not known,
no illustrations, 3 maps, -/35.

Apps: Roll of Honour, H&A, list of former COs, list of former officers.

An account, year by year, for the war period, with some years being
more fully reported than others. The casualty lists give details
by regiment, with dates and locations. A brief but useful source which
covers the activities of: Kathiawar Signal Troop, Hyderabad Lancers,
Mysore Lancers, Bhavnagar Lancers, Patiala Lancers, and 124th Field
Ambulance.
R/4 V/4. AM.


BIKANER AND THE WAR
Being a Brief Narrative of the various Contributions and Efforts of
the Bikaner State towards the successful Prosecution of the War

Anon
The Government Press, Bikaner, for the Government of Bikaner, 31.12.1944
Paper covers, light brown, black, Bikaner State coat of arms on front
cover, 8.0 x 6.0, iv/63.
no illustrations, no maps, no appendixes, Index.

A fairly typical Government-inspired document which extols the personal
efforts and virtues of the Maharajah, but also providing much useful detail
on the financial and practical support he and his people gave to the
Allied cause in WWII. R/4 V/2. AM.


GWALIOR'S PART IN THE WAR

Mohammed Rafiullah
Printed by Hazell, Watson & Viney, London, 1920
Dark blue, gold, ornately embellished, 11.5 x 9.0, xiv/174.
Fp, 56 mono phots, no maps, no appendixes, no Index.

A slightly sycophantic account of the (very generous) activities of
Gwalior's high society in raising funds and doing good works during WWI.
The book contains little information regarding Gwalior's fighting forces
or their services. R/4 V/1. NAM. PJE.

RAJASTHAN STATES FORCES MEMORIAL - JAIPUR

Anon
By Authority ('Official'), Jaipur, n.d. (c.1956)
Seen rebound, details of original binding not known, 8.0 x 6.0, ii/14.
no illustrations, no maps, no Index.

Apps: list of battles fought (by unit), list of contributors to the
memorial.

This little document was published to record the unveiling of a memorial
to the fallen of the Rajasthan States Forces(incorporating Jaipur,
Jodhpur, Udaipur, Bikaner and Alwar). However, the brief narrative does
include some useful historical details regarding the services of these
units. R/4 V/1. AM.


JAMMU AND KASHMIR ARMS
History of the Jammu and Kashmir Rifles

Major General D K Palit VrC
Palit & Dutt, Dehra Dun, 1972
Bright blue, gold, 8.75 x 5.75, xv/305.
Fp, 25 mono phots, 14 half-page litho-graphs of towns and scenes (at the
beginning of each chapter), 6 maps (4 printed in text, 2 printed on end-
papers), Index.

Apps: extracts from the J&K Army List (1944), notes on the regtl crest,
regtl marches, dates of raising of the 14 battalions (8 during the
period of the Raj, 6 post-1947), list of campaigns in which they served.

As previously noted, General Palit is a much-respected military historian,
and this book is a professionally prepared narrative account of a famous
regt. Attractive, nicely illustrated, and well-written. The story covers
the entire period from medieval times through to post-Independence, i.e.
it is a military history of Jammu & Kashmir. Part of the State forces were
dedicated to the IST/ISF arrangement, and these elements served in WWI
(German East Africa and then the Third Afghan War), and in WWII (Iran,
Syria and Burma). The last part of the book deals with the conflicts
with Pakistan. R/2 V/5. IOL. RGB.


MILITARY KAPURTHALA, 1941

Anon
Printed by the Ripon Press, Lahore (presumably for the State), 1941
Light blue, gold, 9.5 x 7.5, -/24.
15 mono phots, no maps, no appendixes, no Index.

Much of the text is devoted to dutiful comments regarding the various
former Maharajahs and their personal virtues. However, it covers the
services of the State forces during the Mutiny and in WWI, and is useful
as a source for dates and events. R/4 V/2. NAM. PJE.

THE HISTORY OF THE KOLHAPUR INFANTRY, 1845-1932

Captain L T Wilcock
The Times of India Press, Bombay, n.d. (c.1932)
Green, blind, 7.5 x 5.0, i/71.
one mono phot (portrait of the Maharajah of Kolhapur), 3 line drawings
(including the regtl badge), no maps, no Index.

Apps: list of former officers, medal roll for the Mutiny, roll of men
who served in WWI.

A fairly brief but interesting account of their services from 1857
(when they declined to join a mutinous HEIC regt at that time stationed
in Kolhapur), through to WWI when many of the sepoys volunteered for
service with the Indian Army. Original title (1845) was the Kolhapur
Fusiliers. The medal roll appendix is particularly useful to medal
collectors. R/4 V/4. RJW.


PATIALA AND THE GREAT WAR
A Brief History of the Services of the Premier Punjab State

Anon ('Compiled from Secretariat and Other Records')
The Medici Society Ltd, London, 1923
Seen only in facsimile form, details of original binding therefore not
known,9.0 x 6.0, iv/91.
Fp, 48 mono phots, no maps, no appendixes, no Index.


Like one or two similar publications, this one makes much of the
Maharajah's personal contribution to the Allied war effort. However, the
narrative does include some useful details concerning the active services
of Patiala units. R/5 V/2. AM.


WAR EFFORT IN JAIPUR

Anon
The Information Bureau, Jaipur, July 1945
Paper covers, illustrated with a photographic portrait of the Maharajah,
8.0 x 6.0, iii/42.
18 mono phots, no maps, no appendixes, no Index.

A useful account of Jaipur's contribution to the Allied cause in WWII.
It is a fairly generalised account, but there are some interesting details
concerning the presentation of gallantry awards to non-ISF soldiers
by His Highness the Maharajah acting on behalf of the King Emperor.
R/4 V/2. AM.

INDIA - MEDICAL SERVICES AND OTHER CORPS


A HISTORY OF THE INDIAN MEDICAL SERVICE, 1600-1913
Volumes I and II

Lieut Col D G Crawford
W Thacker & Co, London, and Thacker Spink & Co, Calcutta, 1914
Dark blue, gold, 10.0 x 6.25, xiv/529 and -/535.
Fps, no illustrations, no maps, no formal appendixes, Bibliography, Index.

This admirable pair of matching books, published simultaneously, is a
very detailed and readable account of the evolution of the IMS over a
period of three centuries. The work has obvious value for research on
India's public health and social histories, but is also of value to
medal collectors and genealogists. Although there are no formal appendixes,
the text includes many lists of IMS personnel with details of their
services, awards, wounds, deaths, places and location of burial, and so
forth. Numerous winners of the VC appear in the story. The Index is
particularly helpful in tracing individual careers. R/4 V/5. PCAL. RP.


ROLL OF THE INDIAN MEDICAL SERVICE, 1615-1930

Lieut Col D G Crawford
W Thacker & Co, London, 1930
Black, gold, 9.75 x 7.0, Li/711.
no illustrations, no maps, a large number of appendixes, Index.

An excellent research tool which lists 6586 former IMS personnel,
giving biographical notes for each, with awards and distinctions,
campaign medal entitlements, etc. It also contains information
regarding Indian medical colleges and places of instruction. R/4 V/5. CSM.
This book was reprinted in facsimile, in a limited edition of 200, in
1986.


SURGEONS TWOE (sic) AND A BARBER
Being an Account of the Life and Work of the Indian Medical Service,
1600-1947

Donald MacDonald
Heinemann, London, 1950
Dark blue, gold, 9.5 x 7.5, ixx/295.
Fp, 11 mono phots, 10 sketches, no maps, Bibliography, list of books
written by IMS officers, Index.

Apps: list of former Heads of the IMS.

A very readable and informative account of the IMS, covering most if not
all campaigns in which the Indian Army took part. The author acknowledges
Crawford's work as 'the definitive history', but the story is here updated
and condensed. R/3 V/4. NAM. PJE.

HISTORY OF THE ARMY SERVICE CORPS

Lieut Col B N Majukdar
Sterling Publishers (Pvt) Ltd, New Delhi, 1976

The details available for this five-Volume history are not complete,
only Volumes II and III having been seen. However, assuming that the three
other Volumes are written to the same standard, this is an extremely
detailed and informative work of reference on the evolution and services
of the Corps.

Volume II:  1858-1913 (numerous accounts of campaigns on the NWF and abroad)
Volume III: 1914-1939 (mainly WWI, Third Afghan War, and Waziristan 1937)

Apart from describing the work of the Corps, there is much helpful
information on the major reforms and re-organisations. R/1 V/5. IOL. RGB.


OFFICIAL HISTORY OF THE INDIAN ARMED FORCES IN THE SECOND WORLD WAR
1939-1945
Technical Services: Ordnance and Indian Electrical & Mechanical Engineers

P N Khara
Combined Inter-Services Historical Section (India and Pakistan), Delhi,1962
Dark blue, gold, 9.5 x 6.5, xxii/479.
22 mono phots, 16 maps (printed in text), Index.

As the title might suggest, this is a detailed factual account of the
IAOC and IEME in WWII. Of value to the specialist researcher. R/2 V/5. PJE.


HISTORY OF THE CORPS OF SIGNALS
Volume I: Early Times to the Outbreak of World War II, 1939

Anon ('The Corps of Signals Committee')
The Military College of Engineering Press, Mhow, 1975
Dark blue, gold, Corps crest on front cover, 9.5 x 6.5, ix/378.
Fp, 30 mono phots, 3 sketches, 11 maps (printed in text), Index.

A detailed history of signals and signalling in almost every campaign in
which HEIC and Indian Army forces took part. This is the first in a
projected three-Volume set. It is not known if Volume II has yet been
published, but it has not been recorded for this bibliography.
R/2 V/5. PJE.

# GURKHAS - GENERAL ACCOUNTS

Given the continuing popularity of the Gurkha soldier with the British public, it is not surprising that several dozens of 'general interest' titles have been published over the past twenty or thirty years. Some are serious historical works, others are less so. Your compiler has selected just six representative titles which he believes complement (rather than duplicate) each other.


THE GURKHAS
Their Manners, Customs and Country

Major W Brook-Northey and Captain S J Morris
John Lane, at the Bodley Head, London, 1928
Green, gold, Coat of Arms of the Maharajahs of Nepal on the front cover,
9.0 x 6.0, xxxvii/282.
68 mono phots, one map (bound in), Bibliography, Index.

Apps: Gurkha festivals, the Kings and Hereditary Prime Ministers of Nepal.

The authors were invited into Nepal by the then Maharajah (a great honour at the time) to write a comprehensive account of the country, its peoples and its customs. Although it does not deal specifically with Nepal's military tradition, and although the passage of time has overtaken the political aspect, this is stated to be still the best reference book on the subject. R/4 V/5. AAM.
It is reported that this book was reprinted in facsimile form by Cosmo Publications of Delhi in 1974.


THE GURKHAS

H D James and D Sheil-Small
Macdonald, London, 1965
Light green, gold, 8.5 x 5.5, viii/283.
37 mono phots, 2 maps (printed on end-papers), no appendixes, Bibliography, Index.

An interesting account of Gurkha service with the pre-1947 Indian Army, the post-Independence British Gurkha involvements in Malaya and Borneo, and the Indian Gurkha operations in the Congo and against the Chinese. R/2 V/3. AAM.


GURKHAS

David Bolt
Weidenfeld & Nicolson, London, 1967
Pale green, gold, 8.75 x 5.5, -/128.
39 mono phots, 5 sketches, one map (printed in text), no appendixes, Bibliography, Index.

Two chapters (pages 1-57) describe the history of Nepal and the rise to power of the Gurkhas pre-1816. The last chapter deals with political matters. The central section (pages 58-103) is a fairly superficial but readable account of campaigns in which Gurkha soldiers fought. A useful introduction to the subject, especially if read in conjunction with Philip Mason's A MATTER OF HONOUR (see page 63). R/2 V/3. AMM.


JOHNNY GURKHA
Friends in the Hills

E D Smith
Leo Cooper, in conjunction with Secker & Warburg, London, 1985
Black, gold, 9.5 x 6.0, xvi/176.
25 mono phots, one map (bound in), no Index.

Apps: notes on the origins of the Gurkha regts and Corps, the Gurkha Welfare Trusts, note on the kukri.

A well-written summary of the Gurkha military ethos. Few individuals are mentioned by name, and there is virtually nothing on campaign services. This is simply a background briefing by a famous Gurkha officer. R/1 V/3. AMM.


A GURKHA BRIGADE IN ITALY
Story of the 43rd Gurkha Lorried Brigade

Anon
The Times of India Press, Bombay, n.d. (c.1946)
Paper covers, green and white, black, embellished on front cover with 'crossed kukris and Italian scene' motif, 6.0 x 3.5, -/32.
Fp, 3 mono phots, one map (printed in the text), no appendixes, no Index.

The Brigade was formed in 1944 with a battalion each from 6th, 8th and 10th Gurkha Rifles expressly for operations on the Adriatic coast of Italy. Formed part of 1st British Armoured Division and fought from Rimini to Trieste over the winter of 1944-1945. A brief but readable account of a year's hard fighting. R/4 V/2. PJE.


Of the many other 'general background' sources, the following titles are recommended: GORKHA, THE STORY OF THE GURKHAS OF NEPAL, by Lieut Gen Sir Francis Tuker (Constable, London, 1957), and THE HANDBOOK OF GURKHAS, by Vansittart (published in 1890 and 1906, revised by Nicolay in 1915 and 1918, by Morris in 1933, 1936 and 1942, and by Leonard in 1965).

210

## GURKHA RIFLES

REGIMENTAL HISTORY OF THE 1st BATTALION, 1st (PRINCE OF WALES'S OWN)
GURKHA RIFLES (THE MALAUN REGIMENT), 1815-1910

H I Money
The Public Printing Press, Kangra, n.d. (c.1910)
This booklet, of 39 pages, has been noted in a catalogue but not seen.
No other details available.


THE 1st KING GEORGE'S OWN GURKHA RIFLES, THE MALAUN REGIMENT, 1815-1921

F Loraine Petrie OBE
Printed by Butler & Tanner Ltd, Frome and London, for the Royal
United Service Institution, 1925
Green, silver, regtl crest on front cover and spine, 12.25 x 9.5, xii/260.
Fp, one mono phot, 14 coloured plates, 33 maps (15 printed in text,
14 bound in, 4 in rear pocket), Index.

Apps: list of former COs, list of former officers (with details of
service), notes on Colours, uniform and equipment.

A big handsome book, typical of the high quality production work of Butler
& Tanner. The narrative is clear, informative and packed with useful detail.
It covers the Sikh Wars, the Mutiny, numerous Frontier campaigns and WWI
(1st Bn in France, Mesopotamia and Palestine, 2nd Bn on the Frontier,
3rd Bn on IS duties and in the Third Afghan War). Approximately half of
the book is devoted to WWI. The maps are excellent, and the appendix
listing former officers includes 345 names. An important book in any library.
R/4 V/5. RP.


THE HISTORY OF THE 1st KING GEORGE V's OWN GURKHA RIFLES (THE MALAUN
REGIMENT, Volume II: 1920-1947

Brigadier E V R Bellers
Gale & Polden Ltd, Aldershot, 1956
Rifle green, silver, regtl crest on front cover, 8.75 x 5.5, xv/358.
Fp, 21 mono phots, 37 maps (printed in text), Index.

Apps: Roll of Honour (WWII), H&A (WWII), list of former COs, list of
former officers, summary of events covered in 'Volume I', notes on actions
behind Japanese lines in Malaya, summary of casualties for WWII.

Although the Loraine Petrie book was not published as Volume I of a series,
this book by Bellers is, as it claims, effectively Volume II of a pair
(even though the dimensions are totally different). The contents follow the
same pattern and, again, the narrative includes plenty of action, with
many individuals mentioned by name. R/3 V/5. IOL. AMM/LM.
It is reported that Volume I was reprinted at The Gondals Press, New
Delhi, in 1965, and it is also thought that Volume II may have been
reprinted (no details available).

HISTORICAL RECORD OF THE SERVICES OF THE 2nd GOORKHA (THE SIRMOOR RIFLE)
REGIMENT

Anon
The Government Central Press, Calcutta, 1876
Paper covers, pink, black, 9.5 x 7.5, -/15/iii.
no illustrations, no maps, no appendixes, no Index.

A modest little publication divided into two parts. The first 15 pages
cover the period 1814-1869 in diary form and deal with such matters as
changes of title, stations and movements, etc. The last 3 pages cover the
years 1870-1876 and include some brief accounts of acts of personal
bravery in the Looshai campaign. R/5 V/1. MODL. AMM.


HISTORY OF 2nd KING EDWARD'S OWN GOORKHA RIFLES
The Sirmoor Rifles, 1815-1910

Colonel L W Shakespear
Gale & Polden Ltd, Aldershot, 1912
Green boards, red leather spine and quarters, regtl crest on front cover,
10.0 x 7.5, xiv/183.
Fp, 22 mono phots, 4 maps (bound in), Bibliography, no Index.

Apps: nine, various, details not recorded.

A good all-round history for the period stated. Although not published as
such, this work became effectively Volume I of a  four-volume series (see
following entries). It is stated that this book was first published in 1910,
and that the 1912 version recorded here was a reprint to satisfy popular
demand. This report is not confirmed, and no 1910 imprint has yet been
sighted. However, it **is** known that the book was reprinted in 1950 with two
colour plates added. R/4 V/4. RGH/RP.


HISTORY OF THE 2nd KING EDWARD'S OWN GOORKHAS
The Sirmoor Rifle Regiment

Colonel L W Shakespear CB CIE
Gale & Polden Ltd, Aldershot, 1924
Rifle green, gold, embellished with broad red band and regtl crest,
10.0 x 7.25, xix/246.
Fp, 29 mono phots, 17 maps (bound in), Bibliography, no Index.

Apps: 12 various, including H&A (WWI, France 1914-15 only), list of COs
(for the period 1911-1920, with details of their services),notes of the
services of officers while detached from the regt.

This is Volume II, and it covers the period 1911-1921 in very great
detail for all three battalions. Individuals appear frequently throughout
the narrative, with details of gallantry awards which otherwise might have
been expected in an appendix. The maps are very good. A first-class
regtl history in every way (barring the lamentable lack of an Index).
R/4 V/4. MODL. AMM.

212

HISTORY OF THE 2nd KING EDWARD'S OWN GOORKHA RIFLES (THE SIRMOOR RIFLES)
Volume III: 1921-1948

Lieut Col G R Stevens OBE
Gale & Polden Ltd, Aldershot, 1952
Rifle green, gold, embellished with broad red band and regtl crest on
front cover to match Volume II (see previous entry, page 211), 10.0 x 7.25,
xv/322.
Fp, 88 mono phots, one coloured plate, 2 line drawings, 18 maps, no Index.

Apps: Roll of Honour (British and Gurkha officers only), summary of H&A
(totals only), list of former COs (1921-1947).

The author sustains the same standards as found in the two earlier Volumes.
The activities of all five battalions are described in very great detail,
with many individuals being mentioned by name in the narrative. The
period covered is 1921-1948, with good accounts of fighting services on
the Frontier and in WWII. The maps are very good. Again, however, Colonel
Stevens has failed to provide an Index (a definite disadvantage in a
book of this length and complexity). R/4 V/4. AMM.


THE STORY OF THE 4th BATTALION, 2nd KING EDWARD'S OWN GURKHA RIFLES

Lieut Col J A Kitson
Gale & Polden Ltd, Aldershot, 1949
Rifle green, gold, regtl crest on front cover, 8.75 x 5.5, xi/51.
Fp, 6 mono phots, 3 maps (printed in text), no Index.

Apps: Roll of Honour (1941-1947), H&A (1941-1947), copy of the recommend-
ation for the award of the VC to Major P R Collins (not conferred).

A very readable narrative account of the Bn's services from 1941 to 1947.
Numerous small actions and individuals mentioned in the text, while three
of the photographs are posed groups (officers with their names in the
captions).R/4 V/4. IOL. MODL. AMM.


2nd KING EDWARD VII's OWN GOORKHA RIFLES (THE SIRMOOR RIFLES), 1857-1957
Centenary of the Siege of Delhi, Based upon the Diaries of Major
Charles Reid

Major Charles Reid
W G Kingham (Printers) Ltd, King's Langley (UK), 1957
Rifle green, gold, embellished with red band and regtl crest, 8.25 x 5.5,
iii/61.
one mono phot, 2 coloured plates, 2 sketches, 2 maps (bound in),
Glossary, no appendixes, no Index.

This slim volume was published to mark the 100th anniversary of the
siege of Delhi at which the Sirmoor Rifles fought with distinction. The
regt was responsible for the defence of the Main Picquet at Hindoo Rao's
house on the Ridge.
R/2 V/3. MODL. AMM.

THE STORY OF THE SIRMOOR RIFLES

Lieut Col E D Smith DSO MBE
Jay-Birch & Co (Pte) Ltd, Singapore, 1969
Rifle green, gold, broad red band and regtl crest on front cover,
9.5 x 7.0, -/58.
Fp, 14 mono phots, 7 coloured plates, no maps, no appendixes, no Index.

A very condensed history of 2nd Gurkha Rifles between 1815 and 1967. The
story is told in simple uncomplicated terms, and the booklet was
probably intended for instructional use within the Regt. The illustrations
are good. R/3 V/2. MODL. AMM.


A PRIDE OF GURKHAS
The 2nd King Edward's Own Goorkhas (The Sirmoor Rifles), 1948-1971

Harold James and Denis Sheil-Small
Printed by Pitman Press, Bath, for Leo Cooper, London, 1975
Olive green, silver, regtl crest on front cover, 8.75 x 5.5, xiv/274.
30 mono phots, no maps, Index.

Apps: H&A, list of former COs.

This is effectively Volume IV of the Sirmoor Rifles histories. The joint
authors are skilled and knowledgeable writers, and this is a good working
account for the period stated. R/1 V/3. VS.
A 1974 edition has been noted, having fewer (251) pages. Not seen.


2nd KING EDWARD VII's OWN GOORKHAS (THE SIRMOOR RIFLES)
2nd Battalion, 1886-1986

Anon
Signland Ltd, Farnham (UK), 1986
Soft card with 'Perfect' binding, green, silver, 5 badges on front cover,
8.0 x 6.0, vi/141.
121 mono phots, 2 coloured plates, one map (Malaya, printed in the text),
no Index.

Apps: Roll of Honour, H&A (all ranks, 1948-1986), list of former COs (for
1st and 2nd Bns), nominal rolls, copies of the two VC citations, plus
citations for three gallantry awards for Borneo.

An extremely detailed history, representing a great deal of research and
compilation by the authors. The Roll of Honour appendix, for example,
lists all ranks KIA and WIA, for 1st and 2nd Bns, under the headings:
1824-1939, 1939-1947, Malaya, Brunei, Sabah and Sarawak. The nominal rolls
appendix lists every officer and Other Rank on the strength of 2nd Bn
at February 1986, with his number, rank, name, Company, Platoon, Section,
or if at the time on Nepal leave. R/1 V/4. TM.

A SHORT HISTORY OF THE 3rd QUEEN'S OWN GURKHA RIFLES

'H.D.H.' (Maj Gen H D Hutchinson)
Hugh Rees Ltd, London, 1907
Green, gold, 'Gurkha rifleman' motif on front cover, 9.5 x 7.5, -/51.
Fp, 19 mono phots, no maps, no appendixes, no Index.

A strange but attractive little book. There are some brief notes on the
regt's history, most of the pages being devoted to pictures. Presumably
the author was a keen photographer. R/5 V/3. IOL. RGH.


HISTORY OF THE 3rd QUEEN ALEXANDRA'S OWN GURKHA RIFLES
From April 1815 to December 1927

Maj Gen Nigel G Woodyatt
Philip Allan & Co Ltd, London, 1929
Dark green, gold, regtl crest on front cover, 9.0 x 5.75, ix/441.
Fp, 5 mono phots, 7 maps (bound in), Index.

Apps: Roll of Honour (2nd Bn only, officers only, Egypt only), H&A (for
2nd, 3rd and 4th Bns), list of former COs (1st and 2nd Bns), idem Subedar-
Majors, list of former officers, notes on arms, notes on the Colours, notes
on dress and establishments.

Generally a good reference source. Readable in style, with much detail for
the earlier campaigns. The WWI period is less well covered. The appendix
for 'former officers' is very useful as, in many cases, it provides
details of individual war services. R/5 V/4. IOL. MCJ.


THE REGIMENTAL HISTORY OF THE 3rd QUEEN'S ALEXANDRA'S OWN GURKHA RIFLES
Volume II: 1927 to 1947

Brigadier C N Barclay CBE DSO
William Clowes & Sons Ltd, London, 1953
Rifle green, gold, regtl crest on front cover, xx/316.
Fp, 43 mono phots, one sketch, 24 maps, Index.

Apps: H&A (WWII only), list of former COs, list of former officers,
summary of events described in Volume I, statistical summary of casualties,
Roll of Honour (British and Gurkha officers KIA and WIA).

Written in narrative style, with many individuals mentioned in the text
by name. The author describes actions on the NWF and during WWII in
great detail and for all four battalions (plus 38th Gurkha Rifles).
R/3 V/5. MODL. AMM.


FLASH OF THE KUKRI
History of the 3rd Gorkha Rifles (1947-1980)

C L Proudfoot
Vision Books, New Delhi, 1984
Green, gold, 9.0 x 5.5, iv/222.
82 mono phots, 2 coloured plates, 17 maps, Index.

Apps: H&A, list of former COs, list of officers and Subedar-Majors at
1947, notes on the Colours, notes on dress flashes, notes on battle
honours.

Although the narrative relates primarily to the post-1947 period,
three early chapters recapitulate the regt's history between 1815 and
1947. R/1 V/4. MCJ.


A HISTORY OF THE 4th PRINCE OF WALES'S OWN GURKHA RIFLES
1857-1937, Volumes I and II

Ranald Macdonnell and Marcus Macaulay
William Blackwood & Sons Ltd, Edinburgh, 1940
Green, black, regtl crest on front cover, 10.0 x 7.5, xvi/433 and viii/247.
Fps, 2 mono phots and 12 maps in Volume I, 10 mono phots and 17 maps in
Volume II, no appendixes in Volume I, various appendixes in Volume II
(see below), no Index in Volume I, full Index in Volume II for both
Volumes. Beautiful illustrations by Colonel G C Borrowman.

Apps (Volume II only): Roll of Honour (WWI), H&A, list of former COs,
list of former officers, numerous notes on the regtl crest, arms, dress,
the band and music, recruiting and trophies.

A lavish and satisfying pair of books which cover the stated period in
uniform and interesting detail. Although Volume I does not contain any
formal appendixes, there are lists of officers and their awards
scattered throughout the narrative. R/4 V/5. MODL. AMM.


A HISTORY OF THE 4th PRINCE OF WALES'S OWN GURKHA RIFLES
1838-1948, Volume III
Colonel J M Macaulay DSO
William Blackwood & Sons Ltd, London, 1952
Green, black, regtl crest on front cover, 10.0 x 7.5, xvii/620.
Fp, 8 mono phots, numerous vignettes, 44 maps, Index.

Apps: Roll of Honour (WWII), H&A (WWII), list of former COs, list of
former officers, anecdotes of battles fought, notes on trophies, dress,
and the regtl memorial.

This lavish third Volume covers the stated period in great detail.
In addition to the information provided in the appendixes, there are lists
of officers and their awards at various points in the main text. All
WWII campaigns, and the involvements of all four battalions (plus 14th
Gurkha Rifles, 1943-1946),are recounted in splendidly lucid style.
R/4 V/5. MODL. AMM.


HISTORICAL RECORD OF THE 5th GOORKHA BATTALION, OR THE HAZARA GOORKHA
BATTALION, PUNJAB FRONTIER FORCE

Anon ('By Authority')
The Punjab Government Press, Lahore, 1886
Black, gold, regtl crest on front cover, 10.5 x 7.0, iv/74.
no illustrations, no maps, no appendixes, no Index.

This is another of the well-known PFF historical records published circa 1885-1887. The text is based upon official and regtl records. It lacks human interest, but is a reliable source for checking dates, stations and movements, etc. R/5 V/4. USII. OSS.


HISTORY OF THE 5th ROYAL GURKHA RIFLES (FRONTIER FORCE)
Volume I: 1858-1928

Anon (several officers of the Regiment)
Gale & Polden Ltd, Aldershot, n.d. (c.1928)
Dark green and black, gold, regtl crest on front cover,10.0 x 7.25, xx/518.
Fp, 65 mono phots, 20 maps (17 bound in, 5 loose in rear pocket), Index.

Apps: Roll of Honour (British officers only), H&A, list of former officers, etc.

A superb regtl history produced to the best of the old Gale & Polden standards. The project was initiated by Colonel H E Weekes, but final compilation was carried through by a number of officers of the Regt. They made an excellent job of it. R/4 V/5. IOL. CSM/VS.


HISTORY OF THE 5th ROYAL GURKHA RIFLES ( FRONTIER FORCE)
Volume II: 1929-1947

Anon (several officers of the Regiment)
Gale & Polden Ltd, Aldershot, 1956
Dark green and black, gold, regtl crest on front cover,10.0 x 7.25, xvii/522.
Fp, 38 mono phots, 22 maps (12 bound in, 10 printed in the text), Index.

Apps: Roll of Honour (British and Gurkha officers), H&A, list of former officers.

Like Volume I (see previous entry), this is a classic regtl history. The first-class narrative covers the stated period in great detail, with accounts of the 1st Bn in Iraq, Syria and Italy, the 2nd Bn in Burma, the 3rd Bn in Burma and Java, and the 4th Bn in Burma and Siam. There is painstaking attention to the finer points, e.g. the Roll of Honour appendix gives full particulars of locations and dates of death for all officers between 1939 and 1945, with the same details for those wounded in action. The H&A appendix includes all ranks for Waziristan 1937 -1939 and WWII, with particulars of the four VC winners. The appendix listing officers who served with the Regt includes many biographical notes. All in all, a very desirable book. R/4 V/5. PCAL. RP.


DESPERATE ENCOUNTERS
Stories of the 5th Royal Gurkha Rifles of the Punjab Frontier Force

Lieut Col R M Maxwell
Douglas Law, at The Portland Press, Edinburgh, 1986
Green, gold, 8.5 x 6.0, vii/260.
8 mono phots, 27 maps (25 printed in the text, 2 printed on the end-papers), no appendixes, no Index.

This is a useful history which covers the whole period from 1858 to 1947 and which concentrates upon the active services of the regt on the NWF and in WWI (Mesopotamia and Gallipoli) and WWII (Burma, Middle East and Italy). Unfortunately the book has no Index. However, it will serve well for any researcher unable to gain access to the rare volumes recorded on page 216. R/1 V/3. FWST.


HISTORICAL RECORD OF THE 6th GURKHA RIFLES
Volume I: 1817-1919

Major D G J Ryan DSO (for 1st Bn), Major G C Strahan OBE (for 2nd Bn), and Captain J K Jones (for 3rd Bn)
Gale & Polden Ltd, Aldershot, 1925
Olive green, silver, regtl crest on front cover, 8.5 x 5.25, xx/331.
Fp, 44 mono phots, 20 maps (bound in), no Index.

Apps: seventeen in all, including H&A, list of former COs, etc.

The three battalions are dealt with separately: 1st Bn in full, for its entire existence through to 1919, 2nd Bn from its formation in 1904 onwards, and 3rd Bn quite briefly because it was formed only in 1917. The narrative is based partly upon official records and partly upon the personal experiences of individual officers. The result is a book easy to read and full of useful information. R/4 V/4. VS/PJE.


HISTORICAL RECORD OF THE 6th GURKHA RIFLES

Lieut Col H K R Gibbs
Gale & Polden Ltd, Aldershot, 1955
Rifle green, silver, regtl crest on front cover, 8.5 x 5.5, xix/320.
Fp, 19 mono phots, 3 sketches, 5 maps (bound in), Index.

Apps: Roll of Honour, H&A (for 1920-1945), list of former COs, list of former officers, notes on dress and equipment from 1817 to 1939.

Although not reported to be imprinted as such, this is Volume II of the regt's history (see previous entry) and covers the period 1919-1948. It is written in a pleasant narrative style, with lots of detail and individual names woven into the text. It covers the inter-war campaigns on the NWF and then the activities of all four battalions in WWII. There is also a brief account of 26th and 56th Gurkha Rifles. A very good history. R/3 V/5. MODL. AMM.


THE HAPPY WARRIORS
The Gurkha Soldier in Malaya, 1948-1958

Brig Gen A E C Bredin DSO MC
The Blackmore Press, Gillingham, Dorset, 1961
Green, gold, 8.5 x 6.0, -/356.
10 plates of mono phots, 2 maps, reported to have no appendixes, no Index.

A highly detailed history of the Gurkha Brigade in the campaign against Chinese Communist gangs in the Malayan jungle, but with a strong emphasis on the services of 6th Gurkha Rifles. R/2 V/4. RJW.


THE STEADFAST GURKHA
Historical Record of the 6th Queen Elizabeth's Own Gurkha Rifles
1948-1982

Charles Messenger
Leo Cooper Ltd, in conjunction with Secker & Warburg, London, 1985
Green, gold, 9.5 x 6.25, xii/147.
19 mono phots, 3 maps (printed on end-papers), Glossary, Index.

Apps: Roll of Honour, H&A, list of former COs, list of Gurkha Majors, list of former officers (including those attached temporarily).

A narrative account based mainly upon personal reminiscences by various officers of their services in Malaya, Malaysia and Hong Kong. Easy reading, with plenty of detail. R/1 V/4. MCJ/AMM.


HISTORY OF 7th DUKE OF EDINBURGH'S OWN GURKHA RIFLES

Colonel J N Mackay DSO
William Blackwood & Sons Ltd, Edinburgh and London, 1962
Green, silver, regtl crest on front cover, 8.75 x 5.75, xxiii/383.
Fp, 48 mono phots, 18 maps (folding, bound in), Index.

Apps: summary of officer casualties, H&A (WWII only), list of former COs, list of former officers, notes on the regtl badge, notes on commemoration dates, notes on the band and regtl music, notes on memorials, etc.

An informative and very readable account of the regt's services from date of formation in 1902 through to 1959. R/2 V/4. DJB/HLL.


EAST OF KATMANDU
The Story of the 7th Duke of Edinburgh's Own Gurkha Rifles
Volume II: 1948-1973

Brig E D Smith DSO OBE
Leo Cooper Ltd, London, 1976
Green, silver, regtl crest on front cover, 8.75 x 5.75, xviii/212.
14 mono phots, 2 drawings, 3 maps, no Index.

Apps: Roll of Honour, H&A, list of former COs, idem Honourary Colonels, idem Gurkha Majors, idem former officers, plus various other notes.

A good detailed history written in narrative style, and covering the regt's services in Malaya, Borneo and Hong Kong. Plenty of individuals mentioned in the text but, sadly, there is no Index. R/1 V/4. IOL. MCJ.

A SHORT HISTORY OF THE 2nd BATTALION, 8th GURKHA RIFLES

Major H J Huxford OBE and Captain H S Gordon
The Curzon Printing Press, Quetta, 1928
Black, yellow, regtl crest on front cover, 8.5 x 5.75, iii/85.
no illustrations,  no maps, no Index.

Apps: H&A, list of former COs, list of former officers (British and
Gurkha), notes on battle honours, list of Subedar Majors

Compiled in diary form, this fairly brief account covers the period 1835-
1927 and details the evolution of the battalion over that time (Assam
Sebundy Corps 1835-1844, 2nd Assam Light Infantry 1844-1891, 43rd Gurkha
Rifle Regiment of Bengal Native Infantry 1891-1903, 7th Gurkha Rifles
1903-1907, thereafter 2/8th Gurkha Rifles. In addition to the formal
appendixes, there are summaries of officer casualties, with names,
scattered throughout. A very helpful research source. R/4 V/4. MODL. AMM.


A BRIEF OUTLINE HISTORY OF THE 8th GURKHA RIFLES

Colonel F H Willasey-Wilsey MC
The Civil & Military Gazette Press, Quetta, 1945
Seen only in photo-copy form, details of original binding not known,
6.75 x 4.5, iv/54.
17 mono phots, 13 drawings, one map (printed in text), no appendixes,
no Index.

This is a brief (very brief) summary of the period 1824 to 1939. Despite
having been published in 1945, there is no mention of WWII. It has been
deleted 'on security grounds'. Given the fact that the booklet was
intended for the instruction of young officers and officer cadets just
joining the regiment, this ruling by the Official Censor must have left
the author speechless. R/4 V/1. MODL. IWM. AMM/RP.


HISTORY OF THE 8th GURKHA RIFLES

Lieut Col H J Huxford OBE
Gale & Polden Ltd, Aldershot, 1952
Green, silver, regtl crest on front cover, 8.75 x 5.5, xix/335.
Fp, 15 mono phots, 17 maps (5 printed in text, 12 bound in), Index.

Apps: summary of honours and awards (no names listed), full citations for
four VC awards, list of former COs.

A very detailed but clearly presented account which is particularly good
for information on 1st, 2nd and 3rd Bns in WWI (France, Mesopotamia and
Palestine), and 1st, 2nd, 3rd and 4th Bns in WWII (Burma, Iraq, North
Africa, Italy, Java and Borneo). The book was produced at a time when Gale
& Polden were trying to maintain their pre-war standards while faced with
post-war shortages of good printing material. The paper is of inferior
'utility' quality, but the binding is very good. An attractive and very
useful work. R/3 V/4. IOL. VS/RP.

GREEN SHADOWS - A GURKHA STORY

Denis Sheil-Small MC
William Kimber, London, 1982
Green, gold, 9.5 x 5.75, -/198.
30 mono phots, 5 maps (printed in text), no formal appendixes, Index.

A very personal account, by an officer who at that time was a Company
Commander, of the services of 4/8th Gurkha Rifles in Burma, and then Java
(1943-1946). Few of his fellow-officers are named in the text, but there
are many good photographs of British officers and campaign scenes. Readable
and interesting. R/1 V/3. MODL. AMM.


A SHORT HISTORY OF THE 38th GURKHA RIFLES, 1943-1946

Lieut Col C W Yeates DSO
The A.V.Press, Dehra Dun, n.d. (c.1946)

38 GR were the training and draft-finding battalion for 3 GR and 8 GR
during WWII. This title has been noted in a catalogue, but not seen. No
other details available.


THE 2nd BATTALION, 9th GURKHA RIFLES, 1904-1923

Anon
Trail & Co Ltd, Calcutta, 1924
Dark green, gold, regtl crest on front cover, 7.5 x 5.0, iv/131.
no illustrations, no maps, no Index.

Apps: extracts from January Army Lists, 1905 to 1923

This is an outline history, written in diary form and presumably based
upon battalion records. Although it has no formal appendixes, the
book contains lists of officers, casualties, awards and distinctions,
relevant to various campaigns and wars, scattered throughout. Readable and
very helpful. R/5 V/4. MODL. AMM.


THE NINTH GURKHA RIFLES
Volume I: 1817-1936

Lieut Col F S Poynder MVO OBE MC
Printed by Butler & Tanner, Frome and London, for the Royal United Service
Institution, for the Regiment, London, 1937
Green and black, silver, regtl crest on front cover, 10.0 x 7.5, xx/275.
Fp, 15 mono phots, 17 maps (bound in), Bibliography, Index.

Apps: Roll of Honour (WWI), H&A (1914-1923), list of former COs, obituary
for British officers who died (1905-1923), officers' war services (1914-
1923), Order of Battle of the Meerut Division (1914), battle honours.

A very full and readable history. The period prior to conversion to a Gurkha regt (1817-1893) is not as fully recorded as the subsequent period, but the WWI services are described exceptionally well. This Volume is assessed by Maggs, the London dealers, as being the rarest of all Gurkha histories. R/5 V/4. IOL. AAM.


THE 9th GURKHA RIFLES
Volume II: 1937-1947

Lieut Col G R Stevens OBE
Printed by Butler & Tanner, Frome and London, for the Regimental Assoc-
iation (UK), 9th Gurkha Rifles, London, 1953
Green and black, silver, regtl crest on front cover, 10.0 x 7.5,
xviii/355.
Fp, 5 mono phots, 12 maps (bound in), no appendixes, Index.

An excellent account, by a skilled researcher and writer, of the period
stated. R/3 V/4. AAM.


9th GURKHA RIFLES
A Regimental History, 1817 to 1947

Lieut Col P Chaudhuri
Printed by Kay Kay Printers, Delhi, for Vision Books (Pvt) Ltd, New Delhi,
for the Regiment, 1984
Green, black, 8.5 x 5.5, v/260.
17 mono phots, no maps, no appendixes, Index.

This is not a reprint but a condensed amalgamation of material from the
two earlier Volumes by Poynder and Stevens. The regt wished to produce a
new book which could be readily studied by young officers who might not
gain access to the original works (certainly Volume I). This work is
also useful for research and general background reading. R/1 V/3. AAM.


CHINESE CHINDITS
Being an Informal Account of Some of the Life of a Wartime Battalion

Anon
Gale & Polden Ltd, Aldershot, 1948
Dark green, black, 8.5 x 5.5, v/53.
no illustrations, one map (bound in), no appendixes, no Index.

This is a personal memoir, written presumably by an officer who served, of
the activities of 4/9th GR on the NWF and in Burma. The Bn was raised
in 1941 and disbanded in 1947. Names of officers appear frequently in
the text, but often without their ranks. The narrative is readable, but
the book lacks form and structure. This is a pity, because the Bn served
with Wingate's Chindits between 1943 and 1945. A more determined effort
by the author could have produced an important historical record.
R/5 V/3. MODL. AMM.

222

HISTORY OF THE 10th GURKHA RIFLES
The First Battalion 1890-1921

Captain B R Mullaly
Gale & Polden Ltd, Aldershot, 1924
Green, gold, regtl crest on front cover, 10.0 x 7.5, -/119.
Fp, 30 mono phots, 7 maps (printed in text), no Index.

Apps: H&A (for the period 1890-1921, complete for WWI but incomplete for
1890-1914), statistics on casualties, notes on other units affiliated to
the regtl depot (1/70 Burma Rifles, 3/70 Kachin Rifles, 4/70 Chin Rifles).

A high quality production, with good paper and binding and well-executed
maps. The narrative covers operations in Burma (1891-1894), Mesopotamia
(1916-1918), and Iraq/Kurdistan (1918-1921). The sub-title should be noted.
This account deals only with the 1st Battalion. It was therefore not
counted as a 'Volume I' when, in 195 , a full history for the complete
regiment was finally published. R/4 V/5. IOL. DH


BUGLE AND KUKRI
The Story of the 10th Princess Mary's Own Gurkha Rifles

Colonel B R Mullaly
William Blackwood & Sons Ltd, Edinburgh, 1957
Green, silver, regtl crest on front cover, 10.0 x 7.5, xvii/492.
Fps, 45 mono phots, one coloured plate, 22 maps (printed in text), Index.

Apps: Roll of Honour (WWII), H&A, notes on regtl customs, notes on the
10th Madras Native Infantry (stated to be not entirely accurate).

A good regtl history,strongest in its coverage of the WWI, WWII, and post-
1947 periods. This is the book which is now regarded as 'Volume I' of
the regt's history because it provides a good account of all three bns
(1st, 2nd, 3rd) in WWI, and all four bns (1st, 2nd, 3rd, and 4th) in WWII.
The regt had the highest number of decorations of the Gurkha Brigade in
WWII, and the second heaviest casualty list. The H&A appendix, in fact,
gives details of all awards from 1893 to 1945. R/2 V/5. DH/MCJ/VS/AS.


BUGLE AND KUKRI
The Story of the 10th Princess Mary's Own Gurkha Rifles, Volume II

Major General R W L McAlister CB OBE
Printed by Vectis Ltd, Newport, Isle of Wight (UK), for the Regimental
Trust of the 10th P.W.O. Gurkha Rifles, 1984
Glazed card covers, green, silver, 'Perfect' binding, 8.5 x 5.5, xii/506.
Fp, 72 mono phots, 21 maps (printed in text), Glossary, no Index.

Apps: Roll of Honour, H&A, list of former COs and Gurkha Majors, notes on
Lahore 1947, notes on the Hong Kong border confrontation, 1967.

This edition was issued in an 'economy' binding, and with a limited print-run of 350 copies, in order to establish what corrections or amendments might be forthcoming from readers. A full hardback edition, of which 650 copies were printed, was then published in 1987. For research purposes, the second version is presumably to be preferred. Apart from any other consideration, it has 24 additional pages at the rear, giving a 'Digest of Services',and including a full Index. The story covers the period 1948-1975, with much detail throughout of daily happenings in 1st and 2nd Bns during their services in Malaya, Borneo, Sarawak, and following their amalgamation in Penang. R/2 V/5. TM/DH.

## OTHER GURKHA FORMATIONS

GURKHA SAPPER
The Story of the Gurkha Engineers, 1948-1970

Major General L E C M Perowne CB CBE
Printed by The Cathay Press Ltd, Hong Kong, for the Regiment, 1973
Dark blue, gold, Gurkha Engineer badge on front cover, 9.25 x 5.75, x/390.
74 mono phots, 3 diagrams, 9 maps (bound in), Index.

Apps: list of former COs, list of former officers.

An immensely detailed work, the narrative full of detail, with many lists of personnel inserted throughout. The pictures, although originally helpful and interesting, have not reproduced well. Otherwise an excellent book. R/2 V/5. MODL. AMM.


THE STORY OF THE ROYAL ARMY SERVICE CORPS AND ROYAL CORPS OF TRANSPORT 1945-1982

Brigadier D J Sutton OBE
Leo Cooper, in conjunction with Secker & Warburg, London, 1983

This is an immense work which deals largely with the matters mentioned in the title. However, the book does contain a chapter (pages 579-604) in which the author describes the structure and work of the Gurkha Army Service Corps.


WITH PEGASUS IN INDIA
The Story of 153 Gurkha Parachute Battalion

Eric Neild
Jay Birch & Co (Pvt) Ltd,Singapore, n.d. (c.1970)
Glazed card, cream, maroon, 'Pegasus' (India) badge on front cover.
Fp, 10 mono phots, 8 maps (bound in), no Index.

Apps: Orders of Battle for 50th Indian Parachute Battalion and 2nd Indian Airborne Division.

This is a very personal account of the formation and subsequent operations
(1942-1945) of the Gurkha Bn of 50 Indian Parachute Brigade. The narrative
flows pleasingly, and is full of incident, but very few members of the bn
are mentioned. This is a pity, given the lack of nominal rolls in
the 'appendixes' section. Even so, a worthwhile record of a little-
known unit. R/3 V/3. IOL. MOD. AMM.

## APPENDIX IV

Designation of Gurkha Regiments
following the re-organisations of 1922

1st King George's Own (The Malaun Regiment)
(re-designated 1st King George V's Own in 1937)

2nd King Edward's Own (The Sirmoor Rifles)
(re-designated 2nd King Edward VII's Own in 1936)

3rd Queen Alexandra's Own Gurkha Rifles

4th Gurkha Rifles
(re-designated 4th Prince of Wales's Own in 1924)

5th Royal Gurkha Rifles (Frontier Force)

6th Gurkha Rifles

7th Gurkha Rifles

8th Gurkha Rifles

9th Gurkha Rifles

10th Gurkha Rifles

Following the granting of Independence in 1947, six of these regiments
were retained in the service of the Government of India and retained
their former numbers (1st, 3rd, 4th, 5th, 8th and 9th Gorkha Rifles).

The four other regiments were transferred to the British Army as a newly
created Brigade of Gurkhas, again retaining their former numbers but,
in the case of three of them, receiving new additional titles, thus:

2nd King Edward VII's Own Gurkha Rifles (The Sirmoor Rifles)

6th Queen Elizabeth's Own Gurkha Rifles

7th Duke of Edinburgh's Own Gurkha Rifles

10th Princess Mary's Own Gurkha Rifles

# PART IV
## Canada

## NEWFOUNDLAND

Newfoundland was Great Britain's oldest Colony until April 1949 when, with
Labrador, it became Canada's tenth Province. Each of the following titles
refer to Newfoundland's pre-1949 military history, and it is for this
reason that they are recorded here under their own heading.


THE FIRST FIVE HUNDRED
A Historical Sketch of the Military Operations of the Royal Newfoundland
Regiment in Gallipoli and on the Western Front during the Great War
(1914-1918)

Richard Cramm
C F Williams & Son Inc, Albany, New York, n.d. (c.1922)
Black, gold, regtl crest on front cover, 10.5 x 8.0, xviii/297.
370 mono phots, 8 maps (7 printed in text, one bound in), no formal
appendixes or Index (but see below).

This is one of the most intimate of unit histories. The population of
Newfoundland in 1914 was very small, and the heavy losses suffered by the
regt had a particularly devastating effect upon local families and the
local economy. The title refers to the first draft of Volunteers (also
known as 'the blue puttees') who crossed over to Europe. The first 109
pages give a reasonably accurate account of the regt's participation in
various battles, with lists of honours and awards for each of those
battles. The second half of the book (193 pages) consists of a biographical
entry for each man with, in many cases, a portrait photograph of him.
The regt gained one VC in WWI - Private (later Sergeant) Thomas Ricketts.
The book contains a good photograph of him, and details of his award.
R/5 V/4. JEB /JBC.


THE TRAIL OF THE CARIBOU
The Royal Newfoundland Regiment, 1914-1918

Major R H Tait
Newfoundland Publishing Co, Boston, 1933
Stiff card covers, red, white, regtl crest on front cover, ix/65.
3 mono phots, no maps, no formal appendixes, no Index.

This is a brief outline history of the regt's services from the date of
inception as a small band of volunteers in August 1914, through to
its last engagement on the Western Front in 1918. Honours and awards, and
casualties, are mentioned in the text. R/4 V/3. JEB.

THE FIGHTING NEWFOUNDLANDERS
A History of the Royal Newfoundland Regiment

Colonel G W L Nicholson CD
Printed by Thomas Nelson (Printers) Ltd, London (UK), for the
Government of Newfoundland, 1964
Ivory, red on gold, 9.75 x 6.25, xix/614.
Fp, 78 mono phots, line drawings of badges, 18 maps (11 printed in text,
5 folding and bound in, 2 printed on end-papers), Bibliography, Index.

Apps: seven in total, including Roll of Honour (WWI, all ranks, with
dates KIA), H&A (all ranks, with dates of engagement for which awarded),
notes on battle honours, notes on the Newfoundland Volunteers (1780).

This is a well-written and very detailed narrative account of the regt
from its origins through to 1964. However, the bulk of the text is
devoted to the period 1914-18 when the Newfoundlanders gained an
outstanding reputation but suffered horrendous casualties in the process.
The photographs have not reproduced well but, in overall terms, this is
a particularly attractive publication. The maps, drawn by E H Wellwand of
the Royal Canadian Engineers, are exceptionally good.
R/3 V/5. PCAL. SB/RP.


MORE FIGHTING NEWFOUNDLANDERS
A History of Newfoundland's Fighting Forces in the Second World War

Colonel G W L Nicholson CD
Printed at Aylesbury (UK), for the Government of Newfoundland, 1969
Ivory, with crests of the three fighting services on the front cover,
9.75 x 6.25, xiii/621.
Fp, 114 mono phots, 16 maps (14 bound in, 2 printed on end-papers),
Index.

Apps: Roll of Honour, H&A, notes on drafts.

As the sub-title indicates, this large and very informative book deals
with the services of Newfoundlanders who served in WWII in the
Army, Navy and Air Force. However, eleven of the sixteen chapters are
dedicated to the two artillery regiments raised in Newfoundland and which
fought in North Africa, Italy and North West Europe. Two chapters
deal with naval services, and one chapter on 125 (Newfoundland) Sqn RAF.
R/2 V/5. SB.

WHAT BECAME OF CORPORAL PITTMAN?

Joy B Cave
Breakwater Books Ltd, St John's, Newfoundland, 1976
Blue, white, 8.0 x 5.5, xiv/180/Lxviii.
10 mono phots, 3 maps (bound in at rear), no Index.

Apps: Roll of Honour (KIA and WIA, on 1.7.1916), nominal roll of survivors.

This is the story of the virtual annihilation of the Newfoundland Regiment
in the disastrous attack on Beaumont-Hamel on the opening day of the Somme
offensive. In a remarkable work, Joy Cave  has constructed nominal rolls
of all the officers and men of the regt who took part: killed that day,
wounded that day, died subsequently of their wounds, or survived.
She provides details of home addresses and locations of burial for
each and every casualty. These appendixes occupy the last 68 pages of the
book. The main narrative (180 pages) is an account of the preparations for
the battle (including the raid of 28 June) and the battle itself.
R/2 V/5. SB.

## CANADA - GENERAL ACCOUNTS

CANADA IN FLANDERS
The Official Story of the Canadian Expeditionary Force
Volumes 1, 2 and 3

Sir Max Aitken (Volumes 1 and 2), Major Charles G S Roberts (Volume 3)
Hodder & Stoughton, London, 1916, 1917 and 1918
Red, gold, 7.5 x 5.0.
Illustrated, no maps, no Index.

The three Volumes record all the battles in which CEF units took part
between 1914 and 28 November 1916. Many unit titles and individual
soldiers are mentioned in the narrative, and the battle descriptions are
good. However, wartime censorship and the speed with which the books
were produced and marketed may not have contributed to their reliability
for research purposes. R/2 V/3. RLP/RP.


CANADIAN EXPEDITIONARY FORCE, 1914-1919
Official History of the Canadian Army in the First World War

Colonel G W L Nicholson
The Queen's Printer, Ottawa, for the Ministry of National Defence, 1962
Red, gold, CEF badge on front cover, 10.0 x 6.5, xiv/621.
Fp, 48 mono phots, 55 line drawings, 16 maps (coloured, 15 bound in,
one printed on end-papers), Glossary, Bibliography, Index.

Apps: seven in total, including lists of units serving in France at
November 1918, notes on battles fought, distinguishing flashes of Canadian
units in the field (coloured fold-out).

After WWI, work was commenced on an eight-Volume Official History of the
Canadian Forces in the Great War. Volume I, by Colonel Duguid, was
published (with a Volume of Appendixes and maps) in 1938, and dealt with
the period from August 1914 to September 1915. A Volume entitled 'The
Medical Services' had already appeared in 1924. After WWII, the project
was abandoned. Colonel Nicholson, a very good historian, was then invited
to pick up the pieces and to produce a single volume in place of the
original eight. Thirty-five years after the events he was expected to
describe, he produced this excellent book which deals primarily with
the war in France and Flanders. The work is very well researched, and
illustrated with excellent maps. R/2 V/5. SB.


AMID THE GUNS BELOW
The Story of the Canadian Corps

Larry Worthington
McClelland & Stewart Ltd, Toronto, 1965
Beige, brown, 'Canadian soldier' motif on front cover, 9.0 x 5.75, xvi/171.
11 mono phots, one map (on end-papers), Bibliography, no appendixes, Index.

A general account of a famous Corps. The author pays over-due credit to
the leadership qualities of General Sir Arthur Currie. The narrative also
includes little-known information regarding Brigadier General Raymond
Brutinel who commanded the Canadian Machine-Gun Corps. An easy and
readable narrative which concentrates upon WWI services in France and
Flanders.  R/1 V/2. JBC.


NOVA SCOTIA'S PART IN THE GREAT WAR

Capt M Stuart Hunt
The Nova Scotia Veteran Publishing Co Ltd, Halifax, Nova Scotia, 1920
Red, black, Provincial armorial bearings on front cover, 9.75 x 5.75,
xii/432.
Fp, many mono phots of officers (named) who were KIA, WIA, or injured,
no maps, no Index.

Apps: Roll of Honour, H&A.

The Province sent volunteers to fill the ranks of many Canadian Army
units during WWI. This book is a compendium of numerous unit histories,
with many individuals named in the text. A useful secondary source when
consulted as a supplement to more complete histories, or to fill gaps in
the published record for: 6th Canadian Mounted Rifles, 9th Siege Battery,
10th Siege Battery, 17th Field Battery, 14th Brigade CFA, the 17th, 25th,
40th, 64th, 85th, 106th, 112th, 185th, 193rd, 219th and 246th Battalions,
CEF. There are condensed histories also of: 1st CGA (Militia), 63rd, 66th
and 94th Composite Battalions (Militia). There are approximately ten to
twenty pages dedicated to the history of each of these units. R/4 V/4. MCJ.

# CANADA – EARLY MILITIA HISTORIES

HISTORICAL RECORD OF THE GOVERNOR GENERAL'S BODYGUARD AND ITS STANDING
ORDERS

Captain Frederick C Denison
Hunter, Rose & Co, Toronto, 1876
Red, gold, ornate Victorian embellishment, 6.0 x 4.75, iii/87.
no illustrations, no maps, no formal appendixes, no Index.

A straightforward account on the War of 1812, the Upper Canada Rebellion
of 1837-1838, and the Fenian Raid of 1866. R/5 V/3. DKD.


THE ORIGIN AND OFFICIAL HISTORY OF THE THIRTEENTH BATTALION OF INFANTRY
And a Description of the Work of the Early Militia of the Niagara
Peninsula in the War of 1812 and the Rebellion of 1837

Lieut Col E A Cruikshank
Printed by E L Ruddy of Hamilton, for the Regiment, 1899
Blue and red, leather spine and quarters, gold, regtl crest on front cover,
10.5 x 8.25, -/88/xL.
Fp, numerous mono phots, no maps, no Index.

Apps: list of former officers, records of rifle shooting competitions.

The sub-title tells it all. R/5 V/3. AMOT. RP.


THE QUEEN'S OWN RIFLES OF CANADA
A History of a Splendid Regiment's Origin, Development and Services,
including a Story of Patriotic Duties well Performed in Three Campaigns

Captain Ernest J Chambers
R G McLean, for E L Ruddy, Toronto, for the Regiment, 1901
Red and green, cloth boards with leather spine, gold, regtl crest on front
cover, 12.0 x 9.0, -/156.
Several mono phots, no maps, no Index.

Apps: list of former officers, with full biographical notes.

Again, the sub-title tells most of the story. A full and interesting
account of Volunteer soldiering in Canada during the 19th century, and
service during the Riel Rebellion and in South Africa for the Boer War.
Written in florid style, but quite readable, and a good source of
information for officers' records of service. R/5 V/4. AMOT. MCJ.

THE GOVERNOR GENERAL'S BODY GUARD OF CANADA
A History of the Origin, Development and Services of the Senior Cavalry
Regiment in the Militia Service of the Dominion of Canada

Captain Ernest J Chambers
E L Ruddy, Toronto, 1902
Blue, gold, regtl crest and 'charging cavalryman' motif on front cover,
12.5 x 10.0, viii/128.
32 mono phots, no maps, no Index.

Apps: list of former officers, muster roll, nominal roll of GGBG personnel
who served in the North West Canada campaign of 1885, nominal roll of
personnel who served in South Africa 1899-1902, list of Staff Sergeants
and Sergeants on the strength of the GGBG, 1902.

This is a much expanded and updated work compared with Denison's book
of 1876 (see previous page). It covers the complete history of the GGBG
from 1793 through the War of 1812, the Upper Canada Rebellion of
1837-1838, the Fenian Raids of 1866 and 1870, the Northwest Canada
campaign of 1885, to the Boer War of 1899-1902.
A well-written story including many personal anecdotes. The names of
junior officers and Other Ranks appear frequently throughout the text.
R/5 V/4. AMOT. DKD/RP.


THE DUKE OF CORNWALL'S OWN RIFLES
A Regimental History of the Forty-third Regiment, Active Militia of Canada

Captain Ernest J Chambers
E L Ruddy, Ottawa, 1903
Cloth board and leather spine, red and blue, gold, regtl crest on front
cover, 11.5 x 9.0, -/70.
many mono phots (studio portraits) of individual officers, no maps,
no appendixes, no Index.

Captain Chambers seems to have earned his living for several years as
a full-time historian for the militia regiments of Canada. He pleased his
clients by inserting lots of photographs of individual officers throughout
each book, and making numerous references to them in the narratives. This
means that his works are today very useful indeed for medal collectors and
genealogists. Also, because the Militia were often engaged in operations
at which no regular British Army regts were present, he describes many
engagements which otherwise might have passed unrecorded. R/5 V/4. AMOT. RP.


THE 5th REGIMENT, ROYAL SCOTS OF CANADA HIGHLANDERS
A Regimental History

Captain Ernest J Chambers
Printed by The Guertin Printing Co, Montreal, for the author, 1904
Red, gold, 12.0 x 9.0, -/90.
Fp, numerous mono portrait studies of officers in uniform (all captioned,
as usual), no maps, no appendixes, no Index.

A detailed account of the early years. The photographs are particularly
useful for details of uniform and personal accoutrement. R/5 V/4. AMOT. RP.

236

THE ROYAL GRENADIERS
A Regimental History of the 10th Infantry Regiment of the Active Service
Militia of Canada

Captain Ernest J Chambers
Printed by Browne Searle Printing Co, Toronto, for E L Ruddy, Toronto, 1904
Cloth boards with leather spine, red and blue, gold, regtl crest on front
cover, 12.0 x 9.25, -/128.
several mono phots, no maps, no Index.

Apps: list of former officers, with biographical notes.

Another of the Chambers' nicely produced Milita histories, with good
coverage of the early years. R/5 V/3. AMOT. RP.


HISTORY OF THE 12th REGIMENT, YORK RANGERS
With Some Account of the Different Raisings of Militia in the County
of York, Ontario

Published in Toronto, c.1912, red cloth, 'numerous illustrations and maps',
noted in a catalogue but not seen.


THE IRISH-CANADIAN RANGERS

Anon
Gazette Printing Co, Montreal, 1916
Green, gold, regtl crest of 199th Bn CEF on front cover, 9.0 x 6.0, i/57.
25 mono phots (including 4 large fold-outs), no maps, no Index.

Apps: list of former officers of the 55th Bn.

This is a short history of the 55th Bn of Canadian Militia. In WWI, it
raised the 199th Bn CEF. Both were known as the Irish-Canadian Rangers.
Concerned mainly with pre-war Militia activities. R/5 V/3. RR.


THE QUEEN'S RANGERS IN THE REVOLUTIONARY WAR

Colonel C J Ingles VD and Lieut Col H M Jackson MBE ED
The Industrial Shops for the Deaf, Montreal, 1956
Green, black, 9.25 x 6.0, xii/301.
Fp, no other illustrations, 20 maps (printed in text), no Index.

Apps: list of former officers (with detailed biographical notes),
nominal roll of all personnel who surrendered at Yorktown.

The regt was raised in 1776 from the loyal population of the Thirteen
Colonies by a retired British Army officer, Major Robert Rogers, to
help put down the rebellion. Highly detailed, and no doubt very useful
for the specialist researcher and for genealogical searches.
R/2 V/3. PCAL. RP.

THE 104th REGIMENT OF FOOT (THE NEW BRUNSWICK REGIMENT), 1803-1817

W Austin-Squires
The Brunswick Press, Fredericton, New Brunswick, 1962
Red, gold, 8.5 x 5.75, xi/246.
11 mono phots (including pictures of uniforms, buttons and badges),
2 maps (printed on the end-papers), Bibliography, no Index.

Apps: list of former officers (with biographical details), nominal roll
of members (with some service details).

A regt recruited partly in Great Britain and partly in British America,
and served in the War of 1812. The narrative is rather uninspiring and
dry, but it includes helpful and otherwise scarce details regarding The New
Brunswick Provincials (also known as The King's New Brunswick Regiment),
and The New Brunswick Regiment of Fencible Infantry. A very good book of
genealogical research and for the specialist military researcher.
The appendixes give officers' services between 1803 and 1817, and
dates of enlistment and discharge for NCOs and private soldiers.
R/1 V/4. PCAL. RP/LM.

THE ORIGIN AND SERVICES OF THE 3rd (MONTREAL) FIELD BATTERY OF ARTILLERY
With Some Notes on the Artillery of By-gone Days, and a Brief History
of the Development of Field Artillery

Captain Ernest J Chambers
E L Ruddy, Montreal, 1898
Black, gold, Battery badge on front cover, 10.5 x 8.25, -/84/xxxvi.
Fp, 25 mono phots, 8 line drawings, no maps, no Index.

Appendix: lists of former and serving officers, list of subscribers (which
the author charmingly entitles 'Roll of Honour'!)

The opening chapters are a eulogy of the Battery's past services and its
senior officers, with some very generalised comments regarding the
evolution of field gunnery. There is then some mention of the Fenian
Raids (in which the Battery played a very minor role) and its various
'aid to the civil power' involvements between 1855 and 1885 (which are
much more interesting). Nominal rolls are scattered throughout the text,
and some of the captioned group photographs are very useful. As usual with
Chamber's works, the last 36 pages are devoted to paid advertisements.
An attractive Militia history which is also an interesting reflection on
Montreal society at the turn of the century. R/5 V/4. MODL. AMM.

THE PRINCE OF WALES'S REGIMENT, by Captain Ernest J Chambers

Yet another Militia history, following his usual format, was produced
cira 1905 for this regt, but no copy has yet been traced. No other details
available.

HISTORICAL RECORD OF THE NEW BRUNSWICK REGIMENT, CANADIAN ARTILLERY
see page 269

## CANADA - MOUNTED AND MECHANISED REGIMENTS

THE 2nd CANADIAN MOUNTED RIFLES
British Columbia Horse in France and Flanders

Lieut Col G Chalmers Johnston
The Vernon News Printing and Publishing Co, Vernon, n.d. (c.1921)
Blue, black, 'regtl and King's Colours' motif on front cover, 9.0 x 6.25,
-/174.
Fp, 13 mono phots, no maps, no Index.

Apps: Roll of Honour, H&A, list of officers who served, nominal roll of
SNCOs and Other Ranks.

An interesting and well-written narrative. R/4 V/4. JEB.


THE 4th CANADIAN MOUNTED RIFLES, 1914-1919

Captain S G Bennett MC
Murray Printing Co Ltd, Toronto, 1926
Dark blue, gold, regtl crest on front cover, 9.75 x 6.75, xiii/336.
14 mono phots, 5 maps (printed in text), no Index.

Apps: list of former COs, nominal roll of all officers and men who served.

This war-time regt was raised in Ontario from Volunteers coming forward
from the local Militia units: Governor-General's Body Guard, 2nd Dragoons,
The Militia Regiment of Ontario, 9th Mississauga Horse and 25th Brant
Dragoons. A good narrative, accurate and interesting. R/4 V/4. JEB.


VANGUARD
The Fort Garry Horse in the Second World War

Anon (by officers of the Regiment)
Vitgevers-Maatschapp C Misset NV (Holland), n.d. (c.1945)
Soft card covers, blue, gold, 9.75 x 6.25, xiv/196.
Fp, 17 mono phots, 2 coloured drawings (regtl crest and badge), 7 maps
(one printed in text, 6 bound in), no Index.

Apps: Roll of Honour, H&A.

Many Allied regts arranged for an account of their WWII adventures to be
written and published in Holland or Germany at the end of the war and
before demobilisation. The majority are quite brief  and poorly produced
(owing to the lack of printing materials in post-war Europe). This book
is one of the exceptions. R/4 V/4. JRT.

THE HISTORY OF THE KANGAROOS
1st Canadian Armoured Carrier Regiment

Anon
SMIT, Hengelo, Holland, n.d. (c.1945)
Paper covers, colours not known, regtl crest on front cover,
8.75 x 6.0, -/11.
Fp, no other illustrations, one map (printed in text), no Index.

Apps: Roll of Honour, list of units carried into battle by the regt at
various times during the advance into North West Europe.

This is the very brief record of a little-known unit first raised in
August 1944 and disbanded in May 1945. R/5 V/3. JLC.


ROYAL CANADIAN DRAGOONS, 1939-45

Anon
Printed in Montreal, for the Regiment, 1946
Red, blue, 9.25 x 6.0, xxiii/233.
Fp, some mono phots, 6 maps (bound in), no Index.

Apps: Roll of Honour (KIA and WIA), H&A.

Interesting and well-written. R/4 V/4. CSM.


AN HISTORICAL ACCOUNT, 7th CANADIAN RECONNAISSANCE REGIMENT
17th Duke of York's Royal Canadian Hussars

Captain Walter G Pavey
Printed in Montreal, for the Regiment, 1948
Grey, blue, regtl crest on front cover, 10.75 x 7.75, -/139.
many photographs, 24 line drawings, 5 maps (printed in text), no Index.

Apps: Roll of Honour, H&A.

This regt served with 3rd Canadian Division in North West Europe and,
like all Canadian units in that campaign, saw much hard action in Normandy
and Holland. The narrative is informative and lucid, while the two
appendixes are very detailed. R/4 V/4. JEB.


STAND TO YOUR HORSES
Through the First Great War with the Lord Strathcona's Horse

Captain S H Williams MC
Printed in Altona, 1961
Blue, gold, 9.5 x 6.5, xi/308.
52 mono phots, 3 maps (printed in text), no Index.

Apps: Roll of Honour, H&A.

Although published in 1961, this book deals exclusively with the regt's services in WWI. We may wonder what prompted its publication after a gap of 42 years, especially as Lord Strathcona's have always attracted much public interest. In the event, the narrative proves to be well-written, interesting and accurate. R/2 V/5. JEB.


THE WESTMINSTER'S WAR DIARY
An Unofficial History of the Westminster Regiment (Motor) in World War II

Major J E Oldfield MC
Printed by Mitchell Press Ltd, Vancouver, for the Regiment, 1964
Maroon, gold, regtl crest on front cover, 9.25 x 6.0, -/209.
Fp, 10 mono phots, 5 line drawings (cartoons), 3 maps (folding, bound in), no appendixes, no Index.

The regt had two frustrating years waiting in the UK before moving to Italy. After a year of hard fighting there, they were brought north for the final advance into Holland and Germany. The author states in his Introduction that his regtl Committee needed 16 years to produce and approve the draft. The narrative is indeed full of exciting incidents and reads well. However, after 16 years of group activity, one could reasonably expect to see an Index and some appendixes, none of which are to be found in this book. The lack of an Index is particularly irksome in this instance because the narrative is packed with dozens of names of officers and Other Ranks. R/2 V/3. RP/LM.


THE 8th HUSSARS
A History of the Regiment

Douglas How
Printed by Maritime Publishing, Sussex, New Brunswick, for the Regiment,1964
Blue, gold, regtl crest on front cover, 9.25 x 6.25, xL/449.
Fp, 65 mono phots (mainly captioned studio portraits of individual officers), 3 line drawings of cap badges, 2 maps (printed on end-papers), Index.

Apps: Roll of Honour, H&A (WWII, with full citations for each award as appropriate), list of former officers, notes on battle honours, table showing regtl organisation and designations from 1848 to 1960.

Their full title is 8th Canadian Hussars (Princess Louise's), and their home Province is New Brunswick. They were the first Canadian regt to become armoured (Spring, 1941), and this is the story of their WWII services in Italy, Belgium and Holland. They fought in Sherman tanks and the narrative is a very readable account of a fine fighting regt. An attractive book in every way. R/3 V/5. AldMM. RP.

HISTORY OF THE CANADIAN GRENADIER GUARDS, 1760-1964


Colonel A Fortescue Duguid DSO OBE TD
Gazette Printing Co Ltd, for the Regiment, 1965
Dark blue, gold, regtl crest on front cover, 9.0 x 5.5, xxiii/520.
Fp, 88 mono phots, 44 maps (all folding, bound in), no Index.

Apps: Roll of Honour (WWI and WWII, all ranks, with dates), H&A (WWI and WWII, all ranks, including MID), notes on battle honours.

A monumental work which covers a very wide variety of service: dealing with raids and rebellions during Canada's early formative years as a new country, WWI infantry service in France, and finally WWII service as an armoured regt in North West Europe. The narrative is packed with names throughout, and ideally they should have been indexed. However, there are numerous lists of names inserted at various points in the body of the book and these partly make up for the deficiency. All in all, a very fine history. R/2 V/4. PCAL. RP.


SINEWS OF STEEL
The History of the British Columbia Dragoons

R H Roy      .
Printed by the Charters Publishing Co Ltd, Brampton, Ontario, for
The Whizzbang Association, 1965
Maroon, gold, 9.25 x 6.25, xiii/468.
Fp, 20 mono phots (including 14 studio portraits of former COs),
7 maps (bound in), no Index.

Apps: Roll of Honour, H&A, notes on unit strengths, notes on battle honours, notes on badges and the Colours.

A generally uniform coverage of their entire history (including their WWI services as 2nd Canadian Mounted Rifles), but strongest for coverage of the 1939-1945 period. Clear accounts of battles and smaller actions, but also some interesting technical detail relating to tanks.
R/3 V/4. MCJ.

THE ELGINS
The Story of the Elgin Regiment (RCAC)

Captain Leonard A Curchin and Lieut Brian D Sim
Printed at the Sutherland Press, St Thomas, Ontario, for the authors, 1977
Blue, gold, regtl crest on front cover, 11.25 x 8.5, vii/150.
Fp, many mono phots, 3 coloured plates, 6 maps (printed in text),
Glossary, Index.

Apps: Rolls of Honour (for the Mackenzie Rebellion, Boer War, WWI), various nominal rolls (as the 91st Elgin Overseas Bn 1914-18, etc).

A superficial but interesting account of the regt from 1866 to 1986. The narrative covers service in Canada, South Africa (Boer War), France (WWI), and in Italy and North West Europe (WWII). The two main strengths of this book are the nominal rolls and the several dozens of photographs of members of the regt (peace-time and war-time, all captioned with names and ranks). R/1 V/4. A1dMM. RP.


ALWAYS A STRATHCONA

W B Fraser
Comprint Publishing Co, Calgary, Alberta, 1986 (reprint of 1976 edition)
Brown, gold, 9.25 x 6.25, -/252.
16 mono phots, 8 coloured plates (uniforms), 6 maps (printed in text), Index.

Apps: Roll of Honour, list of former COs, list of former RSMs, genealogy of the regt, chronology of major events, Honourary officers.

A good history with uniform coverage throughout. The coloured plates are reported to be superb. R/1 V/4. MCJ.


A HISTORY OF THE FIRST HUSSARS REGIMENT, 1856-1980

Anon ('Regimental Committee')
Publisher's detail not stated, n.d. (c.1981)
Blue, gold and silver, 9.25 x 6.25, viii/195.
7 mono phots, 2 maps, Glossary, no Index.

Apps: Roll of Honour (WWII), list of former COs, list of former officers (1939-1945 only), notes on training, notes on the Regtl Association.

The first chapter deals with their early history (formation and service in the Boer War), and a fairly brief summary of their services in WWI. The bulk of the narrative is then devoted to WWII and post-war administrative matters (training, uniforms, equipment, etc). R/2 V/3. MCJ.

# CANADA - EXTENDED HISTORIES

THE HISTORY OF THE PRINCE OF WALES'S LEINSTER REGIMENT (ROYAL CANADIANS)
Volumes 1 and 2

Lieut Col F E Whitton CMG
Gale & Polden Ltd, Aldershot, n.d. (c.1924)
Blue, green, regtl crest on front cover, 8.5 x 5.5, viii/483 and vi/570.
Fps, 3 mono phots and 4 maps in Volume 1, 7 mono phots and 14 maps in
Volume 2, no appendixes in either Volume, Index.

Six regts of the British Army have at different times borne the number
100. The last was the 100th The Prince of Wales's Royal Canadian Regiment.
Raised in 1858 in Quebec and Montreal, it was intended to assist in the
suppression of the Indian Mutiny. In the event, it saw garrison service
in Gibraltar, Malta, England and India before being re-designated the
1st Bn POW's Leinster Regiment (Royal Canadians) in 1881. At the same time,
the 109th Foot (formerly 3rd Bombay European Regt) was re-designated the
2nd Bn POW's Leinster Regiment (Royal Canadians). Volume 1 of this pair of
histories covers the origins and all 18th and 19th century campaigns of
the two founder regts, while Volume 2 deals exclusively with WWI and
then the final disbandment in 1922. An entertaining narrative packed with
information. R/4 V/5. RP.

48th HIGHLANDERS OF CANADA, 1891-1928

Kim Beattie
Printed in Toronto, for the Regiment, by Southam Press Ltd, 1932
Dark blue, gold, regtl crest on front cover, 9.5 x 6.25, -/434.
Fp, 15 composite mono plates, 7 maps (printed in text), no appendixes,
no Index.

As far as it goes, this is an attractive and well-prepared unit history.
The lack of appendixes and an Index severely reduces its worth as a source
of reference. Many individuals, and some of their honours and awards,
are mentioned throughout the text, but tracing them is a laborious task.
Despite the dates mentioned in the title, a major part of the narrative is
devoted to WWI services in France (First and Second Ypres). The regt
was affiliated to the Gordon Highlanders. R/4 V/3. PCAL. RP/LM.

THE WINNIPEG RIFLES
Fiftieth Anniversary 1883-1933
Anon ('Anniversary Committee')
Publisher's detail not shown, Winnipeg, n.d. (c.1933)
Soft card covers, tan, green and black, 10.0 x 8.0, -/59.
52 mono phots, no maps, no Index.

Apps: H&A (VCs only), list of former officers.

A very superficial account, presumably intended as a publicity item rather
than a serious history. R/3 V/2. JRT/RP.

THE ROYAL CANADIAN REGIMENT
Volume I: 1883-1933

R C Featherstonhaugh
Printed by Centennial Print, for the Regiment, 1936
Blue, gold, 9.5 x 6.5, ix/467.
Fp, 27 mono phots, 2 coloured plates, 7 maps (bound in), Index.

Apps: Roll of Honour, list of former COs, list of former officers.

No other information is available for this title. However, with 466
pages, it must presumably be a comprehensive and detailed history. It is
reported to have been reprinted in facsimile in 1981. See page 247 for
Volume II.


THE ARGYLL & SUTHERLAND HIGHLANDERS OF CANADA (PRINCESS LOUISE'S),
1928-1953

Lieut Col H M Jackson MBE ED
Printed by The Industrial School for the Deaf, Montreal, presumably for
the Regiment, 1953
Green, red, regtl crest on front cover, 9.25 x 6.0, -/407.
Fp, 38 mono phots (mainly of named individual officers), 11 maps
(printed in the text), no Index.

Apps: Roll of Honour (with full details, KIA, WIA, DOW, and POW), H&A,
list of former COs, list of former officers, nominal roll (all ranks)
for 1940-1946, full citation for the VC awarded to Sgt Aubrey Cosens.

While the narrative does deal with pre- and post-war regtl business, the
bulk of the book is in fact devoted to the North West Europe campaign,
1944-1945. It is a straightforward account seemingly based upon the War
Diary. Readable and informative. The quality of the paper and binding are
not of the best and, given the lack of an Index, this is a rather
disappointing book to handle. R/2 V/4. PCAL. RP.


WHATEVER MEN DARE
A History of the Queen's Own Cameron Highlanders of Canada, 1935-1960

R W Queen-Hughes
Bulman Brothers Ltd, Winnipeg, 1960
Blue, silver, 9.0 x 6.0, xi/247.
Fp, 61 mono phots, one coloured plate, 8 maps  (printed in the text),
Glossary, no Index.

Apps: Roll of Honour, H&A, list of former COs.

No other details are available for this title, but it is believed to be
a sound conventional unit history, covering the period stated in the
sub-title but with the main emphasis directed at WWII. R/1 V/4. JRT/RP.

THE QUEEN'S OWN RIFLES OF CANADA, 1860-1960
One Hundred Years of Canada

Lieut Col W T Barnard ED CD
Printed by T H Best Printing Co Ltd, for Ontario Publishing Ltd, 1960
Rifle green, silver, 9.25 x 6.0, xiii/398.
Fp, 34 mono phots, 18 maps (9 printed in the text, 7 bound in, 2 printed
on the end-papers), Bibliography, Index.

Apps: Roll of Honour (very detailed, see below), H&A (see below), list
of former COs, notes on battle honours, etc.

This is an admirable history which covers everything the regt did from its
formation in 1860 through to the Korean War and later. The campaigns
in which it took part were: the rebellions and disturbances in pioneering
Canada, the Boer War (1899-1902), North West Europe (1943-1945), and then
in Korea (1953-1954) as part of the Commonwealth forces under UN command.
During WWI they were restricted to recruit-training and draft-finding for
other regts, but many of their own members went on to win fame and glory
elsewhere (including VC awards). The casualty appendix is most unusual
because it lists all the men who died in the Fenian Raid (2.8.1866), in
South Africa (1900), in WWI (with details of the unit in which the man was
then serving), WWII and Korea. The H&A appendix has only a numerical
summary of awards for WWI, but a full list of awards for WWII (including
the full citation for another VC). A splendid research source, with
excellent maps drawn by Capt R A With. R/3 V/5. PCAL. RP.


A CENTURY OF RIFLES
The Halifax Rifles (RCAC)(M)

John Gordon Quigley
Printed by William Macnab & Son Ltd, Halifax, Nova Scotia, n.d. (c.1960)
Stiff card, green, silver, 9.0 x 6.0, xviii/230.
Fp, 26 mono phots (including 3 large fold-outs of the entire regt),
no maps, no Index.

Apps: H&A (incomplete), list of former COs, nominal rolls, notes on local
'regimental families'.

A chronology illustrated with pictures and many stories regarding local
families whose sons and fathers served with this Militia (Volunteer) unit.
It never fought as an integral formation, but several officers served with
other regts during WWII. Of interest mainly as a reflection of the social
history of Halifax and the evolution of the Militia in general.
R/1 V/3. MCJ.


CANADA'S BLACK WATCH - THE FIRST HUNDRED YEARS

Colonel Paul P Hutchison ED
T H Best Printing Co Ltd, Don Mills, Ontario, for the Royal Highlanders
of Canada Armoury Association, 1962
Dark blue, gold, regtl crest on front cover, 9.25 x 6.0, xxiii/340.
Fp, 63 mono phots, 33 line drawings, 2 maps (end-papers), no Index.

Apps: H&A (WWI and WWII), lists of former COs, RSMs, RPMs, and Honorary
Colonels, notes on battle honours.

The regt was founded in 1862. Served in the Fenian disturbances of 1866
and 1870, in WWI (France and Flanders), and in WWII (with a detachment in
the Dieppe raid, and the whole regt then landing in Normandy on 6.7.1944).
As 2nd Royal Highlanders of Canada, they then fought in Korea as part
of the Commonwealth forces under UN command. In addition to the 63 main
photographs, there are about 40 more of individual officers and men (studio
portraits). R/2 V/4. PCAL. JBC/LM.


BATTLE ROYAL
A History of the Royal Regiment of Canada, 1862-1962

Major D J Goodspeed CD
Printed by Charters Publishing Co Ltd, Toronto, for the Regiment, 1962
Blue, silver, regtl crest on front cover, 9.0 x 6.0, -/703.
2 fps, 82 mono phots, 2 coloured plates, 24 maps (2 printed on end-papers,
24 folding, bound in), Bibliography, Index (very detailed).

Apps: Roll of Honour (WWI and WWII), H&A (WWI and WWII), list of former COs,
notes on battle honours.

The Royal Regiment of Canada was formed in 1936 by the amalgamation of
two Militia units - The Royal Grenadiers and The Toronto Regiment. The
early histories of both founder regts are well-described here, but the
bulk of the account is devoted to their individual services in WWI (France
and Flander, 1915-1918), and the new regt's services in WWII (Dieppe and
North West Europe). An outstandingly good source of reference.
R/3 V/5. PCAL. RP.


HISTOIRE DU ROYAL 22e RÉGIMENT

Charles-Marie Boissonnault and Lieut Col L Lamontagne CD
Editions du Pelican, Quebec, pour la Régiment, 1964
Red, gold, regtl crest in gold and silver on front cover, 9.0 x 5.75, -/414.
63 mono phots, 6 coloured plates, one line drawing (cap badge), 16 maps
(2 printed in text, 14 bound in), no Index (but a detailed 'Contents' page
at the rear of the book).

Apps: H&A (all ranks, WWII), list of former COs (with studio portrait
of each).

Written in French, which is the first language of this very famous old
regt recruited from the French-speaking population of Quebec Province
and based in The Citadel, Quebec city. Best known to English-speaking
admirers as 'the Van Dooz'. The opening pages of this book deal with their
early history, but the main part of the narrative is devoted to their
services in Sicily and Italy (1943-1944). They were then withdrawn to join
other Canadian forces in Holland for the final assault on Germany (Spring,
1945). R/2 V/4. PCAL. RP.
100 'de luxe' numbered copies issued, 2900 standard copies.

A CITY GOES TO WAR
History of the Loyal Edmonton Regiment (3 P.P.C.L.I)

Lieut Col G R Stevens OBE
Printed by Charters Publishing Co Ltd, Bramton, Ontario, for The Edmonton
Regiment Associates, 1964
Orange-red, gold, regtl crest on front cover, 10.25 x 6.75, -/431.
Fp, 38 mono phots, 11 maps (folding, bound in), Index.

Apps: Roll of Honour (WWI as 49th Bn CEF, WWII as The Edmonton Regt and
The Loyal Edmonton Regt), H&A (WWI and WWII, as before), list of former
COs (with artist's sketches and biographical notes for each).

An excellently prepared account of services in WWI (France and Flanders)
and in WWII (Sicily, Italy, North West Europe). Very readable, with plenty
of minor actions and ancedotes mentioned in the text. A well-bound book
with particularly good maps. R/2 V/5. AldMM. RP.


HISTORY OF THE CANADIAN GRENADIER GUARDS, 1760-1964

Colonel A Fortescue Duguid DSO OBE CD
Gazette Printing Co Ltd, Montreal, 1965
Dark blue, gold, 9.0 x 6.0, xxiii/520.
Fp, 109 mono phots, 44 maps (bound in), no Index.

Apps: Roll of Honour, H&A, list of former COs, list of former officers.

There is only a sketchy description of the regt's early history (1760-
1914), but the author then launches into a beautifully researched and
very lucid account of their services in the two world wars. Packed with
useful and interesting detail. The appendixes section alone runs to 147
pages! With so many names listed in the appendixes, a formal Index
probably would have been superfluous. R/2 V/5. PCAL. RP.


THE ROYAL CANADIAN REGIMENT
Volume II: 1933-1966

Lieut Col G R Stevens OBE
Printed by The London Printing & Lithographing Co Ltd, London, Ontario,
for the Regiment, 1967
Blue, gold, 10.25 x 7.25, xii/420.
Fp, reportedly no other illustrations and no maps, Index.

Apps: Roll of Honour, H&A, list of former COs, list of former officers.

No further information available for this title.

THE SEAFORTH HIGHLANDERS OF CANADA, 1919-1965

Reginald H Roy CD
Printed by Evergreen Press, Vancouver, for the Regiment, 1969
Beige, gold, regtl crest on front cover, xxiv/559.
53 large captioned group mono phots, plus numerous individual captioned
studio portrait phots of individual officers and men, 2 coloured plates,
8 maps (folding, bound in, very detailed), Index.

Apps: Roll of Honour (KIA, WIA, POW), H&A (a combined list for WWI and
WWII),list of former COs, idem RSMs, idem RPMs, full nominal roll for
all ranks (WWII, with details of individual services, KIA, DOW and
wounded), notes on battle honours for WWI and WWII.

Despite the title,the narrative is devoted almost entirely to WWII
services in Italy and (briefly) Holland and Germany. A magnificent
history, with many individuals mentioned in the text and very detailed
appendixes. Particularly useful for the genealogist and the medal collector,
but a good source for military historians of every hue. Most of the
Canadian Army regtl histories are very good, but this one is outstanding.
R/3 V/5. PCAL. RP.


PRINCESS PATRICIA'S CANADIAN LIGHT INFANTRY

Jeffery Williams
Printed by Compton Press, Salisbury (UK), for Leo Cooper, 1972
Blue, gold, 8.75 x 5.75, xii/110.
Fp, 31 mono phots, no maps, no Index.

Apps: an outline of services, 1914-1972

Like most of Leo Cooper's pleasantly produced 'Famous Regiments' series,
this is an attempt to fill a gap in the market. Colonel Williams is a good
historian, and fought with the regt in WWII and Korea, but commercial
considerations seem to have restricted this work to the 'popular' market,
hence no detailed appendixes, no Index, and only 110 pages to cover the
story of a premier Canadian fighting infantry regiment. The 'Princess Pats'
had a strange beginning. A Captain of Militia, Andrew Hamilton Gault,
was sufficiently wealthy to pay, in 1914, for the raising of a new regt
for service in the European war.He took the name of the daughter of the
Duke of Connaught, Queen Victoria's third and favourite son and at that
time Governor General of Canada. Recruitment came mainly from former
soldiers of the British Army who had emigrated to Canada after the Boer War.
At one stage, every regt of the British Army (bar one) was represented in
the PPCLI's ranks! Most of them were then killed in France by the same
Generals who had commanded them in South Africa. Twenty years later the
regt had a hard and distinguished role in the campaigns in Sicily,
Italy and North West Europe. A useful account, but limited in its scope.
R/1 V/3. RP.

LITTLE BLACK DEVILS
A History of the Royal Winnipeg Rifles

Bruce Tascona and Eric Wells
Frye Publishing, Winnipeg, Manitoba, 1983
Green, white, 9.5 x 6.5, ix/241.
128 mono phots, 6 coloured plates, 11 maps (printed in text), no Index.

Apps: Roll of Honour, H&A, list of former COs.

No other details available for this title.


ONE HUNDRED YEARS, THE ROYAL CANADIAN REGIMENT, 1883-1983

Ken Ball and C P Stacey
Collier MacMillan (Canada), Ontario, 1983
Black, gold, 10.25 x 10.25, -/184.
169 mono phots, 15 coloured plates, no maps, no Index.

Essentially a pictorial history to mark their centenary. The pictures are
of superb quality, but the 'historical' content is fairly limited.
R/1 V/3. DBP-P.


THE LION RAMPANT
A Pictorial History of the Queen's Own Cameron Highlanders of Canada

G C A Tyler
The Public Press, Winnipeg, Ontario, 1985
Blue, gold, 8.75 x 11.25, x/134.
Fp, 212 mono phots, 3 coloured plates, 3 maps (printed in text), no Index.

Apps: H&A, former COs, list of former RSMs, notes on battle honours.

Again, this is basically a centenary celebration publication which relies
mainly upon a good selection of old photographs. They are of interest,
but the purely 'historical' content of the book is quite limited.
R/1 V/2. JRT.

# CANADA - INFANTRY, GREAT WAR

NOVA SCOTIA OVERSEAS HIGHLAND BRIGADE, C.E.F.
A Short History and Photographic Record of the Nova Scotia Overseas
Highland Brigade

Lieut Col A H Borden
The Mortimer Printing Co Ltd, Halifax, n.d. (c.1916)
Brown, red, 4 regtl crests on front cover, 12.5 x 9.5, -/47.
47 pages of mono phots, no maps, no appendixes, no Index.

This is basically a photographic record of the officers and men who
were at that time (c.1916) serving with the Nova Scotia Brigade (85th,
185th, 193rd and 219th Bns, Canadian Expeditionary Force). A massive piece
of war-time research and compilation. The author succeeded in obtaining
a 'head and shoulders' photograph of a very large number of men, each
picture being then captioned with details of the man's name, rank,
service number, unit and home town. Ideal for genealogists and medal
collectors, not so useful to military historians. R/4 V/2. JEB.

FROM THUNDER BAY THROUGH YPRES WITH THE FIGHTING 52nd

W C Millar
Printed in Fort William, Ontario, 1918
Paper covers, brown, black, 7.5 x 5.5, regtl crest on front cover, -/101.
2 mono phots, no maps, no appendixes, no Index.

Private Millar served with the Scout Section of the 52nd Bn CEF and was
invalided in 1917. Basically an autobiographical account and somewhat
limited in scope. However, the author had a good memory for names and
places, and this is as good an account of the regt's services during the
middle years of the war as one is likely to encounter. R/5 V/3. MCJ.

OVER THE TOP WITH THE 25th
25th Battalion, Canadian Expeditionary Force

Lieut R Lewis
H H Marshall, Halifax, Nova Scotia, 1918
White, black, 9.5 x 6.5, -/59.
one mono phot, 2 maps (printed in the text), no appendixes, no Index.

A brief summary of events when one of Nova Scotia's famous WWI regts
fought on Vimy Ridge and at Courcelette. Some officers and men are
mentioned in the text. Limited in scope, but interesting as far as it
goes. R/5 V/2. JEB.

CINQUANTE-QUATRE
A History of the 54th Canadian Infantry Battalion

Bailey John Beswick
Publisher's details not shown, 1919
Stiff card covers, brown, black, regtl crest on front cover, 9.0 x 5.75,
-/108.
one mono phot, 8 sketches, no maps, no Index.

Apps: H&A (all ranks, with details of number, rank, and date of award),
full nominal roll for all ranks.

The regt was recruited from the rural population of British Columbia.
The narrative mentions many individuals by name. A very brief record, but
interesting and certainly useful as a research source. R/5 V/3. JEB.


FROM B.C. TO BAISIEUX
Being a Narrative of the 102nd Canadian Infantry Battalion

L McLeod Gould MSM CdeG
Thomas R Cusack Presses, Victoria, British Columbia, 1919
Dark green, gold, 9.0 x 6.0, -/134/98.
Fp, 8 mono phots, one map (printed in text), no Index.

Apps: the last 98 pages dedicated to a massive nominal roll of every
officer and man who served with the regt in WWI, giving full details of
KIA, WIA, DOW, honours, dates, etc.

Sergeant Gould was the official diarist on the Bn HQ staff and he logged
every single event in the war-time life of the regt. The narrative account
(134 pages) is very good, but the nominal roll appendix (98 pages) must
be almost unique. R/5 V/5. PCAL. LM.


THE 127th BATTALION C.E.F.
2nd Battalion Canadian Railway Troops

Lieut Col H M Jackson
Publisher's details not known, Montreal, n.d. (c.1920)
Green, black, 6.75 x 4.25, -/186.
2 mono phots, no maps, no Index.

Apps: Roll of Honour (detailed), H&A (all ranks, with service numbers,
dates, and some citations), etc. Seven appendixes in total.

A sound history of the regt and its services in France in WWI. Took part
in the Passchendaele debacle. A relatively short history containing a lot
of information. R/5 V/4. JEB.

THE STORY OF THE FIGHTING 26th

R W Gould and S K Smith
St John New Company, St John, New Brunswick, n.d. (c.1920)
Stiff card, grey, red, regtl crest on front cover, 15.0 x 10.75, -/48.
2 mono phots, 38 other illustrations, no maps, no Index.

Apps: nominal roll of original members of the regt when they first sailed
(13.6.1915), with home addresses, next-of-kin, etc.

A brief account, packed with names. R/3 V/3. JEB.


THE HISTORY OF THE 28th BATTALION, C.E.F. (OCTOBER 1914 - JUNE 1919)

Major D G Scott-Calder ED
Published by The Regina Rifle Regiment, n.d. (c.1920)
Stiff card covers, black, silver, 13.0 x 8.0, -/277.
no illustrations, 83 maps (printed in the text), Index.

Apps: Roll of Honour, H&A, list of former COs.

A straightforward factual account. R/5 V/4. JRT.


THE EIGHTY-FIFTH
Nova Scotia's Highlanders in France and Flanders

Lieut Col Joseph Hayes DSO
Royal Print & Litho Ltd, Halifax, Nova Scotia, 1920
Green, gold, regtl crest on front cover, 9.5 x 6.5, -/362.
Fp, 22 mono phots, one map (loose in rear pocket), no Index.

Sometimes known as 'the Highlanders without kilts', they distinguished
themselves at Vimy Ridge when they stormed and held Hill 145. R/4 V/4. JEB.


HISTORY OF THE 72nd CANADIAN INFANTRY BATTALION, SEAFORTH HIGHLANDERS
OF CANADA

Bernard McEvoy and Captain A H Finlay
Cowan & Brookhouse, Vancouver, British Columbia, 1920
Red, gold, regtl tartan and crest on front cover, 9.0 x 6.0, xxiv/311.
Fp, 60 mono phots, 3 maps (folding, bound in), Glossary, no Index.

Apps: 13 in total, including H&A, nominal rolls (various), chronology
of events, etc.

A detailed regtl history, well-produced and containing all the usual
required information. Well-researched and illustrated.R/4 V/4. SB.

THE 116th IN FRANCE

Anon (reportedly a former Adjutant)
The Hunter-Rose Co, Toronto, 1921
Grey, gold, 8.5 x 6.25, -/111.
21 mono phots, 2 maps (printed in the text), no Index.

Apps: Roll of Honour (with service numbers, ranks, and home addresses).

The Bn was raised in Ontario in 1915 and sailed for France on 23.7.1916.
Took part in the Vimy Ridge battle, April 1917. Most of the photographs
depict officers who were killed in action. Very readable. R/4 V/3. JEB.


PRINCESS PATRICIA'S CANADIAN LIGHT INFANTRY, 1914-1919
Volumes I and II

Ralph-Hodder Williams
Printed by R R Clark Ltd, Edinburgh, for Hodder & Stoughton, London, 1923
A matching pair, red and brown, gold, 9.0 x 6.25, ixx/411 and i/391.
Fps, 6 mono phots and 11 maps in Vol I, no phots or maps in Vol II,
Index in Vol II for both Volumes.

Apps: Roll of Honour, H&A, list of former COs, list of former officers,
nominal roll of members, **all** located in Volume II.

A superb source of reference, highly readable but also packed with details
of people and actions. The appendixes are excellent. R/5 V/5. JRD.


RECORDS OF THE FOURTH CANADIAN INFANTRY BATTALION IN THE GREAT WAR, 1914-18

Captain W L Gibson
The Maclean Publishing Co Ltd, Toronto, 1924
Green, gold, 9.75 x 6.5, -/274.
Fp, 16 mono phots, no maps, no Index.

Apps: a nominal roll of every man who served, with his service number, rank,
date of enlistment, details of death or injury (if applicable), awards, and
home address at demobilisation. A separate roll lists all awards, with full
citations in most cases and where applicable.

Very little detail concerning battles, places or dates, but abundant
information on the men who served. R/4 V/3. MCJ.


THE 13th BATTALION, ROYAL HIGHLANDERS OF CANADA, 1914-1919

R C Featherstonhaugh
Privately, by the Regiment, 1925
Black, gold, regtl crest on front cover, 9.0 x 6.5, xv/344.
Fp, 20 mono phots, 3 maps (bound in), no Index.

Apps: Roll of Honour, H&A, list of former COs (with individual portrait photographs).

A useful detailed account of the Bn's movements and engagements in France between February 1915 and November 1918. Most officer casualties are mentioned in the narrative as they happened. The text includes quotations from operational orders and is generally informative. R/4 V/5. MCJ/JBC.


THE ROYAL MONTREAL REGIMENT, 14th BATTALION, C.E.F., 1914-1925

R C Featherstonhaugh
The Gazette Printing Co Ltd, Montreal, 1927
Red, gold, 9.5 x 6.25, xv/334.
Fp, 21 mono phots, 6 maps (printed in text), no Index.

Apps: Roll of Honour, H&A, roll of men commissioned from the ranks, diary of movements and locations, statistics.

A very good general history, with excellent descriptions of specific actions and battles. R/4 V/4. JBF.


THE 24th BATTALION, C.E.F, VICTORIA RIFLES OF CANADA, 1914-1919

R C Featherstonhaugh
Gazette Printing Co, Montreal, for the Victoria Rifles of Canada, 1930
Green (pebbled), gold, 9.25 x 6.25, i/318.
Fp, 13 mono phots, 4 sketches, 8 maps (bound in), no Index.

Apps: Roll of Honour, H&A, list of former officers.

A very detailed - almost 'casualty by casualty' - account of the regt's adventures in France. The appendixes are very complete. R/4 V/4. MCJ.


A SHORT HISTORY OF THE 7th BATTALION, C.E.F.

Major T V Scudamore VD
Anderson & Odlum Ltd, Vancouver, n.d. (c.1931)
Red, black, 8.0 x 5.5, -/55.
no illustrations, no maps, no Index.

Apps: two only. Roll of Honour showing the names of all ranks KIA, DOW, and missing (all with dates), list of officers serving with the Bn in 1914.

Half of the book is taken up with the extensive and detailed Roll of Honour, so the narrative recounting the Bn's services is quite restricted. The book is useful mainly for checking individual casualties and their awards (which are listed in the same Roll). R/3 V/3. MP.

THE 42nd BATTALION, C.E.F., ROYAL HIGHLANDERS OF CANADA IN THE GREAT WAR
.

Lieut Col C Beresford Topp DSO MC
Gazette Printing Co, Montreal, n.d. (c.1932)
Red, gold, regtl crest on front cover, 9.25 x 6.0, xii/412.
21 mono phots, one line drawing, 9 maps (bound in), no Index.

Apps: Roll of Honour, H&A, diary of movements (in great detail),
nominal roll of all ranks.

A well-produced and attractive book containing much useful detail.
R/3 V/4. RP.


SIX THOUSAND CANADIAN MEN
The History of the 44th Battalion, Canadian Infantry, 1914-1919

E S Russenholt
De Montfort Press, Winnipeg, for the Forty-Fourth Battalion Association,
1932
Green, gold, Divisional badge on front cover, 10.0 x 6.5, xii/364.
Fp, 16 mono phots, 10 maps (printed in text), no Index.

Apps: H&A, nominal roll for all ranks.

The Bn was recruited initially in Manitoba, but suffered such heavy losses
that its ranks were later filled with men from New Brunswick. The narrative
is well-written, accurate, and full of interesting detail. R/4 V/4. JEB.


THE HISTORY OF THE 16th BATTALION (THE CANADIAN SCOTTISH), CANADIAN
EXPEDITIONARY FORCE, IN THE GREAT WAR, 1914-1919

H M Urquhart DSO MC ADC
The MacMillan Company of Canada Ltd, Toronto, 1932
Maroon, gold, regtl crest on front cover with wording 'The Sixteenth',
9.5 x 6.5, xx/853.
Fp, 29 mono phots, 11 maps (bound in), no Index.

Apps: Roll of Honour, H&A, nominal roll with details of service,
notes on the Canadian Militia forces 1812-1914, etc (14 in total).

A wonderfully researched history, rich in detail and a goldmine for the
researcher. Half of this massive book's 853 pages are devoted to a
nominal roll of every officer and man who served with the Bn between 1914-
1919, giving dates of joining, death, wounds, awards, etc. The narrative
itself is also full of detail. The Bn won four VCs in WWI, a record for a
Canadian unit in that war. A model history in every way. R/4 V/5. LM/SS.

THE TWENTIETH
History of the 20th Canadian Battalion (Central Ontario Regiment),
C.E.F., in the Great War, 1914-1919

Major D J Corrigall DSO MC
Stone & Cox Ltd, Toronto, for the Trustees of the Twentieth Canadian
Battalion, 1935
Green boards, black spine, gold, 9.5 x 6.5, xvii/589.
Fp (this being a fold-out landscape photograph of the entire battalion, at
Toronto, 1914), 7 other mono phots, one coloured plate (of the Colours),
31 maps (printed in the text), no Index.

Apps: nominal roll (see below), notes on battle honours, notes on the
affiliation with the Queen's Royal Regiment (West Surreys).

This is another massive compilation of names, facts, statistics and
historical narrative. The scholarship is deeply impressive. Of the 589
pages, nearly half are devoted to a nominal roll which lists every officer
and man who served with the Bn in WWI. For each name, there is a note of
his date of joining and leaving, his previous and subsequent services with
other units, his regtl number, his highest rank held, and any awards
gained. As appropriate, there is a note that he was killed, wounded, died
of disease, was presumed dead, or taken prisoner. The other (first) half
of the book is a very good account of the Bn's services in France where
two of its members were awarded the VC (Sgt F Hobson and Lieut W L Algie).
Finally, there is a chapter which recounts the short-lived re-designation
as The West Toronto Regiment, and then the amalgamation in 1925 with the
2nd Bn York Rangers to form The Queen's Rangers (an Active Militia regt).
R/4 V/5.SS/CSM.


HISTORY OF THE 31st CANADIAN INFANTRY BATTALION, C.E.F.
From its Organisation in November 1914 to its Demobilisation in June 1919,
Compiled from its Diaries and other Papers

Major H S Singer and Mr A A Peebles
Published by the 31st Canadian Battalion Association, n.d. (c.1938)
Light blue, black, 9.0 x 6.0, xiv/515.
Fp, 14 mono phots, 8 maps (printed in the text), no Index.

Apps: a large combined Roll of Honour and nominal roll of members of
the regt, list of COs, table of awards gained (no names).

A very readable narrative, with plenty of people and events mentioned in
the text. The extensive nominal roll is useful, but does not include any
dates (died, wounded, decorated, etc). This deficiency, and the lack of
an Index, prevents the book from qualifying as a really first-class source
of reference. R/3 V/4. DJB/JEB.


THE STORY OF THE 64th BATTALION, C.E.F.

Lieut Col G C MacHum
Publisher's details not shown, Montreal, 1956
Red, black, 9.0 x 6.0, -/94.
8 mono phots, no maps, no formal appendixes, no Index.

This fairly slim book has a concise but informative narrative account
of services in France, and then a very large section which is simply
a nominal roll of every officer and man who sailed from Halifax on
31 March 1916. Many officers and Other Ranks are mentioned in the
text, but the book is not nearly as comprehensive as it might have been.
R/3 V/3. JEB/RP.


VANCOUVER'S 29th
A Chronicle of the 29th Battalion, Canadian Infantry, in Flanders Fields

H R N Clyne MC
Tobin's Tigers Association, Vancouver, 1964
Light brown, red, regtl crest on front cover, 8.75 x 5.5, viii/166.
no illustrations, no maps, no Index.

Apps: various, including detailed H&A section.

A straightforward narrative history of the Bn's services in France and
Flanders. R/1 V/2. JEB.


THE SUICIDE BATTALION
46th Battalion, Canadian Infantry, C.E.F.

James L McWilliams and R James Steel
Hortig Publishers, Edmonton, Alberta, 1978
Black, gold, 9.6 x 6.25, -/226.
Fp, no other illustrations, no maps, Index.

Apps: H&A (incomplete), nominal roll (incomplete).

In view of the fact that this book was published sixty-odd years after
the events which it describes, one might have hoped for a more comprehensive work. R/1 V/1. JRT.


THE BANTAMS
The Untold Story of World War One

Sidney Allison
Mosaic Press, Oakville, Ontario, 1982
Grey, red, 9.0 x 6.0, -/287.
27 mono phots, one line drawing, no formal appendixes, Bibliography, Index.

This is not a regtl history, but a valuable secondary source for research
on the WWI recruitment of under-sized Canadian infantrymen into special
'Bantam' units. The author interviewed 300 survivors and made use of
unpublished journals and letters. R/1 V/2. PS.
First published by Howard Baker Press Ltd, Wimbledon (UK), 1981.

THE TWENTY-FIFTH BATTALION, CANADIAN EXPEDITIONARY FORCE
Nova Scotia's Famous Regiment in World War One

F B MacDonald CD and John J Gardiner
J A Chadwick, Sydney, Nova Scotia, 1983
Soft card cover, colours not reported, 8.5 x 5.5, -/211.
Fp, 9 mono phots (including one of badges), no maps, Glossary, no Index.

Apps: H&A (numerical summary only), list of former COs, nominal roll
of all ranks, notes on battle honours.

Apparently this is the only published history for the Bn. The authors have
adopted the unusual technique of compiling a narrative which is based
partly upon the Bn's original War Diary and partly upon personal interviews
with elderly veterans who fought in France. The result is easy reading
and interesting, but the greatest value of the book is probably the
nominal roll and the extracts from the War Diary. R/1 V/2. MCJ.
See also pages 233 and 250 for other (composite) references to this Bn.

## CANADA - INFANTRY, SECOND WORLD WAR

1st BATTALION, THE REGINA RIFLE REGIMENT, 1939-1946

Captain Eric Luxton
Commercial Printers Ltd, for the Regina Rifles Association, n.d.(c.1946)
Spiral bound, soft card covers, black, silver and brown, regtl crest on
front cover, 12.0 x 9.0, -/70.
40 mono phots (of poor quality), one map (badly drawn), no Index.

Apps: Roll of Honour (ranks and names only), H&A, list of COs (with
portrait photographs and biographical notes).

This volume has an unusual format for a regtl history, and generally gives
the impression of having been flung together under the pressures of time
and cost. A great pity, because the narrative, although condensed, is
very readable and informative. The regt went ashore on D-Day as part of
7th Canadian Infantry Brigade, 3rd Canadian Infantry Division, at
Courseulles. They had a hard campaign in Normandy and another in Holland
over the winter of 1944-1945. The author, who presumably served with the
regt, gives a very lucid account of their experiences. R/3 V/3. AldMM. RP.


THE HISTORY OF THE 1st BATTALION, CAMERON HIGHLANDERS OF OTTAWA (M.G.)

Lieut Col Richard M Ross OBE
Publication details not stated, n.d. (c.1947)
Tartan, silver, regtl crest on front cover, 9.25 x 6.0, -/96.
7 mono phots, 6 maps (printed in the text), no Index.

Apps: H&A.

The regt was formed in September 1939 and disbanded in December 1945.
This is a workmanlike account of their services, as a medium machine-gun
regt, in the North West Europe campaign, with many individual officers
mentioned by name in the narrative. R/3 V/3. AMOT. RP.


WEST NOVAS
A History of the West Nova Scotia Regiment

Thomas H Raddall
Published privately (presumably by the Regiment), Toronto, 1947
Brown, gold, regtl crest on front cover, 9.5 x 6.25, -/326.
Fp, 44 mono phots, 10 maps (bound in), no Index.

Apps: Roll of Honour (names and ranks for all KIA).

The regt went overseas as part of the 1st Canadian Division and took part
in the invasion of Sicily and the campaign in Italy. They were then moved
to Holland in the Spring of 1945 for the final assault into Germany. A
good readable account, with plenty of names and small actions mentioned
in the narrative. This first edition was issued in a limited (numbered)
print-run of 1000. There was also a second edition (not seen).
R/4 V/4. JEB.

PRINCESS PATRICIA'S CANADIAN LIGHT INFANTRY, 1919-1957
Volume III

G R Stevens OBE
Published by the Regiment's Historical Committee, Griesbach, Alberta, n.d.
Red, gold, 9.0 x 5.75, xvi/411.
Fp, 32 mono phots, 11 very good maps (bound in), no Index.

Apps: list of former COs, with portraits and biographical notes for each.

The regt was stationed in the UK for 3 years (1940-43) before taking part
in the invasions of Sicily and Italy. In early 1945 they moved up through
France and fought in the final advance into Germany. Two battalions then
served with the UN forces in Korea. This is a long and very detailed
narrative account by a skilled military historian, but it reads more like
an official report than a human narrative. Few individuals are mentioned
in the text, and the lack of appendixes is bewildering in a work of this
scale. R/3 V/3. AldMM. RP.


PRINCESS PATRICIA'S CANADIAN LIGHT INFANTRY

Major R B Mainprize CD
No publisher's detail shown, n.d.
Maroon, gold, 9.5 x 6.25, iii/170.
Fp, no other mono illustrations, one coloured plate, Glossary, no Index.

Apps: Roll of Honour, H&A, nominal roll.

This is a useful narrative account, but the main value of the book is
the nominal roll of all PPCLI men who served in WWII. R/4 V/4. JRT.


NO RETREATING FOOTSTEPS
The Story of the North Nova Scotia Highlanders

Will R Bird
The Kentville Publishing Co Ltd, Kentville, n.d. (c.1951)
Blue, gold, regtl crest on front cover, 9.5 x 6.0, -/398.
Fp, 18 mono phots, 6 maps (printed in the text), no appendixes, no Index.

The regt was formed in Amherst in 1936 and landed in Normandy as part of
2nd Canadian Division. A good narrative account, with many individuals
mentioned by name. The photographs and maps are good. Men from this
regt were taken prisoner and murdered by General Kurt Meyer of the 12th SS
Panzer Grenadiers. R/4 V/4. JEB.
The first edition was restricted to a print-run of 1000 copies. There have
been two subsequent facsimile reprints (not seen).

HISTORY OF THE LINCOLN AND WELLAND REGIMENT

Major R L Rogers
Printed by Industrial Shops for the Deaf, Montreal, for the Regiment, 1954
Red, black, regtl crest on front cover, 9.25 x 6.0, -/465.
Fp, 12 mono phots, 11 maps (printed in the text), Glossary, no Index.

Apps: list of former COs (including those of the original founder regts),
list of former officers (including WWI, with biographical notes),
nominal roll for the regt (1939-1946).

The clear narrative is devoted mainly to combat in North West Europe.
A pleasingly produced book which meets all the usual research requirements.
R/2 V/4. AMOT. RP.


BLOODY BURON

Captain J Allan Snowie
Printed by The Boston Mills Press, Erin, Ontario, 1984
Black, gold, 8.75 x 11.0, -/120.
Fp, 70 mono phots (including 2 large group pictures printed on the end-
papers), 4 maps (printed in the text), Bibliography, Glossary,
Bibliography, no Index.

Apps: Roll of Honour (specifically those killed at Buron), H&A (with full
citations), nominal roll.

Like many modern Canadian regts, the Highland Light Infantry of Canada
has an extraordinarily complicated lineage. In 1965 they were amalgamated
to form the Highland Fusiliers of Canada, but they can trace their roots
back to the North Waterloo Mennonite Teamsters which were raised for
service in the War of 1812. This particular book deals with a specific
battle, the action at Buron, Normandy, when the Bn was ordered to assault
the village in daylight across open ground. It was their baptism of fire,
and a classic infantry action of great intensity. The author describes the
events leading up to the action, and the minutiae of the battle itself.
A most unusual form of regtl history, and of great interest.
R/1 V/4. AldMM. RP.

## CANADA - ENGINEERS AND OTHER CORPS

THE HISTORY OF THE CORPS OF ROYAL CANADIAN ENGINEERS
Volume I   : 1749-1939
Volume II : 1939-1946

Colonel A J Kerry OBE and Major W A McDill CD
Printed by Thornton Press, Toronto, for The Military Engineers Association
of Canada, Ottawa, 1962 (Volume I) and 1966 (Volume II)
Matching pair, blue, gold Corps crest on front cover, xx/389 and xix/711
Fps, 8 maps and 41 mono phots in Volume I, 12 maps and 36 mono phots in
Volume II, Glossary, Bibliography, Indexes.

Apps: H&A (numerical summary only), list of some former officers.

The authors have succeeded in condensing a mass of detailed information in
readily digestible form. The narrative is of interest both to the general
reader and the specialist military engineer. The maps, drawn by Corporal
P Heinrichs of the Royal Canadian Engineers, are exceptionally clear and
attractive. R/3 V/5. PCAL. RP/JEB.


FROM THE RIDEAU TO THE RHINE AND BACK
The 6th Field Company and Battalion, Canadian Engineers, in the Great War

Major K Weatherbe MC
The Hunter-Rose Co Ltd, Toronto, 1928
Blue, gold, Corps badge on front cover, 7.25 x 6.5, xiv/519.
Fp, 135 mono phots, 10 sketches, 27 maps (bound in), no Index.

Apps: Roll of Honour, H&A, nominal roll.

A very complete history for this unit, written by an officer who served
with it, based partly upon his own experiences and partly upon the War
Diary. Many of the photographs are of individual members of the unit, and
the nominal roll is a prime reference source. The maps are in many cases
the official trench maps. R/4 V/5. MCJ.


THE 127th BATTALION, C.E.F.
2nd Bn Canadian Railway Troops

Lieut Col H M Jackson MBE ED
Printed by The Industrial Shops for the Deaf, Montreal, n.d.
Green, black, 6.5 x 4.0, vii/186.
Fp, 3 mono phots, no maps, no Index.

Apps: Roll of Honour (KIA and WIA), H&A (some with citations), list of
attached units.

This is a detailed account of the unit's services in France and Flanders
in WWI. Abundant mention of individual officers and Other Ranks in the
narrative, which is full and informative. R/4 V/4. EDS.

CANADA'S BLACK BATTALION
No2 Construction Bn, 1916-1920
Calvin W Ruck
Black Culture in Nova Scotia, Halifax, 1986
Illustrated card cover, brown, black, 9.0 x 6.0, x/143.
18 mono phots, no maps, no Index.

Apps: nominal roll of all men who served, with ranks and home addresses.

This is the story of the only all-black bn to serve in the Canadian
Army. R/1 V/3. JEB.


HISTORY OF THE ROYAL CANADIAN CORPS OF SIGNALS, 1903-1961

John S Moir
Published by the Committee of the Corps, Ottawa, 1962
Blue, gold, Corps crest on front cover, 10.0 x 6.5, -/366.
Fp, 21 mono phots, 15 maps (2 coloured maps on the end-papers, 2 other
coloured, folding, bound in, and 10 other good mono maps printed in the
text), Glossary, Index (detailed).

Apps: Roll of Honour (all ranks for WWI and Korea), H&A (WWII and Korea),
list of former COs.

A superb Corps history which covers the early days, WWI service in France
and Belgium, WWII service at Dieppe, in Sicily and Italy, in Normandy,
Holland and Germany, in the Pacific theatre, and then finally Korea.
Readable and interesting, even for the non-specialist. R/3 V/5. PCAL. RP.


THE CANADIAN PROVOST CORPS
Silver Jubilee 1940-1965

Lieut Col Q E Lawson, Mr R I Luker, and Major A F Ritchie
Mortimer Ltd, Ottawa, 1965
Blue, silver, Corps crest on front cover, 9.5 x 6.5, -/96.
48 mono phots, no maps, no Index.

Apps: Roll of Honour (rank, name and date of death), H&A (all ranks),
list of former COs.

A quite short but certainly interesting account of this now-disbanded
Corps. The narrative covers WWII, the post-war situation, then the Korean
War and peace-keeping services with the United Nations. R/4 V/4. JEB.


TO THE THUNDERER HIS ARMS
The Royal Canadian Ordnance Corps

William F Rannie
Published privately, Lincoln, Ontario, 1984
'Perfect binding', soft card, ivory, blue, embellished with red/white/
blue diagonal stripes and the Corps crest on the front cover.
8.75 x 5.75, -/360.
53 mono phots, one map (printed in the text), no Index.

Apps: Roll of Honour (all ranks, WWII only, KIA), H&A (WWI and WWII), order of battle 1939-1946, summary of 'milestone' dates in the Corps history.

The narrative traces the history of the Corps from the second half of the 19th century through to disbandment in 1974. An account of WWI service in France and Siberia, WWII service in Sicily, Italy and North West Europe. Post-war, RCOC personnel served with UN peace-keeping forces in Kashmir, Congo, Cyprus, Lebanon, and elsewhere. This is a 'broad brush' description of a long and complicated history, of interest mainly as an account of organisational changes and Corps commitments. R/1 V/4. AldMM. RP.


WAR DIARY, SECOND C.D.A.C.
Second Canadian Divisonal Ammunition Column

Lieut H D Clark
J A McMillan, St John, 1921
Brown, black, 8.5 x 6.0, -/166.
no illustrations, no maps, no Index.

Apps: nominal roll (with details for all ranks of casualties, awards, dates, etc).

The narrative is informative, being devoted mainly to WWI services in France. R/3 V/4. JEB.


WAIT FOR THE WAGON
The Story of the Royal Canadian Army Service Corps

Arnold Warren
McClelland & Stewart Ltd, (Canada), 1961
Dark blue, silver, 9.25 x 5.75, xL/413.
63 main mono phots, with many other small individual studio portrait photographs, no maps, Glossary, Index.

Apps: Roll of Honour (WWI and WWII, listed by year), H&A (WWI, WWII, and Korea).

An account which covers the story of the CASC from its formation on 1901 through to the end of the Korean War. Readable, with some technical and administrative content, but lightened with occasional anecdotes and references to individual actions. R/2 V/5. PCAL. RP.


CANADA'S CRAFTSMEN
The Story of the Corps of Royal Canadian Electrical and Mechanical Engineers, and of the Land Ordnance Engineering Branch

Colonel Murray Johnston
Publisher's details not shown, n.d. (c.1984)
'Perfect' binding, soft card covers, blue, gold, 3 Corps crests
90 mono phots, no maps, Bibliography, Index.

Apps: list of Colonels Commandant and Corps Commanders, order of battle
1939-1945.

The narrative traces the Corps history from 1903 (when it had the title
Canadian Stores Department) through to the 1980s. The Corps, under its
full title of RCEME, was established in 1944 as a 'spin off' from the
Royal Canadian Ordnance Corps. R/2 V/5. AldMM. RP.


HISTORY OF THE CANADIAN FORCES IN THE GREAT WAR
The Medical Services

Sir Andrew MacPhail OBE
F A Acland, for the Government of Canada, Ottawa, 1925
Maroon, gold, 10.0 x 7.0, viii/428.
no illustrations, one map  (bound in), Index.

Apps: Roll of Honour, H&A.

As might be expected, in view of its sponsorship, this is a very
comprehensive history of the Canadian Army's medical branch in WWI.
The book is one of the few tangible results to emerge from the Official
History project mentioned earlier (see page 232). R/4 V/5. JRT.


STRETCHER-BEARERS AT THE DOUBLE
History of the Fifth Canadian Field Ambulance

Frederick W Noyes
The Hunter-Rose Co, Toronto, 1937
Blue, gold, 9.25 x 6.25, -/315.
24 mono phots, 8 maps (bound in), no Index.

Apps: Roll of Honour (covers the period 11.11.1914 to 1.1.1936, with
details of name, rank and date of death), H&A (name, rank, award, and
last known address).

The unit was formed at the outbreak of WWI from the recruitment areas of
Toronto, Hamilton and Owen Sound. This is a good account of its services
in France, written in a pleasant and informative style. R/4 V/5. JEB.


THE INTELLIGENCE SERVICES WITHIN THE CANADIAN CORPS, 1914-1918

Major J E Hahn
The McMillan Co, Toronto, 1930
Red, gold, 9.25 x 6.0, xxii/263.
16 mono phots, 6 maps (printed in the text), no appendixes, no Index.

Possibly of value to the specialist researcher, but less interesting for
the general reader. R/2 V/4. JEB.

THE CANADIAN 'EMMA GEES'
A History of the Canadian Machine-gun Corps

Lieut Col C S Grafton VD
By Hunter Printing, London, Ontario, for the C.M.G.C.Association, 1938
Maroon, black, Corps badge and 'gunner in trench' motif on front cover,
9.75 x 7.0, -/218.
13 mono phots, 3 maps (printed in the text), no formal appendixes,
no Index.

Excellent coverage of the raising and subsequent services of the Corps and
its many sub-units. Although there are no appendixes, there are numerous
nominal rolls of officers scattered throughout the narrative, Company by
Company, and as at 22.2.1918. The organisation of the Corps is explained
in tabular form. A very helpful book. R/3 V/4. MCJ.

## CANADA - POLICE

HISTORY OF THE ROYAL NORTH-WEST MOUNTED POLICE
A Corps History

Captain Ernest J Chambers
The Mortimer Press, Montreal, n.d. (c.1907)
Red and beige, gold, Corps crest and 'mounted police officer' motif on
front cover, 12.0 x 9.0, -/158/xxxvii.
numerous mono phots of early senior officers, no maps, no Index.

Apps: lists of former and serving officers.

The ever-industrious Captain Chambers did not confine his attentions to
Canadian Militia units (see pages 234, 235 and 236). The fact that the
last section of this book (xxxvii) consists entirely of paid advertisements
would suggest that he was one of the few writers to make money out of
history. The basic format of this book is the same as his Militia
histories, and is a useful view of the fore-runner of the RCMP at the turn
of the century. The narrative covers the period from 1873 through to
1906.  R/5 V/3. AMOT. RP.


RIDERS OF THE PLAINS
A Record of the Royal North-West Mounted Police of Canada, 1873-1910

A L Haydon
Andrew Melrose, London, 1910
Seen in rebound form, details of original binding not known, 8.5 x 5.5,
xvi/385.
Fp, 28 mono phots, 4 maps (2 printed in the text, 2 bound in),
Bibliography, Index.

Apps: ten in total, including Roll of Honour (KIA and DOW during the North
West Rebellion), list of former Commissioners, list of some former
officers.

Formed in 1873, the RCMP (as it became later) was the only disciplined
armed force in the wilder tracts of pioneering Canada, and it fulfilled
both a police and para-military role. The citizens for whom they were
responsible were a mixed crowd: fur trappers, gold prospectors, Indians,
lumberjacks, farmer settlers, and so forth. It was during this period
that the Corps gained its romantic popular image which it has never lost.
This book is a detailed historical account of the first 37 years,
a period which witnessed the establishment of modern Canada.
R/5 V/5. PCAL. RP/LM.


THE ROYAL CANADIAN MOUNTED POLICE

L Charles Douthwaite
Blackie & Son Ltd, London & Glasgow, 1939
Red, gold, 8.5 x 5.5, vi/281.
Fp, 15 mono phots, one map (bound in), no Index.

Apps: list of former Commandants.

A good readable account of the force (under its modern title) from 1873 to 1937. The book would have benefitted from an Index and some additional appendixes of names, dates, events, etc, but it is nevertheless a good reference source. R/2 V/3. RLP.


THE LIVING LEGEND
The Story of the Royal Canadian Mounted Police

Allan Phillips
Cassell & Co, London, 1957
Red, gold, 8.5 x 5.5, iv/230.
no illustrations, no maps, no appendixes, Index.

This book is not really a Corps history. It is instead a compendium of incidents and famous cases arising from the 1930s and 1940s. As a research source, it has fairly limited value, but is included here because so little seems to have been published regarding the history of the RCMP. R/1 V/2. RLP.

## CANADA - ARTILLERY

THE ORIGIN AND SERVICES OF THE 3rd (MONTREAL) FIELD BATTERY OF ARTILLERY
See page 237 for details of this title.

HISTORICAL RECORDS OF THE NEW BRUNSWICK REGIMENT, CANADIAN ARTILLERY

Captain John B N Baxter
Privately ('By the Officers of the Regiment')
Printer's details not stated,St John, New Brunswick, 1896
Royal blue, gold, crest of Canadian Artillery on front cover,
8.25 x 5.75, viii/259.
Fp. 23 mono phots, Index.

Apps: list of former COs, list of former officers, nominal roll of all
members.

This handsome book is an account of the oldest Canadian Militia artillery
regiment (and might alternatively have been listed under 'Militia',
see pages 234 to 237). The narrative covers the period 1793 to 1896. The
regt, of ten Companies (later designated Batteries), never saw active
service, but the book is an important example of socio-military history.
It is, in effect, a commentary upon the role and place of the Militia
in the life of the Province during that period. There are some useful
notes on officers and Other Ranks, organisation and designations,
fortifications, the regtl band, and so forth. R/5 V/5. RAI. AMM.


BATTERY ACTION
The Story of the 43rd Battery, C.F.A.

H R Kay, G McGee, and F A McLennan
Warwick Brothers & Rutter, Toronto, n.d. (c.1920)
Red, gold, 7.75 x 5.0, -/305.
Fp, 7 line drawings, one map (bound in), no Index.

Apps: Roll of Honour, nominal roll of those who served overseas.

An Ontario-based battery which served in France in WWI. A pleasantly
readable narrative, with plenty of individuals and incidents mentioned.
The lack of an Index and the paucity of appendixes are a disadvantage in
a book of this length. R/4 V/3. JEB.

THE HISTORY OF THE FIFTY-FIFTH BATTERY, C.F.A.

D C McArthur
H S Longhurst, at the Robert Duncan Press, Hamilton, Ontario, 1919
Leather, blue, gold, 5th Canadian Division sign on the front cover,
7.5 x 5.25, -/94.
Fp, 18 mono phots, 3 maps (bound in), no Index.

Apps: Roll of Honour, list of former officers, nominal roll (with details of awards included).

A straightforward battery history, dealing mainly with movements and engagements. The nominal roll does not include either ranks or service numbers, and this limits its usefulness. R/4 V/3. RAI. AMM.


## THE 60th BATTERY BOOK

Anon
Canada Newspaper Co Ltd, London (UK), for the Battery, 1919
Purple, gold, CFA crest on front cover, 7.25 x 4.75, -/190.
31 mono phots, 7 maps (printed in the text), no Index.

Apps: Roll of Honour, H&A, list of former COs, list of former officers, nominal roll (detailed), notes on 'regimental personalities', notes on the Battery flag.

Produced in the UK, shortly before the unit returned to Canada. A very useful work, with some good photographs. R/4 V/4. RAI. AMM.


## THE STORY OF THE SIXTY-SIXTH C.F.A.

Anon
Turnbull & Spears, Edinburgh, 1919
Red, gold, 7.75 x 5.25, xii/148.
Fp, 13 mono phots, 3 maps (printed in the text), no Index.

Apps: H&A, nominal roll (all ranks, with details and home addresses).

The unit was formed in Montreal in March 1916 and served in the UK and France. Very readable, and a useful source. R/4 V/4. JEB.


## THE SEVENTH
The Seventh Canadian Siege Battery

T W L MacDermont
Published by The Seventh Canadian Siege Battery Association, 1930
Black, gold, Battery badge on front cover, 8.5 x 5.75, -/144.
Fp, 6 mono phots, 8 maps (printed in the text), Bibliography, no Index.

Apps: nominal roll (with details of deaths, wounds, awards, ranks, service numbers).

Like the previous entries (above), this is an account of gunner services in France and Flanders during WWI. The Battery served at Vimy Ridge, Lens, Hill 70, Passchendaele, Arras, Canal du Nord, Valenciennes and Mons. A readable and informative account. R/3 V/4. JEB.

THE SECOND CANADIAN HEAVY BATTERY IN THE GREAT WAR
Chronology of War, 1914 to 1919

Anon
2 C.H.B. Old Boy's Association, Montreal, n.d. (c.1921)
Stiff card covers, red, black, embellished with the Association title,
6.5 x 4.0, -/117.
no illustrations, 2 maps (in rear pocket), no Index.

Apps: nominal roll (all members, with home addresses).

A small book, but listing all the engagements in which the Battery took
part during WWI. The narrative is quite restricted, the bulk of the work
being devoted to the nominal roll. R/3 V/2. JEB.


HISTORY OF THE 11th CANADIAN FIELD REGIMENT, R.C.A.
From 1 September 1939 to 5 May 1945

Captain A G Campbell
Kemink en Zoon NV, Utrecht, Holland, for the 29th Battery RCA Veterans
Association, n.d. (c.1945)
'Perfect' bound, soft card, mottled grey, black, 9.5 x 6.0, -/205.
no illustrations, no maps, no Index.

Apps: Roll of Honour (KIA, WIA, and POW), H&A.

A factual account of the Battery's locations, movements and engagements
during WWII. Dry and terse, but no doubt useful for the specialist RCA
researcher. R/4 V/2. AldMM. RP.


HISTORY OF THE FIFTEENTH CANADIAN FIELD REGIMENT, ROYAL CANADIAN
ARTILLERY, 1941 TO 1945

Captain Robert A Spencer
Elsevier, Amsterdam, Holland, 1945
Green, silver, RCA badge on front cover, 10.5 x 7.5, -/302.
Fp, 12 mono phots, 11 maps, Bibliography, no Index.

Apps: Roll of Honour, H&A, list of former COs, locations, movements, etc.

This was a Western Canadian regt, formed in Winnipeg in 1941. It landed in
Normandy as part of the 4th Canadian Armoured Division. This is a good
account, well-written, with very detailed appendixes of members,
casualties, dates and places. R/4 V/4. JEB.


HISTORY OF THE 7th CANADIAN MEDIUM REGIMENT, R.C.A.
From 1st September 1939, to 8th June 1945

A M Lockwood
Publication details not shown, n.d. (c.1946)
Blue, gold, RCA badge on front cover, 9.5 x 6.0, -/111.
Fp, 7 mono phots, no maps, no Index.

Apps: Roll of Honour, H&A, nominal rolls.

The Regt was formed in London, Ontario, on 1 September 1939, and fought
in North West Europe. The nominal rolls, as with most Canadian regtl
histories, are extremely detailed, with details of KIA and WIA, honours
and awards (with rank, number and date), then a complete roll of officers
and men who served (number, rank and name). There is also a complete roll
of Warrant Officers and Sergeants. R/4 V/4. JEB.


HISTORY OF THE 17th FIELD REGIMENT, R.C.A.

Anon
J Niemeijer's Publishing Company, Groningen, Holland, 1946
Black, gold/red/blue, RCA crest on front cover, 8.5 x 5.5, -/107.
Fp, 29 mono phots, no maps, no Index.

Apps: Roll of Honour (all ranks, with dates), list of officers and Warrant
Officers who served.

The Regt fought in North West Europe as part of the 5th Canadian Armoured
Division, and this is a very good account of their services. It lacks an
appendix for H&A because, according to the Preface, such details were not
available at the time when the book was being published. R/4 V/3. JEB.


THE GUNNERS OF CANADA
The History of the Royal Regiment of Canadian Artillery, 1534-1919

Colonel G W L Nicholson CD
McClelland & Stewart Ltd, for the Royal Canadian Artillery Association,
Toronto, 1967 (Vol I) and 1972 (Vol II)
Dark blue, gold, regtl crest on front covers, 10.0 x 6.25, matching pair,
xiv/478 and xvi/760.
Vol I:   Fp, 48 mono phots, 8 sketches, 18 maps, Index
Vol II:  Fp, 57 mono phots, 5 sketches, 21 maps, Bibliography, Index.

Apps: eight good detailed appendixes in each of the two Volumes, including H&A (for WWI, WWII and Korea), lists of former COs, etc.

These two volumes comprise a set which is a regtl history on the grand
scale. Both are eminently readable throughout, with many references in the
narrative to individuals, to specific actions, to various units and sub-
units, and to particular places and events. The author covers a large
timescale  - commencing with the earliest days of gunnery in Canada and
working his way progressively through the War of 1812, the Fenian Raids,
the Boer War, and the two world wars. Coverage of WWI and WWI is excellent.
The book includes a good range of maps, and the illustrations are all very
interesting and well-produced (many having names of individuals in the
captions). This pair of books is  exemplary in every way.
R/3 V/5+. PCAL. RAI. AMM.

PAR LA BOUCHE DE NOS CANONS
Histoire de 4e Regiment d'Artillerie Moyenne, 4th Canadian Medium
Regiment, Royal Canadian Artillery, 1941-1945

Jacques Gouin
Gasparo Ltee, Quebec, 1970
Stiff card, dark blue, white, 'cannon balls' motif, 10.0 x 8.0, -/268.
63 mono phots, 3 line drawings, 18 maps (bound in), Bibliography, no Index.

Apps: Roll of Honour, H&A, list of former COs, list of former officers,
nominal roll of all members.

Written entirely in French, this is a factual narrative account of a
Quebec-raised artillery regt in the Normandy and North West Europe
campaigns. It covers the first three years of training in Canada and the
UK (1941-44) and the advance through to Germany (July 1944-May 1945).
The Roll of Honour is very detailed, giving each man's name, number,
battery, and the date and cause of death. Of particular interest to
Gunner researchers is the Bibliography (which extends to five pages), and
a 'references' section (which covers another twenty-one pages).
R/4 V/4. RAI. AMM.


BATTERY FLASHES OF W.W.II
A Thumb-nail Sketch of Canadian Artillery Batteries during the
1939-1945 Conflict

D W Falconer
Published privately in Canada (details not shown), 1985
Illustrated stiff card covers, red, white, 9.0 x 6.0, xii/514.
4 mono phots, 4 coloured plates, Bibliography, no formal appendixes,
Index.

The title of this monumental work is very misleading. It does indeed have
a section (well illustrated) which deals with the cloth insignia worn
on battle dress, but the main purpose of the book is to record the
formation, mobilisation, reorganisation, designation, amalgamation,
moves, locations and (where applicable) disbandment of every single
battery of the Royal Canadian Artillery mobilised for service in WWII.
There is an almost incredible amount of information for each battery.
few units receiving less than half a page of print and many having much
more. Every type of battery is covered: anti-aircraft, anti-tank,
coastal, field, medium, heavy and super-heavy, counter battery, Air OP,
training units, holding units, etc. The 'Headquarters' chapter includes,
almost coincidentally, an immense amount of information on the NW Europe
campaign itself. A true labour of love by the author, and a marvellous
source of reference. R/2 V/5+. RAI. AMM.

R.C.H.A. - RIGHT OF THE LINE
An Anecdotal History of the Royal Canadian Horse Artillery from 1871

Major G D Mitchell MC CD
Published by the RCHA History Committee, Ottawa, 1986
Red, gold, 8.75 x 10.75, x/303.
Fp, 175 mono phots, 5 line drawings, 24 maps (printed in the text),
Glossary, Bibliography, Index.

Apps: eight in total, including Roll of Honour, H&A, list of former COs,
former Commandants and former RSMs, notes on the RCHA band, notes on
armament, a diary of significant dates and events, etc.

This is an extremely readable and, at times, moving account of the
Canadian regular artillery, from the time of formation of the first two
Regular Batteries in 1871, to the formation of the RCHA in 1905, and then
to 1986. The narrative covers: North West Canada (1885), South Africa
(1900-1902), WWI (1914-1918), WWI (1939-1945), Korea (1950-1954),
and UN services in Cyprus (1965-1975). Dozens of personal anecdotes and
reminiscences are scattered throughout the story (hence the sub-title of
the book) and almost all of the pictures are captioned with individual
names. An unusual format for a regtl history, but one which works very
well and captures the spirit of the RCHA over a long period of service.
R/1 V/5. RAI. AMM.

# PART V
Australian and New Zealand Forces
in Korea

## AUSTRALIAN AND NEW ZEALAND FORCES
## IN KOREA

16th FIELD REGIMENT, RNZA, 1950-1954

Lieut Col J A Pountney MBE
Unpublished facsimile typescript, no details shown,1954
Seen in stapled card covers, 10.75 x 7.0, -/29.
2 line drawings, 2 maps (printed in the text), no appendix, no Index.

Apps: Roll of Honour, H&A, list of COs.

A brief but interesting account of 16 Field Regt RNZA in Korea for the
period stated. The unit was raised in New Zealand from volunteers at the
outbreak of the war, and then disbanded at the cessation of hostilities.
It saw plenty of action, firing more than three quarters of a million
shells, suffering 89 casualties, and gaining 59 decorations (including
4 DSOs, 11 MCs, 1 DCM, and 7 MMs).It seems likely that this summary of
their services was produced in limited numbers, as a memento for serving
members of the regiment, at RHQ in Korea and as they were preparing to
return to New Zealand. R/5 V/4. SB.


WITH THE AUSTRALIANS IN KOREA

Norman Bartlett
Board of Management of the Australian War Memorial, Canberra, 1960
Blue, 10.0 x 7.25, v/294.
Fp, 123 mono phots, 6 maps (printed in the text), no formal appendixes,
Index.

This book is divided into two parts. The first 140 pages are a narrative
account of the services of Australian troops in Korea as part of the UN
force. Then follow 115 pages containing 18 personal impressions of the
conflict, mainly by official War Correspondents. Interesting and well
illustrated. Useful mainly as background reading. R/3 V/2. SB.


THE KAPYONG BATTALION
Medal Roll of the Third Battalion, The Royal Australian Regiment, Battle
of Kapyong, 23-24 April 1951

James J Atkinson
New South Wales Military Historical Society, 1977
Green and white, white and green, 8.5 x 5.5, -/80.
11 mono phots, 3 maps (printed in the text), no Index.

Apps: Roll of Honour, H&A (with full citations, even for MID), nominal
roll of personnel who took part, Bn medal roll for Korea.

A superb little book, giving an excellent account of the battle followed
by very good appendixes. Much useful detail concerning also the Bn's
movements and services in Korea generally. R/2 V/4. LM/CMF.

# PART VI
Australian and New Zealand Forces
in South Vietnam

## AUSTRALIAN AND NEW ZEALAND FORCES
## IN SOUTH VIETNAM


THE ANZAC BATTALION IN SOUTH VIETNAM, 1967-68
A Record of the Tour of 2nd Bn, The Royal Australian Regiment, and
1st Bn, The Royal New Zealand Infantry Regiment (the Anzac Battalion)
in South Vietnam, 1967-68

Major K E Newman
Printcraft Press, Brookvale, NSW, for the Battalion, 1968
Black, gold, 2 regtl badges (RAR and RNZIR) on front cover, 11.5 x 8.75,
-/175, published in two Volumes.
209 mono phots, 48 coloured plates, 16 maps, Index.

Apps: Roll of Honour, H&A, nominal roll.

A handsome and liberally illustrated pair of matching books which cover
the Bn's activities in Phuoc Tuy Province, with generous mention of all
attached personnel from 108 Battery, 4 Field Regt, RAA, 1 Field Squadron
RAE, and 104 Signals Squadron, RASignals. R/3. V/5. HEC.


MISSION IN VIETNAM
The Tour in South Vietnam of 4 RAR/RNZIR (Anzac) Battalion, and
104 Field Battery, RAA, June 1968 to May 1969

Lieut J R Webb and Pte L A Drake
Times Printers, Singapore, 1969
White, black, 11.25 x 8.5, vi/130.
Very many illustrations, 14 maps (printed in the text), no Index.

Apps: Roll of Honour, chronology of events, Glossary.

A mainly pictorial record of the Bn's second tour in South Vietnam.
A pleasantly readable narrative supported by very good operational maps.
R/2 V/4. HEC.


SEVEN IN SEVENTY
A Pictorial Record of Seventh Battalion, Royal Australian Regiment,
1970-1971

Printcraft Press, Brookvale, NSW, for the Regiment, 1971
maps, illustrations, 207 pages, not seen.   AWM.


THE ANZAC BATTALION

Major A R Roberts
Published by the Regiment, 1972
Stiff card, black, gold, RAR and RNZIR regtl badges on front cover,
dimensions not recorded, -/176.
Many illustrations (including 26 colour plates and numerous line drawings
and cartoons), 3 maps (2 printed on end-papers, one loose in rear pocket).

Apps: Roll of Honour, H&A, nominal roll.

This is reported to be a useful and attractive book, but no other details are available.


THE FIGHTING FOURTH
A Pictorial Record of the Second Tour in South Vietnam by 4 RAR/NZ (ANZAC) BATTALION, 1971-72

Capt L R Sayce, Lieut M D O'Neill, and Pte A Garton
Printcraft Press,Brookvale, NSW, for the Battalion, 1972
Red, gold, 11.0 x 8.5, -/208.
330 mono phots, 11 coloured plates, 36 other illustrations, 9 maps (printed in the text), Index.

Apps: Roll of Honour, H&A, nominal roll.

Like the two previous titles noted for this Bn (see Newman and Webb/Drake on previous page), this is a pictorial and anecdotal record, not a definitive history. As such, however, it is still an excellent reference source and the only one available for this unit during that period. The narrative deals mainly with operations around Nui Dat, against the 274 Viet Cong Main Force Regiment and the 33 North Vietnam Army Regiment. R/3 V/4. HEC.


6 RAR/NZ (ANZAC) BATTALION HISTORY, 1967-70

Major D L Johnson, Pte R J Dorizzi, Pte N S Howarth
Times Printers, Singapore, 1972
Orange, white, 11.5 x 8.5, viii/178.
Very many illustrations (including 8 coloured plates), 19 maps (all loose in rear pocket), no Index.

Apps: Roll of Honour, H&A, nominal roll, notes on pipe tunes.

This publication follows the formula described in respect of the above 4th Anzac Bn, i.e. it is largely pictorial and was produced mainly as a memento for the personnel who served during the campaign. Not a full definitive history, but an excellent reference source. R/3 V/4. HEC. A similar but probably much shorter record was published in 1967 in respect of its first tour in South Vietnam (1966-1967). Not seen.


3 RAR IN SOUTH VIETNAM, 1967-68
A Record of the Operational Service of the Third Battalion, The Royal Australian Regiment in South Vietnam, 12 December 1967 - 20 November 1968

Major R F Stuart
Printcraft Press, Brookvale, NSW, 1968
Grey and green, green and gold, regtl crest on front cover, 11.25 x 8.5, -/104.
Numerous photographs and other illustrations, 13 maps (printed in the text), no Index.

VIETNAM TASK
5th Battalion, Royal Australian Regiment, 1966-67

Major Robert J O'Neill
Cassell Australia Ltd, 1968
Black, gold, regt crest on front cover, 9.0 x 5.75, xvi/256.
30 mono phots, 22 maps (20 printed in the text, 2 printed on the end-
papers), Index.

Apps: Roll of Honour, H&A.

Like other titles of the genre, this book is a graphic and interesting
account of one bn's tour of service in the South Vietnam conflict. Unlike
the books recorded on the previous pages, however, this one relies more
upon a clear descriptive narrative and less upon pictures. R/3 V/4. HEC.


VIETNAM
A Pictorial History of the 6th Bn, Royal Australian Regiment, 1966-67

Captain Iain McLean Williams, Captain B Wickens, Lieut D Sabben, and
Sergeant J Kenna
Printcraft Press, Brookvale, NSW, for the Regiment, 1967
Red, gold, regtl crest on front cover, 11.0 x 8.75, number of pages not
recorded.
Numerous illustrations (including some colour), 7 maps (printed in the
text), no Index.

Apps: Roll of Honour, H&A (with some citations).

A privately produced regtl record intended for the unit's own personnel
rather than public sale. R/3 V/4. HEC.


THE YEAR OF THE TIGERS
The Second Tour of 5th Battalion, Royal Australian Regiment, in South
Vietnam, 1969-70

Captain M R Battle
Printcraft Press, Brookvale, NSW, for the Regiment
Brown, 11.0 x 8.75, -/208.
280 mono phots, 41 coloured plates, 16 maps (bound in), no Index.

Apps: H&A (with full citations where applicable), nominal roll.

Again, this is primarily a photographic record, many of the pictures being
portraits and active service 'snaps' of officers and NCOs of the Bn.
R/3 V/3. JBF.

THE GREY EIGHT IN VIETNAM
The History of Eight Battalion, The Royal Australian Regiment, November
1969 - November 1970

Major A Clunie-Ross
The Courier-Mail Printing Service, Brisbane, 1971
Grey, gold, 11.0 x 9.0, -/160.
155 mono phots, 19 coloured plates, 4 line drawings, 10 maps (printed in
the text), no Index.

Apps: Roll of Honour, H&A, nominal roll of all ranks.

A useful research source for an Australian unit's tour in South Vietnam
during the stated period. The Bn saw much action, gaining one DSO,
2 MCs, 2 MMs, 18 Crosses of Gallantry, 3 Armed Forces Medals (First Class),
and a unique Vietnamese Unit Citation. R/3 V/4. PS.


A HISTORY OF THE SIXTH BATTALION, THE ROYAL AUSTRALIAN REGIMENT,
1965-1985

Nick Welch
Published in Enogera, Queensland, for the Regiment, 1986
Noted as having 'maps, illustrations, 208 pages'. Not seen.


SEVENTH BATTALION, THE ROYAL AUSTRALIAN REGIMENT
Notes on Operations, Vietnam, 1970-71

Anon, publication details not known, n.d. (c.1972)
Noted as having 'maps, illustrations, about 200 pages'. Not seen.


YOURS FAITHFULLY
A Record of Service of the 3rd Battalion, The Royal Australian Regiment
in Australia and South Vietnam, 16 February 1969 - 16 October 1971

Captain Colin J Clarke
Printcraft Press, Brookvale, NSW, for the Regiment, 1972
Green, gold, 11.0 x 8.5, -/203.
392 mono phots, 38 line drawings, 11 maps (printed in the text), no Index.

Apps: Roll of Honour, H&A, nominal roll for all ranks.

As can be seen from the technical specification, this is essentially a
pictorial record which concentrates mainly upon the personnel who served
rather than the finer points of the campaign itself. The book will become
increasingly useful, in future years, to genealogists and medal collectors
(the same being true of most of the other titles recorded here for
Australian and ANZAC units which served in South Vietnam. R/3 V/3. JS.

THE BATTLE OF LANG TAN
The Legend of ANZAC Upheld
Lex McAulay
Century Hutchinson Australia Ltd, Hawthorn, Australia, 1986
Black, white, 8.5 x 5.5, viii/187
55 mono phots, one map, 7 diagrams, Glossary.

Apps: H&A, notes on the artillery, the RAAF, the Viet Cong forces in
Phuoc Tuy Province, etc.

The author tells the story from both sides, Australian and North
Vietnamese. In this fierce engagement, D Company, 6 RAR, gained 2 DSOs,
one MBE, 7 MIDs, and the United States Distinguished Unit Citation.
R/1 V/4. PS.


THE SOLDIER'S STORY
The Battle of Xa Lang Tan, Vietnam, 18 August 1966

Terry Burstall
University of Queensland Press, St Lucia, Queensland, 1986
Paper covers, white, red and black, 7.75 x 5.0, xv/188.
35 mono phots, 2 line drawings, 7 diagrams, 3 maps (printed in the text),
Index.

Apps: Operation Lang Tan, roll of personnel eligible to wear the
Distinguished Unit Citation insignia.

The author took part in the battle, and subsequently interviewed others
who were there. As the title suggests, this is a soldier's eyewitness
account, and as such is both informative and graphic. Recommended
reading, especially in conjunction with the previous entry (McAulay).
R/2 V/4. PS.


VIETNAM GUNNERS
161 Battery, Royal New Zealand Artillery, Vietnam, 1965-71

Lieut S D Newman
Moana Press, Tauranga (NZ), 1988
Stiff card, illustrated, 8.25 x 9.75, -/152.
50 mono phots, 20 coloured plates, 8 maps (printed in the text),
Bibliography, no Index.

Apps: Roll of Honour, H&A, nominal roll, notes on operational deployments.

A sound workmanlike account of the services, at different times within
the stated period, of various 161 Battery detachments in South Vietnam.
R/1 V/4. HEC.

TWELVE IN FOCUS
12th Field Regiment in South Vietnam, 1971. A Memento for All Ranks
of the Tour in South Vietnam.

Major G F B Rickards
Printcraft Press, Brookvale, NSW, for the Regiment, 1971
Red boards with black spine, gold, 'two guns and map of Indo-China' motif
on front cover, 11.0 x 8.25, -/144.
262 mono phots, 3 coloured plates, 9 drawings and cartoons, 2 maps (one
printed in the text, one printed on the end-papers), no Index.

Apps: Roll of Honour, list of former officers, nominal roll.

As the sub-title suggests, this is a pictorial record produced mainly for
the pleasure of those who served with the regt and for the information
of their families. It does not pretend to be a history. However, the
mass of photographs is so great that they coincidentally provide a very
useful coverage of the regt's active services. The book is divided into
sections, each of which deals with a specific Battery or sub-unit, and
this adds to its value as a reference source. A well-produced work.
R/2 V/3. RAI. AMM.

# PART  VII
## New Zealand

# NOTE

In New Zealand, the task of recording each regiment's
active services between 1914-1919 and 1939-1945 is one
which, in most cases, has been met by the War History
Branch of the Department of Internal Affairs. The titles
of books comprising this series nearly all have long
sub-titles commencing 'The Official History of ...'.

The majority of these Volumes were printed for the
authorities by Whitcombe & Tombs Ltd, of Wellington and
Auckland, most of the others coming from the presses of
J Wilkie & Co Ltd (later Coulls, Somerville, Wilkie Ltd)
of Dunedin.

To avoid unnecessary repetition, these books appear in
the following pages without their full sub-titles and
with the publisher's details abbreviated to
'War History Branch'.

Apart from the histories of individual regiments and
Corps, the Government has produced two major series of
Volumes describing all the campaigns and battles in
which New Zealand forces were engaged:

## THE OFFICIAL HISTORY OF NEW ZEALAND'S EFFORT IN THE GREAT WAR

and

## THE OFFICIAL HISTORY OF NEW ZEALAND IN THE SECOND WORLD WAR

These two sets of Volumes, like the official unit
histories, conform to a standard format and contain all
of the information which most researchers are likely
to require. They are highly recommended as
background reading.

## NEW ZEALAND – GENERAL ACCOUNTS

THE NEW ZEALAND ARMY
A History from the 1840s to the 1980s

Major M R Wicksteed (Army Public Relations)
P D Hasselberg, Government Printer, Wellington, 1982
Soft card, red, black, x/101.
103 mono phots, 7 maps (printed in the text), no appendixes, no Index.

Although the narrative does not go into detail, this is an excellent
overview of NZ military activity during the stated period. The pictures
are good, and will be unfamiliar to most readers outside New Zealand.
They illustrate the wide range of services performed worldwide by NZ
soldiers from the earliest pioneering days through to France (WWI), the
Western Desert (including the LRDG NZ Patrol), the SAS in Malaya, and the
monitoring force in Rhodesia/Zimbabwe (1980). R/1 V/3. HEC.

A CHRONOLOGY OF THE NEW ZEALAND ARMY, 1827-1986

Major M E Wicksteed (Army Public Relations)
V R Ward, Government Printer, Wellington, 1986
Soft card, gun-metal, black, viii/43.
no illustrations, no maps, no appendixes, Bibliography, no Index.

Although limited in its scope, this booklet is a useful guide to the key
dates in the evolution and active services of the NZ Army. There are
useful 'quick reference' sections containing details of British regts
which served in New Zealand between 1840 and 1870, and statistics for
the two world wars. It may be noted that 100,444 men served in WWI,
of which 16,697 lost their lives and 41,317 were wounded - a casualty
rate of 58.0%. R/1 V/2. HEC.

THE MAORIS IN THE GREAT WAR
A History of the New Zealand Native Contingent and Pioneer Battalion,
Gallipoli 1915, France and Flanders 1916-1918

James Cowan
Whitcombe & Tombs, Auckland, 1926
Light brown, black, 7.0 x 4.25, -/138.
Fp, 52 mono phots, 8 maps (one printed in the text, 6 folding and
bound in, one loose in rear pocket), Index.

Apps: Roll of Honour, H&A, notes on the Maori recruiting song, notes on the
services of Maori troops in the Gallipoli campaign.

The Maori introduction to modern warfare was the landing at ANZAC Cove and
the battle at Sari Bair. Following the evacuation from Gallipoli they went
directly to the Western Front and took part in most of the major 'pushes'
through to the end of the war. James Cowan had an affinity for the
Maori and wrote warmly of their achievements as warriors (not only in WWI
but also during the battles of the pioneer period). R/3 V/5. HEC.

## NEW ZEALAND – ANGLO-BOER WAR ACCOUNTS

FOURTH CONTINGENT, NEW ZEALAND ROUGH RIDERS
From Otago and Southland

Anon
Joseph Braithwaite, Dunedin (NZ), 1900
Paper covers, illustrated with 'patriotic bunting and flags' motif on
front cover, brown, black, dimensions not reported, -/27 (not numbered).
Fp, 66 mono phots, no maps, no Index.

Apps: nominal roll of members who served in South Africa.

This is a purely photographic record, mostly of members of the Contingent.
The unit's campaign services are barely mentioned, but the pictures are
useful as a source of reference regarding details of uniform, insignia,
and personal accoutrement. R/5 V/2. ATL. JS.


WITH THE FOURTH NEW ZEALAND ROUGH RIDERS

James G Narle Moore
The Otago Daily Times & Witness Newspapers Ltd, Dunedin (NZ), 1906
Maroon, gold, 8.5 x 5.75, -/200.
18 mono phots, 2 sketches, no maps, no Index.

Apps: Roll of Honour, H&A, nominal roll of the Company.

A good workmanlike narrative, with useful appendixes. R/5 V/4. HEC.


ON ACTIVE SERVICE WITH THE SILENT SIXTH

Joseph Linklater
McKee & Co, Wellington (NZ), 1904
Blue, gold, dimensions not reported, -/102.
2 mono phots, no maps, no Index.

Apps: Roll of Honour.

An account of the 6th New Zealand Mounted Rifles in the Anglo-Boer War,
presented in diary form. R/4 V/3. ATL. JS.


THE COLLEGE RIFLES, WELLINGTON
Final Report and Summary of Thirteen Years' Volunteer Service

Anon
City Printing Co, Wellington (NZ), 1911
Paper covers, brown, black, dimensions not reported, iv/25.
no illutrations, no maps, no Index.

Apps: H&A, list of former officers, various nominal rolls.

A small but useful book regarding an obscure Reserve unit. Interesting as a reflection of the socio-military history of the Wellington area, and listed here because it includes a roll of members who volunteered for service in South Africa. R/5 V/3. JS.


THE NEW ZEALANDERS IN SOUTH AFRICA

D O W Hall
War History Branch, Dept of Internal Affairs, Wellington (NZ), 1949
Red, black, 8.75 x 5.5, xviii/97.
Fp, 38 mono phots, 3 maps (bound in), no Index.

Apps: Roll of Honour.

The NZ Government's account of its forces' services in the Boer War, published nearly half a century after the events it describes. The main value of the book is the fact it contains a brief account of the activities of each of Contingents which took part. R/4 V/3. ATL. JS.

# NEW ZEALAND - EXTENDED HISTORIES

TOGETHER ONWARD
A Short History of the Canterbury Regiment, The Nelson, Marlborough and
West Coast Regiment, and the Second Battalion (Canterbury, Nelson,
Marlborough, West Coast) Royal New Zealand Infantry Regiment, 1845-1970

Colonel E G Latter MBE
Published by 2 RNZIR, King Edward Barracks, Christchurch (NZ), 1970
Stiff card, rifle green, white, 9.25 x 7.25, vi/96.
30 mono phots, no maps, no Index.

Apps: list of officers (1964-1970), list of historical relics.

A slim but useful volume which describes the history of one of New
Zealand's six Territorial Battalions and its origins. ATL. JS.


KIA KAHA, A HISTORY OF THE HAURAKIS
Official History, 6th Battalion (Hauraki) RNZIR

L H Barber
Published by Six Battalion (Hauraki) RNZIR, Tauranga, 1978
White, black, 7.5 x 5.25, -/63.
Fp, 10 mono phots, 2 coloured plates, no maps, no Index.

Apps: Roll of Honour (WWI only), list of former COs, chronology of the
Bn's history, notes on the Colours, battle honours, and trophies.

This is a compact but informative history. R/3 V/3. ATL. JS.


SECOND BATTALION, NEW ZEALAND SCOTTISH

Anon (a Regimental committee of seven)
Printing Associates Ltd, Dunedin (NZ), for the ex-Members Assoc., 1981
Red, gold, regtl crest on front cover, xv/62.
157 mono phots, no maps, no Index.

Apps: Roll of Honour, list of former COs, nominal roll, notes on allied
regiments, notes on the Scottish Volunteer units in Otago-Southland
and Canterbury.

The narrative is fairly superficial and not particularly well-written.
It covers the period from the foundation of the regt (shortly before
WWII) through to 1980. The books is nicely printed and bound. Eight
hundred copies were produced, 100 'de luxe' and 700 standard quality.
R/2 V/4. JFS.

SUNDAY SOLDIERS
A Brief History of the Wellington Regiment, City of Wellington's Own

Peter A Lea
Wellington Regiment - 7 RNZIR Association, 1982
Beige, gold, 8.75 x 5.75, x/194.
Fp, 23 mono phots, 2 coloured plates, 2 sketches, no maps, Bibliography,
no Index.

Apps: notes on the RSM's cane, notes on the York & Lancaster Regt
and the Wellington Plate, notes on a rifleman's experiences, etc.

A narrative written in informal style, relying heavily upon stories,
anecdotes and reminiscences by and about former members. Readable,
entertaining and informative, but lacking the cohesion and detail expected
in a conventional regtl history. R/1 V/3. JS/HEC.


THE TARANAKI RIFLE VOLUNTEERS
A Corps with a History

W J Penn
Thomas Avery, New Plymouth (NZ), 1909
Red, black, vii/93.
11 mono phots, one coloured plate, 3 maps (printed in the text), no Index.

Apps: Roll of Honour, Captain Mace's account of Waireka, nominal roll of
all ranks for the Anglo-Boer War.

The Roll of Honour may more precisely be described as the unit's medal
roll for the Maori Wars. Although fairly brief, this is a pleasing
early Volunteer history. R/5 V/3. HEC.


KIWI TROOPER
The Story of the Queen Alexandra's Own 2nd Wellington West Coast Mounted
Rifles

Ted Andrews
Wanganui Chronicle Co Ltd, Wanganui (NZ), 1967
Yellow cloth, 8.75 x 5.75, xiii/273.
Fp, 33 mono phots, one map (bound in), no Index.

Apps: four, but these are of local interest only.

The Regt was raised for the Maori Wars in 1860, and the narrative covers
its history through to 1964. It provided drafts for all ten Contingents
sent by New Zealand to fight in the Boer War, but then served as a
complete unit in WWI (Gallipoli and Mesopotamia). In later years it was
converted to the mechanised role and is now 1st Armoured Squadron, Royal
New Zealand Armoured Corps. A very comprehensive account.
R/2 V/4. VS.

FIRST BATTALION RNZIR JOURNAL
25th Anniversary Commemorative Edition

Major P J Fry
Singapore National Printers (Pte) Ltd, Singapore, 1983
Green, gold, RNZIR badge on front cover, 9.5 x 7.0, -/203.
Fp, numerous other illustrations (including 5 coloured plates), one map
(printed on end-papers), no Index.

Apps: Roll of Honour, H&A, nominal roll (the full Battalion strength in
1983), notes on the band, etc.

One critic states that this book is disappointing and contains too many
errors. Another critic states that it is a brilliant example of what all
regimental histories should be. Your compiler has no further comment.
R/1 V/3.

# NEW ZEALAND - GREAT WAR

2/AUCKLAND, 1918
Being a Partial Record of the War Service in France of the 2/Auckland
Regiment during the Great War

Lieut Col S S Allen CMG DSO
Whitcombe & Tombs, Wellington (NZ), 1920
Buff, black, regtl patch on front cover, 7.5 x 5.0, -/188.
no illustrations, one map (bound in), no Index.

Apps: Roll of Honour (all ranks, KIA, DOW, and missing).

The unit was composed of drafts from various Territorial battalions
amalgamated for service during the closing stages of WWI. The narrative,
therefore, covers only the last few months of the war. A modest book,
printed on paper of poor quality. R/3 V/2. HEC.


THE HISTORY OF TWO CAMPAIGNS
Official History of the Auckland Mounted Rifles Regiment, 1914-1919

Sergeant C G Nichol
Wilson & Horton, Auckland (NZ), 1921
Red, black, 'mounted rifleman' motif on rear cover, 8.5 x 5.5, viii/265.
113 mono phots, one plate of drawings of insignia, 4 maps (loose in rear
pocket), one coloured plate, Index.

Apps: Roll of Honour, H&A.

The narrative deals with the services of the AMR in Gallipoli and
Sinai/Palestine (hence, 'two campaigns'). The Regt was raised in August
1914 from various Territorial units (3rd Auckland Mounted Rifles,
4th Waikato Mounted Rifles, and 11th North Auckland Mounted Rifles). It
finally returned to New Zealand for disbandment in August 1919.
R/4 V/4. HEC/BCC.
It is possible that there may be two versions of this book. A copy, also
dated 1921, has been noted with no Index, and with the 4 maps bound in.


OFFICIAL HISTORY OF THE OTAGO REGIMENT, NEW ZEALAND EXPEDITIONARY
FORCE IN THE GREAT WAR, 1914-1918

Lieut A E Byrne MC
J Wilkie & Co Ltd, Dunedin (NZ), 1921
Mauve, gold, 8.75 x 6.0, xvi/407.
Fp, 55 mono phots, 11 maps (bound in), no Index.

Apps: H&A, notes on the Reserve Battalion.

The narrative covers all the Regt's WWI services (Egypt, Gallipoli, France
and Flanders). Many small actions described in interesting detail, with
frequent mention of officers and men in the narrative. Written by one of
the Regt's officers, and said to be very accurate. A good quality of
production. Sgt Dick Travis VC DCM MM was a member of the Regt.
R/3 V/3. CSM/JFS.

THE AUCKLAND REGIMENT, 1914-1918
Being an Account of the Doings on Active Service of the First, Second
and Third Battalions of the Auckland Regiment

Lieut O E Burton MM
Whitcombe & Tombs Ltd, Auckland (NZ), 1922
Olive green, black, 8.75 x 5.5, xiv/323.
12 mono phots, 14 maps (bound in), no Index.

Apps: Roll of Honour, H&A, chronology of events, notes on unit badges.

A good general history, well-written and readable. Many individuals are
mentioned in the text, so the lack of an Index is an irritation. Printed
on paper of poor quality. The author, who was awarded both the Military
Medal and the Croix de Guerre during WWI, subsequently became a cleric.
In WWII he was imprisoned as a conscientious objector. R/3 V/4. HEC/BCC.


OFFICIAL HISTORY OF THE NEW ZEALAND RIFLE BRIGADE
The Earl of Liverpool's Own

Lieut Col W S Austin DSO
L T Watkins Ltd, Wellington (NZ), 1924
Olive green, black, regtl crest on front cover, 8.5 x 5.5, xx/587.
Fp, 97 mono phots, 11 maps (loose in rear pocket), Index.

Apps: Roll of Honour, H&A, notes on the Training Bn, dress regulations,
notes on the Dunsterforce Expedition, diary of events, etc.

Despite its title, the Regt did not have a traditional affiliation with
the Rifle Brigade of the British Army. It was raised specifically for
WWI service and its four bns served in Egypt, the Senussi campaign, and
in France (Somme, Messines, Ypres, Havrincourt, Cambrai and Le Quesney).
The period covered is 1915-1919. During that time, the Regt gained 2 VCs,
2 CBs, 3 CMGs, 18 DSOs, 1 OBE, 2 MBEs, 93 MCs, 75 DCMs, 310 MMs, and
41 foreign awards. A well-printed and handsomely bound book.
R/3 V/5. HEC/PS.


THE OFFICIAL WAR HISTORY OF THE WELLINGTON MOUNTED RIFLES REGIMENT

Major A H Wilkie
Whitcombe & Tombs, Wellington (NZ), 1924
Buff, black, 3 regtl badges on front cover, 8.25 x 5.5, xiv/259.
3 fps, 106 mono phots, one coloured plate, 22 maps (bound in), no Index.

Apps: Rolls of Honour (one for Gallipoli, another for Palestine, KIA
and WIA), H&A, list of COs.

The Regt was established in 1911, but this book deals solely with WWI
services: Egypt, Gallipoli, and Palestine (Gaza, Beersheba, Jerusalem,
Jordan). The narrative is clear and informative, with much detail and
with many individuals mentioned (especially casualties). Sadly, in a work
of such quality, there is no Index. R/3 V/4. RP/HEC.

THE HISTORY OF THE CANTERBURY MOUNTED RIFLES, 1914-1919

Colonel C G Powles CMG DSO
Whitcombe & Tombs, Auckland (NZ), 1928
Stiff card, maroon, black, 8.5 x 5.75, vii/267.
104 mono phots, 5 maps (bound in), no Index.

Apps: Roll of Honour, H&A, diary of events, notes on remounts.

Reported to be a good reliable history, but no other details available.


THE WELLINGTON REGIMENT, NZEF

W H Cunningham DSO, C A L Treadwell OBE, J S Hanna
Ferguson & Osborn Ltd, Wellington (NZ), 1928
Brown, gold, 8.75 x 6.0, xii/399.
Fp, 38 mono phots, 2 maps (bound in), one fold-out page showing NZEF
strengths at various dates, no Index.

Apps: Roll of Honour, H&A, list of locations through which 1st and 2nd
Battalions passed 'on the march from Beauvois to the German frontier'.

A nicely produced book, well bound, and with a better-than-average
quality of paper. The narrative is clear and informative. This is reported
to be the best of the New Zealand WWI regtl histories. R/3 V/4. AGY/HEC.


PRIMUS IN ARMIS
Journal of the Taranaki Regiment

Anon
Taranaki Daily News, New Plymouth (NZ), 1936
Soft card, red, black, regtl crest on front cover, 10.75 x 8.5, -/94.
24 mono phots, one coloured plate (the Colours), 6 other illustrations,
no maps, no formal appendixes, no Index.

A useful little book, published mainly to mark the presentation of new
Colours, but containing a great deal of information useful to the
researcher. There is a short section recounting the Gallipoli experiences
of the Taranaki Company of the Wellington Regiment, and various notes
regarding members of the regt in the mid-1930s. R/3 V/4. HEC.


POUR DEVOIR
A History of the Northland Regiment and its Forebears

Harry Field
Unity Press Ltd, New Zealand, 1960
Blue, black, dimensions not recorded, vi/122.
Some small mono phots, no maps, no Index.

Apps: notes on the early military history of North Auckland, nominal roll
for WWI, notes on regtl affiliations.

GALLIPOLI TO THE SOMME

Alexander Aitken
Oxford University Press, London, 1963
Grey-green, white and yellow, 8.5 x 5.5, xi/177.
Reported to have no illustrations, no appendixes, one map (folding, bound
in), no Index.

A straightforward narrative account of the Otago Battalion of the New
Zealand Infantry Brigade from August 1915 to 27th September 1916.  No
other information available. RLP.

## NEW ZEALAND – SECOND WORLD WAR

JOURNEY TOWARDS CHRISTMAS
1st Ammunition Company

Peter Llewellyn
War History Branch, 1949
Red, gold, 8.75 x 5.75, xix/461.
Fp, 67 mono phots, 9 maps (bound in), no Index.

Apps: Roll of Honour, H&A, list of COs.

Despite the unpromising title, this story is a microcosm of the New
Zealand experience in the European theatre of war. The Company had Sections
working in their specialised capacity in the UK (Battle of Britain), in
Greece and Crete (the battles and evacuations), in the Western Desert
(Tobruk, Fuka, Bardia, Alamein, etc), and Italy (the Sangro, Cassino,
Florence, Albacina, Forli and the Po). Even for the non-specialist, a very
good source for obtaining the 'feel' of NZ soldiering in WWII. It is
astonishing that a book of such length and complexity should not have been
indexed. R/3 V/4. JFS/HEC.


THE 36th IN THE PACIFIC
The History of a New Zealand Battalion, 1941-1944

G Watson and D H Leigh
War History Branch, n.d.
Paper covers, yellow, black, 10.0 x 7.5, viii/98.
Fp, 45 mono phots, 2 coloured plates, several cartoon sketches, no maps,
no Index.

Apps: Roll of Honour, H&A, biographical notes on the CO, the RSM, and
various other officers.

Reported to be useful, but no other details available.


CALL THE ROLL
The Unofficial History of the 11th Company of the National Military
Reserve of Wanganui

Anon ('Sandy')
Wanganui Chronicle, Wanganui (NZ), 1946
Maroon, gold, dimensions not reported, -/96.
2 mono phots, no maps, no Index.

Apps: Roll of Honour, list of former officers, nominal roll for all
original personnel.

Reported to be useful, but no other details available.

18 BATTALION AND ARMOURED REGIMENT

W D Dawson
War History Branch, 1961
Red, gold, 8.75 x 5.75, xvi/676.
Fp, 66 mono phots, 39 maps (32 printed in the text, 7 bound in), Index.

Apps: Roll of Honour, H&A, list of COs.

The regt served initially in the Western Desert as infantry. They were
the victims of British politics in Greece and Crete, and British general-
ship at Ruweisat Ridge and El Mreir. They were then converted to the
armoured role and fought as such in Italy (Orsogna, Cassino, Florence,
and the Po Valley battles). Best read in conjunction with the first two
Volumes of THE CRUCIBLE OF WAR, by Barrie Pitt, but a first class history
in its own right. R/2 V/5. HEC/RP/JFS


19 BATTALION AND ARMOURED REGIMENT

D W Sinclair
War History Branch, 1954
Red, gold, 8.75 x 5.75, xvi/560.
Fp, 70 mono phots, 30 maps (24 printed in the text, 6 bound in), no Index.

Apps: Roll of Honour, H&A, list of COs.

The Bn served in Greece, Crete, Syria, the Western Desert as infantry, and
then converted to the armoured role for the Italian campaign. Fought in
the Cassino battles before advancing up the Adriatic coast to Faenza
and, finally, Trieste. A very workmanlike regtl history. R/3 V/5. JFS/HEC.


20 BATTALION AND ARMOURED REGIMENT

D J C Pringle and W A Glue
War History Branch, 1957
Red, gold, 8.75 x 5.75, xvi/631.
Fp, 68 mono phots, 41 maps (34 printed in the text, 7 bound in), Index.

Apps: Roll of Honour, H&A (with full citations for the VC awards to
Capt Charles Upham and Sgt John Hinton), list of COs.

An excellent narrative account by two men who served with the Bn. Covers
services in Egypt, Greece, Crete, Western Desert and Italy. Many individual
officers and men are mentioned in the text, often with interesting biographical notes. A high quality production. R/3 V/5. JFS/HEC.


21 BATTALION

J S Cody MM
War History Branch, 1953
Red, gold, 8.75 x 5.75, xv/471.
Fp, 64 mono phots, 22 maps (16 printed in the text, 6 bound in, some
coloured), Index.

Apps: Roll of Honour, H&A, list of COs.

Like many other NZ units, the regt served in Egypt, Greece, Crete, Libya, Syria, Cyrenaica, Tunis and Italy, and thereby experiencing five years of varied and hard campaigning. Apart from having the distinction of capturing General von Ravenstein on 29 November 1941 in the Desert, the Bn could later claim, in Italy, to have captured 6000 German soldiers, various E-boats, one landing ship, a hospital ship, and nearly 20 other vessels. Another first class Volume in the 'Official History' series. R/3 V/5. PS/HEC/JFS.

22 BATTALION

J H Henderson
War History Branch, 1958
Red, gold, 8.75 x 5.75, xvi/487.
Fp, 64 mono phots, 26 maps (19 printed in the text, 7 bound in), Index.

Apps: Roll of Honour, H&A, list of COs, Rugby memories.

Again, a NZ regt which served on Crete, in Egypt, in Syria, at Alamein, and in most of the major Italian battles. They took part in the disastrous but gallant action on Ruweisat Ridge where one of their NCOs, Sgt Keith Elliott, gained the VC when, although wounded, he led a bayonet charge under heavy machine-gun and mortar fire. The author, Jim Henderson, is well known for his historical accuracy and easy writing style. There are many individual officers and men mentioned in the text, often with brief biographical details. A high quality production. R/3 V/5. HEC/JFS.

23 BATTALION

Angus Ross MC (and bar) ED
War History Branch, 1959
Red, gold, 8.75 x 5.75, xii/506.
Fp, 67 mono phots, 37 maps (30 printed in the text, 7 bound in), Index.

Apps: Roll of Honour, H&A, list of COs.

The excellent narrative covers the entire WWII period, with descriptions of the Bn's active services in Egypt, Greece, Crete, Western Desert and Italy. Very readable, with many individuals mentioned in the text. The author served throughout, first as Platoon Commander, then as Adjutant, then as Company Commander. R/3 V/5. JFS.

24 BATTALION

R M Burdon MC
War History Branch, 1953
Red, gold, 8.75 x 5.75, xv/361.
Fp, 62 mono phots, 31 maps (26 printed in the text, 5 folding, part coloured, and bound in), Index.

302

Apps: Roll of Honour, H&A, list of COs.

The Bn fought in Greece, in the Desert (the Sidi Rezegh battles), at
El Alamein, in Cyrenaica, Tunisia, and in the Italian campaign. Like the
rest of this Official series, the book is produced to a high standard,
has very good maps, and detailed appendixes. The original print runs were
seemingly limited to a few hundred, and copies are now much prized.
R/3 V/5. HEC/JFS/PS.


25 BATTALION

Lieut Gen Sir Edward Puttick KCB DSO MC
War History Branch, 1960
Red, gold, 8.75 x 5.75, xvi/654.
Fp, 66 mono phots, 43 maps (37 printed in the text, 6 bound in), Index.

Apps: Roll of Honour, H&A, list of COs.

After the Greek debacle, the Bn fought in the Desert at Sidi Rezegh and
El Alamein, then across North Africa to Tunis, then in Italy (Orsogna,
Cassino, Liri Valley, Rimini, the Savio, and the Senio). A very complete
regtl history of excellent overall quality. R/3 V/5. JFS/HEC.


26 BATTALION

Frazer D Norton
War History Branch, 1952
Red, gold, 8.75 x 5.57, xvi/554.
Fp, 67 mono phots, 47 maps (42 printed in the text, 5 folding, part
coloured, bound in), no Index.

Apps: Roll of Honour, H&A.

Apart from the Crete campaign, this Bn took part in all the actions already
listed in respect of other NZ infantry units. This book, again, is well-
written and nicely produced but, inexplicably, does not have an Index.
R/3 V/4. HEC.


27 (MACHINE-GUN) BATTALION

Robin L Kay
War History Branch, 1958
Red, gold, 8.75 x 5.75, xvi/543.
Fp, 69 mono phots, 48 maps (42 printed in the text, 6 bound in), Index.

Apps: Roll of Honour, H&A, list of COs, notes on the Vickers machine-gun.

The Bn served in Greece, Crete, Egypt, Lebanon, Syria, West Desert, Tunisia
and Italy, seeing much hard action (especially in the Desert and in the
Italian mountains). Towards the end of the war, in Northern Italy, it
reverted to the infantry role. A good detailed history, with many minor
actions and individuals mentioned. R/3 V/5. HEC/JFS.

28 (MAORI) BATTALION

J F Cody
War History Branch, 1956
Red, gold, 8.75 x 5.75, xvi/515.
Fp, 60 mono phots, 32 maps (25 printed in the text, 7 bound in), Index.

Apps: Roll of Honour, H&A (with details of the VC award to 2nd Lieut Moana-Nui-a-Kiwa Ngarimu, Tunis, 4.6.1943), list of COs.

This distinguished Maori infantry battalion served in all the campaigns already noted for other NZ units, including the hard fighting at Orsogna and Cassino. This is another first-class publication in the War History Branch series. R/3 V/5. HEC.


THE TWENTY-FOURTH NEW ZEALAND INFANTRY BATTALION
A Pictorial History

F L Phillips and H R Gilmour
Richards Publishing, Auckland, and Phillips & Gilmour, Hong Kong, 1980
Russet, gold, 11.5 x 8.5, iv/383.
2 fps, very many mono phots, 16 maps (printed in the text), no appendixes, no Index.

A very interesting photographic record of 24 Battalion's services and adventures in WWII. This is not a formal regtl history, but is certainly a most useful secondary source which neatly compliments the official work by Burdon (see page 298). The text is fairly limited, being facsimile typescript and very condensed. There are between one and six photographs, of all kinds, on each of the 370 main pages. R/1 V/4. HEC.


DIVISIONAL CAVALRY

R J M Loughman MBE
War History Branch, 1963
Red, gold, 8.75 x 5.75, xvi/446.
Fp, 66 mono phots, 38 maps (31 printed in the text, 7 coloured and bound in), Index.

Apps: Roll of Honour, H&A, list of COs.

New Zealand armour fought in all the Middle East campaigns, being converted to the infantry role in the final phase of the war (after crossing the Rubicon in Northern Italy). An interesting and highly detailed account. R/3 V/5. HEC.

## NEW ZEALAND - CORPS HISTORIES

OFFICIAL HISTORY OF THE NEW ZEALAND ENGINEERS DURING THE GREAT WAR
1914-1919

Major N Annabel
Evans, Cobb & Sharpe Ltd, Wanganui, 1927
Chocolate brown, black, 8.5 x 5.5, viii/314.
Fp, 30 mono phots, 9 maps (printed in the text), Index.

Apps: Roll of Honour, H&A, list of former officers.

The narrative, which is not always easy to follow, covers services in WWI
rendered by the NZ Field Companies, Field Troops, the Signal Troop and the
Wireless Troop during operations in Samoa (1914-1915), Egypt, Gallipoli,
Sinai and Palestine (1916-1919), and Mesopotamia (1916-1918). Although not
a particularly attractive production, the contents are accurate and
informative. R/3 V/5. JS/HEC.


THE NEW ZEALAND TUNNELLING COMPANY, 1915-1919

J C Neill
Whitcombe & Tombs Ltd, Wellington, 1922
Chocolate brown, black, 7.5 x 5.0, iv/159.
31 mono phots, one line drawing, 6 diagrams, 4 maps (bound in), no Index.

Apps: Roll of Honour (KIA, WIA and DOW), H&A, nominal roll of all ranks.

This is a readable narrative account which describes the formation of the
Company on 12.8.1915, its services in France and Flanders, and its final
disbandment on 23.4.1919. The technical aspects are interesting, even to
the non-specialist. The author explains the differences between the
methods developed by the NZ Engineers and those used by their British Army
counterparts. The New Zealanders operated mainly in the chalk areas around
Arras. They occupied some of the local natural caves which they extended
until they were forty feet in height and several hundred feet in diameter.
Company strength was 19 officers and 500 Other Ranks. Total awards gained
were 4 DSOs, 4 MCs, 6 DCMs, 11 MMs, and 3 MSMs.
R/3 V/5. PS/HEC.


NEW ZEALAND ENGINEERS, MIDDLE EAST

J F Cody
War History Branch, 1961
Red, gold, 8.75 x 5.75, xvi/775.
Fp, 63 mono phots, 49 maps (42 printed in the text, 7 bound in), Index.

Apps: Roll of Honour, H&A, list of Commanders 2nd NZEF Engineers, etc.

An excellent narrative account of their WWII services in Greece, Crete, Egypt, Libya and Italy, with a section on the New Zealand Forestry Companies in the UK. Very readable, with a great many individuals named in the text (often with biographical notes for award winners). The appendixes include descriptions of the work of the NZ Army Postal Service and the Railway Survey Companies. The original print run is reported to have been 5000, but this was never enough to meet demand and copies are rarely available for purchase. R/4 V/5. HEC/JFS.


PACIFIC PIONEERS
The Story of the Engineers of the NZEF in the Pacific

A H & A W Reed, Wellington (NZ), for the Third NZ Divisional Histories Committee, 1945
Buff-orange, black, 8.5 x 5.5, -/169.
54 mono phots, 8 maps (2 printed on the end-papers, 6 printed in the text), no appendixes, no Index.

This book covers the WWII services of the NZ Engineers on Fiji, New Caledonia, the Solomon Islands (Guadalcanal), and Nissan and Mono Islands. There is a brief account for various sub-units, but without any great detail. Although there are no appendixes for casualties and awards, several such lists are scattered throughout the text. R/3 V/3. HEC.


WITH THE NEW ZEALAND TRENCH MORTARS IN FRANCE

Capt W E L Napier MC
Apple Brothers & Co, n.d.
Stiff card, yellow/brown, black, 7.25 x 5.0, -/110.
25 mono phots, one line drawing, 3 diagrams, no maps, no appendixes, no Index.

This is mainly an autobiographical account, but it gives a useful overview of the subject. R/3 V/3. JS.


NEW ZEALAND CHAPLAINS IN THE SECOND WORLD WAR

M L Underhill, S D Waters, J M S Ross, and N E Winhall
War History Branch, 1950
Red, gold, 8.75 x 5.75, xvii/188.
Fp, 37 mono phots, 3 maps (bound in), Index.

Apps: Roll of Honour, H&A.

As the title suggests, this is an account of the work of NZ Chaplains (Army, Navy and Air Force) in all theatres of war during WWII. Interesting and informative. R/3 V/5. HEC.

MEN OF FAITH AND COURAGE
The Official History of New Zealand's Army Chaplains

J Bryant Haigh
The World Publishers Ltd, Auckland, 1983
Red, gold, 8.75 x 5.75, -/216.
134 mono phots, 3 line drawings, no maps, Bibliography, Index.

Apps: eight, including notes on dress, badges, medal rolls (the VD and ED),
list of former Chaplains Commandant.

While complementing the previous entry, this book covers the entire
130 years of New Zealand's military history from the Maori Wars to the
South Vietnam involvement. Many NZ chaplains have been killed in action
and decorated for gallantry, and the author has gathered together many
anecdotes regarding their exploits. Plenty of action and human interest.
The only weak point in the book is the photographs, some of which have
reproduced poorly. R/1 V/3. HEC.


RMT
Official History of the 4th and 6th Reserve Mechanical Transport
Companies, 2nd New Zealand Expeditionary Force

Jim Henderson
War History Branch, 1954
Red, gold, 8.75 x 5.75, xv/369.
Fp, 67 mono phots, 18 maps (12 printed in the text, 6 bound in), Index.

Apps: Roll of Honour, H&A, list of COs, notes on the first New Zealander
to escape from Germany.

A good narrative account which covers all the main WWII campaigns in
the Middle East and Italy. Many officers and men mentioned by name in the
text, with biographical details. A high quality production. R/3 V/5. JFS.


SUPPLY COMPANY

P W Bates
War History Branch, 1955
Red, gold, 8.75 x 5.75, xv/371.
Fp, 65 mono phots, 14 maps (8 printed in the text, 6 bound in), Index.

Apps: Roll of Honour, H&A, list of COs, Index.

One of 2 NZEF's logistical units which served in Greece, Crete, Western
Desert, Tunisia and Italy. This is another in the excellent Official
History series which, despite the rather unpromising title, is full of
interest. R/3 V/5. HEC.

PETROL COMPANY

A L Kidson
War History Branch, 1961
Red, gold, 8.75 x 5.75, xv/363.
Fp, 68 mono phots, 18 maps (11 printed in the text, 7 bound in), Index.

Apps: Roll of Honour, H&A, list of COs.

Again, this is one of the Official History series and, as such, is a
first-class reference source for researchers interested in the
logistical aspect of New Zealand's military effort in the Middle East and
Italy during WWII. R/3 V/5. HEC.


THE FIRST FIFTY YEARS
A Commentary on the Development of the Royal New Zealand Army Medical
Corps from its inception

Anon
Medical Section, Army HQ, Wellington (NZ), 1958
Soft card, maroon, white, Corps crest on the front cover, dimensions not
recorded, vi/24.
20 mono phots, 2 line drawings, no maps, no appendixes, no Index.

A limited summary of the evolution of NZ's military medical services up
to 1958. R/1 V/2. JS.


THE NEW ZEALAND MEDICAL SERVICES IN THE GREAT WAR, 1914-1919

Lieut Col A D Carbery CBE
Whitcombe & Tombs Ltd, Auckland, 1924
Maroon, black, 9.5 x 6.75, xix/567.
Fp, 14 mono phots, 2 maps (loose in rear pocket), Bibliography, Index.

Apps: nominal roll of Colonial Medical Officers (1845-1860), Roll of
Honour (WWI, KIA and WIA), H&A (WWI), specifications for hospital ships,
etc (20 appendix sections and sub-sections in total).

A detailed and interesting analysis of NZ medical services on Gallipoli
and the Western Front. Of value to the medical researcher but also a mirror
of the progress of the Great War and its attendant medical and surgical
problems. The appendixes alone make this book a desirable possession.
R/4 V/5. HEC.


MEDICAL UNITS OF THE SECOND NEW ZEALAND EXPEDITIONARY FORCE IN THE
MIDDLE EAST AND ITALY

J B McKinney
War History Branch, 1952
Red, gold, 8.75 x 5.75, xv/462.
Fp, 63 mono phots, 14 maps (12 printed in the text, 2 bound in), Index.

Apps: Roll of Honour, H&A, list of COs and Matrons.

As the title indicates, this is the official record of the raising of the NZ medical units in 1939 and their subsequent services in Greece, Crete, Libya, Syria, Western Desert, Tunisia and Italy. A good narrative account, of interest to both the specialist researcher and the general reader. R/3 V/5. HEC.


## MEDICAL SERVICES IN NEW ZEALAND AND THE PACIFIC

T Duncan M Stout
War History Branch, 1958
Maroon, gold, NZ Coat of Arms on the front cover, 9.75 x 6.75, xiv/449.
Fp, 61 mono phots, 10 maps (5 printed in the text, 5 bound in), Glossary, no appendixes, Index.

Despite the wording of the title, this detailed Official History covers the activities of NZ medical units (Army, Navy and Air Force) with the New Zealand Brigade on Fiji, with the Third Division in New Caledonia and the Solomons, and with other formations in Greece and Crete, Italy and Germany. Although the book does not have any formal appendixes, there are sections devoted to honours and awards in the text. The final section has a few pages regarding the hospital ships MAUNGANUI and ORANJE. R/3 N/5. HEC.


## THE NEW ZEALAND DENTAL SERVICE (NEW ZEALAND DENTAL CORPS)

T A Anson
War History Branch, 1960
Green, gold, 9.75 x 6.75, xi/422.
30 mono phots, 7 maps (printed in the text), Index.

Apps: H&A.

An Official History which covers the services of the army dental branch during WWII. Well produced and undoubtedly of interest to the health-care specialist researcher. R/2 V/5. PS.


## BY WIRES TO VICTORY
New Zealand Divisional Signals Company, 1914-1918

Roy F Ellis MM
Batley Printing Co Ltd, Auckland (NZ), 1968
Light blue, dark blue, 'signaller reeling out cable' motif on front cover, 8.75 x 5.5, xiii/87.
Fp, 5 mono phots, 3 other illustrations, 2 maps (bound in), no Index.

Apps: Roll of Honour (detailed), H&A.

Although published 50 years after the event, this little book is reported to be useful and informative. R/3 V/3. HEC.

DIVISIONAL SIGNALS

C A Borman
War History Branch, 1954
Red, gold, 8.75 x 5.75, xvii/540.
Fp, 66 mono phots, 18 maps (11 printed in the text, 7 bound in), Index.

Apps: Roll of Honour, H&A, list of COs.

The very readable narrative covers all the main operations in the
Middle East and Italy during WWII. This is a high quality production with
good appendixes. Many officers and Other Ranks are named in the text,
with numerous biographical footnotes. The author himself served with
NZ Divisional Signals for four years. R/3 V/5. JFS.


CRAFTSMEN IN UNIFORM
The Corps of Royal New Zealand Electrical & Mechanical Engineers

Peter Cape
Printed in Wellington (NZ), for the Corps, 1976
Dark blue, gold, RNZEME crest on front cover, 8.5 x 6.0, xi/198.
Fp, 55 mono phots, 2 coloured plates, 4 maps (bound in), no Index.

Apps: Roll of Honour, H&A, list of former COs, roll of personnel
transferred to the RNZEME at its formation on 1.9.1946.

A lively narrative, written in informal style but full of useful
information for the specialist researcher. R/2 V/5. JS.


DARE TO WIN
The Story of the New Zealand Special Air Service

W D Baker
Lothian Publishing Co, Melbourne (Australia), 1987
Dark brown, gold, 11.5 x 8.5, vii/107.
111 mono phots, 16 coloured plates, 3 maps (printed in the text), no
appendixes, no Index.

It was the author's stated intention to cover the evolution and services
of the NZ SAS from the earliest days (as the New Zealand Patrol of the
LRDG in the Western Desert) through to 1986. R/1 V/1. HEC/PS.

310

WITH THE MACHINE GUNNERS IN FRANCE AND PALESTINE
Being the Official History of the New Zealand Machine Gun Corps
1914-1918

Major J H Luxford
Whitcombe & Tombs Ltd, Auckland, 1923
Red, black, Corps crest on front cover, 8.75 x 5.5, -/255.
Fp, 51 mono phots, 9 maps (bound in), no Index.

Apps: Roll of Honour (with details of burial sites), H&A (with citations
in some cases).

A good workmanlike account of the Corps' services in WWI. R/3 V/4. HEC/JS.


THE NEW ZEALAND CYCLIST CORPS IN THE GREAT WAR, 1914-1918

Anon ('by Officers of the Regiment')
Whitcombe & Tombs Ltd, Auckland, 1922
Brown, black, Corps crest on front cover, 8.75 x 5.75, -/139.
Fp, 41 mono phots, one map, no Index.

Apps: Roll of Honour, H&A, nominal roll of the original personnel of
the Corps, notes on reinforcements.

An interesting and complete account of this small unit  which never had
more than 800 officers and men on its strength. Almost the entire
narrative is devoted to their services in France and Flanders where they
fulfilled a variety of tasks (as infantry, working with cavalry, cable
laying, etc).  They saw much hard service, including Passchendaele. The
illustrations include photographs of badges and insignia, and the
nominal rolls are very helpful to medal collectors and genealogists.
R/4 V/5. JS/HEC.


THE WAAC STORY
The Story of the New Zealand Womens Army Auxiliary Corps

Iris Latham
Publisher's details not known, 1986
Green and brown, white, 8.25 x 5.25, vii/214.
52 mono phots, 2 cartoons, no maps, no Index.

Apps: Roll of Honour.

An interesting book, full of anecdotes and personal stories. The
photographs cover a wide range of subjects, from formal parades to coal
shovelling duties. The authoress acknowledges that the Roll of Honour is
incomplete, but this is nevertheless a useful source for social studies
and the impact of WWII on New Zealand women. R/1 V/3. JS.

## NEW ZEALAND - ARTILLERY

'B' BATTERY, NEW ZEALAND FIELD ARTILLERY, 1863-1913

Anon
John McIndoe, Dunedin, 1913
Card covers, beige, red and black, 9.75 x 7.5, -/22.
13 mono phots, no maps, no Index.

Apps: list of former officers (1863-1913), nominal roll, all ranks (1913).

A valuable little book for a Battery which is still in existence as a
Territorial unit. The narrative is concerned mainly with events at the
turn of the century. The photographs are particularly useful for details
of uniform and personal equipment. R/5 V/3. HEC.


NEW ZEALAND ARTILLERY IN THE FIELD
The History of the New Zealand Artillery, 1914-1918

Lieut J R Byrne NZFA
Whitcombe & Tombs Ltd, Wellington, 1922
Dark blue, gold, regtl crest on front cover embellished with red stripes,
8.5 x 5.75, -/314.
Fp, 30 mono phots, 10 maps (folding, bound in, one coloured), no Index.

Apps: H&A.

This is a good attempt at describing a very large subject. The narrative
lacks the finer details, but it is a sound broad description of New
Zealand's artillery at work on Gallipoli and on the Western Front.
R/3 V/3. HEC.


OFFICIAL HISTORY OF THE BAND OF THE ROYAL REGIMENT OF NEW ZEALAND
ARTILLERY (NORTHERN MILITARY DISTRICT)

H F Batley
Auckland Artillery Band Association, Auckland, 1964
Card covers, dark blue, gold, 8.75 x 5.5, -/164.
79 mono phots, no maps, no Index.

Apps: lists of former Directors of Music, Secretaries, and Drum Majors.

An attractive useful little book, particularly for those interested in
the history of military music. Published to celebrate their centenary
in 1964. R/2 V/2. JS.


2nd NEW ZEALAND DIVISIONAL ARTILLERY

W E Murphy
War History Branch, Wellington, 1966
Red, gold, regtl crest on front cover, 8.5.x 5.5, xx/796.
Fp, 120 mono phots, one coloured plate, 5 sketches, 88 maps, Index.

Apps: Roll of Honour (listed by regts), H&A (listed by regts),
Training Directive (1.8.1943), statistical summary of casualties.

This very detailed history covers the story of the Divisional Artillery
Regiments from their raising in 1939-1940, through their services in
Greece and Crete (1941) and North Africa (1941-1943), and finally in
Italy (1943-1945). The maps are very clear and the photographs well
selected and well printed. The narrative is readable and interesting,
with many individuals of all ranks mentioned in the text. R/3 V/5. AMM.


GUNNER'S STORY
A Short History of the Artillery Volunteers of Christchurch, 1867-1967

Guy C Bliss
Canterbury Artillery Officers' Mess, 1970
Card covers, illustrated, red, black, 9.25 x 7.0, -/80.
16 mono phots, no maps, no Index.

Apps: Volunteer Regulations, 1840-1935.

This is a review of Volunteer and Territorial Artillery formations
and their evolution in the Christchurch area over a period of 100 years.
The narrative is of limited interest in the technical sphere, but it is a
worthwhile commentary upon the social history of the district and the
evolution of the Volunteer movement. R/2 V/3. JS.


## NEW ZEALAND - ADDENDA


Immediately after WWII, the 3rd New Zealand Division formed a Histories
Committee with the task of producing a record of service for each of its
constituent battalions. The following titles in this series have been
noted, but not seen. It would seem that they each have a title incorporating the words 'The Unofficial History ...', and were all published in
1947. Each contains a number of photographic illustrations, and has maps
printed on the end-papers. Their most important characteristic, from the
researcher's point of view, is that they contain full nominal rolls (ten
to fifteen pages in length) for all ranks who served. It is understood
that surviving copies of these are relatively scarce.

STEPPING STONES TO THE PACIFIC
The 29th Battalion with the 2nd NZEF in the Pacific (121 pages)

PACIFIC KIWIS
The Story of the Service in the Pacific of the 30th Battalion (150 pages)

THE STORY OF THE 34th
A New Zealand Battalion in the Pacific (159 pages)

THE 35th BATTALION
A Record of Service (143 pages)

PACIFIC SAGA
The Personal Chronicle of the 37th Battalion (114 pages)

# PART VIII
## Australia

314

## NOTE

Despite the generous collaboration of a handful of
bibliophiles in that country, it has not been possible
to obtain full details of all the known Australian
regimental histories.

The following entries are as comprehensive as they
could be within the time-scale allocated to the project.

Most of the titles noted here as 'not seen' are to be
found in the Library of the Australian War Memorial,
Canberra.

The compiler has deliberately left free page space
adjacent to the 'not seen' entries so that users of
the bibliography may enter their own notes,
if they so wish.

For the information of those unfamiliar with the
history of Australia's armed forces, unit titles
which commence with the prefix 'Second' or '2/' are
those which were raised or re-activated for service in
the Second World War.

## AUSTRALIA - GENERAL TITLES

THE LINEAGES OF THE AUSTRALIAN ARMY

Alfred N Festberg
Allara Publishing Pty Ltd, Melbourne, 1972
Soft card covers, gold, white, 10.0 x 12.5, x/118.
no illustrations, no maps.

This useful book sets out the origins and evolution of all Australian
mounted, mechanised and infantry regiments, with details of their battle
honours, other titles, regtl marches, mottoes,etc. There is also an
outline history of the military forces in the Australian Colonies prior
to 1901, and then the development of the Australian Army after that date.
R/1 V/5. PS.

AUSTRALIANS IN THE WAIKATO WAR, 1863-1864

Leonard L Barton
South Press, Marrickville, NSW, 1974
Dark red, gold, 8.75 x 5.5, -/119.
3 mono phots, 4 maps (printed in the text).

Apps: nominal roll (Australians only) of the 1st, 2nd, 3rd and 4th
Waikato Regiments (with details of service number, date of enrolment
and civilian trade), list of officers of the 3rd Waikato Regiment who
were awarded the New Zealand war medal for service with the Imperial
Commissariat Transport Corps.

A nicely researched account, of particular interest to medal collectors
and genealogists, the print run having been limited to 1000 copies.
R/2 V/4. PS.

THE AUSTRALIAN CONTINGENT
A History of the Patriotic Movement in New South Wales and An Account of
the Despatch of Troops to the Assistance of the Imperial Forces in
the Soudan

Frank Hutchinson and Francis Myers
Thomas Richards, Government Printer, Sydney, 1885
285 pages, noted in a catalogue, but not seen.

THE REHEARSAL
Australians in the Sudan War, 1885

K S Inglis
Rigby Publishers, 1985
Red, yellow, 11.0 x 8.0, -/176.
25 mono phots, 67 line drawings, 6 coloured plates, one map (printed in
the text), Bibliography, Index.

As the sub-title indicates, this is the story of the NSW Contingent
in the Sudan campaign of 1885. The author also describes the
reasons for their despatch. R/1 V/4. PS.


BUT LITTLE GLORY
The New South Wales Contingent in the Sudan, 1885

Peter Stanley
Military Historical Society of Australia, Canberra, 1985
Soft card, illustrated, brown, 9.75 x 6.75, vii/79.
14 mono phots, 14 sketches, 4 maps (printed in the text), Bibliography.

Apps: Roll of Honour (detailed).

This is an anthology of eight accounts of the Contingent in the Sudan
campaign. They cover the British military operations in Egypt and the
Northern Sudan, despatches, diary of events, notes on uniforms, weaponry,
and medallic awards. The information on medals (naming, presentations,
survival rates, etc) is particularly detailed. The book is geared mainly
to the needs of the medal collector, but is also a prime source for
genealogists. R/1 V/5. PS.


THE AUSTRALIANS IN NINE WARS
Waikato to Long Tan

Peter Firkins
Robert Hale & Co, London, and Rigby Limited (Adelaide), 1972
Green, gold, 9.5 x 6.5, -/448.
81 mono phots, 8 coloured plates, 27 maps (printed in the text),
no appendixes, Bibliography, General Index and Index of Military
Formations.

Australian soldiers have fought most of the Empire's enemies at one time
or another: Maoris, Dervishes, Chinese Boxers, Germans, Italians,
Japanese, North Koreans, Chinese Communists(and North Vietnamese).This
book provides useful background reading as a framework for the study
of specific regts. R/1 V/4. RP.


WESTERN AUSTRALIAN CONTINGENTS IN THE SOUTH AFRICAN WAR

J Burridge
Publisher's details not stated, 1971
Stiff card, illustrated, 'mounted Trooper' motif on front cover, orange,
black, 8.25 x 6.0, v/49.
5 mono phots, no maps,

Apps: detailed medal rolls for each of the six Contingents which
served in the Boer War, roll of Australian nurses who served, H&A.

Apparently a private publication by the author, containing full details of
medallic awards and much useful information concerning the raising and
active services of each Contingent. R/2 V/4. PS.

FIRST QUEENSLAND MOUNTED INFANTRY CONTINGENT IN THE SOUTH AFRICAN WAR

Major Rex Clark
Military Historical Society of Australia, ACT Branch, 1971
Card, illustrated, 'Trooper with regtl badge' motif on front cover, red,
8.0 x 6.5, iii/26.
10 mono phots, no maps.

Apps: medal roll for all members who served in the Boer War (with full
details, including clasps awarded), H&A (which included 2 CBs, 1 CMG,
2 DSOs, 2 DCMs, and 15 MIDs).

Major Clark compiled a series of these booklets, all similar in format,
and all geared to the needs of medal collectors and genealogists. Amongst
these other titles are: AUSTRALIAN CONTINGENTS TO THE BOXER REBELLION
1900, THE FIRST VICTORIAN CONTINGENT IN THE SOUTH AFRICAN WAR, THE FIRST
NEW SOUTH WALES CONTINGENT IN THE SOUTH AFRICAN WAR, and NEW SOUTH WALES
CONTINGENTS TO SUAKIN, 1885.
R/1 V/4. PS.


TASMANIA'S WAR RECORD, 1914-1918

L Broinowski
J Walch & Sons Ltd, Hobart, for the Government of Tasmania, 1921
Red, gold, 10.0 x 6.25, xvi/370.
Fp, 13 mono phots, one map (printed in the text), no Index.

Apps: statistics on population/enlistments/deaths, nominal roll of all
Tasmanians who served (with ranks, units, awards, casualties, length of
service).

This highly detailed book describes the services of all Tasmanian raised
units and is largely a narrative of places and events. Few names are
mentioned in the main narrative, all of these references appearing in the
nominal roll appendixes. Amongst the units mentioned are: 12th, 15th,
26th, 40th and 56th Bns, and 3rd Light Horse. The story covers their
services in Egypt, Gallipoli, Palestine, France and Belgium. A very good
account, and of obvious value to genealogists. R/4 V/5. MODL. AMM.


VOLUNTEERS AT HEART
The Queensland Defence Forces, 1860-1901

D H Johnson
University of Queensland Press, 1975. Not seen.


OFFICIAL RECORDS OF THE AUSTRALIAN MILITARY CONTINGENTS TO THE WAR
IN SOUTH AFRICA

P L Murray
A J Mullett, Government Printer, Melbourne, 1911. Not seen.

## AUSTRALIA – EXTENDED HISTORIES

THE AUSTRALIAN LIGHT HORSE

Major R J G Hall
W D Joynt & Co Pty Ltd, Blackburn, Victoria, 1967
Black, gold, ALH crest on front cover, 8.5 x 5.5, viii/113.
Fp, 14 mono phots, no maps, no Index.

Apps: notes on lineages.

Although some errors have been detected, this is an excellent reference
source regarding the complicated lineages of the Australian Light Horse.
Covers the entire history, including WWII and after. R/2 V/4. JLC.


THE AUSTRALIAN LIGHT HORSE

Ian Jones
Time-Life Books (Australia), Sydney, 1987
Black, red/black/white, illustrated, 11.0 x 8.75, -/168.
122 mono phots, 9 coloured plates, 13 sketches, 8 maps (printed in the
text), Bibliography, no appendixes, Index.

Like all the Time-Life series, this is a handsome production, prepared
with great care, and giving an accurate (if not profound) account of ALH
services in the Boer War and in WWI (Egypt and Palestine). The coloured
plates are unusual because they are examples of pioneer colour photography
in the field. R/1 V/4. HEC.


HEROES AND GENTLEMEN
Colonel Tom Price and the Victorian Mounted Rifles

Winty Calder
Jimaringle Publications, Melbourne, 1985
In two Volumes:
Vol I:  casebound, x/189, 11.75 x 8.25
Vol II: softbound, iv/56, 11.75 x 8.25
46 mono phots, no maps, Glossary, Bibliography, Index.

Apps: numerous, including notes on unit strength, uniforms, letters,
list of former RSMs, etc.

A pleasantly readable history covering the period 1870-1902 (including
Boer War services), and then 1914-1918. R/1 V/4. DBP-P.


THE ROYAL NEW SOUTH WALES LANCERS, 1885-1960
Incorporating a Narrative of the 1st Light Horse Regiment A.I.F. 1914-1919

P V Vernon
Halstead Press, Sydney, for the Regiment, 1961
Blue, gold, 8.75 x 5.5, xii/380.
Fp, 43 mono phots, 8 maps (printed in the text), Glossary, Index.

Apps: eight in total, including list of former COs.

The NSW Lancers were raised as Volunteer cavalry in 1885, being re-
designated 1st Australian Light Horse Regiment (New South Wales Lancers)
from 1903 to 1912. In that year the title was changed again, to The Light
Horse (New South Wales Lancers), through to 1918, but with some variants,
e.g. 1st Light Horse (Machine Gun) Regiment (New South Wales Lancers).
A squadron was sent to South Africa for the Boer War but, during WWI,
the Lancers' role was restricted to finding drafts for the 1st Light Horse
Regiment AIF which served in Gallipoli, Egypt and Palestine. In WWII,
the regt saw active service, as an integral unit, in New Guinea and
Borneo. A comprehensive and informative history. R/1 V/4. VS.


A HISTORY OF 41st BATTALION, THE ROYAL NEW SOUTH WALES REGIMENT,
1916 TO 1984

J W Alcorn
Publication details not stated
Card, green, black, 11.5 x 8.0, v/24.
no illustrations, no maps, no Index.

Apps: Roll of Honour (WWI), H&A (WWI), list of former COs, notes on
battle honours, notes on Lance Corporal Bernard Sidney Gordon (awarded
the VC and MM for gallantry in France, 1918).

This booklet has been printed in 3 editions. Although very condensed,
it is a useful collection of snippits concerning the stated period.
R/1 V/3. PS.


SADDLE & SPUR
A Photographic Record of Gippsland's Mounted Regiments, 1885-1945

Allan Box (Gippsland Institute of Advanced Education, 1989)
The LV Printers Pty Ltd, for The Centre for Gippsland Studies, Churchill
Soft card, illustrated, sepia and maroon, 11.75 x 8.0, x/110.
75 mono phots, no maps, no Index.

Apps: roll of recipients of Long Service awards to members of Gippsland
Mounted Regiments.

Although it does not conform with the traditional format for a regtl
history, this attractive book contains a mass of useful information. The
author has made an in-depth examination of the Volunteer movement in the
Gippsland area of what was, originally, the Colony of Victoria. Commencing
with 'the Russian invasion scare' of the 1860s, he traces the development
of the Victoria Mounted Rifles from 1885 to 1903, the Gippsland Light
Horse in WWI, and various units carrying that title in WWII. Although
there are no formal appendixes, nominal rolls of officers and men
are scattered throughout the text. The photographs (all fully captioned)
are of particular interest to students of uniform and personal accoutrement.
Sergeant Maurice Buckley VC DCM was a Gippslander who volunteered in 1914,
went overseas with the 13th Light Horse, was returned on medical grounds,
deserted and re-enlisted in the infantry under a false name, and three years
later won the highest award while serving in France. The book contains
many such interesting items. R/1 V/4. DBP-P/RP.

IN ALL THINGS FAITHFUL
A History and Album of the 30th Battalion and New South Wales Scottish
Regiment 1885-1985

T F Wade-Ferrell
Sam Ure Smith, Fine Arts Press Pty Ltd, Sydney, 1985
Black Watch tartan, silver, regtl crest on front cover, 11.25 x 8.5,
xviii/396.
Fp, 492 mono phots, 3 coloured plates, 18 other illustrations, 10 maps
(9 printed in the text, one printed on rear end-paper), Bibliography.

Apps: H&A, list of former COs, 7 nominal rolls, etc.

A very attractive production, printed in double column, very clearly
printed, in a handsome binding. The print run was limited to 750 copies,
individually numbered. Lamentably, in such a high quality work, there is
no Index. R/3 V/4. FC.


ALWAYS FAITHFUL
A History of the 49th Australian Infantry Battalion, 1916-1982

Fred Cranston
Boolarong Publications, Brisbane, 1983
Laminated board, illustrated with 'historical montage', green and black,
9.75 x 6.5, xxviii/243.
117 mono phots, 8 other illustrations, 13 maps (printed in the text),
Bibliography, Glossary, Index.

Apps: Roll of Honour (WWI and WWII), list of former COs, notes on battle
honours,   nominal roll of officers and SNCOs at 1983, etc.

A comprehensive coverage of the Bn's services in WWI (the Western Front),
and WWII (Papua New Guinea and the major action at Sanananda). Produced on
a good quality paper in a fine commercial binding. Some of the photographs
are not of the highest quality, but are totally authentic in time and
location. R/1 V/5. HEC.


HISTORY OF THE LAUNCESTON REGIMENT, 1860 TO 1958

Thomas C T Cooley
Woolston & Son, Launceston, 1959. Not seen.


THE ROYAL NEW SOUTH WALES LANCERS, 1885-1960
Incorporating a Narrative of the 1st Light Horse Regiment, AIF

P V Vernon
Halstead Press, Sydney, 1961. Not seen.

# AUSTRALIA - INFANTRY, FIRST WORLD WAR

THE HISTORY OF THE FIRST BATTALION A.I.F., 1914-1916

B V Stacey
J J Lee, Sydney, 1931. Not seen.


NULLI SECUNDUS
History of the 2nd Battalion A.I.F., 1914-1919

F W Taylor and T A Cusack
New Century Press, Sydney, 1942. Not seen.


WAR BOOK OF THE THIRD PIONEER BATTALION

Major A B B Keatinge MC
The Specialty Press Pty Ltd, Melbourne, 1922
Purple, black, 8.75 x 5.5, -/192.
10 mono phots, 3 maps (printed in the text).

Apps: nominal roll (with details of casualties and enlistment dates), H&A.

This history covers the WWI services of the Bn from the date of its
inception in 1916. It saw action at Messines, Viller Brettoneux, Hamel and
the second battle of Amiens. Members of the Bn gained one VC, 4 DSOs,
10 DCMs, 69 MMs, 9 MSMs, 3 MBEs and one OBE. A very useful unit history.
R/3 V/4. PS.


RANDWICK TO HARGICOURT
History of the 3rd Battalion A.I.F.

Eric Wren
Ronald G McDonald, Sydney, 1935. Not seen.


FORWARD WITH THE FIFTH
The Story of Five Years' War Service, Fifth Infantry Battalion A.I.F.

A W Keown
Specialty Press, Sydney, for the Regtl Assn, 1921
Casebound, 7.5 x 5.0, 326 pages, 24 illustrations.
Noted in a catalogue, but not seen. The Bn served in Egypt, Gallipoli
and France.


SEVENTH BATTALION A.I.F.
A Resume of Activities of the 7th Battalion in the Great War, 1914-1918

Arthur Dean and Eric W Gutteridge
Collingwood, Victoria, 1986. Not seen.

FROM ANZAC TO THE HINDENBURG LINE
The History of the 9th Battalion A.I.F.

Norman K Harvey
William Brooks & Co Pty Ltd, Brisbane, 1941
Brown, black, with blue/black unit patch on front cover, 7.5 x 5.0, vi/300.
26 mono phots, 29 maps (27 printed in the text, 2 bound in), Bibliography,
Index.

Apps: H&A, list of former COs.

A very detailed and informative account, with many individuals mentioned
by name in the text. R/3 V/4. PS.


CAMPAIGNING WITH THE FIGHTING NINTH
In and Out of the Line with the 9th Bn A.I.F., 1914-1919

C M Wrench MC
Boolarong Publications, Brisbane, 1985
Sky blue, white, 9.0 x 6.0, xxvi/598.
Very many mono phots, 4 maps (printed in the text), Glossary, Indexes.

Apps: Roll of Honour, etc

An immensely detailed work, concluding with 30 appendixes and 73
other end notes. Interesting and very readable. The narrative covers
their services in Gallipoli, Egypt and on the Western Front. R/1 V/5. PS.


HISTORY OF THE 10th BATTALION A.I.F.

A Limb
Cassell & Co, London, 1919. Not seen.


THE FIGHTING TENTH
A South Australian Centenary Souvenir of the 10th Bn AIF

C B L Lock
Webb & Son, Adelaide, 1936
Red, black, 8.0 x 5.0, vi/319.
no illustrations, no maps, no Index.

Apps:Roll of Honour, H&A, list of former COs, list of former officers.

This book contains a great deal of biographical information regarding
officers and men who served, with many extracts from Bn Orders and
congratulatory messages worked into the narrative. An unusual format, of
great value to the researcher. The period covered is from 17.8.1914
(date of inception at Morphettville, South Australia) to 17.3.1918
(disbandment at Chatelet, Belgium). R/3 V/4. PS/RP.

LEGS ELEVEN
Being the Story of the 11th Battalion A.I.F.

Walter C Bedford
Imperial Printing Co Ltd, Perth (WA), 1940. Not seen.


THE STORY OF THE TWELTH
A Record of the 12th Battalion AIF During the Great War of 1914-18

L M Newton
J Walch & Sons Pty Ltd, Hobart, Tasmania, for the Regtl Assn, 1925
Grey/blue, blue/black, 6.5 x 4.0, x/508.
21 mono phots, 6 maps (bound in at rear).

Apps: H&A (reported to be incomplete).

A most detailed history, written by an officer who was the Bn's Adjutant
during that period. R/3 V/4. PS.


THE HISTORY OF THE THIRTEENTH BATTALION A.I.F.

T A White
Tyrrells Limited, Sydney, 1924. Not seen.


THE HISTORY OF THE FOURTEENTH BATTALION A.I.F.

Newton Wanliss
The Arrow Printery, Melbourne, 1929
Dark blue, gold, 8.5 x 5.5, xiv/416.
18 mono phots, 16 maps, Bibliography, Index.

Apps: Roll of Honour, H&A, notes on battle honours.

A very detailed and readable history, with many individuals mentioned by
name in the narrative. The appendixes are particularly useful for the
medal collector and the genealogist. R/3 V/4. PS.


HISTORY OF THE 15th BATTALION, AUSTRALIAN IMPERIAL FORCES, 1914-1918

T P Chataway
William Brooks & Co, Brisbane, 1948. Not seen.


THE OLD SIXTEENTH
Being a Record of the 16th Battalion During the Great War, 1914-1918

C Longmore
History Committee of the 16th Bn Association, Perth, 1929. Not seen.

STORY OF THE SEVENTEENTH BATTALION A.I.F. IN THE GREAT WAR, 1914-1918

Lieut Col K W Mackenzie MC
Shipping Newspapers, Sydney, 1946
Green, black, 8.75 x 5.75, -/336.
67 mono phots, 2 maps (printed in the text).

Apps: Roll of Honour, H&A, nominal roll of all members, nominal roll of men who served under assumed names.

The narrative covers the story of the Bn from inception in 1915 through to its active services on Gallipoli and in France. The unit was awarded battle honours for the Somme, Pozieres, Bullecourt, Menin Road, Bapaume 1917, Amiens, Gallipoli, Hindenburg Line and Mont St Quentin.
R/3 V/4. PS.


STORY OF THE TWENTY-FIRST
Being the Official History of the 21st Battalion A.I.F.

A R McNeil
21st Battalion Association, Melbourne, n.d. Not seen.


WITH THE TWENTY-SECOND
A History of the Twenty-Second Battalion AIF

E Gorman, H H Champion, Melbourne, 1919. Not seen.


23rd BATTALION A.I.F. SOUVENIR

G H Knox and W Brazenor
Produced by Corporal H H Ford, on the battlefield, France, 1918. Not seen.


THE RED AND WHITE DIAMOND
Authorised History of the Twenty-Fourth Battalion AIF

Sergeant W J Harvey MM
Alexander McCubbin, Melbourne, for the 24th Battalion Regtl Assn, 1920
Grey paper-covered boards, 8.0 x 5.0, -/340.
23 mono phots, 4 maps.

Apps: Roll of Honour, H&A.

Noted in a catalogue, but not seen. Reported to be a scarce volume.


THE BLUE AND BROWN DIAMOND
A History of the 27th Battalion AIF, 1915-1919

Lieut Col W Dollman and Sergeant H M Skinner
Lonnen & Cope, Adelaide, 1921 (subsequently reprinted, n.d.)
Seen rebound in brown and black, gold, 7.5 x 4.5, ix/213.
30 mono phots, 16 maps (printed in the text).

Apps: Roll of Honour, H&A, details of former COs, tributes from the three COs (1915-1919 period).

Blue and brown were the colours of the Bn cloth insignia. This is a straightforward factual narrative of the Bn's services during the Gallipoli campaign (1915) and on the Western Front (1916-1919), with abundant mention of places, events and individuals.
R/3 V/4. AMM.


THE TWENTY-EIGHTH
A Record of War Service, AIF, 1915-1919 (Volume I)

H B Collett
Trustees, Public Library Museum and Art Gallery, Perth, 1922. Not seen.


THE HISTORY AND REGIMENTAL STANDING ORDERS OF THE 30th INFANTRY
BATTALION, THE NEW SOUTH WALES SCOTTISH REGIMENT

Anon
Battalion Headquarters, Crows Nest,NSW, 1959. Not seen.


THE PURPLE AND GOLD
History of the 30th Battalion AIF

H Sloan
Halstead Press, Sydney, 1938. Not seen.


SHORT HISTORY OF THE 34th BATTALION, A.I.F.

Anon
Illawarra Press, Carlton, for the 34th Battalion AIF Association, 1957.
Not seen.


THE THIRTY-SEVENTH
History of the 37th Battalion AIF

N G McNicol
Modern Printing Co, Melbourne, 1936. Not seen.

326

THE THIRTY-EIGHTH BATTALION A.I.F.
The Story and Official History of the 38th Battalion AIF, 1916-1918

Eric Fairey
Bendigo Advertiser Pty Ltd, Bendigo, Victoria, for the 38th Bn
History Committee, 1920 (subsequently reprinted, n.d.)
Buff, red, 8.5 x 5.5, v/110.
17 mono phots, no maps, no Index.

Apps: Roll of Honour, H&A, list of COs and former officers, nominal roll
of all ranks.

This is almost entirely a narrative account of the Bn's services on the
Western Front. Many individuals are mentioned by name throughout the text,
with some details of citations for gallantry awards. An interesting and
informative history. R/1 (as reprint) V/4. AMM.


THE THIRTY-NINTH
History of the 39th Battalion AIF

A T Peterson
G W Green & Sons, Melbourne, 1934. Not seen.


THE FORTIETH
A Record of the 40th Battalion AIF

F C Green
John Vail, Government Printer, Hobart, for the 40th Bn Assn, 1922
Maroon, white, 8.75 x 5.75, viii/248.
Fp, no other illustrations, 12 maps (bound in), Index.

Apps: H&A, nominal roll for all ranks (including details of KIA and WIA).

This is a very useful unit history. It covers the period from inception,
in Tasmania in 1916, through to the end of the war. The bn served in
the battles of Third Ypres, on the Somme, etc. R/3 V/5. PS.


HISTORY OF THE 41st BATTALION, THE ROYAL NEW SOUTH WALES REGIMENT
1916-1984

J W Alcorn
Published privately, Lismore, NSW, 1984. Not seen.


THE SPIRIT OF THE FORTY-SECOND
Narrative of the 42nd Battalion, 11th Infantry Brigade, 3rd Division,
Australian Imperial Force during the Great War, 1914-1918

Vivian Brahms
W R Smith & Paterson Pty Ltd, Brisbane, 1938
Dark blue, gold, regt crest on front cover, 8.75 x 6.0, -/186.
11 mono phots, 2 sketches, no maps, no Index.

Apps: Roll of Honour, H&A (all ranks, listed alphabetically, many
with full citations), list of former officers, nominal roll of all
ranks).

This is a narrative account of the Bn's services on the Western Front,
with much useful detail of places and events, but almost entirely
devoid of references to individual officers and men. Likewise, the
picture captions do not identify the individuals portrayed. The overall
effect is somewhat impersonal and distant. However, the book is a very
worthwhile historical source. R/1 V/4. AMM. Recently reprinted, n.d.


THE FORTY-THIRD
The Story and Official History of the 43rd Battalion AIF

E J Colliver and B H Richardson
Rigby Limited, Adelaide, 1920. Not seen.


EGGS-A-COOK!
The Story of the Forty-Fourth - War as the Digger saw it

C Longmore
Colortype Press, Perth, Western Australia, 1921. Not seen.


BRIEF HISTORY OF THE 45th BATTALION A.I.F., 1916-1919

J E Lee
45th Battalion AIF Reunion Association, Sydney, NSW, 1962.
Not seen.


STORY OF A BATTALION
48th Battalion AIF

W Devine
Melville & Mullen, Melbourne, 1919. Not seen.


50th BATTALION A.I.F.
A Brief History

R Fisher
Adelaide 50th Battalion AIF Club, Adelaide, n.d.  Not seen.


52nd BATTALION, AUSTRALIAN IMPERIAL FORCE

This title is known to have been published, but no other details
appear in the official AWM catalogue. Not seen.

THE WHALE OIL GUARDS
The 53rd Battalion AIF

J J Kennedy
James Duffy & Co Ltd, Dublin, 1919
Dark green, gold, 7.0 x 5.0, -/144.
No other technical details available. Not seen.


## AUSTRALIA - GREAT WAR, MEDICAL UNITS


Although no details have been reported, it is known that official
histories have been published for the following units:


AUSTRALIAN ARMY MEDICAL CORPS
1st AUSTRALIAN FIELD AMBULANCE
5th AUSTRALIAN FIELD AMBULANCE
7th AUSTRALIAN FIELD AMBULANCE
8th AUSTRALIAN FIELD AMBULANCE
9th AUSTRALIAN FIELD AMBULANCE
11th AUSTRALIAN FIELD AMBULANCE

## AUSTRALIA  - GREAT WAR, OTHER UNIT HISTORIES


Again, although no details are available, it is known that formal
histories have been published for the following units and formations:

6th AUSTRALIAN MACHINE GUN COMPANY
AUSTRALIAN ARMY SERVICE CORPS
18th BATTERY, 6th BRIGADE FIELD ARTILLERY
27th BATTERY (no other details)
1st AUSTRALIAN PACK WIRELESS SIGNAL TROOP

A considerable number of other publications have been noted, but their
titles are too vague for there to be any certainty regarding the contents.

## AUSTRALIA - GREAT WAR, CAVALRY

WESTRALIAN CAVALRY IN THE WAR
The Story of the Tenth Light Horse Regiment AIF, in the Great War

Lieut Col A C N Olden DSO
Alexander McCubbin, Melbourne, 1921 (reprinted 1979)
Red, black, 8.5 x 5.5, x/333 (378 in the reprint edition)
Fp, 86 mono phots, 3 maps, no Index.

Apps: Roll of Honour, H&A (see notes below), operational order for the
final advance on Jerusalem, nominal roll.

A well-written and very helpful unit history. The narrative is at its best
when describing small-scale actions, especially in the section devoted
to the Gallipoli campaign. The nominal roll indicates whether a man was
part of the original regt or whether he joined later as a reinforce-
ment. The original edition of this book continued to be in such keen
demand that it was reprinted in 1979. The second edition has at the rear
a 45-page supplement, compiled by P A Shaw, which covers the history of
the regt from 1901 to 1979. The supplement also gives full details
(with full citations where applicable) for the H&A appendix, lists of
members KIA and WIA on Gallipoli, a list of former COs from 1900
to 1985, and notes regarding changes in the unit title. The narrative
describes the unit's service throughout the Middle East where its
members gained one VC, 3 DSOs, 1 MBE, 17 DCMs, 15 MMs, 6 MSMs, and
4 foreign awards. Of the two editions, the 1979 is to be preferred as a
research source, but it should be noted that only 400 copies were printed.
R/4 V/5. BCC/PS.


HISTORY OF THE SECOND LIGHT HORSE, 1914-1918

Lieut Col G H Bourne
The Northern Daily Leader Printer, Tamworth, NSW, 1926
Light brown boards, red spine, black, 10.0 x 7.0, -/84.
9 mono phots, 4 maps (printed in the text).

Apps: Roll of Honour, H&A.

This is the story of 2 LH in Gallipoli, Upper Egypt, Palestine, the
Jordan Valley and the Hills of Moab during which services 70 awards for
gallantry were gained. Although quite brief, this account is interesting
and a good research source. R/4 V/4. PS.


SAND, SWEAT AND CAMELS
The Australian Companies of the Imperial Camel Corps

George F Langley and E M Langley
Lowden Publishing Co, Kilmore, Victoria, 1976
Red, gold, 9.25 x 6.25, xv/188.
Fp, 32 mono phots, 3 maps (printed in the text), Bibliography, Index.

Apps: Roll of Honour, H&A.

The book tells the story of the 1st, 3rd and 4th Companies which served in the Western Desert, Romani Magthaba, Rafa and Gaza until the Corps was broken up to form the 14th and 15th Light Horse. An interesting account of some little-known actions. R/1 V/4. PS.

3rd LIGHT HORSE REGIMENT A.I.F., 1914-1919

George J Bell
Tasmanian Advocate, Devonport, 1919. Not seen.

STORY OF THE 3rd AUSTRALIAN LIGHT HORSE REGIMENT

Frank M Blackwell and R H Douglas
F Bowden & Sons Ltd, Adelaide, 1950. Not seen.

THE FOURTH AUSTRALIAN LIGHT HORSE REGIMENT
Some Aspects of its War Service

Cyril Smith
Page & Bird Pty Ltd, Melbourne, 1954. Not seen.

HISTORY OF THE FIFTH LIGHT HORSE REGIMENT (AUSTRALIAN IMPERIAL FORCE)
From 1914 to June 1919

L C Wilson
Motor Press of Australia, Sydney, 1926. Not seen.

UNDER FURRED HATS
6th Australian Light Horse Regiment

George Berrie
W C Penfold, Sydney, 1919. Not seen.

HISTORY OF THE 7th LIGHT HORSE REGIMENT A.I.F.

J D Richardson
Eric N Birks, Sydney, 1923. Not seen.

8/13 VICTORIAN MOUNTED RIFLES
8th, 13th and 20th Light Horse Regiments

This title is known to have been published, but no other details appear in the official AWM catalogue.

WITH THE NINTH LIGHT HORSE IN THE GREAT WAR

T H Darley
Hassell Press, Adelaide, 1924. Not seen.


HISTORY OF THE ELEVENTH LIGHT HORSE REGIMENT, 1914-1918

Ernest W Hammond
William Brooks & Co, Brisbane, 1942. Not seen.


NARRATIVE OF OPERATIONS OF THIRD LIGHT HORSE BRIGADE A.I.F. FROM
27th OCTOBER 1917 TO 4th MARCH 1919

L C Wilson
Oriental Advertising Company, Cairo, 1919. Not seen.


HISTORY OF THE FOURTH LIGHT HORSE BRIGADE A.I.F.
The War of 1914-1918, and the Egyptian Rebellion of 1919

G W Nutting
W R Smith & Paterson Pty Ltd, Brisbane, 1953. Not seen.

## AUSTRALIA - SECOND WORLD WAR, CAVALRY AND MECHANISED UNITS

THE 2/7th AUSTRALIAN CAVALRY REGIMENT

M R Birks
2/7th Australian Cavalry Regt Assn, Guildford, NSW, 1974. Not seen.


SANANANDA INTERLUDE
The 7th Australian Division Cavalry Regiment

F K Hartley
Book Depot, Melbourne, 1949. Not seen.


TANKS IN THE EAST
The Story of an Australian Cavalry Regiment

Colin Kerr
Oxford University Press, Melbourne, for the Regiment, 1945
Sky blue, black, 8.5 x 5.5, -/200.
16 pages of small mono phots, 2 maps (printed in the text), no appendixes, no Index.

This aims to be the history of 9th Australian Divisional Cavalry and its services in WWII (mainly Syria and El Alamein). The narrative is mainly anecdotal and is sketchily written. A surprisingly poor effort from such a prestigious publisher. R/2 V/1. RP.


BLACK BERETS
The History and Battles of the 9th Division Cavalry Regiment

Colin Pura
9th Australian Division Cavalry Regt Assn, Melbourne, 1983. Not seen.


TO THE GREEN FIELDS BEYOND
The Story of 6th Australian Division Cavalry Commandos

Shawn O'Leary
Sixth Division Cavalry Unit Historical Committee, Sydney, 1975. Not seen.


STORY OF THE 2/5th AUSTRALIAN COMMANDO SQUADRON A.I.F.

Jack Boxall
Metropolitan Printers, Lakemba, 1961. Not seen.

SPEED AND VIGILANCE
The Story of the 2nd Australian Tank Battalion (AIF), 1939-1944

Anon
New Century Press, Sydney, 1945. Not seen.


HISTORY OF THE 2/6th AUSTRALIAN ARMOURED REGIMENT

Anon
Bulletin Printery Pty Ltd, Southport, 1945. Not seen.


## AUSTRALIA - SECOND WORLD WAR, ARTILLERY


ROUNDSHOT TO RAPIER
Artillery in South Australia, 1840-1984

David Brook
Royal Artillery Association of South Australia, Adelaide, 1986. Not seen.


SIX YEARS IN SUPPORT
Official History of 2/1st Australian Field Regiment

E V Haywood
Angus & Robertson, Sydney, 1959. Not seen.


ACTION FRONT
The History of the 2/2nd Australian Field Regiment, Royal Australian
Artillery

W Cremor
2/2nd Field Regiment Assn, Melbourne, 1961. Not seen.


STORY OF THE 2/4th FIELD REGIMENT
A History of a Royal Australian Artillery Regiment during the Second
World War

Russell L Henry
The Merrion Press, Melbourne, 1950
Blue, gold, 8.5 x 5.75, vii/410.
111 mono phots, 8 maps (printed in the text), no Index.

Apps: Roll of Honour, H&A, list of COs, nominal roll for all ranks.

The Regt served in Egypt and the Syrian campaign before being moved back
to Australia for the New Guinea campaign.  Later it returned again to
Australia before then taking part in the final campaign to clear the
Japanese occupying forces from Borneo. This is a clear and informative
account, with abundant footnotes. Various lists and photographs of officers
are included in the text. R/3 V/4. HEC/AMM.  Recently reprinted, n.d.

GUNS AND GUNNERS
The Story of the 2/5th Australian Field Regiment in World War II

John W O'Brien
Angus & Robertson, Sydney, 1950
Navy blue, gold, 8.75 x 5.5, xvi/267.
Fp, 37 mono phots, 12 maps (printed in the text), Glossary, Index.

Apps: Roll of Honour, H&A.

A good workmanlike regtl history, with many individuals of all ranks
mentioned in the narrative. R/3 V/5. LM.


HISTORY OF THE 2/7th AUSTRALIAN FIELD REGIMENT

David Goodhart
Rigby Limited, Adelaide, 1952. Not seen.


WE WERE THE 2/12th: 1940-1946
2/12th Australian Field Regiment

Max Parsons, McKellar Renown Press, Carnegie, Victoria, 1985. Not seen.


GUNNERS IN THE JUNGLE
A Story of the 2/15th Field Regiment, Royal Australian Artillery,
8 Division, Australian Imperial Force

Cliff Whitelocke
2/15 Field Regt Assn, Eastwood, NSW, 1983. Not seen.


ON YOUR FEET
An Account of 2 Battery of the 2/1st Australian Tank Attack Regiment
in the Wewak Campaign, New Guinea, 1945

R C Searle
W Brooks, Brisbane, 1948. Not seen.


TARGET TANK
A History of the 2/3rd Australian Anti-tank Regiment, 9th Division, AIF

John Silver
Cumberland Newspapers Ltd, Parramatta, 1957. Not seen.


THE STORY OF THE 2/3rd AUSTRALIAN TANK ATTACK REGIMENT (A.I.F.)

Anon
The Reunion Committee, Annerly, Queensland, 1976. Not seen.

ON TARGET
The Story of 2/3rd Australian Light Anti-aircraft Regiment

C J E Rae, A L Harris and R K Bryant
Enterprise Press Pty Ltd, Sale, Victoria, for the 2/3rd Australian Light
Anti-aircraft Regiment Association, 1987
Dark blue, gold on red, 9.75 x 7.0, -/347.
67 mono phots, 4 other illustrations, 13 maps (11 printed in the text,
2 printed on the end-papers), Bibliography, Glossary, no Index.

Apps: H&A, nominal roll of all ranks, notes on the Regtl Assn.

This very good narrative account covers the services in WWII of 7th
Battery (the battle for Crete, Palestine and New Guinea), 8th Battery (as
'Desert Rats' in the Benghazi Handicap and the siege of Tobruk, and then
subsequently New Guinea), and 9th Battery (Western Desert, defence of
the Suez Canal, and subsequently New Guinea and Borneo). The nominal roll
is particularly helpful to researchers, as it gives full details of
personnel killed, wounded and/or taken prisoner. The only adverse
features are the poor reproduction of some of the photographs and, of
course, the lack of an Index. R/1 V/4. FC.

## AUSTRALIA - SECOND WORLD WAR, INFANTRY

FIRST IN WAR
The History of the 2/1st Australian Infantry Battalion

Anon
2/1st Australian Infantry Bn War History Committee, Atarmon, NSW, n.d.
Not seen.


NULLI SECUNDUS LOG
2/2nd Australian Infantry Battalion AIF

A J Marshall
Consolidated Press, Sydney, 1946. Not seen.


PURPLE OVER GREEN
The History of the 2/2nd Australian Infantry Battalion, 1939-1945

Stan Wick
Printcraft Press, for the Battalion Assn, 1977. Not seen.


THE STORY OF THE 2/2nd AUSTRALIAN PIONEER BATTALION

E F Aitken
Publisher's details not known, xiii/288, Roll of Honour, H&A, Index.
No other details available.


WAR DANCE
The Story of the 2/3rd Australian Infantry Battalion, 16th Brigade,
6th Division

Ken Clift
P M Fowler, Kingsgrove, NSW, for 2/3 Battalion Assn, 1980
Green, black, 8.5 x 5.5, xiii/450.
115 mono phots, one sketch, 17 maps.

Apps: Roll of Honour, H&A, nominal roll for all ranks.

The good readable narrative covers the Bn's services in Egypt, Greece,
Syria and New Guinea. R/1 V/4. PS.


WHITE OVER GREEN
The 2/4th Battalion, and Reference to the 4th Battalion

Anon ('Unit History Editorial Committee')
Angus & Robertson, Sydney, for the Battalion Assn, 1963. Not seen.

NOTHING OVER US
The Story of the 2/6th Australian Infantry Battalion

David Hay
Australian War Memorial, Canberra, 1984
Light brown, gold, 9.5 x 7.25, xii/603.
197 mono phots, 4 sketches, 22 maps (printed in the text). no Index.

Apps: Roll of Honour, H&A, nominal rolls of all ranks (various).

A good workmanlike regtl history, with much detail regarding individual
services (including WIA and POW). The Bn was formed in Victoria in 1939
and served subsequently in the Western Desert, Greece, Crete, and New
Guinea. The total awards to the Bn were 4 DSOs, 15 MCs, 5 DCMs, one MBE,
one BEM and 59 MIDs. The author, Sir David Hay, himself served with the
Bn, gaining the DSO and the MBE. R/1 V/4. PS/FC.


THE FIERY PHOENIX
The Story of the 2/7th Australian Infantry Battalion, 1939-1946

W P Bolger and J G Littlewood
2/7th Battalion Association, Parkdale, Victoria, 1983. Not seen.


THE SECOND EIGHTH
A History of the 2/8th Australian Infantry Battalion

Anon
2/8th Battalion Association, Melbourne, 1984. Not seen.


PURPLE AND BLUE
The History of the 2/10th Battalion AIF (The Adelaide Rifles), 1939-1945

Lieut Col Frank Allchin MM
Published by a Battalion Committee, printer's details not shown,
Adelaide, 1958
Royal blue, gold, 9.5 x 6.0, xxviii/454.
Fp, 31 mono phots, 7 maps (bound in), Index.

Apps: Roll of Honour, H&A, nominal roll for all ranks (with details of
casualties).

An excellently compiled account, written by many hands, some in a 'chatty
Digger' style, but clearly very well researched. R/3 V/5. HLL.


THE 2/11th (CITY OF PERTH) AUSTRALIAN INFANTRY BATTALION, 1939-1945

Anon
H M Binks, Perth, 1984. Not seen.

BAYONETS ABROAD
A History of the 2/13th Battalion AIF in the Second World War

G H Fearnside
Waite & Bull, Sydney, 1953. Not seen.


THE SECOND FOURTEENTH BATTALION
A History of an Australian Infantry Battalion in the Second World War

W B Russell
Halstead Press Pty Ltd, for Angus & Robertson, Sydney, 1948
Blue, gold, Bn flash on front cover, 8.75 x 5.75, xv/336.
Fp, 92 mono phots, 14 sketches, 2 line drawings, 11 maps, Glossary, Index.

Apps: Roll of Honour, H&A, statistical summary of casualties.

A very good history, with abundant footnotes and many individuals
mentioned by name in the text. Private Bruce Steel Kingsbury VC was a
member of this Regt, his Cross being awarded posthumously for great
gallantry at Isurava, Papua New Guinea, on 29.8.1942.
R/4 V/5. HEC.


A THOUSAND MEN AT WAR
The Story of 2/16th Battalion AIF

Malcolm Uren
William Heinneman, Melbourne, 1959. Not seen.


17th BATTALION, NORTH SYDNEY REGIMENT SOUVENIR
Photograph Album

Anon
A K Murray, Sydney, n.d.  Not seen.


THE GRIM GLORY OF THE 2/19th BATTALION AIF

R W Newton ('and others')
2/19th Battalion AIF Assn, Sydney, 1975 (2nd edition, 1976)
Green, gold, cap badge motif on front cover, 10.75 x 8.75, xvi/837.
306 mono phots, 44 maps (printed in the text), no Index.

Apps: Roll of Honour, H&A, nominal roll for all ranks.

This massive work is printed in facsimile typescript which, although full
of interesting detail, is occasionally difficult to follow. The lack of an
Index in a book of this size is a very severe disadvantage to the
researcher. More time spent on editing and indexing would have been very
beneficial. Even so, this is a wonderfully complete reference source.
R/3 V/4. HEC.

ETCHED IN GREEN
The History of the 22nd Australian Infantry Battalion, 1939-1946

Graeme Macfarlan
22nd Australian Infantry Battalion Assn, Melbourne, 1961. Not seen.


MUD AND BLOOD
Albury's Own Second Twenty-third Australian Infantry Battalion

Pat Share Heritage Book Publications, Frankston, Victoria, for the 2/23rd
Australian Infantry Battalion Association, 1978
Red, white, 8.75 x 6.0, xvi/464.
134 mono phots, 4 coloured plates, 8 maps, Index.

Apps: Roll of Honour, H&A.

This very complete narrative covers the history of the Bn from 1940
through to the end of WWII. It served in the Western Desert (Tobruk and
El Alamein) before being moved back to Australia to re-train for service
in the South West Pacific theatre. It subsequently saw much action
in the jungles of New Guinea (which provided a sharp contrast to the
sands of the Western Desert). Total awards to the Bn were 4 DSOs, 11 MCs,
4 DCMs, 20 MMs, one MBE and 35 MIDs. An exemplary publication. R/3 V/5. PS.


THE SECOND TWENTY-FOURTH AUSTRALIAN INFANTRY BATTALION OF THE NINTH
DIVISION: A HISTORY

R P Searle
The Jacaranda Press, Brisbane, for the 2/24th Battalion Assn, 1963
Olive green, white, 9.75 x 6.75, xiv/378.
Fp, 20 mono phots (with 2 phots printed on the end-papers), 10 maps
(printed in the text), Glossary, Index.

Apps: a combined Roll of Honour and list of Honours and Awards.

A sound narrative account of the Bn's services in New Guinea between 1943
and 1945. Complete and informative, with a good quality of production.
R/3 V/5. HEC.


THAT'S THE WAY IT WAS
A History of 2/24th Australian Infantry Battalion AIF

George Christensen
The Craftsman Press Pty Ltd, Hawthorn, Victoria, 1982
Brown, gold, 9.25 x 5.5, xx/364.
73 mono phots, 3 line drawings, 11 maps (printed in the text), Glossary,
Index.

Apps: Roll of Honour (with places of burial), roll of WIA, nominal roll of
all ranks who served.

This book covers the same ground as that covered in the book by Serle (see previous entry, page 339), but extends the history further into the post-war period. Also, it seems probable that, having been published 20 years later, Christensen's researches will have contributed some fresh information to the story. R/1 V/5. PS.


THE BROWN AND BLUE DIAMOND AT WAR
The Story of the 2/27th Battalion AIF

John Burns
2/27th Battalion Association, Adelaide, 1960. Not seen.


SECOND TWENTY-EIGHTH
The Story of a Famous Battalion of the Ninth Australian Division

Philip Masel
2/28th Battalion and 24th Anti-Tank Company Assn, Perth, 1961. Not seen.


HISTORY OF THE 2/29th BATTALION, 8th AUSTRALIAN DIVISION A.I.F.

R W Christie and Robert Christie
2/29th Battalion Assocation, Malvern, Victoria, 1983. Not seen.


UNOFFICIAL HISTORY OF THE 29/46th AUSTRALIAN INFANTRY BATTALION A.I.F.

Rupert Charlott
Halstead Press, Melbourne, 1952. Not seen.


GALLEGHAN'S GREYHOUNDS
The Story of the 2/30th Australian Infantry Battalion

A W Penfold, W C Bayliss and K E Crispin
2/30th Battalion Association, Sydney, 1949. Not seen.


THE FOOTSOLDIERS
The Story of the 2/33rd Australian Infantry Battalion AIF

William Crooks
Printcraft Press, Brookvale, NSW, 1971
Red, gold, 9.5 x 6.0, xxii/528.
196 mono phots, 8 line drawings, 54 maps (printed in the text), Glossary, Index.

Apps: Roll of Honour, H&A, roll of POWs, notes on battle honours, notes on 33rd Bn AIF (1915-1918), details of 'the Liberator crash, New Guinea, 7.9.1943',various statistics.

This is a very detailed account of the Bn's WWII services in Syria, Palestine, New Guinea and Borneo. As can be seen from the technical specification shown overleaf, the book contains a mass of detailed inform- ation and is a first-class reference source. The Bn gained 2 DSOs, 6 MCs, 11 MMs, and 29 MIDs during the course of the war. R/3 V/5. PS.


THE 36th AUSTRALIAN INFANTRY BATTALION 1939-1945
The Story of an Australian Infantry Battalion and its Part in the War against Japan

Stan Brigg and Les Brigg
36th Battalion (St George's English Rifle Regiment) Association
Sydney, 1967. Not seen.


STORY OF THE 42nd AUSTRALIAN INFANTRY BATTALION

S E Benson
Dymock's Book Arcade, Sydney, for the 42nd Australian Infantry Battalion Association, 1952. Not seen.


THE SECOND FORTY-THIRD AUSTRALIAN INFANTRY BATTALION, 1940-1946

Gordon Combe
Second 43rd Battalion AIF Club, Adelaide, 1972. Not seen.


TOBRUK TO TARAKAN
The Story of 2/48th Battalion AIF

John G Glenn
Rigby Limited, Adelaide, 1960. Not seen.


THAT MOB
The Story of the 55/53rd Australian Infantry Battalion AIF

F M Budden
Published privately, Sydney, 1973. Not seen.


MILITIA BATTALION AT WAR
The History of 58/59th Australian Infantry Battalion in the Second World War

Russell Mathews
Halstead Press, Sydney, 1961 (reprinted in soft covers in Hong Kong, 1987)
Green and white, black, 8.0 x 5.25, xii/236.
42 mono phots, 2 coloured plates, 7 maps (printed in the text).

Apps: Roll of Honour, roll of WIA, H&A, operation order for the Hongorai river crossing.

This is a very competent narrative account of the Bn's services in
New Guinea between 1943 and 1945. A good reference source, well produced.
R/1 (in reprint format) V/4. PS.

STORY OF THE 2/2nd AUSTRALIAN PIONEER BATTALION

E F Aitken
2/2nd Pioneer Battalion Association, Melbourne, 1953. Not seen.

MUD AND SAND
Being the Official War History of the 2/3rd Pioneer Battalion AIF

J A Anderson and J G T Jackett
NSW 2/3rd Pioneer Battalion Assn, Sutherland, 1963. Not seen.

MUZZLE BLAST
A Pictorial Story of Six Years of War with the 2/2nd Australian Machine
Gun Battalion

Edwin Ernest Oaks
2/2nd Australian Machine Gun Battalion Association War History Committee,
Sydney, 1980. Not seen.


FROM SNOW TO JUNGLE
A History of the 2/3rd Australian Machine Gun Battalion

John Bellair
Allen & Unwin (Australia) Pty Ltd, North Sydney, NSW, 1987
Grey, gold, 9.25 x 6.0, xxviii/298.
74 mono phots, 12 maps (printed in the text).

Apps: Roll of Honour, H&A, nominal roll of all ranks, notes on the Vickers
machine-gun, notes on the organisation of a machine-gun battalion in WWII,
list of COs.

The battalion was formed in 1940 and served in the Middle East before
moving to Java where many of its members became prisoners of the Japanese.
It was then reformed in Australia and subsequently took part in the New
Guinea, Hollandia and Aitape campaigns. A good working history.
R/1 V/4. PS.


LOST LEGION
Mission 204 and the Reluctant Dragon

William Noonan
Printed in Singapore for Allen & Unwin, Sydney, 1987
Brown, silver, 9.75 x 6.25, xv/235.
Fp, 44 mono phots, 5 maps (printed in the text), Bibliography, Index.

Apps: notes on the composition of a mixed Chinese and British Guerilla
Battalion, notes on the Mission operation orders.

In 1942 a small group of soldiers volunteered to undertake the longest
overland deep penetration behind enemy lines ever attempted in the
history of the world's armed forces. Mission 204 was a secret cadre of
demolition and guerilla experts, despatched from Burma to China to cause
mayhem on the Japanese lines of communication. This book is the first
full account of that episode. The title is listed here because most of the
European personnel came from the ranks of 2/19th and 2/20th Australian
Infantry Battalions. A most interesting and unusual account. R/1 V/4. HEC.

INDEPENDENT COMPANY
2/2nd and 2/4th Australian Independent Companies in Portuguese Timor
1941-1943

Bernard J Callinan DSO MC
William Heineman Ltd, Melbourne, 1954
Light green, green on dark blue, 8.75 x 5.75, xv/235.
Fp, 37 mono phots, 8 maps (2 printed on the end-papers, 6 printed in
the text), Index.

Apps: list of officers who served.

In February 1942, the Japanese landed 6000 assault troops in Portuguese
Timor. They were opposed by just 300 Australian troops. This small unit,
forced into the mountains, then operated in the guerilla role. With
the assistance of some Timor natives, they lived off the land and carried
their wounded with them. They were thus, at a crucial stage in the war,
the only Allied unit anywhere between India and New Guinea which was still
in direct action with the enemy. At one stage, they were immobilising
30,000 Japanese troops (upon whom they inflicted considerable losses). The
survivors of the unit were evacuated back to Australia before the end of
the war. A fascinating and little-known campaign. R/3 V/5. HEC/JRS.

## AUSTRALIA - SECOND WORLD WAR, MEDICAL FORMATIONS

Although no details are available, it is known that authorised
histories have been published for the following units:

2/4th AUSTRALIAN GENERAL FIELD HOSPITAL
2/6th AUSTRALIAN GENERAL FIELD HOSPITAL
2/9th AUSTRALIAN GENERAL FIELD HOSPITAL
2/10th AUSTRALIAN FIELD AMBULANCE, 8th DIVISION
AUSTRALIAN ARMY NURSING SERVICE

## AUSTRALIA - ENGINEERS

THE GALLIPOLI DIARY OF SERGEANT LAWRENCE OF THE AUSTRALIAN ENGINEERS,
1st A.I.F., 1915

Cyril Lawrence with Sir Ronald East CBE
Melbourne University Press, Carlton, Victoria, 1981
Light brown, gold, 8.0 x 6.0, xi/167.
4 mono phots, 6 maps (printed in the text), Index.

Apps: war diary of the 2nd Field Company, Royal Australian Engineers AIF,
at Gallipoli.

This edited diary records the activities and personal observations of
a non-commissioned officer of 2nd Field Company from the time of his
arrival at Suez through to the evacuation from Gallipoli. Although
basically autobiographical, the book is a valuable soldier's record of
military engineering activities during that campaign. R/1 V/3. EDS.


THE ROYAL AUSTRALIAN ENGINEERS

Maj Gen R R McNicoll CBE
Royal Australian Engineers Corps Committee. Canberra
Blue, gold, 9.25 x 6.0
Published in four Volumes, of which three are recorded here:
Volume I:    THE COLONIAL ENGINEERS, 1835-1902, xviii/203, 40 mono phots
Volume II:   MAKING AND BREAKING, 1902-1919, xix/ 232, 49 mono phots
Volume III:  TEETH AND TAIL, 1919-1945, xix/432, 55 mono phots
All three Volumes having Bibliographies and Indexes, with maps.
Publication dates were 1977, 1979 and 1982 respectively, but the
bindings and general format are the same in each case.

The narrative covers the entire history of military engineering in
Australia, commencing with the early pioneering days in Van Diemen's Land
and New South Wales. Officers of the Royal Engineers were in charge of
such works in the various Colonies, and their names are recorded here.
Volume II covers the Great War period (Gallipoli, the Western Front, and
Palestine), while Volume III is concerned mainly with operations in
the Western Desert, Syria, and the South West Pacific. Each Volume is
provided with detailed appendixes. This is an important reference source
produced to a high standard in all respects. R/3 V/5. HEC.


CORPS OF ROYAL AUSTRALIAN ENGINEERS IN THE SECOND WORLD WAR, 1939-1945

Anon
Specialty Press, Melbourne, 1946. Not seen.

# AUSTRALIA - OTHER CORPS HISTORIES

AUSTRALIAN ARMOUR
A History of the Royal Australian Armoured Corps, 1927-1972

Maj Gen R N L Hopkins CBE
Australian War Memorial and Australian Government Publication Service,
Netley, South Australia, 1978
Khaki, red, 10.0 x 7.25, xvii/371.
Fp, 62 mono phots, 11 line drawings, 16 maps (printed in the text),
Bibliography, no appendixes, Index.

This is an authoritative history which traces the modest beginnings of
the Corps during the Depression years, its increasing importance in the
late 1930s, and then the rapid expansion (and formation of the 1st
Australian Armoured Division) in 1941-1942. During WWII, Australian armour
served mainly in the South West Pacific theatre, and these services are
covered in detail. There is brief mention of the Korean War, but the final
70 pages are devoted to the Corps'involvement in the Vietnam conflict
(where it fought in Centurion tanks and armoured personnel carriers).
R/1 V/4. HEC/RP.


SIGNALS
Story of the Australian Corps of Signals

Anon ('Written and Prepared by Members of the Australian Corps of Signals')
Halstead Press Ltd, Sydney, NSW, 1953
Dark green, black, 11.0 x 8.5, -/196.
109 mono phots, 2 coloured plates, 74 sketches, 4 maps.

Apps: H&A (up to February, 1945).

This book is an anthology of 61 short pieces concerning the Corps of
Signals during WWII. Useful and well illustrated, but not a complete
history. R/2 V/3. PS.


SIGNALS
A History of the Royal Australian Corps of Signals, 1788-1947

Theo Barker
Brown Prior Anderson Pty Ltd, Burwood, Victoria, for the Royal Australian
Corps of Signals, 1987
Blue, gold, 9.5 x 6.0, xiii/361.
51 mono phots, 4 line drawings, 11 diagrams, 23 maps, Glossary, Index.

Apps: Roll of Honour (WWI and WWII), H&A (WWI and WWII), biographical notes
on various senior Signals officers, list of former Directors (to 1948),
Signals Troops 1912, notes on organisation.

This very comprehensive account describes the evolution of military communications in Australia from the time of the arrival of the First Fleet in 1788, through to 1947. All aspects of the Corps' activities are covered - technical and operational. It is understood that a second Volume is in course of preparation, which will bring the story forward from 1947 to the present time. R/1 V/5. PS.


GETTING THROUGH
The Unit War History of 3rd Australian Division Signals, 1939-1945

Anon ('Members of 3/66 Club Unit Association')
Kenwalk Printing, Dandenong, Melbourne, 1987
Soft card, green, black, 8.5 x 5.75, vi/199.
30 mono phots, 3 diagrams, 3 line drawings, 4 maps (printed in the text), Glossary.

Apps: H&A, nominal roll of all ranks.

This is a short history of the unit's services between 1916 and 1939, and then its WWII services in Australia (1943-1944), in New Guinea (1943-1944), and then on the Solomon Islands and Bougainville(1945). R/1 V/4. PS.


LEBANON TO LABUAN
A Story of Mapping by the Australian Survey Corps, World War II

Brig Gen Lawrence FitzGerald OBE
J G Holmes Pty Ltd, Melbourne, for 2/1st Survey Association, 1980
White, blue, regtl crest on front cover, 11.5 x 8.75, xii/124.
Fp, 79 mono phots, 5 other illustrations, 11 maps (9 printed in the text, 2 printed on the end-papers), Index.

Apps: list of former officers, schedule of operations June 1941 to January 1942, GHQ Mapping Directive.

A very interesting work which deals with an obscure but vitally important aspect of modern warfare. This book must be of great interest to all cartographers. The story cover the unit's services in Palestine, Jordan and Syria, and then subsequently in the South West Pacific. A first-class history. R/3 V/5. HEC.


PADRE
Australian Chaplains in Gallipoli and France

Michael McKernan
Printed by Koon Wah Printing Pte Ltd, Singapore, for Allen & Unwin Australia Pty Ltd, Sydney, NSW, 1986
Dark blue, gold, 9.25 x 6.25, xv/190.
32 mono phots, no maps, no appendixes, Index.

This is an anthology of extracts from letters and diaries written by numerous Australian chaplains who served with AIF forces on Gallipoli and on the Western Front. The graphic personal accounts give a unique insight into the work of these men during WWI. R/1 V/3. HEC.

## AUSTRALIA - ADDENDUM

TO KOKODA AND BEYOND
The Story of the 39th Battalion, 1941-1943

Victor Austin
Printed by Prior Anderson Pty, for Melbourne University Press, 1988
Brown, yellow and red, 8.5 x 5.5, xviii/267.
24 mono phots, 10 maps (printed in the text), Index.

Apps: Roll of Honour, H&A, nominal roll for all ranks.

The Bn was formed at Darley in November 1941, and sailed for Port Moresby aboard the AQUITANIA. It subsequently saw much sharp action at Isurava, Buna and Sanananda before being disbanded. Although written more than forty years later, this is a good workmanlike account, with much detail in the narrative. The nominal roll includes details of casualties incurred in each area of action, e.g. Kokoda, Sanananda, Port Moresby. R/2 V/5. HEC.

## AUSTRALIA - POLICE

THE TROOPER POLICE OF AUSTRALIA
A Record of Mounted Police Work in the Commonwealth from the Earliest Days of Settlement to the Present Time

A L Haydon
Published in London (details not known), 1911, xviii/431, 'photographs, maps and diagrams', noted thus in a catalogue but not seen.

# MISCELLANEOUS AND ADDENDA

HISTORICAL RECORDS OF THE 76th 'HINDOOSTAN REGIMENT'
From its Formation in 1787 to 30th June 1881

Lieut Col F A Hayden DSO
The Johnson's Head, Lichfield, 1909
Red, gold, 8.5 x 5.5, xiv/195.
no illustrations, 7 maps (folding, bound in), no Index.

Apps: list of officers at 1788 and 1881, notes on uniforms, notes on
the Colours.

This is a British Army history, but it is listed here because the
Regt spent so many of its early years in India (1788-1805, 1864-1868, and
Burma 1868-1870). It was amalgamated in 1881 with the 33rd Regiment to
become 2nd Bn Duke of Wellington's (West Riding) Regiment. This is a
very detailed account, and produced to a better-than-average standard
for the period. Sadly there is no Index, but various rolls of casualties
(with details of date and location) are woven into the text. Likewise,
although there is no formal appendix for Honours & Awards, the relevant
details do appear in the text (including the Boer War awards).
R/4 V/4. PCAL. RP.


HER MAJESTY'S ARMY - INDIAN AND COLONIAL FORCES
A Descriptive Account of the Various Regiments now Comprising the
Queen's Forces in India and the Colonies

Walter Richards
Publisher's details not known, London, n.d. (c.1887)
Red, gold, decorated, dimensions unknown, vi/376.
Coloured fp, 14 other coloured plates, no other details known. Noted thus
in a catalogue, not seen.


THE HISTORY OF KING EDWARD'S HORSE
The King's Overseas Dominions Regiment

Lieut Col Lionel James
Sifton Praed, London, 1921
Grey, gold, regtl crest on front cover, 8.75 x 5.75, xv/401.
Fp, 14 mono phots, 8 maps (bound in), no Index.

Apps: Roll of Honour.

This regt was raised in 1900 as THE KING'S COLONIALS from Colonials
resident in the area of London, then renamed as KING EDWARD'S HORSE
in 1910. In WWI, the regt served in France as Divisional Cavalry with
notable distinction. Although this was a British Army unit (and to quote
from the Preface) 'there was no Dominion, Dependency, Colony, nor
portion of the globe where the British tongue is spoken that had not a
representative in the uniform of King Edward's Horse'. R32 V/4. VS.

THE COLONIAL POLICE

Sir Charles Jeffries KCMG OBE
Max Parrish, London, 1952
Pale blue, gold, 8.5 x 5.5, -/232.
no illustrations, no maps, Bibliography, Index.

Apps: the police forces of 42 Colonial Territories, with details of
personnel by rank.

The interesting narrative covers the period 1835-1951 and is an excellent
general account of policing and peace-keeping in the Caribbean, the Far
East, West Africa, East and West Africa, and all of the island Colonies.
Very useful indeed as background reading. R/3 V/4. RP.


THE LAND FORCES OF THE BRITISH COLONIES AND PROTECTORATES

Compiled by the Intelligence Division, War Office, 1902, Revised by the
General Staff, War Office, 1905
His Majesty's Stationery Office, London, 1905
Red, gold, 'For Official Use Only' on front cover, 9.5 x 6.25, viii/424.
no illustrations, no maps, no Index.

Apps: tables of strengths and establishments for each Colony and
Protectorate.

This book gives brief details of the constitution and organisation of all
forces (including Armed Police) which had received training in the use of
firearms. Arranged aphabetically from Australia to the Windward Islands.
A superb statistical and factual research source. R/4 V/5. VS.
It is reported that the print runs for both editions (1902 and 1905)
were limited to 1800 copies. Of the two, the 1905 edition is presumably
to be preferred.


ACTIVITIES OF THE BRITISH COMMUNITY IN THE ARGENTINE REPUBLIC DURING THE
1939-1945 WAR

Anon
The British Community Council in the Argentine Republic, Buenos Aires,
July 1953
Soft card, beige, black, 8.5 x 5.5, iv/127.
no illustrations, no maps, Bibliography, Index.

Apps: Roll of Honour, H&A, various rolls.

This unusual but most informative publication contains a complete list of
all those Argentine nationals who volunteered to fight with British forces
during WWII. The rolls give full details of rank, unit and awards, and
include a Roll of Honour for those who lost their lives. Additionally,
there is much information concerning the fund-raising activities of the
British Community Council which led to the creation of the 'Argentine-
British' Squadron, RAF, in 1942. A unique source. R/4 V/5. APR.
This report contributed by Alberto Peralta-Ramos,until recently a Staff
Officer of the Argentine armed forces.

IMPERIAL SUNSET
Frontier Soldiering in the 20th Century

James Lunt
Macdonald Futura Publishers, London, 1981
Beige, gold, 9.5 x 6.0, xvii/422.
41 mono phots, 4 maps (printed in the text), no appendixes, Bibliography,
Index.

This superb book is recommended to users of this bibliography on two counts.
First, the author was both a professional soldier and a professional
historian. He was able, therefore, to convey in his writings both the
spirit and the fact of Empire soldiering in clear and accurate terms.
Secondly, his book is divided into sections each of which deal with a
military formation of the type described elsewhere in REGIMENTS OF THE
EMPIRE. Not all of those units ever succeeded in having published a full
account of their evolution and active services. James Lunt's book serves
to fill in those gaps. Some of the units which would otherwise have gone
unrecorded are: THE TRANS-JORDAN FRONTIER FORCE, THE TRUCIAL OMAN SCOUTS,
THE ADEN PROTECTORATE LEVIES, THE HADHRAMI BEDOUIN LEGION, THE SOMALILAND
CAMEL CORPS and SOMALILAND SCOUTS, and THE HONG KONG REGIMENT.
R/2 V/5. RP.


HISTORICAL RECORD OF THE KUMAON RIFLES

Major J F A Overton
Published privately, UK, 1983
Card covers, stapled, light green, black, regtl crest on front cover,
11.75 x 8.25, xiii/159.
44 mono phots (photo-copied), 23 maps (printed in the text), Bibliography,
Index.

Apps: H&A, list of former COs, idem Adjutants, idem Subadar-Majors,
idem all former officers (British and Indian, 1917-1947), nominal roll
for all ranks (June 1941), nominal roll for Mortar Platoon (1944), etc.

The regt was first raised, as 1/50th and 2nd/50th Kumaon Rifles, as a
war-time expedient in 1917. Recruitment came exclusively from the Kumaonis,
hillsmen who quickly made a name for themselves and who took great pride
in the wearing of the kukri and their light infantry drill of 140 paces
to the minute. They served briefly at the end of WWI in Palestine and on
the North West Frontier. The 2nd Bn was disbanded in 1922, but 1st Bn
served in Hong Kong in the 1930s before returning west to take part in
the landings at Abadan in 1941 and the protection of Persia and Iraq
until 1945. In 1946 they were in Malaya but then returned for Aid to the
Civil Power duties at the time of Partition. The Bn retained all its special
distinctions until 1950 when it ceased to be a Rifles unit. It was then
absorbed, as infantry of the line, into the Kumaon Regiment (see page 157)
and became 3rd Battalion (Rifles) The Kumaon Regiment.

This record was prepared by the son of a former officer, but never
formally published. Fifty photo-stat copies were made, and copies are
held by the NAM, IOL, IWM, and AMOT. It is an extremely detailed work,
containing all of the supplementary information which any researcher is
likely to require. R/5 V/5. RP.

## NOTE ON INDEXES

Every regiment and other type of military unit mentioned
in the preceding pages has been indexed according to the
country in which it was raised, or in which it normally
operated. For example, even though the ADEN TROOP was an
element of the Indian Army, it has been indexed under ADEN.
Similarly, although Burma did not become autonomous from
India until 1937, and even though Assam never did form
part of Burma, it has been found convenient to index
Assam and Burma together.

Newfoundland has been allocated its own heading in the
preceding pages because, despite having become Canada's
tenth Province in 1949, it was still a British Colony
during the years covered by its regimental history books.
For the purposes of indexing, however, it has been
merged with Canada.

The user of this bibliography may encounter other similar
anomolies. Cross-referencing has reduced these, it is
hoped, to a minimum. However, the evolution and structure
of the Empire was neither symmetrical nor constant,
and this fact should be taken into account when
consulting the indexes.

In the event that a particular regiment cannot be
traced in the indexes, two possible explanations should
be considered, i.e. the unit in question does not have
a published record of its former services, or the
existence of such a record has been overlooked by
the compiler.

Most military librarians and specialist book dealers
will be pleased to give further advice concerning
unrecorded regiments.

## ARRANGEMENT OF INDEXES

To locate a particular regiment or country, please
consult either the introductory 'Contents' list (page 9)
or the 'Index of Indexes' (page 378).

## ARRANGEMENT OF APPENDIXES

To locate one of the four appendixes, please
consult the 'Index of Indexes' (page 378).

**Part 1 - Colonies, Protectorates, and other Territories (page 11)**

FIJI

CHINA

## Part II - Africa (page 27)

## Part III — INDIA (page 61)

GENERAL BACKGROUND TITLES, AND
BRITISH ARMY REGIMENTS HAVING THEIR ORIGINS IN INDIA

Note:

Punjab Frontier Force component regiments are listed and indexed under the appropriate headings of Cavalry, Infantry, Mountain Artillery, etc. For comprehensive or general background titles regarding the P.F.F., see pages 161 and 162.

See Appendix I (page 74) for information regarding British Army infantry regiment lineages.

See Appendix II (page 108) for information regarding Indian Cavalry regiment designations.

INFANTRY

Infantry under various numbering systems:

See Appendix III (page 160) for information regarding Indian Infantry regiment designations.

## ARTILLERY

## EUROPEAN VOLUNTEER AND AUXILIARY FORCES

| | |
|---|---|
| Assam-Bengal Railway Battalion | 197 |
| Behar (or Bihar) Light Horse | 191.192 |
| Bengal Yeoman Cavalry | 190 |
| Bombay Light Horse | 196 |
| Bombay Motor Patrol | 196 |
| Bombay Volunteer Rifles | 196 |
| Calcutta Light Horse | 193 |
| Calcutta & Presidency Battalion | 194 |
| Calcutta Volunteer Cavalry | 193 |
| Cossipore Artillery Volunteers | 192 |
| Khakee Ressalah | 190 |
| Kolar Gold Fields Battalion | 195 |
| Lumsden's Horse | 191.197 |
| Madras Volunteer Guards | 195 |
| Meerut Volunteer Horse | 190 |
| Volunteer Force, The | 194 |
| Soubah Behar Mounted Rifles | 191 |
| Surma Valley Light Horse | 196 |

## POLICE, ARMED POLICE, TRIBAL MILITIAS, FRONTIER SCOUTS

| | |
|---|---|
| Assam Rifles | 19 |
| Burma Military Police | 20 |
| Chin Hills Battalion | 20 |
| Chitral Scouts | 200 |
| Frontier Militias (NWF) | 199 |
| Frontier Scouts (NWF) | 199 |
| Gilgit Scouts | 200 |
| Indian Police, The | 198 |
| Kachin Levies | 20 |
| Khandesh Bhil Corps | 201 |
| Khyber Rifles | 200 |
| Kurram Militia | 200 |
| Malwa Bhil Corps | 201 |
| Meywar Bhil Corps | 200 |
| Military Police, The Corps of | 199 |
| Pishin Scouts | 200 |
| Punjab Police Battalions | 199 |
| Samana Rifles | 200 |
| South Waziristan Scouts | 200 |
| Tochi Scouts | 200 |
| Zhob Militia | 200 |

GURKHA REGIMENTS, CORPS, FORMATIONS, AND CONNECTIONS

See Appendix IV (page 225) for information regarding Gurkha
unit designations.

**Part VII - NEW ZEALAND (page 287)**

2nd New Zealand Expeditionary Force - Infantry and Armour

See also

Part V (page 275) - AUSTRALIAN forces which served in KOREA

Part VI (page 279) - AUSTRALIAN forces which served in SOUTH VIETNAM

379

## INDEX OF INDEXES

## APPENDIXES

## ACKNOWLEDGEMENTS

Publication of this bibliography would have been impossible without the practical support and specialised knowledge of many private individuals and public institutions. Detailed reports have been received from seventy-one book collectors and dealers, and they are listed overleaf. Correspondence has been received from approximately eighty other individuals who, either as bibliophiles or as former officers of the regiments concerned, have been able to contribute additional information.

It is accepted that the lists of titles noted in REGIMENTS OF THE EMPIRE are not complete. With new regimental histories being published almost every month, and with rare old records being discovered every year, it is debatable whether such a work ever could be one hundred percent complete. Your compiler can only offer the thought that this bibliography is as comprehensive as a network of nearly two hundred people, reporting from fourteen different countries, could achieve in the span of less than three years.

A particular debt of gratitude is due to those who have shown exceptional determination in their efforts on behalf of the project: Michael Johnson and James Bradbury in Canada, Paul Street in Australia, Howard Chamberlain in New Zealand, the late Neil Orpen in South Africa, Cliff Parrett in France, and Patric Emerson and Maxwell Macfarlane here in the United Kingdom.

Several people with specialist knowedge of particular countries and specific areas of military research have eliminated the compiler's most blatant errors by checking parts of the draft: John Arnold (East Africa), Howard Chamberlain (New Zealand), and Sir John Chapple (the Gurkhas). To Maxwell Macfarlane has fallen the arduous task of not only checking the Artillery titles (of which he has an intimate knowledge) but also of proof-reading the entire work. While thanking them each for their individual contributions to the whole, the compiler accepts that any outstanding deficiencies in the bibliography are entirely his own responsibility.

Several professional book dealers have supported the project, either by providing details of books in their stocks or by giving valued advice and guidance. They are Brian Maggs of Maggs Brothers Limited (London), Chris Buckland of London Stamp Exchange (London), Jack St Aubyn of Woolcott Books (Gillingham, Dorset), Henry Lloyd (of Twyford, Winchester), and Gaston Renard (of Collingwood, Victoria).

Thanks are due for their cooperation to the Librarians and staffs in charge of several important collections: the Army Museums Ogilby Trust (Aldershot, UK), the Prince Consort's Army Library (Aldershot, UK), the Australian War Memorial (Canberra, Australia), the National Army Museum (London, UK), the South African Library (Cape Town, RSA), and the United Services Institution of India (Delhi, India).

It is likely that this book would have remained no more than a glint in the compiler's eye for several years more if the project had not had the unswerving and always cheerful support of Lieut Col Patric Emerson, Honorary Secretary of the Indian Army Association. To him must go the final vote of thanks.

KEY to contributors as initialled in the main entries

| | | | | |
|---|---|---|---|---|
| AAM | Lieut Col A A Mains | | JRT | John Thyen |
| AGB | Major A G Bond | | JS | Jeremy Seed |
| AGY | A G Young | | JWW | Capt J W Webb |
| AJW | Lieut Col A J Ward | | | |
| AM | Anthony McClenaghan | | LBR | Lelia Ryan |
| AMM | Lieut Col A M Macfarlane | | LD | Lionel Digby |
| AN | A Nath | | LM | Laurie Manton |
| AS | Major Anthony Sudlow | | | |
| | | | MCJ | Michael Johnson |
| BCC | Bruce Cazel | | MGHW | M G H Wright |
| BDM | Brian Maggs | | MP | Max Powling |
| BWR | Brian Ritchie | | MW | M Wright |
| CJP | Cliff Parrett | | NO | Lieut Col Neil Orpen |
| CMF | C M Fagg | | NKR | Maj N K Rampal |
| CRDG | Lieut Col C R D Gray | | | |
| CSM | Colin Message | | OSS | O S Sachdeva |
| DBP-P | David Picton-Phillips | | PJE | Lieut Col Patric Emerson |
| DCSD | Col D C S David | | PS | Paul Street |
| DH | David Harding | | | |
| DJB | David Barnes | | RGB | Ronald Baxter |
| DKD | David Dorward | | RGH | R G Harris |
| DM | Lieut Col D Milman | | RJW | Lieut Col R J Wyatt |
| | | | RLP | Ron Platt |
| EDS | Lieut Col E DeSantis | | RP | Roger Perkins |
| EPM | Maj E S Straus | | RR | R Rolleg |
| | | | RS | Lieut Col Robin Stewart |
| FC | Finola Chamberlain | | | |
| FRB | Dr Frank Bradlow | | SB | Stuart Barr |
| FWST | F W S Taylor | | SDC | Maj S D Clarke |
| | | | SS | S Snelling |
| GB | Gordon Bickley | | | |
| GC | Gene Christian | | TA | Capt Timothy Ash |
| | | | TM | Timothy Mole |
| HEC | Howard Chamberlain | | | |
| HLL | Henry Lloyd | | VS | Victor Sutcliffe |
| HRC | Lieut Col H R Carmichael | | | |
| | | | WEL | Lieut Col W Elliott Lockhart |
| JA | John Arnold | | WMTM | Brig W M T Magan |
| JBC | Joy Cave | | | |
| JBF | Maj Jeffrey Floyd | | | |
| JEB | James Bradbury | | | |
| JFS | J F Sutherland | | | |
| JHG | J H Girling | | | |
| JLC | Gen Sir John Chapple | | | |
| JMAT | John Tamplin | | | |
| JPR | Brig J P Randle | | | |
| JRD | John R Devereau | | | |
| JRS | Maj Jack St Aubyn | | | |

382

KEY to Libraries as initialled in the main entries


AldMM      Aldershot Military Museum, Aldershot (UK)
AMOT       Army Museums Ogilby Trust (UK)
ATL        Alexander Turnbull Library, Wellington (NZ)
AWM        Australian War Memorial, Canberra (Aus)

BM         British Museum (UK)

IOL        India Office Library & Records, London (UK)

IWM        Imperial War Museum, London (UK)

MODL       Ministry of Defence Library, London (UK)

NAM        National Army Museum, London (UK)

PCAL       Prince Consort's Army Library, Aldershot (UK)

RAI        Royal Artillery Institution, London (UK)
RMAS       Royal Military Academy Sandhurst (Central Library)
           Camberley (UK)

SAL        South African Library, Cape Town (RSA)
SSL        Sherborne School Library, Sherborne (UK)

USII       United Services Institution of India, Delhi (India)
UWM        University of Wisconsin, Madison Library (USA)


In addition, helpful correspondence has been received from a number of
other libraries, including:

Australian Defence Force Academy, University of New South Wales (Aus)
London Library, London (UK)
Police Staff College, Bramshill (UK)


For the information of those intending to pursue their own studies, it
must be mentioned that some of these libraries are privately funded or
exist mainly to meet a specialised requirement. They are not 'open to the
public' in the general sense of that phrase. However, in broad terms,most
Librarians are prepared to grant access to their holdings whenever they
receive an enquiry from a bona fide researcher and providing that
advance notice is given.